DAMIAN HARPER
DAVID EIMER

BEIJING
CITY GUIDE

INTRODUCING BĚIJĪNG

Beijingers drink and stroll on a balmy Saturday night, Houhai Lake (p138)

Capital of the country set to dominate the 21st century, Běijīng has transformed itself into one of the world's great cities at a speed few other metropolises could ever hope to match.

Ten years ago, Běijīng was a dowdy backwater of a capital. Now, the world looks on enviously at the futuristic buildings that loom over a buzzing, buoyant city that has embraced consumerism as eagerly as it once championed communism. Yet for all its fancy new trimmings, Běijīng is in many ways the same city that was once ruled by emperors and has been invaded by everyone from Genghis Khan to the former colonial powers.

It's that contrast between the distant past and super-charged present that makes Běijīng such a captivating destination. Tower blocks dot the skyline, but the *hútòng* (ancient alley-ways that criss-cross the heart of the city) still teem with life, as they did hundreds of years ago. Temples and shopping malls coexist, as do five-star restaurants and hole-in-the-wall dumpling joints, or you can sip a cocktail in a trendy rooftop bar while gazing over the Forbidden City. And just a couple hours away, the majestic Great Wall snakes its way across the hills north of Běijīng.

But as well as some of the most essential sights in all of China, it's Běijīng's fizzing energy that makes it such a unique place. Summer is hot and humid, and winter is freezing, making autumn and spring the best times to visit, but whenever you come you'll get to experience a city intoxicated by the spirit of change. It's never boring in Běijīng.

BĚIJĪNG LIFE

Beijingers are a stoical people. But even the most reserved of the city's 17 million–odd inhabitants have been left gasping, as well as proud, at the way Běijīng has reinvented itself in recent years. If the staging of the hugely successful 2008 Olympics was the catalyst for this remarkable overhaul, then the pace has hardly let up since. New buildings, shopping malls and subway lines spring up almost weekly.

'A buzzing, buoyant city that has embraced consumerism as eagerly as it once championed communism.'

That feeling of being in permanent flux can be disorientating and the changes have resulted in millions of people decamping to the ever-expanding suburbs of this huge, sprawling city. The centre of the capital is now lined with the office blocks and shopping malls that stand as temples to the twin gods of money and status that many Beijingers worship. Moving up the social ladder is an obsession for everyone.

Constant change also means that most people look forward rather than back. The capital's former reputation as a conservative city is a fast-fading memory as rising incomes and the rapidly increasing numbers of restaurants, bars and clubs fuel a vibrant nightlife. And with the latest fashions in the shops and new cars on the streets, Beijingers are quickly shrugging off any feelings of inferiority to the West.

Nevertheless, the widening gap between the rich and the poor is evidence that not everyone has benefited from Běijīng's boom. The city's 20-somethings might party till late with the latest mobile phones clamped to their ears, but the elderly, the unemployed and the huge army of migrant workers in the capital exist in a parallel universe where life is far less sweet.

Politics, though, is hardly mentioned, at least not in public. For most people, especially the young, the knowledge that they can enjoy lives radically different and more prosperous than ever before is enough to satisfy them. But almost all Beijingers possess an overwhelming confidence that life can only get better. They know that this is their city's time.

Taichi is practised in the Temple of Heaven Park (p80)

HIGHLIGHTS

IMPERIAL BĚIJĪNG

These glorious buildings stand as silent witnesses to 500 years of dynastic rule. Still hugely significant today, their very presence resonates deep into the Chinese psyche.

❶ Forbidden City
The heart of China for 500 years (p56)

❷ Summer Palace
Marvel at the Long Corridor and gaze out over Běijīng (p127)

❸ Great Wall
Snaking away over the hills, the most iconic monument of them all (p97)

MUSEUMS

Browse bronzes and Buddhist statues, or check out the latest trends in the iconoclastic galleries of the 798 Art District.

❶ Capital Museum
Stunning outside and in (p92)

❷ 798 Art District
Frequently irreverent, sometimes infuriating, always interesting (p133)

❸ Poly Art Museum
Some of the rarest Chinese art from early dynasties (p75)

TEMPLES

Dating from the time when Buddha was big in Běijīng, temples are scattered throughout the city. Not just for tourists, they still attract the devout and anyone seeking divine assistance from the deities.

❶ Temple of Heaven
Flawless design at this utterly unique temple (p80)

❷ Lama Temple
Former prince's palace, now Beijing's biggest Buddhist temple (p70)

❸ Confucius Temple
Scholars congregated here in the shadow of the great sage (p71)

ARCHITECTURE

Běijīng has been transformed in recent years by the work of leading avant-garde architects. In total contrast, the courtyard houses in the hútòng *(alleyways) will transport you back to old Běijīng.*

❶ CCTV Building
Eye-popping example of modern architecture at its best (p113)

❷ Hútòng
Explore *sìhéyuàn* (courtyard houses) in the ancient alleyways that criss-cross the central city (p46)

❸ National Grand Theatre
Vast, dome-like sci-fi structure (p91)

DINING & DRINKING

Home to the very best of Chinese cuisine, Běijīng's restaurants are a sight to behold. Dine in the historic Legation Quarter and then finish the evening in a designer bar.

❶ LAN
Try a nightcap in this Philippe Starck–designed temple to extravagance (p185)

❷ Maison Boulud
World-class cuisine in the newly restored Legation Quarter (p169)

❸ Beijing Dadong Roast Duck Restaurant
The place to sample the capital's most iconic dish (p164)

CONTENTS

THE AUTHORS

Damian Harper

Damian first arrived in Běijīng in 1992 via a degree in Chinese from London's School of Oriental African Studies. Since then he has shacked up in a *sìhéyuàn* (courtyard house), worked as a Beijing Radio presenter, lived in Shànghǎi, wrestled with the Cantonese dialect in Hong Kong, chewed the fat with Shaolin monks and knocked back bags of beer in Qīngdǎo. Married to an outstanding Shāndōng lass, Damian has been authoring for Lonely Planet for over 12 years, exploring China with a constant swarm of deadlines *(Beijing, China, China's Southwest, Shanghai, Hong Kong, Lonely Planet's Best in Travel)* in pursuit.

DAMIAN'S TOP BĚIJĪNG DAY

I like to rise early to join the shuffling queue for *yóutiáo* (deep-fried dough stick) to chew en route to practising several forms of *tàijíquán* (taichi) in the park. The pulse-quickening Yang-style long form (108 moves) takes around 20 minutes to perform. For fresh coffee afterwards, I'll make my way to Nanluogu Xiang after picking up a copy of 参考消息 *(Reference News)*, one of the few Chinese-language newspapers worth reading. Fortified by caffeine I'll disappear into the city's *hútòng* (alleyways), which is *the* best way to rummage through Běijīng's past. I'll always find something extraordinary buried away here whether I'm deliberately exploring or just idly meandering. I'll certainly go temple hunting in the *hútòng*, as some temples – such as Huguo Temple in Xīchéng district – are well disguised, their disparate halls divided up among live-in residents or converted for other functions. Others, such as Zhihua Temple (p77), are authentic and almost neglected. To catch up with currents in Chinese art, I'll bookmark the 798 Art District (p133) but for hiking I'll opt for Bādàchù (p134) or Fragrant Hills Park (p133). In fact in spring or autumn, I may devote the entire day to visiting Jiankou Great Wall (p103) for absolute tranquillity and premier views of the brick bastion. Tiananmen Square (p66) at twilight is a magical spot to stop if I've time, and I'll always visit the Forbidden City beforehand –

you can never explore the palace enough. I'll have dinner with friends in the Hòuhǎi area before sinking late-night drinks in Nanluogu Xiang again and chatting till the witching hour and beyond.

Contributing Author
DAVID EIMER

David made his first trip to China in 1988, when both Westerners and cars were in short supply. After graduating with a law degree from University College London, he abandoned the idea of becoming a barrister for a career as a freelance journalist. That took him from London to LA for five years, where he wrote for a variety of newspapers and magazines. Back in London, David began to be intrigued by the world's increasing focus on China. Returning there for the first time in 14 years, he found a country that had changed beyond almost all recognition. He moved to Běijīng in early 2005, where he contributes to the *Sunday Telegraph* and the *South China Morning Post*. He co-wrote the previous editions of *Beijing* and *Shanghai* for Lonely Planet, as well as working on the last edition of the *China* guide.

GETTING STARTED

From backpacking expeditions to luxury stopovers and every point in between, Běijīng caters to each and every budget. First you'll need a visa (p253), and you'll also need to know when to go (below) and what weather to expect. Běijīng doesn't do the English language at all well (this is no Thailand or Malaysia), so you'll need to prepare for excruciating lingo problems – consult the Language chapter (p256) at the back of the book and the language section in the Background chapter (p45). We have put a considerable amount of written Chinese in this book. When in doubt, showing the Chinese characters to local passers-by is far more immediate than trying to pronounce Chinese (unless you can speak the language). Try to allow time to explore China outside Běijīng; engineering an itinerary is an excellent idea. If you plan on visiting Tibet, check on any travel restrictions. For essentials, you should be able to find most of what you need in Běijīng, but it's advisable to take along any prescription medicines and cannot-live-without reading material. Last but not least, Běijīng is often surprising and endlessly fascinating – so don't forget to pack a sense of adventure!

WHEN TO GO

'Climate is what you expect; weather is what you get.'

Robert A Heinlein

Climate-wise, autumn (September and October) is Běijīng's finest, but shortest, season. Skies are blue, the weather is cooling down and the mad summer rush has exhausted itself, so fewer visitors are in town. Locals muse that this is the season of 'tiāngāo qìshuǎng', literally 'high skies and the air is fresh', with trademark blue skies and crisp air. Arid spring (March to April/May) can be pleasant, apart from the scouring sandstorms (see the Dust Devil boxed text, p42) gusting in from Inner Mongolia, and the ubiquitous static electricity discharging everywhere. Spring also sees the snow-like liǔxù (willow catkins) wafting through the Běijīng air. Summer (May to August) is a blistering, drawn-out event, but it's also the peak tourist season. From May onwards the mercury can surge above 30°C, reaching over 40°C in midsummer; heavy rainstorms appear late in the season. Face-numbing winter (November to February/March) sees far fewer tourists in town, and some hotels may offer substantial discounts – but it's glacial outside (dipping as low as -20°C) and the northern winds cut like a knife through bean curd. Heating in public buildings is officially turned on only in mid-November, no matter how cold it gets. Air pollution can be very harsh in both summer and winter (see p120).

Avoid visiting the capital during the first week of October and the first three days of May (p245), as the entire nation is on holiday – rooms are in short (and expensive) supply and attractions are swamped. Be warned that the Spring Festival (below) is China's biggest holiday and transport outside Běijīng can be hellish; many people take a week off work. But it can also be a great time to see the Chinese celebrating with all stops out – be sure to book your room in advance.

FESTIVALS & EVENTS

China follows both the yánglì (Gregorian) and the yīnlì (lunar) calendars. Traditional Chinese festivals are calculated according to the lunar calendar and fall on different days each year according to the Gregorian calendar. The three huge holiday periods begin with the Spring Festival, on 1 May and 1 October, respectively.

January & February

WESTERN NEW YEAR
1 Jan

元旦 Yuándàn

The Spring Festival is China's big New Year's bash, but the Western New Year is also wildly celebrated throughout town.

SPRING FESTIVAL
14 Feb 2010 & 3 Feb 2011

春节 Chūn Jié

As big in China as Christmas in the West, the family-oriented Spring Festival celebrates the arrival of the new lunar New Year. The festival commences on the first day of the first month in the lunar calendar, which usually falls sometime between late January and mid-February, ushering in one of the 12 animals of the Chinese zodiac. The long build-up to the festival is an explosion of colour, with *chūnlián* (spring couplets) pasted on door posts, door gods brightening up *hútòng* (alleyways) and shops glistening with red and gold decorations. Work colleagues and relatives present each other with red envelopes of *hóngbāo* (money), the streets ring with cries of '*gōngxǐ fācái*' ('congratulations – make money'). At midnight of the New Year a long cavalcade of fireworks illuminates the sky. The White Cloud Temple (p93), the Lama Temple (p70) and other temples in Běijīng stage entertaining *miàohuì* (temple fairs). Celebrations are also held in parks, such as Ditan Park (p79).

VALENTINE'S DAY   14 Feb
情人节 **Qíngrén Jié**

China's traditional festival for lovers (the seventh day of the seventh lunar month) simply doesn't attract the same kind of dewy-eyed fascination. Jewellery stores are busy with white-collar suits blowing a month's salary on rings, while flower shops do a roaring trade in roses (in bunches of eleven, symbolising loyalty). If eating out, book early or make do with a takeaway. With fortuitous synchronicity, Valentine's Day in 2010 exactly coincides with the first day of the Spring Festival (so book that table *months* ahead).

LANTERN FESTIVAL 28 Feb 2010 & 17 Feb 2011
元宵节 **Yuánxiāo Jié**

Celebrated two weeks after the first day of the Spring Festival, this family-oriented festival is not a public holiday, but can be a very colourful time to visit Běijīng. The Chinese devour gorgeous *yuánxiāo* (glutinous rice dumplings with soft, sweet fillings) while evening firework shows explode over town.

March & April
INTERNATIONAL LITERARY FESTIVAL   Mar
国际文学节 **Guójì Wénxué Jié**

This excellent festival sees writers, readers and bibliophiles convening at the fabulous Bookworm (p148) – where else? – for a two-week bonanza of readings and discussions. Hosting a gaggle of prize-winning international authors and local writers, the event has been going strong since 2006. The festival sells out quickly so bookmark it early for tickets: see www.chinabookworm.com for details.

GUANYIN'S BIRTHDAY
                          3 Apr 2010 & 23 Mar 2011
观世音生日 **Guānshìyīn Shēngrì**

Held on the 19th day of the second moon, the birthday of Guanyin, the Buddhist Goddess of Mercy, is a fine time to visit Buddhist temples. Dedicated to the goddess, Puning Temple (p222) in Chéngdé province holds suitably big celebrations.

TOMB SWEEPING DAY
                          5 Apr (4 Apr in leap years)
清明节 **Qīngmíng Jié**

A day for worshipping ancestors, the festival falls near the date of Easter. People visit and clean the graves *(sǎomù)* of their departed relatives, placing flowers on tombs and burning ghost money for the departed. There may be increased vigilance in Tiananmen Square during the festival, as public displays of mourning for the dead of 4 June 1989 remain sensitive. The festival has now become an official public holiday.

May
MAY DAY   1 May
五一 **Wǔyī**

May Day kicks off a much-needed three-day national holiday for Chinese, who swamp tourist sights the length and breadth of the nation.

GREAT WALL MARATHON   May
长城马拉松 **Chángchéng Mǎlāsōng**

The hike up Sīmǎtái is like a walk to the local shops compared to the thigh-juddering,

ADVANCE PLANNING

Scroll through some of Běijīng's top websites (p15) and scope government travel-health websites (p243). Check whether your trip coincides with popular festivals or clashes with the big Chinese holiday periods (opposite). Make sure your passport and visa are in order (p253). Check that your vaccinations are up-to-date and make a start at learning some Mandarin. If you're going to Běijīng on business, make sure you've got some business cards.

Give some thought to possible excursions (p218) outside of town. Scout around for good hotel deals and make a room reservation. On the day before you leave, reconfirm your fight (and cancel the milk).

knee-wrecking agony of this main and half marathon. See www.great-wall-marathon .com.

September

MID-AUTUMN FESTIVAL
22 Sep 2010 & 12 Sep 2011

中秋节 Zhōngqiū Jié

Also known as the Moon Festival, the Mid-Autumn Festival is marked by eating tasty *yuèbǐng* (moon cakes), gazing at the full moon and gathering together with relatives for family reunions. It is also a traditional holiday for lovers. It takes place on the 15th day of the eighth lunar month.

October & November

NATIONAL DAY
1 Oct

国庆节 Guóqìng Jié

Crowds flock to Tiananmen Square for a huge party, followed by a massive week-long national holiday where the Chinese blow their hard-earned savings on travelling and enjoying themselves in what is known as Golden Week.

BEIJING MUSIC FESTIVAL
Oct & Nov

北京国际音乐节 Běijīng Guójì Yīnyuè Jié

Usually staged around October and November, this classical-music festival (www .bmf.org.cn) sees foreign orchestras and musicians coming to town for a five-week range of musical events.

December

CHRISTMAS DAY
25 Dec

圣诞节 Shèngdàn Jié

Not an official Chinese festival perhaps, but the birthday of baby Jesus is a major milestone on the commercial calendar, when Běijīng's big shopping zones sparkle with decorations and glisten with snow. Yuletide is celebrated more by expats and young Chinese than by more elderly locals.

COSTS & MONEY

Běijīng is no longer cheap. In the good-old, bad-old communist days (up to around 15 years ago), you could have survived in town on a pittance and lived like a lord; nowadays you can wince when forking out Y45 for a latte or Y50 for a bowl of noodles at Capital Airport.

BĚIJĪNG'S ECONOMIC STATS

GDP US$151 billion (2008)

Per capita GDP $9000 (2008)

Per capita income US$1573 (2008)

Expenditure on real estate US$25.77 billion (2008)

Hotels are the biggest expense, but food and transport can quickly add up, too. Dorm beds start at around Y35 a night, but you will probably pay at least around Y200 for a double room. The underground system is very good value indeed (Y2 flat fee) and taxis are reasonable; hiring a bike is also cheap. Eating at street stalls and small hole-in-the-wall restaurants is cost-effective, and you can eat this way for around Y40 per day or less.

Bank on spending from around Y500 a day for midrange comfort (accommodation, dining and sightseeing). This figure can rapidly expand depending on where you choose to eat and sleep. Further up the spectrum, five-star hotel rooms can cost over Y1500 a night and stylish restaurant meals can cost from Y150.

Entertainment is no longer cheap. Beer bought from corner shops is cheaper than the equivalent size of bottled water, however, costing around Y2.5 for a bottle of Beijing or Yanjing Beer. Bars are far pricier, with small bottles of Tsingtao retailing for around Y15 to Y25 (although we have listed some budget-bracket watering holes); imported beers cost much more. Unlike in countries such as the UK, where prices for cigarettes are by and large the same, there is great variation in Chinese cigarette prices (Y3 to Y70 per pack).

HOW MUCH?

Bāozi (steamed meat buns) from street stall Y3

Bus ticket Y1

Metro ticket Y2

Hour in internet cafe Y2-4

Large bottle of Yanjing Beer from a shop Y2.50

Local SIM card Y100

Lamb kebab from Y1

Chinese-language newspaper Y0.50

0.5L bottle of mineral water Y2

Taxi rate (for first 3km) Y10

Great Wall cotton T-shirt from Y15

BEST BLOGS

Beijing Boyce (www.beijingboyce.com) Ins-and-outs of Běijīng's bar and club scene with an avalanche of detail.

Bezdomny ex patria (http://wangbo.blogtown.co.nz) 'Ramblings of an expat Kiwi living in one small corner of Beijing'; on learning Chinese and all things Běijīng.

China Blog List (www.chinabloglist.org) A list of China-related blogs.

Danwei (www.danwei.org) Resourceful reflections on Chinese media, advertising and urban life; translations into English from Chinese media.

Pomfret's China (http://newsweek.washingtonpost.com/postglobal/pomfretschina) 'A Foreign Devil's take on the Middle Kingdom' by the former *Washington Post* Běijīng bureau chief.

Quirky Beijing (www.quirkybeijing.com) Does what it says on the packet.

The China Blog (http://china.blogs.time.com) Articles and observations from *Time* magazine's China correspondents.

Zhongnanhai Blog (www.zhongnanhaiblog.com) News, opinion, analysis and articles on China from contributors living in China.

Cinema ticket prices are similar to those in the West, so most locals buy pirate DVDs instead, which cost between Y5 and Y10.

Be extra vigilant against being lured to tea houses or art galleries in tourist areas (p251). We have read endless tales of travellers being duped of their entire holiday budgets in extortionate tea houses. Remember, as a foreigner you can be preyed upon and targeted for your hard-earned cash. There's little point in pinching your pennies while shopping only to be conned big time elsewhere.

Běijīng is one of those wonderful cities where tipping is not the norm. This applies throughout China. Midrange restaurants and above have closed the gap with a service charge (*fúwùfèi*), however, so there is no need to indulge them with a tip. Porters at upmarket hotels will, of course, expect a tip. Taxi drivers certainly do not expect a tip and will often refuse.

INTERNET RESOURCES

Beijinger (www.thebeijinger.com) The low-down on Běijīng entertainment.

Beijingpage (www.beijingpage.com) Informative online directory with reams of practical info on the city.

CTrip (www.english.ctrip.com) Discounted hotels and ticketing; recommended.

Lonely Planet (www.lonelyplanet.com) Useful summaries on travelling through China, plus tips from travellers on the Thorn Tree travel forum.

Wild Wall (www.wildwall.com) Great Wall expert William Lindesay's informative website on the crumbling fortification.

Zhongwen (www.zhongwen.com) Handy primer for students of written Chinese.

SUSTAINABLE BĚIJĪNG

From the city's growing water woes and encroaching desertification to caustic atmospheric pollution and a long history of environmental neglect, Běijīng is hardly a paragon of environmental sustainability. However, recent initiatives (such as the banning of free plastic grocery bags) are having an effect, and China is a world leader in harnessing solar energy. You can help to lessen the human impact on the environment by buying your own reusable chopsticks, avoiding shark's fin soup (if it's genuine) and getting around town as much as you can by bicycle.

BACKGROUND

HISTORY
THE RECENT PAST

The 2008 Olympic Games marked Běijīng's modern coming-of-age and the climax of China's greatest urban program since the 14th century. After former president Jiang Zemin launched the project in 1998, China spent at least US$200 billion, not counting more than US$40 billion specifically for the 2008 Summer Olympic Games. By lavishing three times the amount Athens spent on hosting the 2004 games, the 2008 games were the costliest in history. Běijīng began ticking the requisite first-world boxes at blinding speed: a well-developed and growing underground network, the world's largest airport terminal, sparkling skyscrapers, a surging immigrant population, world-class sports facilities, traffic gridlock and a stupefying haze.

The Olympic Games themselves went swimmingly (particularly for Michael Phelps who netted eight gold medals) as China topped the medals table with commendable professionalism. The opening ceremony – choreographed masterfully by Zhang Yimou – drew gasps of amazement from across the globe and Běijīng bathed in the bright glow of international admiration. Fears of a polluted Olympics were blown away as scads of cars were forced off the road and further Draconian measures kept the smog at bay.

Accusations of fakery (fake fireworks and singing at the opening ceremony) could hardly dent the upbeat mood, but other hiccups pointed to deep-rooted problems. Běijīng residents and expats complained about the city being in a virtual state of lockdown as the hands-on government sought to present a suitably squeaky clean Olympics. Hobos were sent packing and the streets were lined by ranks of silent volunteers in the run-up to the games, creating a suffocating mood of vigilance. Chinese embassies kept a tighter hold on visas, visa extensions were hard to acquire and expat numbers fell. Free Tibet campaigners were instantly arrested and the unfettered access to the internet promised to journalists was only fitfully provided.

Recently Běijīng has found itself increasingly preoccupied with the global financial crisis and troubles on China's western frontiers. The deadly 2008 riots in Lhasa and 2009 unrest in Ürümqi prompted Běijīng to point its finger at external enemies, accusations that many Western analysts agree may do little to defuse deep-seated ethnic and social tensions.

HISTORY BOOKS

- *The City of Heavenly Tranquility: Beijing in the History of China* (Jasper Becker) An authoritative and heartbreaking rendering of Běijīng's transformation from magnificent Ming capital to communist-capitalist hybrid.
- *The Penguin History of Modern China: The Fall and Rise of a Great Power 1850–2008* (Jonathan Fenby) Highly readable account of the paroxysms of modern Chinese history.
- *The Siege at Peking* (Peter Fleming) Celebrated account of the Boxer Rebellion and the historic siege of the Foreign Legation Quarter.
- *The Dragon Empress* (Marina Warner) Riveting biography of the scheming Empress Dowager and the fall of the Qing dynasty.

BACKGROUND HISTORY

TIMELINE

500,000 BC	pre-11th century BC	5th century–3rd century BC
Peking man (Sinanthropus pekinensis), an example of Homo erectus, inhabits the Běijīng region; Peking man fossils were excavated at Zhōukǒudiàn in Běijīng municipality between 1923 and 1927.	The first settlements in the Běijīng area are recorded (evidence suggests Paleolithic cultures living in the central areas of Běijīng).	Yānjīng, capital of the state of Yan, is located near Běijīng. Yānjīng (which means 'Capital of Yan') was also known as Ji and was later moved to Xiàdū in today's Yixian Country (Héběi province) during the Warring States period.

FROM THE BEGINNING

As a youth in the 14th century, the future Emperor Yongle was sent by his father to live as the Prince of Yan in the abandoned ruins of the former capital of the Yuan dynasty (present-day Běijīng), established by Kublai Khan (1215–94). The Mongols called the city Khanbalik, and it was from here that the descendants of Genghis Khan ruled over the largest land empire in history. This is where Marco Polo, one of many thousands of foreigners drafted to help the Mongols govern China, came to serve as an official. Běijīng was really only the winter capital for Kublai Khan, who chose to spend the summer months at Běijīng's sister city, Xanadu, which lay to the north, 1800m up on the steppes. This was called the 'Upper Capital', or 'Shàngdū' in Chinese, while Běijīng was 'Dàdū' or 'Great Capital'.

Běijīng seems a curious place to select as the capital of the Yuan empire, or indeed any empire. For one thing, it lacks a river or access to the sea. It is on the very outer edge of the great northern plain, and very far indeed from the rich rice granaries in the south and the source of China's lucrative exports of tea, silk and porcelain. Throughout history the Han Chinese considered this barbarian territory, home to a series of hostile predatory dynasties such as the Liao (907–1125) and the Jin (1115–1234). To this day Chinese historians describe these peoples as primitive 'tribes' rather than nations, perhaps a prejudice from the ancient antipathy between nomadic pastoralist peoples and the sedentary farmers who are the Chinese.

Běijīng first became a walled settlement in AD 938 when the Khitans, one of the nomadic 'barbarian tribes', established it as an auxiliary southern capital of their Liao dynasty. It was sometimes called Yānjīng, or the 'City of Swallows', and this is still the name of a beer produced by a local brewery. When they were overthrown by Jurchens from Manchuria, the progenitors of the Manchus, it became Zhōngdū or 'Middle Capital'. Each of these three successive barbarian dynasties enlarged the walled city and built palaces and temples, especially Buddhist temples. They secured a supply of water by channelling streams from the dry limestone hills around Běijīng, and stored it in the lakes that still lie at the heart of the city.

The Khitans relied on the Grand Canal to ship goods like silk, porcelain, tea and grain from the Yangtze Delta. Each successive dynasty shortened the Grand Canal. It was originally 2500km long when it was built in the 5th century by the Chinese Sui dynasty to facilitate the military conquest of northeast China and Korea. From the 10th century it was used for a different purpose: to enable these northern peoples to extract the wealth of central China. Běijīng's role was to be the terminus.

For 1000 years, half a million peasants spent six months a year hauling huge barges from Hángzhōu up the Grand Canal to Běijīng. You can still see the canal after it enters the city from Tōngzhōu, now a suburb of Běijīng, and then winds around the Second Ring Rd. The tax or tribute from central China was then stored in huge warehouses, a few of which still remain. From Běijīng, the goods were carried out of the West Gate or Xīzhí Mén (where Xizhimen Station is today), and taken up the Tanqin Gorge to Bādálǐng, which once marked the limits of the Chinese world. Beyond this pass, the caravans took the road to Zhāngjiākǒu, 6000ft above sea level where the grasslands of inner Asia begin. The Mongols referred to Zhāngjiākǒu as Kalgan; 'the Gate'.

This pass was also the favourite route chosen by invaders, such as Genghis Khan, who wanted to attack China. The ultimate aim of Khitans, Jurchens, Mongols and Manchus was to control the lucrative international trade in Chinese-made luxuries. Chinese dynasties like the Song faced a choice of paying them off or staging a bloody resistance. The Southern Song did attack and destroy Běijīng, but when it failed to defeat the Liao dynasty of the Khitans it resorted to

AD 938	1153	1215
Běijīng is established as auxiliary capital of the Liao dynasty. Běijīng's oldest street – Sanmiao Jie, or Three Temples St – dates to this time, when it was known as Tanzhou Jie.	Běijīng becomes capital of the Jin dynasty where it becomes known as Zhōngdū or 'Middle Capital'; the city walls are expanded and paper currency enters circulation.	In their war against the Jurchen Jin, the Mongols, under Genghis Khan, break through the Great Wall at several points and sack Zhōngdū, razing it to the ground and slaughtering its inhabitants.

a strategy of 'using the barbarian to defeat the barbarian'. It made a pact with the Jurchen, and together they captured Běijīng in 1125. But instead of just helping to defeat the Khitans, the Jurchen carried on south and took the Song capital at Kāifēng. The Jurchens, however, chose not to try to govern China by themselves and instead opted to milk the Southern Song dynasty. The Mongols became the first 'barbarian' tribe to attempt to rule China. They ruled from Běijīng for just short of a century, from 1272 to 1368.

Ming-Dynasty Běijīng

Běijīng can properly be said to be a Chinese city only during the Ming dynasty (1368–1644), when the Emperor Yongle – whose name means perpetual happiness – used over 200,000 prisoners of war to rebuild the city, construct its massive battlements, rebuild the imperial palace and establish the magnificent Ming Tombs (p229). He forced tens of thousands of leading Chinese families to relocate from Nánjīng, the capital founded by his father, and unwillingly settle in what they considered an alien land at the extremity of the Chinese world. Throughout the Ming dynasty it was constantly under attack by the Mongols, and on many occasions their horsemen reached the very gates of Běijīng. Mongol bandits roamed the countryside or hid out in the marshes south of the city, threatening communications with the empire.

Everything needed for this gigantic enterprise, even tiles, bricks and timber, had to be shipped up the Grand Canal, but in time Běijīng grew into a city of nearly a million residents. Although farms and greenhouses sprang up around the city, it always depended on the Grand Canal as a life-line. Most of the canal was required to ship the huge amounts of food needed to supply the garrison of more than a million men that Yongle press-ganged into building and manning the new Great Wall (p97). This Wall, unlike earlier walls, was clad in brick and stone, not pounded earth, and the Ming emperors kept enlarging it for the next 250 years, adding loops, spurs and watchtowers. For long stretches, the fortifications run in two parallel bands.

Běijīng grew from a forward defence military headquarters into an administrative centre staffed by an elite corps of mandarins. They had to pass gruelling examinations that tested candidates' understanding of classical and Confucian literature. Then they were either assigned to the provinces or selected to work in the central government ministries, situated in what is now Tiananmen Square, south of the Meridian Gate and the entrance to the Forbidden City (p56). Each day the mandarins and the generals entered the 'Great Within' and kowtowed at an audience before the emperor. He lived inside, like a male version of a queen bee, served by thousands of women and eunuchs. Ming emperors were the only males permitted to live in the palace. Yongle established rigid rules and dreary rituals, and many of his successors rebelled against the constrictions.

Under later Ming emperors, the eunuchs came to be more trusted and more powerful than the mandarins. There were 100,000 by the end of the Ming dynasty – more than any other civilisation in history. A few became so powerful they virtually ruled the empire, but many died poor and destitute. Some used their wealth to build grandiose residences and tombs, or to patronise temples and monasteries located in hills outside the walls. The eunuchs tended to be Buddhists (while the mandarins honoured Confucius), as it gave them hope they would return as whole men in a future reincarnation.

1260	1368	1368–1644
The first Yuan emperor, Kublai Khan, transforms the city and names it Dàdū, also called Tatu. In Marco Polo's travels, the Italian explorer refers to Dàdū as Cambuluc (Khanbaliq) – Mongolian for 'Great Residence of the Khan'.	Zhu Yuanzhang takes Dàdū and proceeds to level its palaces, renaming the city Běipíng ('Northern Peace') and establishing the Ming dynasty. The last Khan flees to Xanadu (Shàngdū).	The great city walls are reshaped and the Great Wall is rebuilt and clad with bricks, while the basic layout of modern Běijīng is established. Běijīng becomes the world's largest city.

Over time Běijīng became the most important religious centre in Asia, graced by more than 2000 temples and shrines. Daoists and Buddhists vied for the favour of the emperor who, as a divine being, was automatically the patron of every approved religious institution in the empire. As the residence of the emperor, Běijīng was regarded by the Chinese as the centre of the universe. The best poets and painters also flocked to Běijīng to seek court patronage. The Forbidden City required the finest porcelain, furniture and silverware, and its workshops grew in skill and design. Literature, drama, music, medicine, map-making, astrology and astronomy flourished, too, so the imperial city became a centre for arts and sciences.

Although early visitors complained about the dust and the beggars, as they do now, most were awed and inspired by the city's size, magnificence and wealth. Ming culture was very influential in Japan, Korea, Vietnam and with other neighbouring countries. By the close of the 15th century the Ming capital, which had started out as a remote and isolated military outpost, had become a wealthy and sophisticated Chinese city.

Despite the Great Wall, the threat from the north intensified. The Manchus (formerly the Jurchens) established a new and powerful state based in Shěnyáng (currently the capital of Liáoníng province) and watched as the Ming empire decayed. The Ming had one of the most elaborate tax codes in history, but corrupt eunuchs abused their growing power. Excessive taxation sparked a series of peasant revolts. Silver, the main form of exchange, was devalued by the import of silver from the new world, leading to inflation.

One peasant rebel army, led by Li Zicheng (1606–45), actually captured Běijīng. The last Ming emperor, Chongzhen (1611–44), called on the Manchus for help and after crossing the Great Wall at Shānhǎiguān (p224) they helped rout Li Zicheng's army. The Manchus then marched on Běijīng, where Emperor Chongzhen hung himself on a tree on Coal, or Prospect, Hill (p92), which overlooks the Forbidden City. Chongzhen lies buried in the Ming tomb a short distance from the grander Ming tomb complex, and now there's a small artificial snowfield near his tomb.

Qing-Dynasty Běijīng

The Manchus established their Qing dynasty in 1664, although it took several decades before they completed the conquest of the Ming empire. As a foreign dynasty, they took great pains to present themselves as legitimate successors to the Chinese Ming dynasty. For this reason they kept Běijīng as their capital and changed very little, effectively preserving Yongle's city. The Manchu imperial family, the Aisin Gioro Clan, moved in to the Forbidden City, and imperial princes took large courtyard palaces.

Soon the Aisin Gioro family began to feel that living inside the confines of the Forbidden City was claustrophobic. The great Emperor Kangxi (1654–1722) effectively moved the court to what is now called the Old Summer Palace (p131), a vast parkland of lakes, canals and palaces linked to the city by the Jade Canal. The Manchus, like the Mongols, enjoyed hunting, riding, hawking, skating and archery. In summer, when Běijīng became hot and steamy, the court moved to Chéngdé (p218; formerly Jehol or Rehol), a week's ride to the north. At Chéngdé the court spent three months living in felt tents (or yurts) in a walled parkland.

The Manchu army was divided into regiments called banners, so the troops were called Bannermen (Qírén). Each banner had a separate colour by which it was known and settled in a particular residential area in Běijīng. The Embroidered Yellow Bannermen, for example,

1403–21	1420	1465
Emperor Yongle moves the capital south to Nánjīng ('Southern Capital'), where the imperial palace is built. Běijīng is reinstated as capital in 1421 when the Forbidden City is completed (1406–20).	The Temple of Heaven is constructed at the same time as the Forbidden City. The Gate of Heavenly Peace is completed and is called Chengtianmen, only to be burned down after a lightning strike in 1457.	The Gate of Heavenly Peace is rebuilt but is again torched by peasant rebels in 1644 prior to the arrival of Manchu soldiers. The reconstruction of the gate is completed in 1651.

A BEASTLY AFFAIR

In February 2009 there was an uproar in China about the sale of two bronze animal heads by the auction house Christie's. The sale was the latest twist in a saga stretching back to 1860, when the Old Summer Palace (p131) was torched by Anglo-French troops and the animal heads were presumably pilfered.

The 12 heads belonged to a dozen statues with human bodies and animal heads (representing the 12 animals of the Chinese zodiac) that jetted water from their mouths for two hours in a 12-hour sequence and formed part of a structure called the Hǎiyàntáng.

Four of the original 12 animal heads have been repatriated (by being bought at auction or donated) and can be seen at the Poly Art Museum (p75). Of the eight still abroad, the rat and rabbit heads that appeared at Christie's became the focus of a powerful Chinese sense of injustice.

A convincing moral argument exists that the animal heads should be returned to China; however some people have pointed to the lack of conclusive evidence that the animal heads were stolen by French or British troops; the possibility exists, others argue, that they were plundered by Chinese eager to get back at Manchu rule or to sell to international clients.

Although it is probable French or British troops carried off the booty, the evidence is largely circumstantial. The torching of the Old Summer Palace was a shocking act of vandalism (revenge for killing a correspondent from the *Times*) and most of the wooden Chinese-style buildings were burned to the ground. But the Old Summer Palace's famous Jesuit-designed Western-style palaces were built of stone and far harder to destroy. It is these that we can still see today in their jumble of ruins in the northeast corner of the palace park. Records indicate that a considerable number of these buildings survived the torching, but progressive theft by locals over the subsequent decades gradually reduced what remained.

The heads themselves are perhaps a peculiar choice of national ire for the Chinese, considering they are Western in fashion, styled by the Jesuits, who also designed the Western palace buildings at the Old Summer Palace. It has also been suggested that the Empress Dowager disliked the heads so much that she had them pulled down; if that story is true, where were they stored?

What is evident is that the ruins, and the animal heads, have become symbols of China's humiliation at the hands of foreign powers, and icons that increasingly resonate as the country assumes a more central role in international affairs.

lived near the Confucius Temple (p71), and a few are still there today. Only a minority were actually ethnic Manchu – the rest were Mongols or Han Chinese.

Běijīng was a Manchu city and foreigners used to call it the 'Tartar City': 'Tartars' being the label given to any nomadic race from inner Asia. The Han Chinese, forced to wear their hair in a queue (pigtail) as a symbol of their subjugation, lived in the 'Chinese city' to the south of Tiananmen Square. It was the liveliest, most densely populated area, packed with markets, shops, theatres, brothels and hostels for provincial visitors. If Chinese people wanted to get to north Běijīng, they had to go all the way round the outside walls. The Bannermen posted at the gates prevented anyone from entering without permission. Up to 1900, the state provided all Bannermen families with clothing and free food that was shipped up the Grand Canal and stored in grain warehouses.

It was the Manchu Bannermen who really created a Běijīng culture. They loved Beijing opera, and the city once had over 40 opera houses and many training schools. The sleeveless *qípáo* dress is really a Manchu dress. The Bannermen, who loved animals, raised songbirds and pigeons and bred exotic-looking goldfish and miniature dogs such as the Pekinese. And after the downfall of the Qing empire, they kept up traditional arts such as painting and calligraphy.

Through the centuries of Qing rule, the Manchus tried to keep themselves culturally separate from the Chinese, speaking a different language, wearing different clothes and following differ-

1644	1850–68	1900
Manchu troops pour through the pass at Shānhǎiguān to impose the Qing dynasty on China; Emperor Chongzhen hangs himself from a tree in Jingshan Park. Běijīng is known in Manchu as Gemun Hecen.	The quasi-Christian Taiping Rebellion blazes north and east across China from Guǎngxī province, killing an estimated 20 million people in the process. Rebels fail to reach Běijīng, but establish their 'Heavenly Capital' in Nánjīng.	Boxer rebels commence the long siege of the Foreign Legation Quarter. The Hanlin Academy is accidentally burned down by rebels trying to flush out besieged foreigners in the British Legation.

ent customs. For instance, Manchu women did not bind their feet, wore raised platform patens (shoes), and wore their hair coiled in distinctive and elaborate styles. All court documents were composed in the Manchu script; Manchu, Chinese and Mongolian script were used to write name signs in such places as the Forbidden City.

At the same time, the Qing copied the Ming's religious and bureaucratic institutions. The eight key ministries (Board of Works, Board of Revenue, Board of State Ceremonies, Board of War, Board of Rites, Board of Astronomy, Board of Medicines and Prefecture of Imperial Clan Affairs) continued to operate from the same buildings in what is now Tiananmen Square. The Qing dynasty worshipped their ancestors at rites held in a temple, which is now in the Workers Cultural Palace (p72), south of the Forbidden City. They also built a second ancestral temple devoted to the spirits of every Chinese emperor that ever ruled. For some time it was a girls' school but it has since been turned back into a museum.

The study of Confucius was encouraged in order to strengthen the loyalty of the mandarins employed by the state bureaucracy. And the Manchus carried out the customary rituals at the great state temples, such as the Temple of Heaven (p80). By inclination, however, many of the Manchu emperors were either Shamanists or followers of Tibetan Buddhism. The Shamanist shrines have disappeared, but Běijīng is full of temples and stupas connected with Tibetan Buddhism. The Emperor Qianlong considered himself the incarnation of the Bodhisattva Manjusri and cultivated strong links with various Dalai Lamas and Panchen Lamas. Many visited – a round trip usually lasted three years, and special palaces were built for them. The Dalai Lama's ex-palace is now rented out by the government of the Tibet Autonomous Region. The Manchus deliberately fostered the spread of Tibetan Buddhism among the war-like Mongols in the hope of pacifying them. Běijīng therefore developed into a holy city attracting pilgrims of all kinds.

Of course, the arrival of the first Jesuits and other Christians made Běijīng an important centre of Christianity in China. Emperor Qianlong employed many Jesuits who, among other things, built for him the baroque palaces that can still be seen in the ruins of the Old Summer Palace (Yuánmíng Yuán; the Garden of Perfect Happiness; p131), which was burnt down by a combined force of British and French troops in 1860 during the Second Opium War.

Foreign Devils & Empress Dowager Cixi

After the military defeats of the Opium Wars (1839–42 and 1856–60), the Western nations forced the Qing emperors to allow them to open formal embassies or legations in the capital. Hitherto, the emperor had had no equal in the world – foreign powers could only send embassies to deliver tribute, and they were housed in tributary hostels.

The British legation was the first to open after 1860. It lay on the east side of Tiananmen Square and stayed there until the 1950s when its grounds were taken over by the Ministry of State Security. By 1900, there were a dozen legations in an odd foreign ghetto with an eclectic mixture of European architecture. The Foreign Legation Quarter (p74) never became a foreign concession like those in Shànghǎi or Tiānjīn, but it had banks, schools, shops, post offices, hospitals and military parade grounds. Much of it was reduced to rubble when the army of Boxers (a quasi-religious cult) besieged it in the summer of 1900. It was later rebuilt. The last of these foreign embassies did not leave until 1967 and much of the Legation Quarter has been destroyed during the past decade.

The Empress Dowager Cixi (1835–1908), a daughter of a Bordered Blue Bannermen, was a young concubine when the Old Summer Palace was burned down by foreign troops in 1860.

1908	1911	1916
Empress Dowager Cixi bequeaths power to two-year-old Puyi, the last emperor, who rules till 1911 when he is forced to abdicate.	The Qing dynasty collapses and the modernisation of China begins in earnest; Sun Yat-sen is declared president of the Republic of China.	Yuan Shikai dies less than a year after attempting to establish himself as the Hongxian emperor. Yuan's monarchical claims prompted widespread resistance from Republicans.

Cixi allowed the palace to fall into decay, associating it with a humiliation, and instead built herself the new Summer Palace (Yíhé Yuán; p127). She was left with a profound hatred and distrust of the Western barbarians and their ways.

Over the four decades in which Cixi ruled China 'from behind the curtain' through a series of proxy emperors, she resisted pressure to change and reform. After a naval defeat at the hands of the Japanese in 1895, young Chinese officials put forward a modernisation program. She had some of them executed outside Běijīng's walls then imprisoned their patron and her nephew, Emperor Guangxu (1871–1908). She encouraged the Boxers to attack Westerners, especially foreign missionaries in northern China, and when Boxers besieged the Foreign Legation Quarter in 1900, she stood by. When the allied forces marched in to Běijīng to end the siege, she fled in disguise, an ignominious retreat that marked the final humiliation that doomed the Qing dynasty. When Cixi returned in disgrace a year later, China's modernisation had begun in earnest, but it was too late to save the Qing dynasty – it fell in 1911.

Republican China

After 1900, the last tribute barges arrived in Běijīng and a railway line ran along the traditional invasion route through the Juyong Pass to Bādálǐng. You can see the handsome clocktower and sheds of Běijīng's first railway station (Qian Men Railway Station), recently restored, on the southeast corner of Tiananmen Square. Běijīng never became an industrial or commercial centre – that role went to nearby Tiānjīn, as it lies on the coast. Yet it remained the leading political and intellectual centre of China until the late 1920s. China's first (and only) parliament was established in Běijīng in what was once the imperial elephant house, now out of sight in the sprawling headquarters of Xinhua, the state news agency.

In the settlement imposed after 1900, China had to pay the victors heavy indemnities. Some of this money was returned to China and used to build the first modern universities, including what are now the Oxford and Cambridge of China – Qinghua and Peking Universities. Běijīng's university quarter is in the Hǎidiàn district, near the Old Summer Palace (some campuses are actually in the imperial parkland). Intellectuals from all over China continued to gravitate to Běijīng, including the young Mao Zedong, who arrived to work as a librarian in 1921.

Běijīng students and professors were at the forefront of the 1919 May Fourth Movement. This was at once a student protest against the Versailles Treaty, which had awarded Germany's concessions in China to Japan, and an intellectual movement to jettison the Confucian feudal heritage and Westernise China. Mao himself declared that to modernise China it was first necessary to destroy it. China's intellectuals looked around the world for models to copy. Some went to Japan, others to the USA, Britain, Germany or, like Deng Xiaoping and Zhou Enlai, France. Many, of course, went to study Marxism in Moscow.

As the warlords marched armies in and out of Běijīng, the almost medieval city began to change. Temples were closed down and turned into schools. The last emperor, Puyi, left the Forbidden City in 1924 with his eunuchs and concubines. As the Manchus adapted to the changes, they tried to assimilate and their presence faded. Western-style brick houses, shops and restaurants were built. City gates were widened and new ones added, including one at Jianguomenwai to make way for the motorcar. Běijīng acquired nightclubs, cinemas, racecourses and a stock exchange; brothels and theatres flourished. Despite political and diplomatic crises, this was a period when people had fun and enjoyed a unique period of individual freedom.

4 May 1919	1927	1928
Students demonstrate in Běijīng against foreign occupation of territories in China and the terms that conclude WWI. The date of the protests leads to the name of the movement.	The first shots of the Chinese Civil War are fired between the KMT and the communists. The war was to continue on and off until 1949.	The Nationalists move the capital to Nánjīng and Běijīng is again renamed Běiping. This is the first time the capital of the entire nation has been in Nánjīng ('Southern Capital') for almost 500 years.

Generalissimo Chiang Kaishek united most of the country under Chinese National Party (KMT or Kuomintang in Chinese) rule and moved the capital to Nánjīng. Even after 1928, Běijīng's romantic air of decaying grandeur attracted Chinese and Western writers and painters trying to fuse Western and Chinese artistic traditions. Some of 20th-century China's best literature was written in Běijīng in the 1920s and 1930s by the likes of Lao She, Lin Huiyin, Xu Zhimou, Shen Congwen and Qian Zhongshu.

It all came to end when Japan's Kwantung Army moved down from Manchuria and occupied Běijīng in 1937. By then most people who could had fled – some to Chóngqìng in Sìchuān province, which served as Chiang Kaishek's wartime capital. Others joined Mao Zedong in his communist base in Yán'ān. Many universities established campuses in exile in Yúnnán province. And the collection of imperial treasures was secretly removed, eventually ending up in Taiwan where they can still be seen in a Taipei museum.

The Japanese stayed in Běijīng for eight years and, before their WWII defeat in 1945, had drawn up plans to build a new administrative capital in an area to the west of the city walls near Gōngzhǔfén. It was a miserable time for Běijīng, but the architecture was left largely untouched by the war. When the Japanese surrendered in August 1945, Běijīng was 'liberated' by US marines. The city once again became a merry place famous for its parties – the serious events took place elsewhere in China. When the civil war broke out in earnest between nationalists and communists in 1947, the worst fighting took place in the cities of Manchuria.

In 1948, the Communist Eighth Route Army moved south and encircled Běijīng. General Fu Zuoyi, commander-in-chief of the Nationalists Northern China Bandit Suppression Headquarters, prepared the city for a prolonged siege. He razed private houses and built gun emplacements and dugouts along the Ming battlements. Nationalist planes dropped bags of rice and flour to relieve the shortages, some hitting skaters on the frozen Beihai Lake. Both sides seemed reluctant to fight it out and destroy the ancient capital. The rich tried to flee on the few planes that took off from a runway constructed at Dongdan on Changan Dajie (Changan means 'Avenue of Eternal Peace'). Another airstrip was opened at the Temple of Heaven by cutting down 20,000 trees, including 400 ancient cypresses.

On 22 January 1949 General Fu signed a surrender agreement, and on 31 January his KMT troops marched out and the People's Liberation Army (PLA) entered. A truck drove up Morrison St (now Wangfujing Dajie) blasting a continuous refrain to the residents of Běijīng (or Peiping as it was know then): 'Welcome to the Liberation Army on its arrival in Peiping! Congratulations to the people of Peiping on their liberation!' Behind it marched 300 soldiers in battle gear. A grand victory parade took place on 3 February with 250 assorted military vehicles, virtually all US-made and captured from the KMT over the previous two years.

Mao's Běijīng

'Communism is not love. Communism is a hammer which we use to crush the enemy'

Mao Zedong

In the spring of 1949 Mao Zedong and the communist leadership were camped in the Western suburbs around Bādàchù (p134), an area that is still the headquarters of the PLA. On 1 October

7 July 1937	1 October 1949	1950s & 1960s
The Marco Polo Bridge Incident signals the beginning of the Japanese occupation of Běijīng and the start of the Second Sino-Japanese War, which does not end till September 1945.	With the communist victory over the KMT, Mao Zedong announces the founding of the People's Republic of China from the Gate of Heavenly Peace.	Most of Běijīng's city walls, gates and decorative arches are levelled to make way for roads. Work commences on Běijīng's labyrinthine network of underground tunnels.

1949, Mao mounted the Gate of Heavenly Peace (p67) and declared the founding of the People's Republic of China, saying the Chinese people had stood up. He spoke only a few words in one of the very few public speeches he ever made.

Mao then moved into Zhōngnánhǎi, part of the chain of lakes and gardens dating back to Kublai Khan. Marshal Yuan Shikai (1859–1916) had lived there too during his short-lived attempt to establish his own dynasty after 1911.

Nobody is quite sure why he chose Běijīng as his capital – nor why he failed to carry out his intention to raze the Forbidden City and erect new party headquarters on the site. Designs were drawn up in the late 1960s but never implemented. The Forbidden City was closed for nearly 10 years and became overgrown with weeds.

After 1949 many of new China's top leaders followed Mao's cue and moved their homes and offices into the old princely palaces (wángfǔ) – inadvertently preserving much of the old architecture. Mao wished to turn Běijīng from a 'city of consumption into a city production.' 'Chairman Mao wants a big modern city: he expects the sky there to be filled with smokestacks,' said Peng Zhen, the first Party Secretary of Běijīng, to China's premier architectural historian, Liang Sicheng, as they stood on the Gate of Heavenly Peace looking south.

Thousands of factories sprang up in Běijīng and quite a few were built in old temples. In time Běijīng developed into a centre for steel, chemicals, machine tools, engines, electricity, vinegar, beer, concrete, textiles, weapons – in fact everything that would make it an economically self-sufficient 'production base' in case of war. By the 1970s Běijīng had become one of the most heavily polluted cities in the world.

The move to tear down the city's walls, widen the roads and demolish the distinctive páilou (ceremonial arches) started immediately after 1949, but was fiercely contested by some intellectuals, including Liang Sicheng, who ran the architecture department of Qinghua University. So in the midst of the demolition of many famous landmarks, the municipal authorities earmarked numerous buildings and even old trees for conservation. However, it was all to no avail – Mao's brutal political purges silenced all opposition. In the 1958 Great Leap Forward, the last qualms about preserving old Běijīng were abandoned. A new plan was approved to destroy 80% of the old capital. The walls were pulled down, but the series of ring roads planned at the time were never built.

Those intellectuals who escaped persecution in the 1950s were savagely dealt with during the Cultural Revolution (1966–76). Qinghua University became the birthplace of the Red Guards (a mass movement of young radicals, mobilised by Mao). In the 'bloody August' of 1966, Běijīng's middle-school students turned on their teachers, brutally murdering some of them. In August and September of 1966, a total of 1772 people were killed in the capital, according to a report published by the Beijing Daily after 1979. The number excludes those beaten to death as they tried to escape Běijīng on trains – their registration as residents of Běijīng was suddenly cancelled. The headquarters of the Cultural Revolution in Běijīng was in the Jianguomenwai embassy area, and has since been demolished. The site is now occupied by the Si-tech Department Store.

By 1969 Mao had fallen out with Moscow and he prepared China for a nuclear war. The remaining population was turned out to build tunnels and nuclear fallout shelters. Bricks from the city walls and even the Old Summer Palace were used to build these. You can still visit the tunnels and shelters built during those years in many places, such as Ditan Park (p79), where the tunnels are used as an ice rink, and at Yuetan Park, where the tunnels have been converted into a shopping arcade. This underground city is connected by road and rail tunnels, which still allow the top leadership to move around Běijīng in secret; see p85 for more information about the capital's underground city.

1956–57	1958	16 May 1966
The Hundred Flowers Movement promises to presage an era of intellectual freedom, but instead leads to a purge of intellectuals, artists and thinkers who are labelled rightists and persecuted.	The Great Leap Forward commences but the plans to rapidly industrialise China result in a disastrous famine that kills millions of Chinese.	The Great Proletarian Cultural Revolution is launched by Mao Zedong in Běijīng; in August millions of Red Guards pack into Tiananmen Square. The police are powerless to stop the Red Guards: from August to September 1772 Beijingers are killed.

In Mao's time the geomantic symmetry of Běijīng was radically changed. The north–south axis of the Ming City was ruined by widening Changan Dajie into a 10-lane, east–west highway. This was used for huge annual military parades or when visiting dignitaries arrived and the population was turned out to cheer them. In the 1950s, the centre was redesigned by Soviet architects and modelled on Moscow's Red Square. Three major gates and many other Ming buildings, including the former government ministries, were demolished, leaving the concrete expanse of Tiananmen Square you see today.

Mao used the square to receive the adulation of the millions of Red Guards who flocked to Běijīng from 1966 to 1969, but after 1969 Mao exiled the Red Guards, along with 20 million 'educated youth', to the countryside. From 1976 the square became the scene of massive antigovernment protests – when Premier Zhou Enlai died in 1976 the large and apparently spontaneous protest in the square was quelled by the police. In 1976, Mao himself died.

Reform & Protest

Deng Xiaoping (1904–97), backed by a group of veteran generals, seized power in a coup d'état and threw Mao's widow, Jiang Qing (1914–91), and her ultraleftist cronies into the notorious Qincheng prison outside the city, where Mao had incarcerated so many senior party veterans. This still exists not far from the Ming Tombs.

At the third plenum of the 11th Party Congress, Deng consolidated his grip on power and launched economic reforms. At the same time thousands of people began putting up posters along a wall west of Zhōngnánhǎi, complaining of injustices under the 'Gang of Four' (Jiang Qing and her three associates) and demanding democracy. The Democracy Wall in Xīdān has now disappeared and been replaced by a shopping mall. Deng initially appeared to back political reforms, but soon the activists were thrown in jail, some in the Beijing No 1 Municipal Prison. This famous prison no longer exists, it was demolished in the mid-1990s.

Many of the activists were former Red Guards or exiled educated youth. After 1976 they drifted back to the city but could only find jobs in the new private sector running small market stalls, tailor shops or restaurants. After the universities opened conditions remained poor and the intelligentsia continued to be treated with suspicion. Frustrations with the slow pace of reforms prompted fresh student protests in the winter of 1986. Peasants did well out of the first wave of reforms, but in the cities many people felt frustrated. Urban life revolved around 'work units' to which nearly everyone was assigned. The work unit distributed food, housing, bicycles, travel permits and almost everything else. Běijīng was still a rather drab dispiriting place in the 1980s; there was much more to eat but everything else was in a lamentable state. For 30 years, there had been little investment in housing or transport.

In January 1987 the party's conservative gerontocrats ousted the pro-reform party chief Hu Yaobang and, when he suddenly died in the spring of 1989, Běijīng students began assembling on Tiananmen Square. Officially they were mourning his passing but they began to raise slogans for political reform and against corruption. The protests snowballed as the Communist Party leadership split into rival factions, causing a rare paralysis. The police stood by as the protests spread across the country and workers, officials and ordinary citizens took to the streets. When the military tried to intervene, Beijingers surrounded the tanks. The students set up tents on Tiananmen Square and went on a hunger strike. When the premier Li Peng held a dialogue with the students that was aired live on TV, student leaders sarcastically upbraided him.

1976	1977–79	June 1989
The death of Premier Zhou Enlai sparks spontaneous protests in Tiananmen Square, an event that becomes known as the Tiananmen Incident; the mighty Tángshān earthquake is blamed on a cosmic correction after the death of Mao Zedong in September.	With the death of Mao, the 'Běijīng Spring' sees the first shoots of nascent political freedom and the appearance of the short-lived 'Democracy Wall' in Xīdān. Deng Xiaoping's reformist agenda commences in 1979.	Democracy protestors fill Tiananmen Square as parallel protests are held across the land. Běijīng imposes martial law and on the evening of 3 June and the early hours of 4 June soldiers clear the streets, killing hundreds (perhaps thousands) in the process.

The students created the first independent student union since 1919 and celebrated the anniversary of the May Fourth Movement (p22) with a demonstration in which over a million took to the streets. For the first time since 1949, the press threw off the shackles of state censorship and became independent. When Soviet leader Mikhail Gorbachev entered on a state visit, and was enthusiastically welcomed as a symbol of political reform, it seemed as if the Chinese Communist Party (CCP), too, would embrace political change. Party General Secretary Zhao Ziyang led the reformist faction, but the older-generation leaders, led by Deng Xiaoping, feared the worst. They decided to arrest Zhao and retake the city with a military assault. On the night of 3 June, tens of thousands of troops backed by tanks and armoured personnel carriers entered the city from four directions, bulldozing aside the hastily erected barricades.

Many people died, and by the early hours of 4 June the troops were in control of Tiananmen Square. In the crackdown that followed across the country, student leaders escaped abroad while the Communist Party arrested thousands of students and their supporters. In the purge of party members that followed, China's reforms seemed to be going into reverse. The 1989 pro-democracy protests were the largest political demonstrations in Chinese history.

Rapid Development

Things only began to change when Deng Xiaoping emerged from the shadows and set off in 1991 on a so-called 'southern tour', visiting his special economic zones in the south and calling for more and faster reform. Despite opposition in the party, he won the day. China began a wave of economic reforms but did not alter the political system. Reforms transformed urban China and brought new wealth and opportunities to most urban residents. At the same time some 40 million workers in state-owned factories lost their jobs. Deng's reforms pulled in a tide of foreign investment, creating two economic booms, after 1992 and 1998. Stock markets reopened, state companies privatised and private enterprise began to flourish, especially in the service sector, creating millions of new jobs. Over 100 million peasants left the countryside to work on construction sites or in export-processing factories. The factories were moved out of Běijīng, a city that has once again become a 'centre of consumption'.

The economy was given a huge impetus by decisions to rebuild all major cities virtually from scratch, privatise housing, and sell 50- or 70-year land leases to developers. There was resistance by Party Secretary Chen Xitong to the destruction of Běijīng's centre. During the '80s and early '90s, Chen approved redevelopment plans that aimed to preserve and restore Běijīng's historic centre and characteristic architecture. Chen had earlier helped persuade many army and civilian work units to vacate historical sites they'd occupied during the '70s. However, in 1995, he was ousted by Jiang Zemin who had him imprisoned on corruption charges in the same year.

Once the Party apparatus was under his direct control, President Jiang approved plans to completely rebuild Běijīng and relocate its inhabitants. This was part of the nationwide effort to rebuild the dilapidated and neglected infrastructure of all Chinese cities. The 'trillion-dollar' economic stimulus package has been carried out with remarkable speed. In Běijīng more than a million peasants, housed in dormitories on construction sites, have worked round the clock. New shopping malls, office blocks, hotels and luxury housing developments have been thrown up at astonishing speed. Nothing so fast or on such a big scale could have happened in any other country in the world. Only a dictatorship with the vast human and industrial resources of China at its command could ever have achieved this.

1997	2001	2008
Deng Xiaoping dies before having the chance to see Hong Kong returned to Chinese rule in the same year. The reconstruction of Běijīng is launched.	Work commences on the immense National Grand Theatre west of the Great Hall of the People, Běijīng's futuristic answer to the Shanghai Grand Theatre. The building is not completed for a further seven years.	Běijīng hosts the Olympic Games with a dramatic opening ceremony and a bravura performance that sees China topping the gold medals table; restrictions on international media are temporarily lifted.

Jiang wanted to turn Běijīng into another Hong Kong, with a forest of glass-and-steel skyscrapers. The new municipal leadership threw out the old zoning laws, which limited the height of buildings within the Second Ring Rd. It revoked existing land deeds by declaring old buildings to be dilapidated slums. Such regulations enabled the state to force residents to abandon their homes and move to new housing in satellite cities. Under the new plan, only a fraction of the 67-sq-km Ming city will be preserved. The city boasted over 3679 historic *hútòng* (alleyways) in the 1980s, but only 430 were left according to a field survey in 2006 by the Beijing Institute of Civil Engineering & Architecture.

Some see the rebuilding as a collective punishment on Běijīng for its 1989 rebellion, but others see it as the continuing legacy of Mao's Cultural Revolution and the late Qing dynasty reformers. Many in the current leadership are engineers and ex-Red Guards, including President Hu Jintao, who graduated from Qinghua University during the Cultural Revolution. They are determined to jettison everything from the past and bury recent history. Běijīng's new architecture is designed to embody their aspiration to create a new, forward-looking, hi-tech society, and mark the realisation of the goal of a new modern China.

RELIGION

Mao Zedong made an abortive attempt to exorcise the nation of religious impulses: today, an estimated 400 million Chinese adhere to a particular faith. The bankruptcy of communism as a popular ideology coupled with wide-ranging social problems, from vast income disparities to a sense of powerlessness in a one-party state, has encouraged people to turn to other

CHRISTIANITY IN CHINA

The explosion of interest in Christianity in China over recent years is unprecedented except for the wholesale conversions that accompanied the tumultuous rebellion of the pseudo-Christian Taiping in the 19th century. The history of Christianity in China dates to the arrival of Nestorians in the 7th century but it was with the fall of the Qing dynasty in the early 20th century that the religion began to successfully proliferate, as China increasingly drew upon foreign ideologies and practices. The Cultural Revolution and growing secularism of China under the communists was a spectacular reversal for the faith, but it has flourished in the relatively liberal social climate that followed the death of Mao Zedong.

The economic reforms of the past three decades have brought riches to many urban Chinese, but the spiritual vacuum at the heart of contemporary Chinese life – coupled with the hardships still endured by huge sections of the population – provides an ideal environment for the flourishing of faith. The associations between Christianity and a strong work ethic combined with the progressive standing of Christian nations around the world have only added to its allure. Christianity is furthermore seen as being tolerant and able to accommodate, and to a degree inspire, scientific endeavour. That Chinese Christians made up a considerable proportion of the volunteers helping with relief efforts after the huge Sìchuān earthquake of May 2008 provides an indication of the increasing penetration of the religion into modern Chinese society.

It is hard to calculate the total number of Christians in China. Estimates of 70 million Chinese Protestants and up to 20 million Chinese Catholics (the latter including around 10 million members of the state sanctioned church) are hard to verify; what is undeniable however is the huge number of house churches operating in China, attracting legions of adherents. Being free of government control, unregistered house churches – although essentially illegal in China – attract most worshippers, who prefer them to the official state churches. Increasingly concerned about losing ideological ground to a competing system of thought, the Communist Party has responded by closing numerous house churches, but this has done little to stem the tide. For more details on the Chinese house church movement, go to www.backtojerusalem.com. A fascinating article from the *Times* can be read at: www.timesonline.co.uk/tol/news/article5960010.ece.

Visitors to China increasingly report being stopped by English-speaking Chinese Christians; some are zealously evangelising, an activity that is forbidden. As with the Taiping, whose leader Hong Xiuquan claimed he was the Son of God, the lack of trained priests can create room for the appearance of heresies and other complications.

Jesus in Beijing (*How Christianity is Changing the Global Balance of Power*) by David Aikman argues that China is approaching a tipping point that will transform the land into a largely Christian domain over the next 30 years. However unlikely the scenario, such an achievement would surely owe much to the communist secularisation of China, which has turned the nation's soul into a blank sheet of paper to be written upon.

beliefs. The overemphasis on the temporal world and the pseudo-scientific (un-)certainties of Marxist-Leninism may also have driven people back into the religious fold. And it's certainly not just the Chinese poor who are turning to religion: the drift to spiritual belief has occurred across the income spectrum.

The Chinese were traditionally either Buddhist, Taoist or Confucian; other major faiths in Běijīng are Islam and Christianity. But while religious freedom exists in China, this is freedom with Chinese characteristics. Belief systems (eg Falun Gong) can be banned overnight if Běijīng's leaders sense a threat to their political hegemony. Religious leaders of the major faiths are also cherry-picked by Běijīng. Proselytising is banned, although this is having limited effect on the spread of Christianity.

Indeed, if any religion faces a bright future in China, it is Christianity. By wiping the slate clean, Mao Zedong allowed the monotheistic religion – which had an indecisive presence in China since the 7th century – to flourish in a land that suddenly found itself unsure what to believe in. Most Chinese Christians belong to illicit house churches, rather than the state-recognised Protestant or Catholic churches, so the precise number of Christians is hard to fathom, although figures of over 100 million have been posited.

ARTS

Unlike China's media (p44), Běijīng's arts scene has flourished over the past two decades, fuelled by the oxygen of opening up and reform. Lobotomised during the Cultural Revolution, Běijīng's creative faculty is no longer totally antithetical to communist rule and has found room to grow. But political taboos and suspicion of artistic endeavour among the *lǎobǎixìng* (common people) keeps the artistic ceiling low.

Although the once underground Běijīng artistic community emerged long ago, like anyone with a subterranean upbringing, long shadows are cast across the work of artists over the age of 40. And while there is no doubt that young artists are riding a wave of creative energy that has lifted many of them onto the international map, the context of their existence within a one-party dictatorship needs to be addressed. Although some of the arts (eg fine arts, dance and, to an extent, cinema) exploit ambiguity and interpretative difficulties to fashion risqué commentary, serious limits to what can and cannot be said remain in all of the arts.

Běijīng is certainly edgier and grittier than Shànghǎi – itself hypnotised by money-making, venture capital and sky-scraping skylines – but the northern capital is hardly anti-establishment, despite its revolutionary DNA. Popular energy still goes into commerce and money-making in Běijīng. The Confucian educational system is ill-suited to nurturing creative talent, out-of-the-box thinking or the techniques of inventive criticism. Nonetheless, and despite being a more authoritarian city and the headquarters of communist power, Běijīng tends to attract China's creative talent more than anywhere else.

From a visitor-perspective Běijīng has excellent cinema, theatre, music and visual arts venues and is a fantastic place to catch the enduring vitality of Chinese traditional and contemporary arts.

LITERATURE

In keeping with its well-read and creative reputation among ordinary and educated Chinese, Běijīng has been home to some of China's towering modern literary figures. The literary landscapes of Lao She, Lu Xun, Mao Dun and Guo Moruo are all forever associated with the capital. Venue of the inspirational May Fourth Movement (p22), the first savage stirrings of the Red Guards and the democracy protests of 1989, Běijīng's revolutionary blood has naturally seeped into its literature: over the past century, Běijīng writers have penned their stories of sorrow, fears and aspirations amid a context of ever-changing trends and political upheaval.

Běijīng remains one of China's most important literary centres, with a dynamic group of writers, many young and upcoming, who are further turning the Chinese writing scene on its head. With the relaxation of state controls and the explosion of the internet there has been an enormous flurry of literary activity, ranging from politics to pulp and from blogs to porn.

BĚIJĪNG BOOKSHELF

- *Beijing Coma* (Ma Jian, 2008) Novel revolving around protagonist Dai Wei's involvement with the democracy protests of 1989 and the political coma that ensues.
- *Diary of a Madman and Other Stories* (Lu Xun, translated by William Lyell) Classic tale of mental disintegration and paranoia, and a critique of Confucianism in prerevolutionary China from the father of modern Chinese literature. China's first story published in *báihuà* (colloquial speech), save the first paragraph.
- *Camel Xiangzi* (Lao She, translated by Shi Xiaoqing, 1981) A masterpiece by one of Běijīng's most beloved authors and playwrights about a rickshaw puller living in early-20th-century China.
- *Blades of Grass: The Stories of Lao She* (translated by William Lyell, 2000) This collection contains 14 stories by Lao She – poignant descriptions of people living through times of political upheaval and uncertainty.
- *Black Snow* (Liu Heng, translated by Howard Goldblatt, 1993) Compelling novel about workers in contemporary Běijīng. Superbly written – a fine translation.
- *Empress Orchid* (Anchee Min, 2004) Historical novel about Empress Cixi and her rise to Empress of China during the last days of the Qing dynasty. Good historical background of Běijīng and entertaining to read.
- *Peking Story: The Last Days of Old China* (David Kidd, 2003) A true story of a young man who marries the daughter of an aristocratic Chinese family in Běijīng two years before the 1949 Communist Revolution. The writing is simple, yet immersive.
- *Beijing: A Novel* (Philip Gambone, 2003) A well-written account of an American working in a medical clinic in Běijīng who falls in love with a local artist. One of the few books out there to explore in-depth the intricacies of Běijīng gay subculture.
- *The Noodle Maker* (Ma Jian, translated by Flora Drew, 2004) A collection of interconnected stories as told by a state-employed writer during the aftermath of the Tiananmen Square massacre. Bleak, comical and unforgettable.
- *Sounds of the River: A Young Man's University Days in Beijing* (Da Chen, 2003) A humorous account of the author's life as a student in Běijīng. The writing is lyrical and uplifting.
- *Lake with No Name* (Diane Wei Liang, 2004) An intelligent memoir of a young woman's involvement in the events leading up to 4 June 1989. The author writes movingly of her relationships with many of the activists involved.
- *Foreign Babes in Beijing: Behind the Scenes of a New China* (Rachel Dewoskin, 2005) An easygoing account of a young woman's five years spent in Běijīng during the mid-1990s.

The Birth of Modern Chinese Literature

Until the publication of Lu Xun's short story *Diary of a Madman* in 1918, Chinese literature had been composed in classical Chinese *(gǔwén)*, a kind of Shakespearian language far removed from colloquial speech *(báihuà)*. Rendering of texts in classical Chinese maintained divisions between educated and uneducated Chinese, putting literature beyond the reach of the common person and fashioning a cliquey *lingua franca* for officials and scholars. For Lu Xun to write his short story – itself a radical fable of palpable terror – in the spoken vernacular was dynamite.

The opening paragraph of Lu's seminal story uses classical (archaic) language. The stultified introduction – peppered with archaic character use and the excruciatingly paired down grammar of classical Chinese – continues as one solid block of text, without any new paragraphs or indentation. Then suddenly the passage concludes and the reader is confronted with the appearance of fluent colloquial and vernacular – *spoken* – Chinese:

今天晚上，很好的月光 *Tonight there is good moonlight*

The effect on Chinese readers was explosive – rather like David Bowie pitching up in the middle of a Latin hymn recital. Chinese people were at last able to read language as it was spoken and the short story's influence on creative expression was electric. Lu Xun's tale records the diary entries of a man descending into paranoia and despair. Fearful that those around him are engaging in cannibalism, the man's terrifying suspicions are seen as a critique of the self-consuming nature of feudal society. It is a haunting and powerful work, which instils doubts as to the madness of the narrator and concludes with lines that offer a glimmer of hope.

From this moment on, mainstream Chinese literature would be written as it was thought and spoken: Chinese writing had been modernised. The text of *Diary of a Madman* in Chinese (minus the classical Chinese introduction) can be downloaded at www.gutenberg.org/etext/25423. Lu Xun's works can be picked up in translation at the Lu Xun Museum (p95).

Pre-1989 Literature

Contemporary Chinese literature is commonly grouped into two stages: pre-1989 and post-1989. The 1949 ascendency saw literature gradually became a tool of state control and most work in this period echoed the Communist Party line, with dull, formulaic language in a socialist realist framework. Writers were required to inject their work with stock phrases and cardboard characters that embodied political ideals. Inseparable from propaganda, literary production was banal and unimaginative, with creative inspiration making way for Maoist political correctness; publishing was nationalised. Literature had taken a step sideways and two steps back.

The Hundred Flowers Movement (1956–57) promised a period of open criticism and debate, but instead resulted in a widespread crackdown on intellectuals, including writers. During the Cultural Revolution (1966–76), writers either toed the line or were mercilessly purged. Běijīng writer Lao She (1899–1966; p78) was badly beaten and humiliated by Red Guards in August 1966 and committed suicide the next day in a Běijīng lake.

After Mao's death in 1976, Chinese artists and writers threw off political constraints and began to write more freely, exploring new modes of literary expression. Western books began to appear in translation, including works by authors such as Faulkner, Woolf, Hemingway and DH Lawrence. The Chinese also developed a taste for more mainstream fare such as Kurt Vonnegut and even Jackie Collins. This deluge of Western writing had a great impact on many Chinese authors who were exposed for the first time to a wide array of literary techniques and styles.

An important writer to emerge during this period was Zhang Jie, who first drew the attention of literary critics with the publication of her daring novella *Love Must Not Be Forgotten* (1979). With its intimate portrayal of a middle-aged woman and her love of a married man, the book challenged the traditional mores of marriage. Chinese authorities disparaged the book, calling it morally corrupt, but the book was extremely popular with readers and won a national book award. Zhang went on to write the novels *Heavy Wings* (1980) and *The Ark* (1981). *The Ark,* about three women separated from their husbands, established Zhang as China's 'first feminist author'. Shen Rong was another talented female author; she appeared during the 1980s. Her novella *At Middle Age* (1980), tells the plight of a Chinese intellectual during the Cultural Revolution who must balance her family life with her career as a doctor.

Freer of the fear of persecution, several literary movements flowered during the late 1970s and 1980s, including 'Scar Literature', where writers dared to explore the traumatic events of the Cultural Revolution, and 'New Realism', which delved into previously taboo issues, such as AIDS, party corruption and other topical social problems. One of the most controversial novels to appear in the 1980s was *Half of Man is Woman,* by Zhang Xianliang and translated into English by Martha Avery. The novel is a candid exploration of sexuality and marriage in contemporary China and went on to become an international bestseller. Another of Zhang's works in English translation is *Getting Used to Dying* (1989), about a writer's new-found sexual freedom (also translated by Martha Avery).

Post-1989 Literature

The tragic events of 1989 inspired the desire for a more 'Realist' type of literature, paving the way for a new group of writers, such as the now internationally recognised 'hooligan author' Wang Shuo, a sailor turned fiction writer, famous for his satirical stories about China's underworld and political corruption. Wang's stories – dark, gritty and taking jabs at just about every aspect of contemporary Chinese society – have not endeared him to the Chinese authorities, who see him as a 'spiritual pollutant'. One of Wang's most contentious novels, *Please Don't Call Me Human,* first published in 1989, was written after the Tiananmen Square democracy protests and provides a mocking look at the failures of China's state security system. Wang's works appeal to a broad spectrum of Chinese society, despite being banned. He has written over 20 books as well as screenplays for TV and film. Books available in English include *Playing for Thrills* (2000) and *Please Don't Call Me Human* (1998), both translated by Howard Goldblatt.

The literature that emerged in the 1990s was a far cry from the socialist realist Maoist tracts of earlier years. The 1990s witnessed an explosion in experimental writing that probed the boundaries of risqué and often controversial subject matter. Wang Meng, former minister of culture, became celebrated for his stream-of-consciousness style of writing and his satirical take on everything from politics to Chinese medicine. His collection of short stories, *The Stubborn Porridge and Other Stories* (1994), translated by Zhu Hong, is a smart, scathing look at modern Chinese society. The composer, playwright and author Liu Sola, who began writing in the mid-1980s, became internationally recognised a decade later with her novel *Chaos and All That* (1994), translated by Richard King, about a Chinese woman in London who pens a novel about growing up in Běijīng during the Cultural Revolution.

In recent years, China's rampant commercialisation and excessive materialism have given an emerging generation of authors a brand new platform and a new round of ammunition. Younger authors, who remember nothing about the Cultural Revolution and who only have dim memories of the Tiananmen democracy protests, write instead about the loneliness and decadence of modern city life. Escapism is a common theme in contemporary novels, often through sex, drugs and alcohol. The provocative novel *Beijing Doll* (2004) by Chun Shu (Sue), translated by Howard Goldblatt, is written by a high school dropout who lives a life fuelled by drugs, sex and booze. Called a 'punk memoir', the book is currently banned in China for its disturbing account of teenagers caught up in Běijīng's dark underbelly. Annie Wang's *The People's Republic of Desire* (2006) also holds nothing back with its candid exploration of sexuality in modern Běijīng. The acclaimed novelist Ma Jian also picks up on the theme of escapism, but infuses his work with a sense of nostalgia. *Red Dust* (2004) by Ma Jian, translated by Flora Drew, is a poignant story of the author's three-year trek through Guìzhōu, Myanmar and Tibet. Memories of the Tiananmen era have not completely faded for this younger generation of writers, however, and are explored in Ma Jian's *Beijing Coma* (2008), an incisive retrospective novel exploring the events of June 1989.

One of the most moving works to appear in English within the past few years is *A Thousand Years of Good Prayers* (2006) by Yiyun Li. The short stories in this collection, winner of the Guardian First Book Award in 2006, reveal the lives of ordinary Chinese caught up in the sweeping cultural changes of the past 20 years and are told in haunting prose.

The unstoppable internet has recently given rise to a vibrant, alternative literary scene. Legions of established and wannabe authors are posting their poetry, personal diaries and even novels online and attracting huge numbers of readers.

If in town in spring, make sure you get your literary fix at the Bookworm International Literary Festival (p13), held at the Bookworm (p148). Numerous local and international authors are invited to talk; among luminaries at the 2009 festival were Mo Yan, Ian Buruma, Jasper Becker, Blake Morrison and the renowned Chinese–English translator Howard Goldblatt.

VISUAL ARTS

In the mid-1970s, local artists still aspired to master the skills of socialist realism, a vibrant communist-endorsed style that had its roots in non-Chinese neo-classical art, the life-like canvases of Jacques Louis David and, of course, the output of Soviet Union painters. Infused with political symbolism and dripping with propaganda, the vibrant artistic style was produced on an industrial scale, with mechanical rules governing content and style. The same techniques were applied to most literary production as creativity became subservient to the ideals of the communist state.

Traditional precepts of Chinese classical painting were sidelined and Chinese art instead found itself importing foreign artistic techniques wholesale. Washes on silk were replaced with oil on canvas while a Realist attention to detail supplanted China's traditional obsession with the mysterious and ineffable. The entire course of Chinese painting – which had evolved in glacial increments over the centuries – was redirected virtually overnight. Vaporous landscapes, in which people played a minor or incidental role, were replaced with harder-edged panoramas in which

top picks

BĚIJĪNG ART GALLERIES & NEIGHBOURHOODS

- **798 Art District** (p133) Modern Chinese art's premier zone, a former factory site converted to house up-to-the-minute art works.
- **Cǎochǎngdì** (p134) Concentration of cutting-edge art galleries in the orbit of 798 Art District.
- **Courtyard Gallery** (p77) Basement, minimalist contemporary Chinese art gallery handily tucked away by the Forbidden City moat.
- **Red Gate Gallery** (p86) One of Běijīng's best-known galleries, an innovative feature of the landmark Southeast Corner Watchtower.
- **Chinese Contemporary Beijing** (p133) This gallery shows mainly group exhibitions of contemporary Chinese artists.
- **China Art Museum** (p78) This was the first gallery in Běijīng to exhibit modern Western artworks and remains a pivotal institution in China's contemporary art scene.

humans occupied a central, commanding position. Human activity in these paintings was directed towards the glory of the Communist Revolution and as such the individual artistic temperament was subscripted to the service of the state. According to the communist vision, man was now the governor of his destiny and art was another foot soldier in this quest. Chinese art consequently became art for the masses.

It was only with the death of Mao Zedong in September 1976 that the shadow of the Cultural Revolution – when Chinese aesthetics was conditioned by the threat of violence – began its retreat. The individual artistic temperament was once again allowed more freedom to explore beyond propaganda. Painters such as Luo Zhongli employed the Realist techniques they learned in China's art academies to portray the harsh realities etched in the faces of contemporary peasants. Others escaped the suffocating confines of socialist realism to explore new horizons, experimenting with a variety of contemporary forms.

A voracious appetite for Western art put further distance between traditional Chinese aesthetics and artistic endeavour. One group of artists, the Stars, found retrospective inspiration in Picasso and German expressionism. The ephemeral group had a lasting impact on the development of Chinese art in the 1980s and 1990s, leading the way for the New Wave movement that emerged in 1985. New Wave artists were greatly influenced by Western art, especially the iconoclastic Marcel Duchamp, and further challenged traditional Chinese artistic norms. The New Wave artist Huang Yongping, destroyed his works at exhibitions, in an effort to escape from the notion of 'art'. Some New Wave artists adapted Chinese characters into abstract symbols, while others employed graphic images in a bid to shock viewers. Political realities became instant subject matter with performance artists wrapping themselves in plastic or tape to symbolise the repressive realities of modern-day China.

The pivotal turning point for contemporary Chinese art came in February 1989 when Běijīng's China Art Museum (p78) sponsored an exhibit devoted exclusively to Chinese avant-garde art for the first time, inviting all of the important artists of the preceding decade to exhibit. On the opening day of the exhibition, artists Tang Song and Xiao Lu fired pistol shots at their own installations and the exhibition closed. Both artists were arrested but released several days later.

The disturbing events during and after June 1989 created artistic disillusionment with the political situation in China and hope soured into cynicism. This attitude is reflected through the 1990s in artworks permeated with feelings of loss, loneliness and social isolation. Many artists left China to find greater artistic freedom in the West. Two of the most important Běijīng artists to characterise this period of 'Cynical Realism' are Fang Lijun and Yue Minjun. Both created grotesque portraits of themselves and friends that convey a sense of boredom and mock joviality.

Experiments with American-style pop art were another reaction to the events of 1989. Inspired by Warhol, some artists took symbols of socialist realism and transformed them into kitschy visual commentary. Images of Mao appeared against floral backgrounds and paintings of rosy-cheeked peasants and soldiers were interspersed with ads for Canon cameras and Coca-Cola. Artists were not only responding to the tragedies of the Tiananmen massacre but also to the rampant consumerism that was sweeping the country.

Reaction to the rapid modernisation of China has been a consistent theme of much Běijīng art from the 1990s to the present day. Urban development and accompanying feelings of isolation and dislocation are themes of Běijīng video artist Zhu Jia. In his video titled 'Double Landscape', a man is being served coffee by a mannequin dressed as a woman. The banality of the video and its lack of drama or narrative suggest the meaningless patterns of urban existence. The artist Yin Xiuzhen has become internationally renowned for her installations that are artistic commentaries on globalisation, urban waste and the destruction of Běijīng's traditional architecture.

Throughout the 1990s, artists who felt marginalised from the cultural mainstream found escape from political scrutiny by setting up their own exhibitions in non-official spaces outside of state-run institutions. Many relied on the financial support of foreign buyers to continue working. Despite political pressure from authorities, some artists began to receive international attention for their art, sparking a worldwide interest in Chinese contemporary art. A defining moment for artists was in 1999, when 20 Chinese artists were invited to participate in the Venice Biennale for the first time.

Chinese art's obsessive focus on contemporary socio-economic realities makes much creativity from this period parochial and predictable, but more universalist themes have become apparent over recent years and the art climate in Běijīng has changed dramatically. Many artists who left China in the 1990s have returned, setting up private studios and galleries. Government censorship remains, but artists are branching out into other areas and moving away from overtly political content and China-specific concerns.

CHINA'S CONTEMPORARY ART SCENE David Eimer

When Brian Wallace arrived in China as a backpacker in 1984 there was no visible contemporary art scene. Artists were viewed with suspicion and were frequently subject to harassment and worse by the authorities. They showed their work to each other and their friends only inside the safety of their own homes. But just as China has transformed itself into an economic powerhouse, so Chinese artists have made the long march from obscurity to global recognition and their work has become prized by both mainland Chinese art collectors and foreigners.

Part of that success is due to Wallace, an Australian who grew up in a small country town in New South Wales. Having returned to China to live in 1986, he opened the Red Gate Gallery (p86), Běijīng's first space devoted to contemporary art, in the imposing Southeast Corner Watchtower in 1991. In 2005, he opened his second gallery in the flourishing 798 Art District in Dàshānzi (p133).

Wallace represents, or has represented, just about every contemporary Chinese artist of note. His role in helping develop China's booming art scene means he's often referred to as the 'father of contemporary Chinese art'. 'Other people have said that. I would never say it,' protests the amiable, bearded Wallace. In fact, when he started out in the late '80s, it was a simple case of helping out mates. 'My friends were artists and in those days there were no galleries, so we started to organise exhibitions for them.'

Things have changed dramatically since then. Paintings by artists such as Fang Lijun, Zhang Xiaogang and Yue Minjun can fetch US$1 million at auction, as the advent of mainland Chinese buyers has helped drive prices up. 'In the last couple of years, galleries overseas have started to pick up on contemporary Chinese artists, museums have started to buy and now the auction houses have kicked in. Their job is to talk up the market of course, which they've been doing quite well,' says Wallace.

Painters and sculptors are the artists who've benefited the most from the boom. 'The more traditional forms are the most popular. The market for photography has eased off a bit. Mainland buyers, who make up 20% of our customers, are more conservative than overseas buyers. They like the contemporary work, but they stick to paintings rather than the more conceptual stuff,' points out Wallace. Nor have female artists prospered as much as the men. 'I think it's more difficult for women artists. They don't necessarily hold up half the sky in the art world.'

In the past, Chinese artists were often accused of being derivative and in thrall to their Western contemporaries. Wallace believes that's no longer the case. 'They went through a period where they absorbed everything, but now they're much more confident and appreciative of the attention they're getting. The stamp of approval gives them a lot of confidence. There's a lot of gutsy stuff out there now.'

While China's film-makers and writers are still subject to stringent censorship, the visual arts have been treated more leniently. 'The government has accepted, or realised, that young artists aren't going to bring down the country,' says Wallace. 'But we know the political limits and we have had to take shows down in the past when they've been over-the-top politically.'

With an ever-increasing range of art available, visitors to Běijīng who want to buy a piece can find something to suit every taste and price range. 'You can get some very valuable prints by very important artists for hundreds of dollars, or we can sell you a large oil painting for US$200,000,' says Wallace. With the demand for Chinese art set to continue, you could end up with a bargain.

Dàshānzi, a factory-turned-gallery zone in northeastern Běijīng, is a mandatory destination for artists and buyers. Created in 2001, this once quiet enclave has transformed into a thriving neighbourhood of lofts, galleries, bookshops, design studios, cafes and bars, all tucked into a small section of Dàshānzi called 798 Art District (p133) – named after Factory 798, a disused electronics factory complex built in the 1950s by East German architects. Here, Mao's ideals are reinterpreted through the artistic works of China's new visionaries, resulting in a lively, enigmatic and sometimes controversial community that attracts artists, dealers and critics from around the world. For an excellent behind-the-scenes look at the vibrant Dàshānzi art community, be sure to get your hands on *Beijing 798: Reflections on Art, Architecture and Society in China*, edited by Běijīng artist Huang Rui. Nearby Cǎochǎngdì is a further domain of cutting-edge galleries.

With scores of private and state-run galleries and a booming art market (p153), Běijīng is a fantastic city to witness the changing face of contemporary Chinese art. While traditional Chinese art is still practised in the capital, Běijīng has fully surrendered to the artistic currents that sweep the international sphere. Today's Běijīng is home to a vibrant community of artists practising a diverse mix of art forms, from performance art, installation and video art to film. Běijīng artists compete internationally in art events, and joint exhibitions with European and North American artists are frequent. Western artists have also flocked to Běijīng in an aesthetic *entente cordiale*. BritArt supremo Tracy Emin's *My Bed* may have been deemed too squalid for local tastes at Capital Museum in 2007 (and was substituted with a less ghastly version of her living quarters), but her work was shown alongside other luminaries from the contemporary British art scene.

The capital hosts several art festivals, including the Dashanzi International Arts Festival (every spring) and the Beijing Biennale, held every two years in September/October, which attract artists, dealers and critics from around the world.

MUSIC
Traditional Music
Traditional Chinese musical instruments include the two-stringed fiddle (*èrhú*) – famed for its desolate wail – the two-stringed viola (*húqín*), the vertical flute (*dòngxiāo*), the horizontal flute (*dízi*), the four-stringed lute (*pípa*) and the Chinese zither (*zhēng*). To appreciate traditional music in Běijīng, catch performances at the Lao She Teahouse (p193).

Popular Music
China was a definite latecomer to popular music. By the time Elvis was dead, London Mods were snapping up third-hand Lambrettas for their late 1970s revival and New Romantics were set to generate a worldwide shortage of firm-hold hair gel, Beijingers were still tapping their feet to 'The East is Red'. Like all of the arts, music was tranquilised during the Cultural Revolution as China's self-imposed isolation severed creative ties with the outside world.

In 1986 during a 'World Peace' music concert held in Běijīng, a young trumpet player named Cui Jian walked on stage, strapped on a guitar and played a song that would forever change the sound and look of Chinese popular music. With its distinctly abrasive vocal style and lyrics describing feelings of loneliness and alienation, 'Nothing To My Name' ('Yi Wo Suo You') was unlike any song ever performed by a mainland Chinese musician.

For early Chinese rock bands like Tang Dynasty and Black Panther, the riffs and power chords of heavy metal from the '70s and '80s (ie Led Zeppelin and Rush) provided the inspiration to pick up guitars, grow long hair and start a band. This 'first generation' of Chinese rockers took inspiration from classic rock, heavy metal, and punk's aggression and abrasiveness.

Since those early days, Běijīng has gained the reputation as China's rock-music mecca. Overexposure to the saccharine confections of mainstream Cantopop and Mandopop may be like drinking gallons of extra-sugary Fanta, but the infusion of new styles and sounds has left an indelible impression on China's aural landscape and created a potent new subculture. Young Chinese people might be razor-sharp when it comes to the latest Chinese sounds, but few are more than dimly aware of the roots of all modern popular music – whether it's Chinese punk, syrupy Mandopop or rock – in American blues and jazz.

DJ culture has also come to China with Běijīng's new wave of clubs. Club-goers can now get their grooves on to the booming sounds of hip-hop, house, drum and bass, techno and trance in addition to the popular sounds of home-grown Chinese house music.

Rock festivals worth looking out for include the open-air MIDI Music Festival at the Beijing MIDI School of Music (☎ 6259 0101, 6259 0007), which is held every October. Another excellent festival is the Beijing Pop Festival (www.beijingpopfestival.com/music) held every September in Chaoyang Park. Catch Běijīng's up-and-coming acts as well as more established names such as post-punk outfit SUBS, Brain Failure, Carsick Cars, rockers PK14, Snapline and popsters Hedgehog at Běijīng's numerous live-music venues (see p188).

For classical music and opera lovers, the five-day International Music Festival is held every May and attracts internationally renowned composers from China and abroad. Performances are held at the Central Conservatory of Music and the Beijing Concert Hall (p192). The Beijing Music Festival (www.bmf.org.cn; p14) is held for around 30 days during the months of October and November and features music performances by opera, jazz and classical artists from around the world. For a list of opera venues in the capital, see p193.

CINEMA

Cinema in China dates to 1896, when a Spaniard (Galen Bocca) with a film projector blew the socks off crowds in a Shànghǎi tea-house garden. Although Shànghǎi's cosmopolitan gusto would help make the city the capital of China's film industry, China's first movie – *Conquering Jun Mountain* (an excerpt from a piece of Beijing opera) – was actually filmed in Běijīng in 1905.

Like all the arts, China's film business went into steep decline after 1949; the dark days of the Cultural Revolution (1966–76) were particularly devoid of creative output. While Taiwan's and Hong Kong's movie industries continued to flourish, China's cinema business was coerced into satisfying political agendas with output focused on propaganda and glorification of the Communist Party. The film industry in China has yet to recover: taboo subjects still have directors walking on egg shells and criticism of the authorities remains hazardous. Contemporary Chinese TV dramas are often wooden and artificial – signs of creative uncertainty across the industry.

Western audiences awoke to a new golden age of Chinese cinema in the 1980s and 1990s when the lush palettes and lavish tragedies of the Fifth Generation directors stimulated the right aesthetic nerves. The cinematic output of the Fifth Generation – directors such as Chen Kaige and Zhang Yimou – perfectly dovetailed with China's nascent opening up and escape from Mao-era constraints. Garlanded with praise, received with standing ovations and rewarded with several major film awards, rich works such as *Farewell My Concubine* (Chen Kaige; 1993) and *Raise the Red Lantern* (Zhang Yimou; 1991) redefined Chinese cinema, radiating a beauty that entranced Western cinema-goers and made their directors the darlings of Cannes. Chinese cinema-goers admired their artistry, but saw Fifth Generation output as pandering to the Western market.

Sixth Generation film directors collectively shunned the exquisite beauty of the Fifth Generation, taking the opposite tack to render the angst and grimness of modern urban Chinese life. Their independent, low-budget works put an entirely different spin on mainland Chinese film-making, but their dour subject matter and harsh film style (frequently in black and white) left many Western viewers cold.

The Beijing Film Academy graduate Zhang Yuan set a precedent for gritty, independent film-making with *Mama* (1990), a beautiful but disturbing film about a mother and her autistic child. This small film, created without government sponsorship, had a large influence on future film-makers. Zhang followed up with *Beijing Bastards* (1993), which focussed on the preoccupations and drug-taking lifestyle of Běijīng's youth. Another important film, *Frozen* (1995), directed by Wang Xiaoshuai, also strayed into controversial territory with its disturbing examination of suicide. *Beijing Bicycle* (2001), also directed by Wang Xiaoshuai and inspired by De Sica's *Bicycle Thieves*, is a tale of a Běijīng youth seeking to recover his stolen bike.

Today, except for a few directors who are able to attract domestic and overseas investments, such as Zhang Yimou and Chen Kaige, Chinese film-makers are constantly dealing with funding problems, small audiences and high ticket prices. To cap it all off, many Sixth Generation films went unseen inside China. Both Fifth and Sixth Generation directors ran into problems with

BEST FILMS ABOUT BĚIJĪNG

- *Beijing Bicycle* (2001) Eschewing the lavish colour of Fifth Generation directors and viewing Běijīng through a Realist lens, Wang Xiaoshuai's film follows young and hapless courier Guo on the trail of his stolen mountain bike.
- *The Last Emperor* (1987) Bernardo Bertolucci's celebrated (seven Oscars including best director, best costume design and best cinematography) and extravagant epic charts the life of Henry Puyi during his accession and the ensuing disintegration of dynastic China.
- *Beijing Bastards* (1993) Starring rocker Cui Jian, Yuan Zhang's documentary-style cinematography tags along with a rock band in Běijīng, grittily capturing the energy of Běijīng's alienated and discontented youth.
- *The Gate of Heavenly Peace* (1995) Using original footage from the six weeks preceding the Tiananmen massacre, Richard Gordon and Carma Hinton's moving three-hour tribute to the spirit of the student movement and its annihilation is a must-see.
- *Farewell My Concubine* (1993) Charting a dramatic course through 20th-century Chinese history from the 1920s to the Cultural Revolution, Chen Kaige's film is a sumptuous and stunning narrative of two friends from Beijing opera school whose lives are framed against social and political turmoil.
- *The Making of Steel* (1998) Lu Xuecheng directed this intriguing film about a rebellious young man and his involvement in Běijīng's underground music scene during the 1970s and 1990s.
- *The World* (2005) Jia Zhangke's social commentary on the effects of globalisation is set in a Běijīng theme park called 'World Park', where workers and visitors play out their lives among replicas of the world's monuments.
- *Blooming Flowers in Springtime* (2002) This exquisitely beautiful short film by Chang Zheng tells the story of a young deaf-mute couple in Běijīng and the trials of bringing up their hearing son.
- *Shower* (1999) Though at times overly sentimental, this endearing film about a bathhouse owner and his sons warmed the hearts of both Chinese and foreign audiences. Directed by Zhang Yang.
- *For Fun* (1992) Directed by Ning Ying, China's most renowned female film-maker, this film follows the life of a retired custodian at a Beijing opera theatre and his humorous attempts to transform a group of grumpy senior citizens into opera singers.

the authorities and the most controversial films were clipped by the censors or banned outright. Other retaliatory measures included revoking their passports so they could not attend foreign film festivals. Regardless, the movie industry carries on, producing surprisingly high-quality films on tiny budgets.

Two of the most intriguing movies of the past few years include *The Banquet* (2006), a lavish historical epic directed by Feng Xiaogang and starring China's leading lady Zhang Ziyi, and Zhang Yimou's *Curse of the Golden Flower*. Both point to historical dramas becoming the default position for Chinese cinema; even Hong Kong's John Woo has chipped into the lucrative genre with *Red Cliff* (Parts 1 and 2; 2008 and 2009) starring Tony Leung. Chinese cinema's gravitation towards historical epics is largely due to the safety of the material and the fascination Chinese people have with their nation's history.

On a much simpler note, Zhang Yuan's *Little Red Flowers* (2006) is a poignant story of a young boy adapting to the rigid conformity of Chinese kindergarten and is well worth seeing. A film that caused a buzz at international film festivals is Jia Zhangke's *The World* (2005), which follows the lives of youth and migrant workers employed at a Běijīng theme park. *The Knot* (2006), a tragedy revolving around separation, saw considerable success in China. *Still Life* by Jia Zhangke was awarded the Golden Lion for Best Film at the 2006 Venice Film Festival, while *Tuya's Marriage* won the Golden Bear for Best Film at the 2007 Berlin Film Festival.

A good place to see Chinese films by established and emerging directors is at the Beijing Student Film Festival, a 20-day event held every April. Films are shown at various venues around the city – you can check the *Beijinger* (www.thebeijinger.com) for screen times.

Chinese cinema is under constant threat from piracy, which effectively pulls the plug on many smaller, independent productions. With cinema tickets costing over 10 times the price of a pirate DVD (available on the streets within days of the film's first screening), fewer and fewer Chinese film-makers see movie production as a viable money-making proposition.

THEATRE

Theatre (p194) in China was traditionally sung in the form of opera. Spoken drama is a far more recent introduction and remains an emerging art. An increasing number of theatrical companies are coming to Běijīng from abroad, however, and local theatre companies are staging more and more productions, many of which are influenced by Western technique and content. For stage events in Běijīng, consult the stage listings of the *Beijinger* (www.thebeijinger.com).

BEIJING OPERA

Beijing opera is still regarded as the *crème de la crème* of all the opera styles in China and has traditionally been the opera of the masses. Intrigues, disasters or rebellions are common themes, and many opera narratives have their source in the fairy tales, stock characters and legends of classical literature.

The style of music, singing and costumes in Beijing opera are products of its origins. In the past opera was performed on open-air stages in markets, streets, tea houses or temple courtyards. The orchestra had to play loudly and the performers had to develop a piercing style of singing, which could be heard over the throng. The costumes were a garish collection of sharply contrasting colours because the stages were originally lit by oil lamps.

The movements and techniques of the dance styles of the Tang dynasty were similar to those used in today's opera. Provincial opera companies were characterised by their dialect and style of singing, but when these companies converged on Běijīng they started a style of musical drama called *kunqu*. This developed during the Ming dynasty, along with a more popular variety of play-acting pieces based on legends, historical events and popular novels. These styles gradually merged by the late-18th and early-19th centuries into the opera we see today.

The musicians usually sit on the stage in plain clothes and play without written scores. The *èrhú*, a two-stringed fiddle that is tuned to a low register and has a soft tone, generally supports the *húqín*, a two-stringed viola tuned to a high register. The *yuèqín*, a sort of moon-shaped four-stringed guitar, has a soft tone and is used to support the *èrhú*. Other instruments are the *shēng* (a reed flute) and the *pípa* (lute), as well as drums, bells and cymbals. Last but not least is the *ban,* a time-clapper that virtually directs the band, beats time for the actors and gives them their cues.

Apart from the singing and the music, the opera also incorporates acrobatics and mime. Few props are used, so each move, gesture or facial expression is symbolic. A whip with silk tassels indicates an actor riding a horse. Lifting a foot means going through a doorway. Language is often archaic Chinese, music is ear-splitting (bring some cotton wool), but the costumes and make-up are magnificent. Look out for a swift battle sequence – the female warriors involved are trained acrobats who leap, twirl, twist and somersault in attack.

There are numerous other forms of opera. The Cantonese variety is more 'music hall', often with a 'boy meets girl' theme. Gaojia opera is one of the five local operatic forms from the Fújiàn province and is also popular in Taiwan. It has songs in the Fújiàn dialect but is influenced by the Beijing-opera style.

If you get bored after the first hour or so, check out the audience antics – spitting, eating apples, plugging into a transistor radio (important sports match perhaps?) or loud tea slurping. It's lively audience entertainment fit for an emperor. For recommended theatres that stage performances of Beijing opera, see p193.

ARCHITECTURE

Whether it's the Great Wall, the Forbidden City or the brand spanking new CCTV Building, Běijīng's shape-shifting architecture wows visitors across the generations. From its warren-like *hútòng* to the Soviet-style monuments of the 1950s, imperial palace buildings and frayed temple halls, Běijīng's architectural vernacular is as unique to the capital as the local dialect or the aromas of Peking duck. In the space of a few minutes, you can amble from an ancient *hútòng* past the vermillion Forbidden City (p56), trot alongside the mind-numbing Great Hall of the People (p91) and arrive at the vast and glittering sci-fi style National Grand Theatre (p91). In the process you will have spanned an architectural narrative at least six-centuries long and seen

RELIGIOUS ARCHITECTURE

With today's religious renaissance (p27) drawing legions of Chinese to prayer, Běijīng's temples and shrines are increasingly busy places of worship.

Buddhist, Taoist and Confucian temples may appear complex, but their layout and sequence of deities tend to follow quite strict schematic patterns, so it helps to understand some basic principles. Temples are virtually all arranged on a north–south axis in a series of halls, the main door of each hall facing south, in the same way as courtyard houses and the halls of the Forbidden City.

Chinese temples are strikingly different to Christian churches because of their open plan and succession of halls; buildings follow a hierarchy and are interspersed with breezy open-air courtyards. This allows the weather to permeate the empty spaces, changing the mood of the temple depending on the climate. The open-air layout also allows the *qì* (energy) to circulate, dispersing stale air and allowing incense to be liberally burned.

Large numbers of Běijīng's temples have vanished since the Qing dynasty. Many surviving shrines and churches were damaged, left empty or employed for another purpose during the Cultural Revolution (1966–76): some served as warehouses or factories while others were requisitioned for public use or to house families.

Today, many temples have been restored to their original purpose, but others have disappeared (such as Big Buddha Temple off Dafosi Dongjie; p142), are still occupied by residents (Fire God Temple; p71) or the military (Dagaoxuan Temple; p141), or have been converted to offices (Bailin Temple; p71). Some, such as the small Guanyin Temple just off Dazhalan Xijie (p140), are due for restoration while others are either currently shut (Guangfuguan Taoist Temple; p138) or plan to reopen as hotels (Songzhuyuan Temple).

Buddhist Temples

Although there are notable exceptions, most Buddhist temples tend to follow a predictable layout. The very first hall is frequently the Hall of Heavenly Kings (Tiānwáng Diàn), where a sedentary statue of the smiling and podgy bodhisattva Maitreya (Mílèfó), also known as the Monk with the Bag or the Laughing Buddha, is flanked by the ferocious Four Heavenly Kings. Behind is the first courtyard, where the drum and bell towers often stand – if the temple is large enough – and smoking braziers for the burning of incense may be positioned. The largest hall is usually named the Great Treasure Hall (Dàxióngbǎo Bǎodiàn) where you will often discover a golden trinity of statues, representing the historic, contemporary and future Buddhas. You can often find two rows of nine *luóhàn* (Buddhist, especially a monk, who has achieved enlightenment and passes to nirvana at death) on either wall to the side. In other temples the *luóhàn* appear in a crowd of 500, housed in a separate hall; the Azure Clouds Temple in Fragrant Hills Park (p133) has an example.

A statue of Guanyin (the Goddess of Mercy) often stands at the rear of the main hall, facing north, atop a fish's head or a rocky outcrop. The goddess may also be venerated in her own hall and often has a multitude of arms, such as at Chéngdé's outstanding Puning Temple (p222). The rear hall may house sutras (Buddhist scriptures) in a building

how the continuity of vision has collapsed. Since 1949, China's communist rulers have read from an eclectic design compendium and given little thought to integrating new architecture in a thoughtful or sensitive fashion.

TRADITIONAL ARCHITECTURE

Běijīng may date from the Yuan dynasty but traditional architecture in the capital is largely a legacy of the Ming and Qing dynasties (1368–1911). A few fitful fragments have somehow struggled through from the Mongol era, but they are rare. The communists were accomplished destroyers: when the mighty gate of Xīzhí Mén was levelled in 1969, the Yuan dynasty gate of Héyì Mén was discovered within the later brickwork; they were both brought down.

Standout structures from early dynasties include the magnificent Forbidden City (p56), the Summer Palace (p127), and the remaining *hútòng* and courtyard-style homes in the centre of the city. Most historic buildings, however, date from the Qing dynasty (1644–1911) and indeed from the latter part of the Manchu dynasty; little survives from the Ming dynasty, although the conceptual plan of the city dates to Ming times. Old buildings were constructed with wood and paper, so fire was a perennial hazard (spot the huge bronze water vats dotted around the Forbidden City for extinguishing flames that could rapidly reduce halls to smoking mounds). Because buildings were not durable, even those that escaped fire were not expected to last long.

called the Scripture Storing Hall (Cángjīnglóu). A pagoda (tǎ) may rise above the main halls or may be the last vestige of a vanished temple, such as at the Yongyousi Pagoda (p221) in Chéngdé. Originally built to house the remains of Buddha and later other Buddhist relics, pagodas were also used for storing sutras, religious artefacts and documents. Some pagodas can still be climbed for excellent views, but others may be out of bounds; Zhèngdìng (p227) is notable for its large crop of pagodas.

Taoist Temples

As Taoism predates Buddhism and connects to a more primitive and distant era, Taoist shrines are more netherworldly and project more of an atmosphere of superstition and magic. Nonetheless, Taoist temples appear – in the arrangement of their halls – very similar to Buddhist temples.

You will almost certainly see the shape of the circular bāguà (eight trigrams) reflected in eight-sided pavilions and diagrams. The yīn/yáng Taiji diagram is also a common motif. Effigies of Laotzu, the Jade Emperor and other characters popularly associated with Taoist myths, such as the Eight Immortals and the God of Wealth, are customary.

Taoist temple entrances are often guarded by Taoist door gods, similar to those in Buddhist temples, and the main hall is usually called the Hall of the Three Clear Ones (Sānqīng Diàn) and devoted to a triumvirate of Taoist deities.

Taoist monks and nuns are easily distinguished from their shaven-headed Buddhist confrères by their long hair, twisted into topknots, straight trousers and squarish jackets. China's soft martial arts (taichi, bāguà zhǎng and xíng yì quán) are Taoist in inspiration, so you may see monks practising movements and patterns (see p114 for more information).

Confucian Temples

Confucian temples are not as colourful as their Taoist or Buddhist cousins, and can appear musty and neglected. Confucius has ridden a roller-coaster ride of successive adulation and condemnation throughout Chinese history. Confucianism is currently enjoying an upswing after being thoroughly humiliated during the Cultural Revolution when Red Guards savaged the teachings as one of the 'Four Olds'. However, today's communists have seen the benefits of endorsing the harmonising message of Confucius and are actively trying to promote the Confucius Institute abroad. Foreign governments are increasingly seeing the merits of the Confucian vision in fields from education to the workplace.

Confucian temples bristle with steles celebrating local scholars, some supported on the backs of bìxì (mythical tortoise-like dragons). A statue of Kongzi (Confucius) usually resides in the main hall, overseeing rows of musical instruments and flanked by disciples. A mythical animal, the qílín (a statue exists at the Summer Palace), is commonly seen. The qílín was a hybrid animal that appeared on earth only in times of harmony. Běijīng's Confucius Temple (p71) is China's second largest after the temple in Qūfù in Shāndōng, the birthplace of the sage.

The oldest standing structure in the Běijīng municipality is the Great Wall (see p97). Although the wall dates to the 3rd century BC, most of what you will see is the work of Ming dynasty (1368–1644) engineers, while the tourist sections have largely been rebuilt over the past 30 years or so. The largest architectural complex in China is the Forbidden City (p56), covering 72 hectares.

Fine examples of temple architecture can be seen at Beihai Park (p87), the Lama Temple (p70) and at Chéngdé (p218).

One of the best places to see the ancient architecture of China is at the Beijing Ancient Architecture Museum (p117), which has exhibits of architecture ranging from early mud huts to examples of Ming and Qing palaces.

Most residences in old Běijīng were once sìhéyuàn, houses situated on four sides of a courtyard. The houses were aligned exactly – the northern house was found directly opposite the southern, the eastern directly across from the western. Sìhéyuàn can still be found within the Second Ring Rd, and although many have disappeared, an increasing number have appeared as hotels.

Traditionally the Chinese followed a basic ground plan when they built their homes. In upper-class homes as well as in palaces and temples, buildings were surrounded by an exterior wall and designed on a north–south axis, with an entrance gate and a gate built for spirits that might try to enter the building. Behind the entry gates in palaces and residential buildings was a public hall and behind this were private living quarters built around a central court with a garden. The garden area of upper-class gentry and imperial families spawned an entire subgenre of 'recreational architecture', which included gardens, pavilions, pagodas, ponds and bridges.

REBUILDING BĚIJĪNG

For first-time visitors to Běijīng, the city can be an energising and inspiring synthesis of East and West, old and new. After 1949 the characteristics of the old city of Běijīng – formidable and dwarfing city walls, vast and intimidating gates, unbroken architectural narrative and commanding sense of symmetry – were flung out of the window. Many argue (such as author Wang Jun in *Story of a City*) that the historic soul of Běijīng has been extirpated, never to return. In a dismal irony, in its bid to resemble a Western city Běijīng has lost a far larger proportion of historic architecture than Western cities such as London or Paris. And many argue the loss was avoidable.

Although Běijīng has been radically altered in every decade since 1949, the current building mania really picked up pace in the 1990s, with a housing renovation policy that resulted in thousands of old-style homes and Stalinist concrete structures from the 1950s being torn down and replaced by modern apartment buildings. During the 1990s Běijīng destroyed so much of its architectural heritage it was denied a World Heritage listing in 2000 and 2001. This prompted the government to establish 40 protection zones throughout the older parts of the city to protect the remaining heritage buildings. Despite these attempts at protection, Unesco claims that since 2003 a third of the 62-sq-km area that made up the central part of the old city has now been destroyed, displacing close to 580,000 people. After Běijīng was awarded the Olympics, demolition increased dramatically.

One of the hardest hit areas was the central neighbourhood of Qiánmén, once the home of scholars and opera singers. Preservationists and residents have petitioned for government protection but even after a new resolution was passed in 2005 to protect Běijīng's historic districts, many places like Qiánmén weren't included because they were approved for demolition before the order was passed. Road widening has bulldozed its way through the area, but Qianmen Dajie has been restored in a mock historic style and the word is that Dashilan Dajie is next in line.

The Olympic building frenzy helped stir up plenty of controversy in other areas, too. Some local architects were resentful of foreign architectural firms hired to design the Olympic buildings and many wonder how the city will ever pay for the elaborate structures, which include the National Stadium (Bird's Nest; p114), National Gymnasium, National Aquatics Center (Water Cube; p114), Convention Center, Olympic Village, and the Wukesong Cultural and Sports Center.

Běijīng's new buildings could well have your eyes on stalks, but their often senseless deployment could also have you blinking in bafflement. The vast Legendale Hotel on Jinbao Lu is a kitsch, outsize interpretation of a Parisian apartment block curiously plonked in central Běijīng. The glass grill exterior of the hip Hotel Kapok (p209) on Donghuamen Dajie is a jab in the eye of the staid and yesteryear Jade Garden Hotel next door. The opinion-dividing National Grand Theatre (p91), designed by French architect Paul Andreu, is perhaps Běijīng's most controversial building.

The eventual consequences of this great urban reshaping cannot be estimated. The growing self-respect and self-belief among ordinary Chinese has seen the pendulum begin to swing the other way, initiating a movement to reinstate traditional Chinese architectural aesthetics. The rebuilding of Yǒngdìng Mén and the decorative arches of Qiánmén and Xīdān indicates this process is underway, but many question why they were felled in the first place.

ENVIRONMENT & PLANNING

THE LAND

Situated on a plane, urban Běijīng's terrain is as flat as a Peking duck pancake. In the countryside the landscape frequently lifts more dramatically into hills and mountains, cut by valleys and sometimes capped with remnants of the Great Wall (p97) that roller coasters up and down peaks and ridges. Běijīng's largely arid climate leaves the earth freeze-dried in winter, desiccated in spring and hard as a brick most of the year. One of the few hills in central Běijīng is

top picks

BĚIJĪNG'S MOST NOTABLE BUILDINGS

- National Stadium (p114) More famously known as the Bird's Nest, this iconic lattice-work stadium symbolised the 2008 Olympic Games.
- CCTV Building (p113) Designed by Rem Koolhaas, this futuristic building is shaped like a gigantic 'Z' and has generated a huge amount of controversy over its shape – to many Chinese it resembles a person kneeling.
- National Grand Theatre (p91) Běijīng's most loved/hated building – Paul Andreu's creation is either a masterpiece or a blot on the landscape. You decide.
- Forbidden City (p56) China's incomparably majestic imperial palace – the largest collection of dynastic architecture in the land.
- Capital Museum (p92) A cutting-edge example of modern Chinese museum design.
- Legation Quarter (p74) Recently restored collection of impressive legation-era buildings.
- Terminal Three Building (p232) Norman Foster–designed – the world's largest airport terminal building.
- Great Hall of the People (p91) Erected during the Great Leap Forward, this Soviet-inspired building would look right at home in the heart of Pyongyang.
- National Aquatics Center (p114) This iridescent 'cube' of water has won international awards for its innovative design, including 'The Most Accomplished Work in Atmosphere' at the 2004 Venice Biennale.
- Hall of Prayer for Good Harvests (p83) The *ne plus ultra* of Ming-dynasty design and a feast for the eyes.

Jingshan Park (p92), heaped up from the soil excavated from the Forbidden City moat. It not only interrupts the perpetual flatland of Běijīng, but was also designed to shield the emperor from negative *fēngshuǐ* streaming down from the north.

GREEN BĚIJĪNG

A possible oxymoron, but you are less likely to choke on your dumplings at the notion of a green Běijīng than five years ago. While preparing for the Olympic Games, Běijīng boosted its green credentials by sprucing up the city with as much green grass as possible while banishing polluting industries to the suburbs. But Běijīng's sulphurous haze makes it one of the world's most polluted cities and with China now the world's largest producer of carbon dioxide, international attention is swinging to the fuggy skies over town. When pollution is measured by micrograms of particles of pollution dust per cubic metre, Běijīng's level is 142, compared to the averages for Paris (22), London (24) and New York (27). The World Health Organization (WHO) guideline is 20.

Sustainable development policies have long taken a back seat to the economic-growth-at-any-cost model, which saw provinces competing against each other. The CCP knows that its popularity depends on providing jobs and generating economic growth, but the resulting damage to the environment and long-term costs are finally hitting home. China knows it is sitting on an environmental time bomb. At the time of writing, however, it was uncertain how much the financial crisis of 2009 would impact environmental initiatives.

China's unparalleled economic growth over the past few decades has imposed immense strains on the environment. China uses energy at an astonishingly inefficient rate. It is estimated that China uses three times the world energy average to generate US$1 of GDP in industrial production. To produce US$10,000 worth of goods, China draws on seven times the amount of resources as Japan. The equivalent of 10% of China's GDP is frittered away by pollution and environmental degradation. Analysts also suggest that one of the reasons China was able to keep manufacturing costs low was because environmental protection regulations were so inadequately enforced. More and more Chinese are tuning in to environmental issues – there are now over 2000 environmental groups in China – but the laws for protecting the environment are often not rigorously applied, or are flouted at the local level by corrupt cadres.

However, Běijīng made impressive progress before the Olympic Games, encouraging the use of natural gas and electricity rather than the traditional circular coal briquettes (*fēngwōméi*) for winter heating, replacing diesel buses with ones powered by natural gas, and closing heavily polluting industries, or moving them out of the city. However, China as a whole remains largely dependent on the burning of coal for power.

DUST DEVIL

You've heard of the Gobi and you may have heard of the Takla Makan, but did you know that Běijīng may one day be another of China's deserts? The Gobi Desert is just 150km from Běijīng and winds are blowing the sands towards the capital at a rate of 2km a year, with dunes up to 30m high wriggling ever closer.

In 2006, Běijīng was hit by eight major sandstorms that coated the city in choking yellow dust. One particularly vicious storm dumped 330,000 tonnes of dust on the capital. Experts blame overgrazing, deforestation and worsening drought; without grassland and tree cover, and with a dropping water table, the deserts are on a roll, overwhelming villages in northern China. Global warming further exacerbates the underlying problems. The Gobi Desert is expanding towards the south at a rate of 2.4% per year, swallowing grasslands. Every month, 200 sq km of arable land in China becomes desert.

According to the United Nation's Office to Combat Desertification and Drought (UNSO), a third of China is subject to desertification – the process by which previously semi-arable or arable land gradually becomes depleted of plant and animal life.

The Chinese government has been jolted into pledging a massive US$6.8 billion to stop the spread of the sand. A green wall that will eventually stretch 5700km is being planted in northeastern China to keep back the sand, though some experts argue that it is not tree but grass cover that best binds the soil.

BACKGROUND GOVERNMENT & POLITICS

Anyone visiting Běijīng outside summer will that know it's drier than a terracotta warrior's armpit. It can be a source of eternal puzzlement how anything can grow from the hard, baked earth. Environmentalists argue that water scarcity around Běijīng and north China is largely a consequence of its unsustainable use as a resource. To placate peasant farmers, water has long been kept at an unrealistically low price, but this has merely encouraged overuse, while underground aquifers are quickly draining and water tables dropping. The epic sandstorms that gust into Běijīng every spring – some carrying particles as far as Taiwan – are yearly proof of north China's expanding deserts. The mammoth south–north water transfer project will be bringing water up to Běijīng from the flood-prone Yangzi River, but some experts warn that may not be enough. In 2009, Běijīng declared a water emergency during north China's worst drought for 50 years; no rain fell on Běijīng for over 100 days. The city is so arid that old anti-aircraft guns positioned around Běijīng routinely fire shells containing rain-inducing chemicals into the clouds; in February 2009 they prompted snow to fall on the city centre. Crisis point could come in 2010 when Běijīng's population is expected to top 17 million, three million more than available resources can supply.

GOVERNMENT & POLITICS

'A revolution is not a dinner party, or writing an essay, or painting a picture, or doing embroidery; it cannot be so refined, so leisurely and gentle, so temperate, kind, courteous, restrained and magnanimous. A revolution is an insurrection, an act of violence by which one class overthrows another.'

Mao Zedong

Běijīng is the seat of political power in China and all the important decisions that affect the rest of the land are made here.

The entire system of state power is controlled by the CCP. The highest authority rests with the Standing Committee of the Politburo of the CCP. Including the president, Hu Jintao, and premier Wen Jiabao, its nine members are in effect China's cabinet. Beneath them are another 25 members and below them is the 210-member Central Committee, made up of younger party members and provincial party leaders. At the grass roots level the party forms a parallel system to the administrations in the army, universities, government and industries. Real authority is exercised by the party representatives at each level in these organisations. They, in turn, are responsible to the party officials in the hierarchy above them, thus ensuring strict central control.

The day-to-day running of the country lies with the State Council, which is directly under the control of the CCP. The State Council is headed by the premier and beneath the premier are four vice-premiers, 10 state councillors, a secretary-general, 45 ministers and various other agencies. The State Council implements the decisions made by the Politburo.

Approving the decisions of the CCP leadership is the National People's Congress (NPC), the principal legislative body that convenes in the Great Hall of the People (p91). It comprises a 'democratic alliance' of party members and nonparty members, including intellectuals, technicians and industrial managers. In theory they are empowered to amend the constitution and to choose the premier and State Council members. The catch is that all these office holders must first be recommended by the Central Committee, thus the NPC is only an approving body.

The Chinese government is also equipped with a massive bureaucracy. The term 'cadre' is usually applied to bureaucrats, and their monopoly on power means that wide-ranging perks are a privilege of rank for all and sundry – from the lowliest clerks to the shadowy puppet masters of Zhōngnánhǎi. China's bureaucratic tradition is a long one.

The wild card in the system is the armed forces, the People's Liberation Army (PLA). Comprising land forces, the navy and the air force, it has a total of around 2.3 million members. Another 1.1 million serve in the People's Armed Police. China is divided into seven military regions, each with its own military leadership – in some cases with strong regional affiliations.

China's president, Hu Jintao, is also chairman of the Central Military Commission and so head of the PLA. Therefore, along with his status as the General-Secretary of the CCP, Hu holds the three most powerful positions in China. Born in 1942 in Ānhuī province and trained as an engineer (like many of China's most senior politicians) at Běijīng's prestigious Tsinghua University, Hu is the first of China's presidents to have joined the CCP after the 1949 revolution.

Although Hu, who is said to have a photographic memory and to be a keen ballroom dancer, often appears enigmatic in his public appearances, he has consistently shown his ability to out-manoeuvre his political opponents. Having inherited a government packed with previous president Jiang Zemin's supporters, known as the 'Shanghai Gang' (because so many of them rose to power in Shànghǎi), Hu has edged some of them out while promoting his own protégés who, like him, began their careers in the Communist Youth League.

He has also shown a fierce determination to reinforce the CCP's dominant position in China and has promoted his vision of a 'Harmonious Society', which owes much to the teachings of Confucius. In 2006, he launched the 'Eight Honours and Eight Disgraces' (Bā Róng Bā Chǐ) campaign in an effort to restore the Chinese people's faith in the CCP. The campaign calls on party members to avoid greed and corruption, while thinking always of society's needs rather than those of the individual.

Premier Wen Jiabao has capitalised on a responsive public disposition towards him. This was especially reinforced after the May 2008 Sìchuān earthquake when Wen – endearingly called 'Grandfather Wen' – made numerous tearful appearances in the disaster zone and won the hearts of the population.

The CCP's 70 million members need a similar image overhaul. Rising discontent over official corruption, along with anger over illegal land seizures and damage to the environ-

BOOKS ON THE ECONOMY & POLITICS

- *The Writing on the Wall: China and the West in the 21st Century* (Will Hutton, 2008) Will Hutton's incisive look at the vast challenges facing China and, consequently, the world economy.
- *China Shakes the World: The Rise of a Hungry Nation* (James Kynge, 2006) China's growing ascendancy and how it will shape world affairs.
- *Mr China: A Memoir* (Tim Clissold, 2004) An amusing post-mortem of ruined business aspirations in China during the 1990s.
- *Chinese Lessons: Five Classmates and the Story of the New China* (John Pomfret, 2006) A former Běijīng bureau chief for the *Washington Post,* Pomfret offers a moving narrative of what happened to five of his 1981 classmates from Nanjing University over the last 25 years, offering invaluable insights into the reality of life in contemporary China.
- *Mao: The Unknown Story* (Jung Chang and Jon Halliday, 2005) Hugely controversial biography of Mao that paints a picture of a man consumed by egotism and indifferent to the fate of the Chinese people. Banned in China.
- *The China Dream: The Elusive Quest for the Greatest Untapped Market on Earth* (Joe Studwell) Sober, balanced and cautionary perspective on the Chinese economy and how it all fits together.
- *The Tiananmen Papers* (compiled by Zhang Liang, edited by Andrew Nathan and Perry Link, 2001) A 2in-thick compilation of Politburo memos, minutes and documents, this publication blows away the smoke screen hanging over 4 June 1989.

ment, routinely spills over into violence. There were 74,000 violent protests across China in 2004 according to the government. That number declined by 22% in 2005, but included one protest over the construction of a power station in Guǎngdōng province that saw members of the People's Armed Police open fire on demonstrators for the first time since the student protests in Tiananmen Square in June 1989.

While such a harsh reaction is uncommon, the authorities continue to be ruthless in their treatment of those they regard as their enemies. Environmental activists, crusading lawyers, investigative journalists, Tibetan activists and members of banned groups, such as the Falun Gong, all risk imprisonment because of their activities. But thanks to mobile phones and the spread of the internet, it is now far harder for the government to prevent news and videos of protests from leaking out. And with an ever-growing gap between the rich and the poor fuelling discontent, it will only get harder for the CCP to maintain its grip on China. The bloody 2008 riots in Lhasa and 2009 disturbances in Xīnjiāng are also signs that things are not harmonious in China's twitchy west and northwest borderland territories.

To mask its own foibles and to promote itself, the CCP has also fostered nationalism among China's citizens that some argue may swing out of control. It is common to read heated nationalist diatribes on Chinese blogs and the success of *China is Unhappy,* a nationalist bestseller in 2009, points to potentially powerful currents of xenophobia.

It is notoriously difficult for foreigners to discuss Chinese politics with Chinese people. They may sink the knife into the CCP in private but Chinese people frequently become defensive of their leaders under Westerners criticism.

MEDIA

'Lies in newspapers are like rat droppings in clear soup. Not only disgusting but obvious.'

The media in China is tightly controlled and frequently functions as a government contrivance for manipulating public opinion and diverting attention away from, or throwing a blanket over, negative domestic developments. The Chinese media has long drawn international attention for deliberately not reporting events, presenting news with a heavy bias or simply serving as a propaganda tool. Although China is the world's largest producer of daily newspapers (with over 2200 of them on sale each day), few are worth reading. Newspapers stick to a diet of good news and while you may see numerous cartoons lampooning foreign leaders, China's politicians are untouchable. Foreign journalists in China are subject to tight control and domestic journalists are routinely harassed. Every year, China features near the bottom of Reporters Without Borders' annual World Press Freedom Index.

Specific taboos (such as the Tiananmen protests of 1989 or direct criticism of the CCP) further limit editorial autonomy and as a consequence many newspapers adopt a tabloid tone, with graphic pictures of car crashes competing with celebrity gossip and UFO abduction stories. The capital's papers are no exception. The most reputable is the *Beijing News,* but unless you read Chinese you will be limited to the government's English-language flagship, the anodyne *China Daily* (see p249 for more on newspapers and magazines). Even Běijīng's otherwise savvy expat magazines need to rigorously toe the line or face closure. Fake newspapers also periodically make an appearance on the streets of Běijīng (p117). Many Chinese people see the Western media as being overly critical of China, although analysts argue that an uninterrupted diet of upbeat news fed to Chinese by local media helps create this impression; in comparison, Western media is negative about most subjects.

It's a similar story with the state-run China Central TV (CCTV), the national media group that initially failed to report the huge fire that destroyed a flagship building (p113) at its own Běijīng headquarters in 2009 (even though everyone could see the building in flames). Its English-language outlet is the bland CCTV 9, where the latest government directive or meeting is always given top billing on the news. Other stations, such as Beijing TV (BTV), offer an uninspiring mix of soap operas, reality TV, game shows and sport. Just like in the West really.

only with censored news. More with-it TV channels such as Phoenix have moved things forward, importing a kind of Hong Kong–style quality control, but taboo areas still need to be skirted, so real autonomy remains impossible.

If the print and TV media are a lost cause, then hope can be found in the blogosphere. The Chinese are fanatical bloggers. There were some 35 million blogs out there at the last count and they're written by everyone from movie stars to school kids. It's through reading the blogs that you can get a sense of what people in this vast country are preoccupied with, angry about and what their hopes for the future are. There are websites that provide English translations of the most popular ones; www.danwei.org has a list of these. See p15 for a list of the best blogs in China.

But despite the much-vaunted 'Great Firewall of China', the government's grip on cyberspace is not nearly as tight as is sometimes assumed. Proxy servers enable people to access sites that are routinely blocked, while file-sharing websites offer free downloads of foreign TV shows that would never pass the censors. Nonetheless, the authorities can restrict direct access to sites at the flick of a switch; in 2008 access to YouTube was restricted after a video of police brutality during the crackdown on Tibetan rioters was put online and numerous international newspapers were either partially or entirely inaccessible for periods during 2008.

LANGUAGE

Běijīnghuà (literally 'Běijīng language') is held aloft across China as the Queen's English of the People's Republic. Wherever Beijingers traipse across their home country, they are immediately identified by the nation's most recognisable accent. Despite its notorious trickiness, foreign students of Mandarin all aim – at some stage – to live in the capital and immerse themselves in the rich sounds of the Běijīng dialect: to chortle in Mandarin with a Běijīng accent has winning cachet. To learn Mandarin in Fúzhōu or some other peripheral city on China's perimeters could impregnate your Chinese with an accent you may never shift. Běijīng is where it's at.

Although Mandarin is very loosely based on the Běijīng dialect, Běijīnghuà is markedly different from the standard Mandarin spoken by prim newscasters across the nation. As it needs to be commonly understood across China, standard Mandarin comes with limited slang and a necessary clarity, but the Běijīng dialect is richly endowed with a colloquial argot and a famously tricky accent.

Perhaps the most distinctive idiosyncrasy of Běijīnghuà is its adding of a unique "er" ending to many words, in a phenomenon known as '*érhuà*'. Words such as *mén* (door) become *mér*, *shuǐ* (water) become *shuǐr* and *dài* (bag) becomes *dàir*. To students of Mandarin *érhuà* can be off-putting at first encounter.

Běijīng people are perhaps uniquely scornful of other Chinese dialects. Aware of the central position of the Běijīng dialect, Beijingers tend to mock southern Chinese dialects mercilessly, affording endless material for stand-up comedy shows and cross-talk quipping.

For more information on language and some helpful phrases, see p256.

HISTORIC HÚTÒNG

The essence of Běijīng is its distinctive *hútòng* (胡同), the alleyways that criss-cross the centre of town. Not only do these enchanting passageways offer a very real glimpse of what Běijīng was like before the bulldozers and construction crews got to work in earnest, but they are still home to around 20% of the residents of inner Běijīng. Immersing yourself in the *hútòng* is an essential part of any visit to the capital and by far the best way to experience Běijīng street life. Nor will you struggle to find them. As the Chinese saying goes: 'There are 360 *hútòng* with names and as many nameless *hútòng* as there are hairs on a cow.' If you get lost, it won't be for long as you'll never be far from a main road.

ORIGINS OF THE HÚTÒNG

Hútòng first appeared in Běijīng in the Yuan dynasty, in the wake of Genghis Khan's army. With the city, then known as Zhōngdū, reduced to rubble in characteristic Mongol fashion, it was redesigned with *hútòng* running east–west. By the Qing dynasty, more than 2000 *hútòng* riddled Běijīng, leaping to over 6000 by the 1950s. But the construction of the office buildings and apartment blocks that now dominate central Běijīng, as well as the widening of roads, resulted in the demolition of many of them.

Around 2000 remain, with the oldest being the 900-year-old Sanmiao Jie (三庙街; Three Temple St) in Xuānwǔ district, which dates to the Liao dynasty (907–1125). Despite all that history, the origins of the word '*hútòng*' are hazy. Originally a Mongolian term, the name derives from the time when the Khan's horsemen camped in the new Yuan-dynasty capital. It might have referred to a passageway between *gers* (or 'yurts', the Russian term). Or it might come from the word '*hottog*' (a well) – wherever there was water in the dry plain around Běijīng, there were inhabitants.

Most *hútòng* lie within the loop of the Second Ring Rd. The most famous are the ones to the immediate east and west of the Forbidden City. With proximity to the centre of power a sign of status, they were reserved for aristocrats and the city elite. These *hútòng* have the oldest and grandest *sìhéyuàn* (courtyard houses). Further away, to the north and south of the Forbidden City, were the homes of merchants and artisans, which feature more functional design with little or no ornamentation. Other *hútòng* sprung up still further from the city centre, and much later, and have little aesthetic value.

HÚTÒNG TODAY

Now, *hútòng* land is a hotchpotch of the old and the new, where Ming- and Qing-dynasty courtyards come complete with modern brick outhouses and stand alongside grim apartment blocks. Adding to the lack of uniformity is the fact that many *sìhéyuàn* were subdivided in the 1960s so that they could house more people. The shortage of space, as well as the paucity of modern facilities, such as heating, proper plumbing and sometimes private bathrooms and toilets, is the main reason many *hútòng* dwellers have been happy to leave the alleyways for newly built high-rise flats.

Older residents are more reluctant to abandon the *hútòng*, citing the sense of living in a real community, as opposed to a more isolated existence in the suburbs. And there are now increasing signs that many will be able to see out their days in them because, despite having enthusiastically consigned so many *hútòng* to history in the near past, the city authorities seem to have cottoned onto their worth as one of the principal attractions of Běijīng.

Some alleyways are now protected by law, while others have become tourist hubs. The successful remodelling of Nanluogu Xiang (p48) into a nightlife hotspot is being replicated elsewhere: some of the *hútòng* behind the Drum Tower (p74) and off Gulou Dongdajie and Andingmennei Dajie in Dōngchéng district have started to sprout more and more bars and restaurants. While not exactly preservation in its strictest sense, the adaptation of the *hútòng* for commercial use will undoubtedly aid their future survival.

THE HÚTÒNG OF THE IMPERIAL CITY

The Imperial City failed to survive the convulsions of the 20th century, but the *hútòng* that threaded through the imperial enclave survive. Many bore names denoting their former function during imperial days. Zhonggu Hutong (钟鼓胡同; Bell and Drum Alley) was responsible for the provision of bells and drums to the imperial household. Jinmaoju Hutong (巾帽局胡同; Cloth and Cap Department Alley) handled the caps and boots used by the court, while Zhiranju Hutong (织染局胡同; Weaving and Dyeing Department Alley) supplied its satins and silks. Jiucuju Hutong (酒醋局胡同; Wine and Vinegar Department Alley) managed the stock of spirits, vinegar, sugar, flour and other culinary articles.

Also scattered within the Imperial City were numerous storehouses, surviving in name only in such alleys as Lianziku Hutong (帘子库胡同; Curtain Storehouse Alley), Denglongku Hutong (灯笼库胡同; Lantern Storehouse Alley) and Duanku Hutong (缎库胡同; Satin Storehouse Alley). Candles were vital items during Ming and Qing times, their supply handled by the Làkù, which operated from Laku Hutong (蜡库胡同; Candle Storehouse). The Jade Garden Hotel (☎ 5858 0909; 1 Nanheyan Dajie; 南河沿大街1号) sits on the former site of the Ciqikù (Porcelain Storehouse), which kept the Forbidden City stocked with porcelain bowls, plates, wine cups and other utensils.

West of Beihai Park (p87), the large road of Xishiku Dajie (西什库大街; West Ten Storehouse St) gets its name from the various storehouses scattered along its length during Ming times. Among items supplied to the Imperial City from warehouses here were paper, lacquer, oil, copper, leather and weapons, including bows, arrows and swords.

There are also the *hútòng* named after the craft workers who supplied the Forbidden City with its raw materials, such as Dashizuo Hutong (大石作胡同; Big Stonemason's Alley), where stonemasons fashioned the stone lions, terraces, imperial carriageways and bridges of the Imperial City.

Now-vanished temples are also recalled in *hútòng* names, such as the Guangming Hutong (光明胡同), south of Xi'anmen Dajie, named after the huge Guāngmíng Diàn (Guangming Temple) that is no more.

For a bird's-eye panorama of Běijīng's *hútòng* universe, take a look at the diorama of the modern city at the Beijing Planning Exhibition Hall (p86). The Beijing Cultural Heritage Protection Center (www.bjchp.org) website has useful information on the efforts to preserve the remaining *hútòng*.

Apart from wandering them on foot or by bike, you can experience these delightful lanes to the full by spending a night in a *hútòng* courtyard hotel. See the boxed text on p211 for a list of Běijīng's top courtyard hotels. Dōngchéng is also now home to a number of fine courtyard restaurants, which allow you to dine inside a *sìhéyuàn*.

OLD WALLED COURTYARDS

Sìhéyuàn (四合院) are the building blocks of the *hútòng* world. Some old courtyards, such as the Lao She Museum (p78), have been quaintly mothballed as museums, but many of them remain inhabited and hum with domestic activity inside and out. Doors to communal courtyards are typically left open, while from spring to autumn men collect outside their gates, drinking beer, playing chess, smoking and chewing the fat. Inside, trees soar aloft, providing shade and a nesting place for birds.

Most old courtyards date from the Qing dynasty, although some have struggled through from the Ming. Particularly historic and noteworthy courtyard homes boast a white marble plaque near the gates identifying them as protected structures.

Prestigious courtyards are entered by a number of gates, but the majority have just a single door. Venerable courtyards are fronted by large, thick, red doors, outside of which perch either a pair of Chinese lions or drum stones (*bǎogǔshí*; two circular stones resembling drums, each on a small plinth and occasionally topped by a miniature lion or a small dragon head). A set of square *méndāng* (wooden ornaments) above the gateway is a common sight. You may even see a set of stepping-on stones (*shàngmǎ shí*) that the owner would use for mounting his steed.

Many of these impressive courtyards were the residences of Běijīng's officials, wealthy families and even princes; Prince Gong's Residence (p92) is one of the more celebrated examples.

Běijīng's more historic courtyard gates are accessed by a set of steps, both topped with and flanked by ornate brick carvings. The generosity of detail indicates the social clout of the courtyard's original inhabitants.

THE CHANGING FACE OF NANLUOGU XIANG

Thirty-five-year-old Beijinger Wang Haiyan and her husband opened the Passby Bar (p181) in Nanluogu Xiang (South Drum Alley) in 1999. Its success as the first bar to open in the historic 800-year-old *hútòng* sparked a deluge of bars, restaurants and shops that have turned the area into one of Běijīng's hot spots.

Why did you open the Passby? At the time we were living in a *hútòng* just off Nanluogu Xiang and we wanted to open a comfortable place where our friends could drink. There were no bars around here then and the ones in Sānlǐtún were all aimed at foreigners. It was a totally different area then, really quiet. Taxi drivers didn't know where it was. It was all local families living here, some of whom had been here for generations. They thought I was crazy to open the bar because they didn't think we'd make any money. They said, 'You can buy a beer for Y1, so why would people pay Y10 for one?'

How has Nanluogu Xiang changed since 1999? The atmosphere is totally different. It's not a *lǎo* (old) Běijīng *hútòng* anymore. It's like a fake *hútòng* now. Most of the families have moved out, there are only three or four left. They've rented out their houses to bars and shops and it's a good deal for them. I think the locals are very happy because they never imagined that they could rent their houses for so much money. It's impossible to buy a *sìhéyuàn* around here now, because the locals know they can make more by renting them.

Do you feel guilty about the way the hútòng has been transformed since you opened? It's similar to what happened to Hòuhǎi. We call it 'mushroom business'. One place opens and does well and then suddenly there are lots of them. But you can't stop it; we can never go back to the way the *hútòng* used to be. The local government likes it, too, because they get more tax from all the businesses. And if the government likes it, then it can't be stopped.

Do you miss living in the hútòng? No, I don't. The outside bathrooms were really cold in winter. But although we've thought about moving the bar to a quieter area with fewer tourists, we don't want to. This bar is like an apple tree for me. I've put a lot of effort into watching it grow and I don't want to lose it now.

Courtyards used to house just one noble or rich family, but many were appropriated by work units to provide housing for their workforce. Others belong to private owners, and a few are now the private residences of top officials, but the state ultimately owns all property in China, which has made it easy for local authorities to subdivide or demolish so many *hútòng*.

Foreigners long ago cottoned on to the charm of courtyard life and breached this conservative bastion, although many are repelled by poor heating, dodgy sanitation and neighbours who can be too close for comfort by Western standards. In addition, some *hútòng* homes still lack toilets, explaining the malodorous public loos strung along many alleyways. But other homes have been thoroughly modernised and sport such features as varnished wooden floors, fully fitted kitchens and air-conditioning. Converted courtyards are prized and are much more expensive to buy or rent than even the swishest apartments.

While large numbers of old courtyard houses have been divided into smaller units, many of their historical features remain, especially their roofs. Courtyard communities are served by small shops and restaurants spread throughout *hútòng*, which also house schools and government offices. For informative displays on Běijīng's courtyard houses, visit the Beijing Ancient Architecture Museum at Xiannong Altar (p117).

WIND-WATER LANES

By far the majority of *hútòng* run east–west, ensuring that the main gate faces south, so satisfying *fēngshuǐ* requirements. This south-facing aspect guarantees maximum sunshine and protection from negative forces prevailing from the north. This positioning mirrors the layout of all Chinese temples, which nourishes the *yáng* (the male and light aspect) while checking the *yīn* (the female and dark aspect).

Less significant north–south running alleyways link the main alleys. The resulting rectangular waffle-grid pattern stamps the points of the compass on the Běijīng psyche. You may hear older Běijīng locals exclaiming, '*wǒ gāoxìng de wǒ bù zhī běi le*', meaning 'I was so happy, I didn't know which way was north' (an extremely disorientating state of joy). In cities without this plethora of parallel roads (such as Shànghǎi), it's far easier to lose your way.

Some courtyards used to be further protected by rectangular stones bearing the Chinese characters for Tài Shān (Mt Tai) to vanquish bad omens. Other courtyards preserve their screen walls or spirit walls (yǐngbì) – fēngshuǐ devices erected in front of the main gate to deflect roaming spirits. Běijīng's two most impressive spirit walls are the Nine Dragon Screens at the Forbidden City (p56) and in Beihai Park (p87).

Trees provide qì (energy) and much-needed shade in summer, and most old courtyards have a locust tree at the front, which would have been planted when the sìhéyuàn was constructed.

HÚTÒNG NAMES

Some hútòng are christened after families, such as Zhaotangzi Hutong (赵堂子胡同; Alley of the Zhao Family). Other hútòng simply took their names from historical figures, temples or local features, while a few have more mysterious associations, such as Dragon Whiskers Ditch Alley. Many reflect the merchandise that is for sale at local markets, such as Ganmian Hutong (干面胡同; Dry Flour Alley), while some hútòng, such as Gongbei Hutong (弓背胡同; Bow Back Hutong), have names derived from their shape.

Some rather unusual industries coalesced around the Forbidden City. Wet Nurse Lane was full of young mothers who breastfed the imperial offspring; they were selected from around China on scouting trips four times a year. Clothes Washing Lane was the residence of the women who did the imperial laundry. The maids, having grown old in the service of the court, were packed off to faraway places until their intimate knowledge of royal undergarments was out of date and no longer newsworthy.

Hútòng Name Changes

During the Cultural Revolution, selected hútòng and roads were rechristened in obeisance to the changing political climate. Nanxiawa Hutong (南下洼胡同) was renamed Xuemaozhu Hutong (学毛著胡同), literally 'Study Mao's Writings Hutong'. Doujiao'er Hutong (豆角儿胡同) became Hongdaodi Hutong (红到底胡同), 'Red to the End Hutong', and Andingmen Dajie (安定门大街) unfortunately became known as Dayuejin Lu (大跃进路) or 'Great Leap Forward Road', an unconscious but prophetic description of the way Běijīng's roads would become clogged with traffic.

Other hútòng names conceal their original names, which were considered either too unsavoury or unlucky, in homophones or similarly sounding words. Guancai Hutong (棺材胡同), or 'Coffin Alley', was instead dropped for Guangcai Hutong (光彩胡同), which means 'Splendour Hutong'. Muzhu Hutong (母猪胡同), 'Mother Pig Hutong' or 'Sow Hutong', was elevated to the much more poetic Meizhu Hutong (梅竹胡同), or 'Plum Bamboo Hutong'.

HÚTÒNG DIMENSIONS

Despite an attempt at standardisation, Běijīng's alleys have their own personalities and proportions. The longest alley is Dongjiaomin Xiang (东交民巷), which extends for 3km (see the Tiananmen Square & Foreign Legation Quarter Walk, p135), while the shortest – unsurprisingly called Yichi Dajie (一尺大街; One Foot St) – is a very brief 25m. Some people contest that Guantong Xiang (贯通巷; Guantong Alley), near Yangmeizhu Xijie in Xuānwǔ district (east of Liulichang Dongjie), is even shorter, at 20m.

Some hútòng are wide and leafy boulevards, whereas others are narrow, claustrophobic corridors. Běijīng's broadest alley is Lingjing Hutong (灵境胡同; Fairyland Alley), with a width of 32m, but the aptly named Xiaolaba Hutong (小喇叭胡同; Little Trumpet Alley) is a squeeze at 50cm. And chubby wayfarers could well get wedged in Qianshi Hutong (钱市胡同), situated not far from Qiánmén and Dàzhàlan – its narrowest reach is a mere 44cm. The alley with the most twists and turns is Jiuwan Hutong (九湾胡同; Nine Bend Alley), while another of Běijīng's oldest hútòng is Zhuanta Hutong (砖塔胡同; Brick Pagoda Alley). Dating from Mongol times, it can be found west off Xisi Nandajie.

HÚTÒNG TOURS

Exploration of Běijīng's *hútòng* is an unmissable experience. Go on one of our walking or cycling tours, such as the Běijīng Bike Ride (p140), and delve deep into this alternately ramshackle and genteel, but always magical, world. Or wander off the main roads in the centre of Běijīng into the alleyways that riddle the town within the Second Ring Rd.

Good places to plunge into are the *hútòng* behind the Drum Tower (p74), the area around Nanluogu Xiang (p74) or the roads branching west off Chaoyangmen Beixiaojie and Chaoyangmen Nanxiaojie, east of Wangfujing Dajie. Most significant *hútòng* have red enamel street signs, sporting the alley name (in Chinese and Pinyin) in white. If you can't find the *hútòng* street sign, the *hútòng* name in Chinese also appears on a small metal plaque above doorways strung along each alley.

Hire a bike and explore this historic world on two wheels (p234); if you want to join a tour, the China Culture Center (☎ 6432 9341; www.chinaculturecenter.org) runs regular tours, or can arrange personalised ones. Call for further details, or check the website. Many hotels also run tours of the *hútòng*, or will point you in the direction of someone who does. Alternatively, any number of pedicab touts infest the roads around the Shichahai Lakes. Such tours typically cost Y250 to Y300; you'll do better spending the money on a bike to head off on your own.

NEIGHBOURHOODS

top picks

- **Forbidden City** (p56)
  Vast, long-abandoned palace that's the stuff of legend.
- **Temple of Heaven Park** (p80)
  Sacred geometry, cosmic symbolism, classic architecture.
- **National Grand Theatre** (p91)
  'Socialism with Chinese characteristics' in one chrome-plated nutshell – a truly extraterrestrial design.
- **Lama Temple** (p70)
  Infusion of incense, mystery and the supernatural.
- **Nanluogu Xiang** (p74)
  Ancient alleyway swinging with bars and restaurants.
- **Capital Museum** (p92)
  Eye-catching modern architecture and ancient treasures.
- **798 Art District** (p133)
  Derelict industrial wilderness injected with cutting-edge art.
- **Summer Palace** (p127)
  Buddhist architecture, lakes, breathtaking walks.
- **Foreign Legation Quarter** (p74)
  Grand district of former embassy buildings.

What's your recommendation? www.lonelyplanet.com/beijing

NEIGHBOURHOODS

Plonked on a mammoth plain that ranges south as far as the Yellow River around 250km away, Běijīng benefits from not being near either a major river or the sea. Without its strategic location on the edge of the North China Plain it would hardly be an ideal place to locate a major city, let alone a national capital.

A colossal metropolis without major rivers or natural hills in its central neighbourhoods, Běijīng is very much a city designed by humans. Unlike other modern-day Chinese cities such as Shànghǎi and Hong Kong, where water draws the line between two entirely different domains and states of mind, Běijīng is largely an uninterrupted continuum of flat land. To fathom how Běijīng fits together as a city, we need to look at its history.

'A colossal metropolis without major rivers or natural hills in its central neighbourhoods, Běijīng is very much a city designed by humans.'

The Forbidden City acts as the cartographic and physical focus of Běijīng, the bull's-eye around which the city's historic sights cluster and the city's six ring roads radiate concentrically. Běijīng's most ancient quarters surround the Forbidden City and Tiananmen Square, within the looping boundary of the Second Ring Rd.

Glance at the Neighbourhoods map of Běijīng and notice how the city's central districts (Xīchéng, Dōngchéng, Xuānwǔ and Chóngwén) divide by neighbourhoods into east and west. A dissecting hinge runs along the meridian line that cleaves Běijīng on a north–south axis, running from the gate of Yongding Gate (Yǒngdìng Mén) in the south due north through Front Gate (Qián Mén), bisecting Tiananmen Square and the Forbidden City and continuing up to the Drum and Bell Towers, then scorching a trail all the way to the gates of Olympic Forest Park. A purely human construct and an imaginary line that dates to the city's Ming-dynasty conception, the symmetry created expresses a desire for order.

The city's neighbourhoods also owe their shape and extents to another human creation: the mighty walls that once ringed Běijīng. Felled by the communists in the 1950s and 1960s, the city walls have left their ghostly patterns not only along major roads that follow their footprint and underground Line 2, which tracks their original course, but also in the extents of the city's districts. An inexact science perhaps, but the presence of the Tartar City Wall, the Chinese City Wall and the dividing axis of the north–south meridian line essentially shape the outlines of Běijīng's central districts.

Xīchéng and Dōngchéng extend west and east of the Forbidden City respectively, forming Běijīng's most historic domain and the area most closely associated with the Manchu quarters of the Qing-dynasty city. Striated with ancient *hútòng* (alleyways), these two districts are the most charming the city has to offer. Both Xīchéng and Dōngchéng are the city's core districts, containing Běijīng's most ancient monuments and famous lakes and enclosing the former Imperial City.

For all practical purposes, north and south Běijīng are separated by Chang'an Jie (divided into Dongchang'an Jie and Xichang'an Jie; becoming Jianguomennei Dajie and Jianguomenwai Dajie in the east, and Fuxingmennei Dajie and Fuxingmenwai Dajie in the west), along which runs Line 1 of the subway. The southern wall of the Tartar City once ran along this street, so again the now-vanished city wall acts as a boundary. To the south of this line are the districts of Chóngwén, where the Temple of Heaven is found, and Xuānwǔ, both of which were contained within the historic Chinese City south of the Tartar City.

The districts of Cháoyáng and Hǎidiàn both sprawl more wildly beyond the old, more self-contained central districts that were within the city walls. Within mammoth Hǎidiàn district, Wǔdàokǒu is a lively student neighbourhood of bars and restaurants.

CHÁOYÁNG (p109)

Sānlǐtún Embassy Area

Cháoyáng

Jiànguóménwài Embassy Area

DŌNGCHÉNG (p56)

Dōngchéng

Chóngwén

CHÓNGWÉN (p80)

XĪCHÉNG (p87)

Xīdān

Xīchéng

XUĀNWǓ (p116)

Xuānwǔ

Hǎidiàn

HǍIDIÀN (p121)

Wǔdàokǒu

WǓDÀOKǑU (p124)

Fēngtái

0 ___ 2 km
0 ___ 1 miles

ITINERARY BUILDER

Your prime sightseeing zone should be Dōngchéng, where fantastic restaurants and bars also converge with the best selection of hotels in town. You'll find yourself straying into Cháoyáng for shopping and for its plentiful variety of watering holes, clubs and sleeping options. Běijīng's other districts contain a wide range of sights, shops, restaurants, bars, clubs and hotels, so explore at will.

AREA	ACTIVITIES	Sights	Shopping	Eating
	Dōngchéng	Forbidden City (p56)	Oriental Plaza (p146)	Dīng Dīng Xiāng (p164)
		Tiananmen Square (p66)	Grifted (p146)	Dali Courtyard (p164)
		Lama Temple (p70)	Plastered T-Shirts (p147)	Crescent Moon Muslim Restaurant (p167)
	Chóngwén	Temple of Heaven Park (p80)	Hongqiao (Pearl) Market (p147)	Dūyíchù (p171)
		Southeast Corner Watchtower & Red Gate Gallery (p86)		Liqun Roast Duck Restaurant (p170)
		Qianmen Dajie (p84)		
	Xīchéng	National Grand Theatre (p91)	77th Street (p148)	Hàn Cāng (p172)
		Beihai Park (p87)		Café Sambal (p171)
		Capital Museum (p92)		Hutong Pizza (p171)
	Cháoyáng	CCTV Building (p113)	Bookworm (p148)	Hatsune (p172)
		Bird's Nest & Water Cube (p114)	Shard Box Store (p150)	Three Guizhou Men (p175)
		Dongyue Temple (p109)	Silk Market (p149)	Pure Lotus Vegetarian (p173)
	Xuānwǔ	Dashilar (p116)	Ruifuxiang (p152)	
		Fayuan Temple (p116)	Maliandao Tea Market (p152)	
		Niujie Mosque (p117)	Neiliansheng Shoe Shop (p152)	
	Hǎidiàn, Wǔdàokǒu & Greater Beijing	798 Art District (p133)	Panjiayuan Market (p153)	Salt (p178)
		Summer Palace (p127)	Spin (p154)	Golden Peacock (p177)
		Old Summer Palace (p131)	Beijing Curio City (p153)	Isshin Japanese Restaurant (p177)

HOW TO USE THIS TABLE

The table below allows you to plan a day's worth of activities in any area of the city. Simply select which area you wish to explore, and then mix and match from the corresponding listings to build your day. The first item in each cell represents a well-known highlight of the area, while the other items are more off-the-beaten-track gems.

Drinking	Entertainment	Sleeping
Passby Bar (p181)	Mao Livehouse (p189)	Hotel Côté Cour SL (p207)
Drum & Bell (p181)	Yúgōng Yíshān (p189)	Raffles Beijing Hotel (p206)
Yin (p182)		City Walls Courtyard (p211)
Bed Bar (p183)	What? Bar (p189)	Ritz-Carlton Beijing, Financial Street (p212)
La Baie des Anges (p183)	Beijing Concert Hall (p192)	Sleepy Inn (p212)
No Name Bar (p183)	National Centre for the Performing Arts (p192)	Red Lantern House (p213)
Face (p185)	Cargo (p190)	Opposite House Hotel (p213)
LAN (p185)	World of Suzie Wong (p190)	St Regis (p213)
Q Bar (p186)	Mix (p190)	Hotel G (p214)
	Liyuan Theatre (p194)	Qianmen Hostel (p214)
	Tianqiao Acrobatics Theatre (p191)	Changgong Hotel (p215)
	Huguang Guild Hall (p193)	Autumn Garden Hotel (p215)
Lush (p187)	D-22 (p188)	Shangri-La Hotel (p215)
	2 Kolegas (p188)	Aman at Summer Palace (p216)

DŌNGCHÉNG 东城区

Eating p162; Shopping p145; Sleeping p206

If you need instant pointers to how Běijīng is cobbled together from a cartographic and existential viewpoint, Dōngchéng (East City) – and its roughly symmetrical sibling Xīchéng to the west – holds the key. Although it spills over a stretch of the Second Ring Rd in the north and northeast, and a stub pokes south of Chang'an Jie, Dōngchéng is largely contained within what can be called Běijīng's eastern old town. Once marking the hub of Yuan-dynasty Běijīng, a city whose east–west axis later shifted south, the Drum and Bell Towers rise up from an area deeply striated with *hútòng* (alleyways) and knee-deep in historic charm.

Virtually every Chinese town with a history of over 100 years has its 'old town', but – as in the case of Shànghǎi and Luòyáng – it is usually a mere fragment in the overall mosaic. Běijīng's huge old town ranges across several districts, with Dōngchéng the most charming and sight-intensive. Dōngchéng was part of what was termed the Inner City (Nèichéng), pointing to its proximity to the seat of Manchu power and the imperial palace.

Běijīng's heart is indeed the Forbidden City, magnificently lodged into the southwest corner of Dōngchéng. The Second Ring Rd traces the form of the now-vanished city walls, whose outline reflects the positioning of the Forbidden City at the core of town. Progressively larger squares and parallelograms of streets radiate out from the Forbidden City, culminating in the boxlike boundary of the Second Ring Rd and rippling on to successive ring roads beyond. In the west, Dōngchéng's boundary line follows Jiugulou Dajie just west of the Drum and Bell Towers, before running due south from the Drum Tower to skirt Jingshan Park, then lassoing in the Forbidden City and Tiananmen Square before coming to a halt at Front Gate (Qián Mén).

The top right corner of the old Imperial City, the eastern boundary of which ran along Donghuangchenggen Nanjie and Donghuangchenggen Beijie and then west along Di'anmen Dongdajie and Di'anmen Xidajie, is in Dōngchéng. None of the four gates of the Imperial City Wall survive, but a few fragments of Dōngān Mén can be seen near the Forbidden City's east gate (Dōnghuá Mén). Many of Běijīng's most famous temples naturally belong in Dōngchéng, even though many have vanished. Dōngchéng also hosts Běijīng's premier shopping street: Wangfujing Dajie, with its host of top-name shops and malls.

Speeding around Dōngchéng is simple, thanks to Line 2 of the underground, and Line 5, which now splices the district in two on a north–south axis. Dōngchéng is also one of the most attractive parts of Běijīng if you want to sling a bicycle between your legs and explore.

FORBIDDEN CITY Map pp58-9

紫禁城 Zǐjìn Chéng

☎ 6513 2255; www.dpm.org.cn; adult Nov-Mar/Apr-Oct Y40/60, Clock Exhibition Hall & Hall of Jewellery Y10 each, audio guide Y40; ⏰ 8.30am-4pm May-Sep, 8.30am-3.30pm Oct-Apr; ⊕ Tiananmen Xi or Tiananmen Dong

The astonishing Forbidden City, so called because it was off-limits to commoners for 500 years, occupies a primary position in the Chinese psyche. To communists, the Forbidden City is a contradictory symbol. It's a politically incorrect yarn from a pre-Revolutionary dark age, but it's also one spun from the very pinnacle of Chinese civilisation. It's therefore not surprising that violent forces during the Cultural Revolution wanted to trash the place. Perhaps hearing the distant tinkle of the tourist dollar, Premier Zhou Enlai did the right thing by stepping in to calm down the Red Guards.

Even though less than half of the palace (430,000 sq metres) is actually open to visitors and it is possible to explore the Forbidden City in a few hours, a full day will keep you occupied and the enthusiast will make several trips. Areas not open to the public include much of the western part of the Forbidden City and a lot of the southeast section. A massive chunk remains, and whatever you do, don't miss the delightful courtyards, pavilions and mini-museums within them on each side of the main complex.

As you approach the ticket office you may be encircled by a swarm of pushy guides. Note that their English levels vary and the spiel can often be tedious, formulaic and parrot-fashion. The better and cheaper alternative is to rent a funky automatically activated audio tour instead, which comes in 30 languages.

Don't confuse the Gate of Heavenly Peace with the Forbidden City entrance.

Some visitors purchase a Gate of Heavenly Peace admission ticket by mistake, not realising that this admits you only to the upstairs portion of the gate. The Forbidden City ticket booths are on either side of Meridian Gate – walk north until you can't walk any further without paying and you will spot the queues nearby.

Restaurants, cashpoints and toilets can be found within the Forbidden City and the sound of ping pong may unexpectedly emerge from some halls. Exterior photography is no problem, but photographing the interior of halls is often prohibited. Wheelchairs (Y500 deposit) are free to use, as are strollers (Y300 deposit). Smoking is not permitted in the Forbidden City.

History

Constructed on the site of a palace dating to Kublai Khan and the Mongol Yuan dynasty, the Ming emperor Yongle established the basic layout of the Forbidden City between 1406 and 1420, basing it on the now-ruined Ming-dynasty palace in Nánjīng. The grandiose emperor employed battalions of labourers and craftspeople – by some estimates there may have been up to a million of them – to build the Forbidden City. The palace once lay at the heart of the Imperial City, a much larger, now-vanished walled enclosure reserved for the use of the emperor and his personnel. The wall enclosing the Forbidden City – assembled from 12 million bricks – is the last intact surviving city wall in Běijīng.

This gargantuan palace complex – China's largest and best-preserved cluster of ancient buildings – sheltered two dynasties of emperors, the Ming and the Qing, who didn't stray from their pleasure dome unless they absolutely had to. A bell jar dropped over the whole spectacle maintained a highly rarefied atmosphere that nourished its elitist community. A stultifying code of rules, protocol and superstition deepened its otherworldliness, perhaps typified by its twittering band of eunuchs. From here the emperors governed China, often erratically and haphazardly, with authority occasionally drifting into the hands of opportunistic court officials and eunuchs. It wasn't until 1911 that revolution eventually came knocking at the huge doors, bringing with it the last orders for the Manchu Qing and dynastic rule.

Its mystique diffused (the Běijīng authorities prosaically call the complex the Palace Museum, or gùgōng bówùguǎn; 故宫博物馆), entry to the palace is no longer prohibited. In former ages the price for uninvited admission would have been instant death; these days Y40 to Y60 will do. The final ignominy came in 2001 when a Starbucks opened just north of Jingyun Gate (Jǐngyùn Mén) within the palace; it eventually closed, but was later replaced by a Chinese no-name cafe.

Most of the buildings you see now are post-18th century: the largely wooden palace was a tinderbox and fire was a constant hazard – a lantern festival combined with a sudden gust of Gobi wind would easily send flames dancing in unexpected directions, as would a fireworks display. Fires were also deliberately lit by court eunuchs and officials who could get rich off the repair bills. Originally water was provided by 72 wells in the palace (only 30 have been

TRANSPORT: DŌNGCHÉNG

Subway The Yonghegong-Lama Temple stop on Line 2 serves the Lama Temple and the Confucius Temple, and Ditan Park is a short walk north. Also on Line 2, get off at Dongsishitiao Station for the Poly Art Museum and buses east to Sānlǐtún; alight at Dongzhimen Station for the Airport Express and Line 13. Line 2 intersects with Line 1 at Jianguomen Station (for the Ancient Observatory). Line 5 intersects with Line 2 at Yonghegong-Lama Temple in the north and Dongdan in the south, running through Dengshikou, Dongsi, Zhangzizhonglu and Beixinqiao Stations. Running east–west along Dongchang'an Jie, Line 1 stops at Tiananmen Dong, Dongdan, Wangfujing and Jianguomen.

Bus Bus 5 travels from Deshengmen to the Bell Tower, down to Di'anmen Xidajie and Jingshan Houjie (for Jingshan Park), on to Beihai Park and Xihuá Mén (West Gate of the Forbidden City), before heading further south to Zhongshan Park and Qiánmén; bus 13 runs from the Lama Temple along Di'anmen Xidajie to Beihai Park (north gate); bus 103 runs from Sundongan Plaza on Wangfujing Dajie to Dengshikou, on to the China Art Museum, the Forbidden City (north entrance), Jingshan Park and Beihai Park; and bus 107 runs from Beihai Park to the Drum Tower then along to Jiaodaokou Dongdajie via Nanluogu Xiang to Dongzhimen Station.

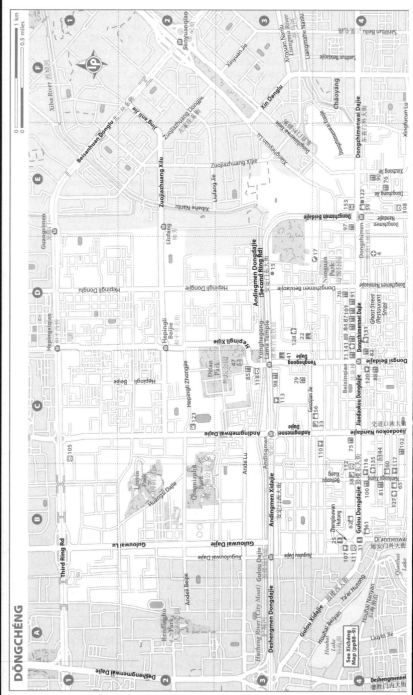

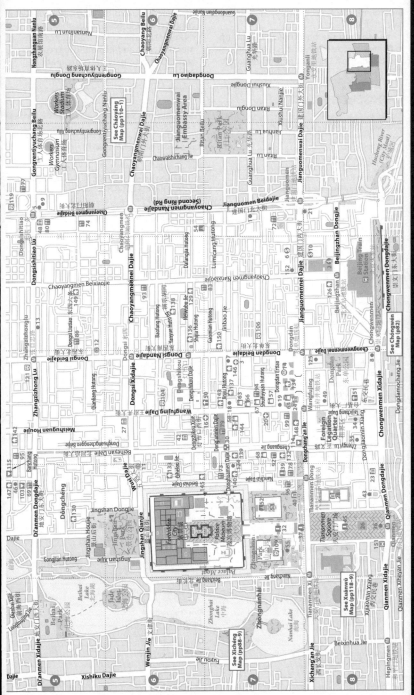

preserved), while a complex system took care of drainage.

It wasn't just the buildings that went up in flames, but also rare books, paintings and calligraphy. Libraries and other palace halls and buildings housing combustible contents were tiled in black; the colour represents water in the *wǔxíng* (five-element) theory, and its symbolic presence was thought to prevent conflagrations.

DŌNGCHÉNG (pp58–9)

In the 20th century there were two major lootings of the palace by Japanese forces and the Kuomintang (KMT; Chiang Kai-shek's Nationalist Party, the dominant political force after the fall of the Qing dynasty). Thousands of crates of relics were removed and carted off to Taiwan, where they remain on display in Taipei's National Palace Museum (worth seeing). Some say this was just as well, since the Cultural

Revolution reduced much of China's precious artwork to confetti.

Layout

Ringed by a picturesque 52m-wide moat that freezes over in winter, the rectangular palace is laid out roughly symmetrically on a north–south axis, bisected by a line of grand gates and ceremonial halls that straddle the very axis that cleaves Běijīng in two. The palace is so unspeakably big (over 1 million sq metres, with 800 buildings and 9000 rooms) that restoration is a never-ending work in progress; but despite the attentions of restorers, some of the hall rooftops still sprout tufts of grass. A pre–Olympic Games heavy-duty refit saw several signature halls and gates undergoing extensive repair. Many halls have been repainted in a way that conceals the original pigment; other halls, such as the Hall of Mental Cultivation (Yǎngxīn Diàn), however, possess a more threadbare and faded authenticity.

You can enter the Forbidden City by Meridian Gate in the south or Shenwu Gate (Shénwǔ Mén) in the north of the complex. You can exit from either gate or via Donghua Gate in the east (but you cannot enter the palace through Donghua Gate).

Restored in the 17th century, Meridian Gate (Wǔ Mén) is a massive portal that in former times was reserved for the use of the emperor. Gongs and bells would sound imperial comings and goings, while lesser mortals used lesser gates: the military used the west gate, civilians the east gate. The emperor also reviewed his armies from here, passed judgement on prisoners, announced the new year's calendar and oversaw the flogging of troublesome ministers.

The Golden Stream (Jīn Shuǐ), delightfully fringed by willows, runs through here and into the courtyard in front of the Gate of Supreme Harmony (Tàihé Mén), where it is shaped to resemble a Tartar bow and spanned by five marble bridges. Contrast the newly painted vibrant colours on the exterior of the gate with the far less colourful and fainter colours of the interior.

The dwarfing courtyard beyond the gate could hold an imperial audience of 100,000 people. For an idea of the size of the restoration challenge, note how the crumbling courtyard stones are stuffed with dry weeds, especially on the periphery. Within the Hongyi Pavilion (Hóngyì Gé) to the west is an exhibition of the ceremonial music system of the imperial palace.

Three Great Halls 三大殿

Raised on a three-tier marble terrace with balustrades are the Three Great Halls (Sān Dàdiàn), the heart of the Forbidden City. The recently restored Hall of Supreme Harmony (Tàihé Diàn) is the most important and largest structure in the Forbidden City. Built in the 15th century and restored in the 17th century, it was used for ceremonial occasions, such as the emperor's birthday, the nomination of military leaders and coronations. Inside the Hall of Supreme Harmony is a richly decorated Dragon Throne (Lóngyǐ), from which the emperor would preside over trembling officials. The entire court had to touch the floor nine times with their foreheads (the custom known as kowtowing) in the emperor's presence. At the back of the throne is a carved Xumishan, the Buddhist paradise, signifying the throne's supremacy.

Bronze vats – once full of water for dousing fires – stand in front of the hall; in all, 308 such vats were dotted around the Forbidden City, draped in quilts or warmed with fires in winter to keep them from freezing over. The large bronze turtle in the front symbolises longevity and stability. It has a removable lid, and on special occasions incense was lit inside it so that smoke billowed from its mouth.

To the west of the terrace is a small pavilion with a bronze grain measure and to the east is a sundial; both are symbolic of imperial justice. On the corners of the hall's roof, as with other buildings in the city, there's a mounted figure with his retreat cut off by mythical and actual animals, a story relating to a cruel tyrant hanged from one such eave.

Note the fascinating exhibitions strung out along a string of halls on the eastern flank of the Three Great Halls. In sequence, exhibitions cover the gates and guards in the Forbidden City and a fascinating collection detailing the emperor's Tibetan Buddhist beliefs. In all there were 10 Buddhist chapels in the northwest of the Forbidden City; among them were the Big Buddha Hall (大佛堂; Dàfó Táng), the Rain and Flower Pavilion (雨花阁; Yǔhuā Gé) – a copy of the Gold Hall from Tholing Monastery in Tibet – and

BEHIND THE WALL

If ceremonial and administrative duties occupied most of the emperor's working hours, it was the pursuit of pleasure behind the high walls of the Forbidden City that occupied much of his attention during the evenings. With so many wives and consorts to choose from, a system was needed to help the emperor choose his bedtime companion. One method was to keep the names of royal wives, consorts and favourites on jade tablets near the emperor's chambers. By turning the tablet over the emperor made his request for the evening, and the eunuch on duty would rush off to find the lucky lady. Stripped naked (and therefore weaponless), the little foot-bound creature was giftwrapped in a yellow cloth, piggybacked over to the royal boudoir and dumped at the feet of the emperor, the eunuch recording the date and time to verify the legitimacy of a possible child.

Aside from the emperor's frolicking, all this activity had a more serious purpose: prolonging the life of the emperor. An ancient Chinese belief that frequent sex with young girls could sustain one's youth even motivated Mao Zedong to follow the same procedure.

Financing the affairs of state probably cost less than financing the affairs of the emperor, and keeping the pleasure dome functioning drew heavily on the resources of the empire. During the Ming dynasty an estimated 9000 maids of honour and 70,000 eunuchs served the court. As well as the servants and prize concubines, there were also the royal elephants to maintain. Pocketing the cash was illegal, but selling elephant dung for use as shampoo was not – it was believed to give hair that extra sheen. Back in the harem the cosmetic bills piled up to 400,000 *liang* of silver. Then, of course, the concubines who had grown old and were no longer in active service were still supposed to be cared for. Rather than cut back on expenditure, the emperor sent out eunuchs to collect emergency taxes whenever money ran short.

As for the palace eunuchs, the royal chop was administered at the Eunuch Clinic near the Forbidden City, using a swift knife and a special chair with a hole in the seat. The candidates sought to better their lives in the service of the court, but half of them died after the operation. Mutilation of any kind was considered grounds for exclusion from the next life, so many eunuchs carried around their appendages in pouches, believing that at the time of death the spirits might be deceived into thinking them whole.

the Fragrant Clouds Pavilion (香云亭; Xiāngyún Tíng), none of which is currently open. Within the Fanzong Building (梵宗楼; Fànzōng Lóu) once stood a statue of the fierce multi-armed Yamantaka (the 'Destroyer of Death'), while the Baohua Hall (Bǎohuá Diàn) was the principal hall for Tibetan Buddhist rites during the Qing dynasty. The now ruined Hall of Rectitude (中正殿; Zhōngzhèng Diàn), destroyed by fire in 1923, was once lavishly furnished with Buddhist figures and ornaments. Further along in the sequence is an exhibition dedicated to ancestor worship in the palace and the imperial harem and the lives of imperial concubines. In the next hall along is a detailed diorama of the entire Forbidden City.

Halls west of the Three Great Halls exhibit treasures from the palace. Running from south to north the exhibitions cover: scientific instruments (astronomical devices, telescopes etc) and details of Jesuit scientists who attended the Qing court, articles of daily use (including imperial hunting guns, chessboards and ceramics), objects presented as tribute and objects made by the imperial workshop.

Behind the Hall of Supreme Harmony is the smaller Hall of Middle Harmony (Zhōnghé Diàn), which was used as the emperor's transit lounge. Here he would make last-minute preparations, rehearse speeches and receive close ministers. On display are two Qing-dynasty sedan chairs, the emperor's mode of transport around the Forbidden City. The last of the Qing emperors, Puyi, used a bicycle and altered a few features of the palace grounds to make it easier to get around.

The third hall is the Hall of Preserving Harmony (Bǎohé Diàn), used for banquets and later for imperial examinations. The hall has no support pillars, and to its rear is a 250-tonne marble imperial carriageway carved with dragons and clouds, which was transported into Běijīng on an ice path. The emperor was conveyed over the carriageway in his sedan chair as he ascended or descended the terrace. The outer housing surrounding the Three Great Halls was used for storing gold, silver, silks, carpets and other treasures.

Other Halls

The basic configuration of the Three Great Halls is echoed by the next group of buildings. Smaller in scale, these buildings were more important in terms of real power, which in China traditionally lies at the back door or, in this case, the back gate.

FORBIDDEN CITY

0   200 m
0   0.1 miles

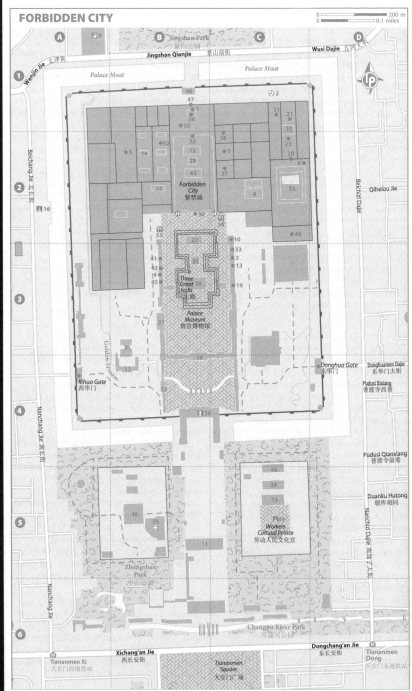

The first structure is the Palace of Heavenly Purity (Qiánqīng Gōng), a residence of Ming and early Qing emperors, and later an audience hall for receiving foreign envoys and high officials.

Immediately behind it is the Hall of Union (Jiāotài Diàn), which contains a clepsydra – a water clock made in 1745 with five bronze vessels and a calibrated scale. There's also a mechanical clock built in 1797 and a collection of imperial jade seals on display. The Palace of Earthly Tranquillity (Kūnníng Gōng) was the imperial couple's bridal chamber and the centre of operations for the palace harem.

At the northern end of the Forbidden City is the Imperial Garden (Yù Huāyuán), a classical Chinese garden with 7000 sq metres of fine landscaping, including rockeries, walkways, pavilions and ancient, carbuncular and deformed cypresses. Look out for the lump tree, the Elephant Man of the cypress world. Before you reach the large Shenwu Gate, note the pair of bronze elephants whose front knees bend in an anatomically impossible fashion just before you reach Shunzhen Gate (Shùnzhēn Mén).

The western and eastern sides of the Forbidden City are the palatial former living quarters, once containing libraries, temples, theatres, gardens and even the tennis court of the last emperor. Walk east and you can access the Hall of Jewellery (Zhēnbǎo Guǎn; admission Y10; 🕙 8.30am-4pm summer, 8.30am-3.30pm winter), tickets for which also entitle you to glimpse the Well of Concubine Zhen (Zhēn Fēi Jǐng), into which the namesake wretch was thrown on the orders of Cixi, and the glazed Nine Dragon Screen (Jiǔlóng Bì). The treasures on view are fascinating: within the Hall of Harmony (Yíhé Xuān) sparkle Buddhist statues fashioned from gold and inlaid with gems, and a gold pagoda glittering with precious stones, followed by jade, jadeite, lapis lazuli and crystal pieces displayed in the Hall of Joyful Longevity (Lèshòu Táng). Further objects are displayed within the Hall of Character Cultivation (Yǎngxìng Diàn), but at the time of writing the further sequence of halls to the south was empty. The Changyin Pavilion (Chàngyīn Gé) to the east was formerly an imperial stage.

The Clock Exhibition Hall (Zhōngbiǎo Guǎn; admission Y10; 🕙 8.30am-4pm summer, 8.30am-3.30pm winter) is one of the unmissable highlights of the Forbidden City. Located at the time of writing in the Fengxian Hall (Fèngxiàn Diàn), the exhibition contains an astonishing array of elaborate timepieces, many gifts to the Qing emperors from overseas. Many of the 18th-century examples are crafted by James Cox or Joseph Williamson (both of London) and imported through Guǎngdōng from England; others are from Switzerland, America and Japan. Exquisitely wrought, fashioned with magnificently designed elephants and other creatures, they all display astonishing artfulness and attention to detail. Standout clocks include the 'Gilt Copper Astronomy Clock' equipped with a working model of the solar system, and the automaton-equipped 'Gilt Copper Clock with a robot writing Chinese characters with a brush'. The Qing court must surely have been amazed by their ingenuity. Time your arrival for 11am or 2pm to see the clock performance in which choice timepieces strike the hour and give a display to wide-eyed children and adults.

TIANANMEN SQUARE Map pp58-9
天安门广场 Tiān'ānmén Guǎngchǎng
Ⓜ Tiananmen Xi, Tiananmen Dong or Qianmen
Flanked to the east and west by stern 1950s Soviet-style buildings and ringed by white perimeter fences that channel the hoi polloi towards periodic security checks and bag searches, the world's largest public square (440,000 sq metres) is a vast desert of paving stones at the heart of Běijīng. The square is also a poignant epitaph to China's hapless democracy movement, which got a drubbing from the People's Liberation Army (PLA) in June 1989. The designated points of access and occasional security checks immediately suggest that this is no Trafalgar Square. Unlike London's famous plaza, Tiananmen Square is cut off somehow from the city – it is obsessively monitored to quickly suffocate any signs of dissent, beggars and vagrants are kept at bay, and a tangible mood of restraint and discipline reigns. In some ways the square symbolises the China of today.

Which means the square is hardly a relaxing place, but there's more than enough space to stretch a leg and the view can be simply breathtaking, especially on a clear, blue day and at nightfall when the square is illuminated. Height restrictions mean that surrounding buildings are all low, allowing largely uninterrupted views of the dome of the sky (unlike Shànghǎi's People's Square). Kites flit through the sky, children stamp around on the paving slabs and Chinese out-of-towners huddle together for the obligatory photo opportunity with the great helmsman's portrait. On National Day (1 October), Tiananmen Square is simply packed.

Tiananmen Square as we see it today is a modern creation and there is precious little sense of history. During Ming and Qing times part of the Imperial City Wall (Huáng Chéng) called the Thousand Foot Corridor (Qiānbù Láng) poked deep into the space today occupied by the square, enclosing a section of the imperial domain. The wall took a 'T' shape, emerging from the two huge, now absent, gates that rose up south of the Gate of Heavenly Peace – Chang'an Zuo Gate and Chang'an You Gate – before running south to the vanished Daming Gate (Dàmíng Mén). Called Daqing Gate during the Qing dynasty and Zhonghua Gate during the Republic, the Daming Gate had three watchtowers and upturned eaves and was guarded by a pair of stone lions. It was pulled down after 1949, a fate similarly reserved for Chang'an Zuo Gate and Chang'an You Gate. East and west of the Thousand Foot Corridor stood official departments and temples, including the Ministry of Rites, the Ministry of Revenue, Honglu Temple and Taichang Temple.

Mao conceived the square to project the enormity of the Communist Party, so it's all a bit Kim Il Sung–ish. During the Cultural Revolution, the chairman, wearing a Red Guard armband, reviewed parades of up to a million people here. The 'Tiananmen Incident' is the term given to the near riot in the square that accompanied the death of Premier Zhou Enlai in 1976. Another million people jammed the square to pay their last respects to Mao in September that year. In 1989 army tanks and soldiers forced pro-democracy demonstrators out of the square. Although it seems likely that no one was actually killed within the square itself, hundreds,

top picks

BEIJINGERS' FAVOURITE HISTORIC SIGHTS

- Forbidden City (p56) The magnificent Forbidden City, so called because it was off-limits to commoners for 500 years, occupies a primary position in the Chinese psyche.
- Summer Palace (p127) The huge regal encampment of the Summer Palace in the northwest of town is one of Běijīng's foremost sights.
- Great Wall (p97) You can't see it from the moon, but you can from north of town.
- Drum Tower (p74) First built in 1272, the Drum Tower marked the centre of the old Mongol capital Dàdū.
- Bell Tower (p73) Fronted by a Qing-dynasty stele, the Bell Tower – originally built in 1272 – sits along an alley behind the Drum Tower.

possibly thousands, were slaughtered outside the square. During the 10th anniversary of the 1989 demonstrations, the square was shut for renovations.

Despite being a public place, the square remains more in the hands of the government than the people; it is monitored by closed-circuit TV cameras, and plain-clothes police can move faster than the Shànghǎi maglev if anyone strips down to a 'Free Tibet' T-shirt.

Like historic Běijīng, the square is laid out on a north–south axis. Threading through Front Gate to the south, the square's meridian line is straddled by the Chairman Mao Memorial Hall, cuts through the Gate of Heavenly Peace (Tiānānmén) – the gate that lends its name to the square – to the north, and cleaves through the Forbidden City.

In the square, one stands in the symbolic centre of the Chinese universe. The rectangular arrangement, flanked by halls to both east and west, to some extent echoes the layout of the Forbidden City. As such, the square employs a conventional plan that pays obeisance to traditional Chinese culture, but its ornaments and buildings are largely Soviet-inspired.

West of the Great Hall of the People, the National Grand Theatre (p91) – with its controversial styling and out-of-place looks – resembles something from another solar system.

If you get up early you can watch the flag-raising ceremony at sunrise, performed by a troop of PLA soldiers drilled to march at precisely 108 paces per minute, 75cm per pace. The soldiers emerge through the Gate of Heavenly Peace to goosestep faultlessly across Chang'an Jie as all traffic is halted. The same ceremony in reverse is performed at sunset. Ask at your hotel for flag-raising/-lowering times so you can get there early, as crowds can be quite intense.

Unless you want a map you'll have to sidestep determined map sellers and their confederates – the incessant learners of English – and just say no to the 'poor' art students press ganging tourists to view their exhibitions; fending them off can be draining. Avoid invitations to tea houses, unless you want to pay in excess of US$400 dollars for the experience.

Bicycles cannot be ridden across Tiananmen Square, but you can walk your bike. Traffic is one way for north–south avenues on either side of the square.

GATE OF HEAVENLY PEACE Map pp58-9

天安门 Tiānānmén

adult Y15; 🕗 8.30am-4.30pm; 🚇 Tiananmen Xi or Tiananmen Dong

Hung with a vast likeness of Mao, the double-eaved Gate of Heavenly Peace, north of Tiananmen Square, is a potent national symbol. Built in the 15th century and restored in the 17th century, the gate was formerly the largest of the four gates of the Imperial City Wall. Called Chéngtiān Mén during the Ming dynasty, it was renamed Tiānān Mén during Emperor Shunzhi's reign in 1651. The gate is guarded by two pairs of Ming stone lions; one of the creatures apocryphally blocked the path of Li Chuangwang as he invaded Běijīng at the end of the Ming dynasty. Li fended the lion off by stabbing its belly with his spear while on horseback, leaving a mark that can still be seen. Other locals dispute this story, arguing that it is a bullet hole from allied-force guns when troops entered Běijīng to quell the Boxer Rebellion in 1900. In the 1950s, electric trams used to pass in front of the gate. Until 1952, the two large gates of Chang'an Zuomen and Chang'an Youmen stood south of the Gate of Heavenly Peace, at right angles to it.

PITCHER PERFECT

The portrait of a benign Mao Zedong still hangs exultantly from the Gate of Heavenly Peace in the same way that public statues of the Great Helmsman still keep guard over cities across China, from Dāndōng on the North Korean border to the far-flung central-Asian outpost of Kashgar and the ethnic Naxi town of Lìjiāng in Yúnnán. Mao's Běijīng portrait has been reportedly vandalised just twice during its long vigil overlooking Tiananmen Square: once in 1989 and again in 2007. During the democracy protests of 1989, three men from Mao's home province of Húnán pitched paint-filled eggs at the portrait, while in 2007 burning material was thrown at the painting, scorching it in the process. Several copies of the portraits exist and replacement versions were speedily requisitioned in both instances. Such dissent is severely dealt with in China: the three egg throwers paid for their crime with spells in jail. One of them was journalist Yu Dongyue, who was jailed for over 16 years, emerging mentally ill upon his release in 2006. Two of the egg throwers fled China in 2009 to seek sanctuary in the US.

There are five doors to the gate, fronted by seven bridges spanning a stream. Each of these bridges was restricted in its use, and only the emperor could use the central door and bridge. The soldiers performing the punctilious daily flag-raising and flag-lowering ceremony on Tiananmen Square emerge through the gate.

Today's political coterie watches mass troop parades from here, and it was from this gate that Mao proclaimed the People's Republic of China on 1 October 1949. The dominating feature is the gigantic portrait of the ex-chairman (see boxed text, above), to the left of which runs the poetic slogan 'Long Live the People's Republic of China' and to the right 'Long Live the Unity of the Peoples of the World'.

If entering the palace from the south, you pass through the gate on your way to the Forbidden City. Climb up for excellent views of Tiananmen Square, and peek inside at the impressive beams and overdone paintwork; in all there are 60 gargantuan wooden pillars and 17 vast lamps suspended from the ceiling. Within the gate tower there is also a fascinating photographic history of the gate (but only in Chinese) and Tiananmen Square; no prizes for guessing which monumental historical episode from the late 1980s makes a non-appearance. Yawn-inducing patriotic video presentations celebrating communist events round off the picture.

There's no fee for walking through the gate, but if you climb it you'll have to buy an admission ticket and pay (Y2 to Y6) to store your bag (one hour maximum) at the kiosk about 30m northwest of the ticket office. As the gate is a state symbol, security here can be intense and locals are scrupulously frisked. Note that the gate ticket office only sells tickets for the gate; if you want to visit the Forbidden City, continue north until you can go no further.

CHAIRMAN MAO MEMORIAL HALL
Map pp58-9

毛主席纪念堂 **Máo Zhǔxí Jìniàntáng**
admission free, bag storage Y2-10, camera storage Y2-5; 8am-noon Tue-Sun; Tiananmen Xi, Tiananmen Dong or Qianmen

Mao Zedong died in September 1976 and his memorial hall was constructed on the southern side of Tiananmen Square soon afterwards. The hallowed epicentre of China's inexorable empire of Mao memorabilia and merchandise, this squat, Soviet-inspired mausoleum lies on Běijīng's north–south axis of symmetry on the footprint of Zhonghua Gate (Zhōnghuá Mén), a vast and ancient portal flattened during the communist development of Tiananmen Square.

Domestically feted so his achievements forever eclipse his darker and more ruinous experiments, Mao is still revered across much of China. His portrait still hangs over living rooms throughout the land and graces drum towers in far-off Guǎngxī villages and beyond. Mao's personality cult is recalled in the statues of the chairman that rise up across China while mute Mao-era slogans (see boxed text, p75) still fight the class war from crumbling walls in villages across the Middle kingdom.

To this day the Chinese show deep respect when confronted with the physical presence of Mao. You are reminded to remove your hat and you can fork out Y3 for a flower to lay at the foot of a statue of the Great Helmsman. Further on, Mao's mummified corpse lies in a crystal cabinet, draped in an anachronistic red flag emblazoned with hammer and sickle, as guards in white gloves impatiently wave the hoi polloi on towards further rooms, where a riot of Mao kitsch – lighters, bracelets, statues, key rings, bottle openers, you name it – ensues. Don't expect to stumble upon Jung Chang signing copies of her *Mao, the Unknown Story* (see boxed text, p43). At certain times of the year the body requires maintenance and is not on view. Bags need to be deposited at the building east of the memorial hall across the road from Tiananmen Square (if you leave your camera in your bag you will be charged for it).

FRONT GATE Map pp58-9
前门 Qián Mén
☎ 6525 3176; adult Y10; ◷ 8.30am-4pm;
Ⓜ Qianmen

Front Gate actually consists of two gates. The northernmost of the two gates is the 40m-high Zhengyang Gate (正阳门城楼; Zhèngyáng Mén Chénglóu), which dates from the Ming dynasty and was the largest of the nine gates of the Inner City Wall separating the inner, or Tartar (Manchu), city from the outer, or Chinese, city. Partially destroyed in the Boxer Rebellion around 1900, the gate was once flanked by two temples that have since vanished. With the disappearance of the city walls, the gate sits out of context, but it can be climbed for views of the square. Similarly torched during the Boxer Rebellion, the Zhengyang Gate Arrow Tower (正阳门箭楼; Zhèngyángmén Jiànlóu) to the south also dates from the Ming dynasty and was originally connected to Zhengyang Gate by a semicircular enceinte (demolished last century). To the east is the old British-built Qian Men Railway Station (老车站; Lǎo Chēzhàn), until recently taken over by shops and restaurants but at the time of writing it was set to become the Beijing Railway Museum.

BĚIJĪNG ON FOOT

The city itself may appear uncontrollably huge, but Běijīng is a city of orderly design (unlike Shànghǎi). Think of the city as one giant grid, with the Forbidden City at its centre.

Street signs in Běijīng are marked in both Chinese characters and Pinyin (romanised Chinese). Even so, understanding a little basic Chinese will help to make some sense of street names. It is also useful to refer to the detailed maps in this chapter, where many roads are labelled with Chinese characters. We have also frequently added road names in Chinese in the text to assist you around town.

The majority of Běijīng's larger streets are affixed with the word *jiē* (街), which means 'street', as in Wangfujing Dajie (Dajie here means 'big street', 'avenue' or just 'street') – 'Wangfujing St'. Occasionally the world *lù* (路) is also used, meaning 'road', as in Zhangzizhong Lu – 'Zhangzizhong Rd'. Běijīng's plentiful alleyways in the centre of town are called *hútòng* (胡同); a minority are called *xiàng* (巷), which means 'alley'. Another term used is *lǐ* (里), meaning 'neighbourhood'.

Many road names are also compound words that place the road in context with others in the city, by using the points of the compass. The following words are used in compound street names:

běi	north	北
nán	south	南
dōng	east	东
xī	west	西
zhōng	central	中

So, Gulou Dongdajie means 'Gulou East St' and Dongdan Beidajie means 'Dongdan North St'.

However, some Běijīng street names have a few local idiosyncrasies. Jianguomenwai Dajie means 'the avenue outside (外; *wài*) Jianguo Gate (建国门; Jianguomen)' – that is, outside the old wall – whereas Jianguomennei Dajie (建国门内大街) means 'the avenue inside Jianguo Gate'. The gate in question no longer exists, so it survives in name alone.

Unlike countless other Chinese cities, Běijīng is one place where you won't find a Jiefang Lu (Liberation Rd), Renmin Lu (People's Rd), Zhongshan Lu (Zhongshan Rd) or a Beijing Lu (Beijing Rd). Six ring roads circle the city centre in concentric rings, while a seventh is forming.

LAMA TEMPLE Map pp58–9
雍和宫 Yōnghé Gōng
28 Yonghegong Dajie; adult Y25, audio guide Y20;
⏰ 9am-4pm; ⓔ Yonghegong-Lama Temple

Běijīng's foremost Buddhist temple, the Lama Temple is also one of the most magnificent Tibetan Buddhist temples outside of the Land of Snows. With three richly worked archways and five main halls (each one taller than the preceding one), revolving prayer wheels (propel them clockwise), multicoloured glaze tiles, magnificent Chinese lions, tantric statuettes and hall boards decorated with Mongolian, Manchu, Tibetan and Chinese, the sumptuous temple is a profound introduction to Tibetan Buddhist lore.

The temple was once the official residence of Count Yin Zhen, who became emperor in 1723 and traded up to the Forbidden City. His name changed to Yongzheng, and his former residence became Yonghe Palace (Yōnghé Gōng). In 1744 it was converted into a lamasery (a monastery of lamas) and became home to legions of monks from Mongolia and Tibet.

In 1792 the Emperor Qianlong, having quelled an uprising in Tibet, instituted a new administrative system involving two golden vases. One was kept at the renowned Jokhang Temple in Lhasa, to be employed for determining the reincarnation of the Dalai Lama, and the other was kept at the Lama Temple for the lottery used for choosing the next Panchen Lama. The Lama Temple thus assumed a new importance in ethnic minority control.

Premier Zhou Enlai – seemingly single-handedly responsible for saving what he could of China's heritage during the Cultural Revolution – stepped in when the Red Guards focused their iconoclastic attentions on the temple. Today the temple is an active place of worship, attracting pilgrims from across the land and thronging with worshippers, some of whom prostrate themselves at full length within its halls.

The first hall, Yonghe Gate (雍和门; Yōnghé Mén), houses a statue of Maitreya, the future Buddha, flanked by celestial guardians. Above the statue of Maitreya (also called Milefo) is a board inscribed with the characters '心明妙现', which literally means 'If the heart is bright, the wonderful will appear'.

In the courtyard beyond is a pond with a bronze mandala depicting Xumishan, the Buddhist paradise. Glimpses of the more abstruse nature of the temple can be seen in the hall on the right after Yonghe Gate: the Esoteric Hall (密宗殿; Mìzōng Diàn) contains the fierce, multi-armed deity Deweidejingang. Opposite is the Exoteric Hall (讲经殿; Jiǎngjing Diàn), where sutras were studied and recited.

With its air of peaceful reverence, the second hall, the huge Yonghe Hall (雍和殿; Yōnghé Diàn), contains a trinity of gilded effigies representing the past, present and future Buddhas.

The third hall, Yongyou Hall (永佑殿; Yǒngyòu Diàn), contains statues of the Buddha of Longevity and the Buddha of Medicine (to the left). Peek into the East Side Hall (东配殿; Dōngpèi Dian) for its esoteric gathering of cobalt-blue Buddhas and two huge dog-like creatures. Note how the tantric statues have been partially draped to disguise their couplings.

Within the Hall of the Wheel of the Law (法轮殿; Fǎlún Diàn) is a large bronze statue of a benign and smiling Tsong Khapa (1357–1419), founder of the Gelukpa, or Yellow Hat, sect, robed in yellow and illuminated from a skylight above. Also within the hall is a throne that seated the Dalai Lama when he lectured sutras here, while at the rear is a carved wooden bowl into which are thrust mounds of cash.

Don't miss the collection of bronze Tibetan Buddhist statues within the Jiètái Lóu (戒台楼; Jiètái Lóu). Most effigies date from the Qing dynasty, from languorous renditions of Green Tara and White Tara to exotic, tantric pieces (such as Samvara) and figurines of the fierce-looking Mahakala. Also peruse the collection of Tibetan Buddhist ornaments within the Bānchán Lóu (班禅楼; Bānchán Lóu): there's a fantastic array of dorje (Tibetan ritual sceptres), mandalas, tantric figures, and an impressive selection of ceremonial robes in silk and satin.

Towards the rear, Wanfu Pavilion (万福阁; Wànfú Gé) has a stupendous 18m-high statue of the Maitreya Buddha in his Tibetan form, clothed in yellow satin and reputedly sculpted from a single block of sandalwood. Each of the bodhisattva's toes is the size of a pillow. You may find yourself transported to Tibet, where the wood for this statue originated, thanks to the smoke curling up from yak-butter lamps. Galleries can be seen above, but sadly you cannot climb up to them. Behind the statue is the Vault of Avalokiteshvara (观音洞; Guānyīn

Dòng), from where a diminutive and blue-faced statue of Guanyin peeks out. The Wanfu Pavilion is linked by an overhead walkway to the Yansui Pavilion (延绥阁; Yánsuí Gé), which encloses around a huge lotus flower that revolves to reveal an effigy of the longevity Buddha.

At the very rear, worshippers gather to worship White Tara and Green Tara in the Suicheng Hall (绥成殿; Suíchéng Diàn).

Photography is not permitted inside the temple buildings. English-speaking guides (Y80) can be found in the office to the left of the entrance gate or loitering near the temple entrance. The street outside the temple entrance heaves with shops piled high with statues of Buddha, talismans, Buddhist charms and keepsakes, picked over by pilgrims. Exiting the temple and walking east along Xilou Hutong brings you to the former Bailin Temple (Bǎilín Sì; Map pp58–9; 1 Xilou Hutong) at the bend in the alley, its temple halls now converted to offices and its northernmost wall still daubed with the outline of Maoist slogans (the guard at the gate may not let you in, however).

CONFUCIUS TEMPLE & IMPERIAL COLLEGE Map pp58-9
孔庙、国子监 Kǒng Miào & Guózǐjiàn
13 Guozijian Jie; adult Y20, tour guide Y80;
🕑 8.30am-5pm; ◎ Yonghegong-Lama Temple

With over 30 Confucius Institutes world-wide, the Shāndōng sage is currently enjoying yet another upswing after bouts of anti-Confucian violence (the last one erupted in August 1966) singled him out for Chinese spleen. An incense stick's toss away from the Lama Temple, China's second-largest Confucian temple has had a recent refit, but the almost otherworldly sense of detachment is seemingly impossible to shift. Antediluvian bixi (mythical tortoise-like dragons) glare from repainted pavilions while lumpy and ossified ancient cypresses claw stiffly at the dusty Běijīng air. A mood of impassiveness reigns and

the lack of worship reinforces a sensation that time has stood still. This is made all the more palpable by the mute forest of 190 stelae recording the 13 Confucian classics in 630,000 Chinese characters at the temple rear. Also inscribed on stelae are the names of successful candidates of the highest level of the official Confucian examination system. It was the ambition of every scholar to see his name engraved here, but it wasn't easy. Each candidate was locked in one of about 8000 cubicles, measuring roughly 1.5 sq metres, for a period of three days. Many died or went insane during their incarceration.

Like everywhere in town, skeletons lurk in the temple cupboard and a distasteful footnote lurks unrecorded behind the tourist blurb. Běijīng writer Lao She (p78) was dragged here in August 1966, forced to his knees in front of a bonfire of Beijing opera costumes to confess his anti-Revolutionary crimes, and beaten. The much-loved writer drowned himself the next day in Taiping Lake (one of the thousands of Běijīng deaths in August and September of '66).

But in its tranquillity and reserve, the temple is a lovely sanctuary from Běijīng's congested, smoggy streets and snarling traffic and is a true haven of peace and quiet. Some of Běijīng's last remaining páilou (decorated archways) bravely survive in the hútòng outside (Guozijian Jie) and the entire area of hútòng now swarms with small cafes and a fascinating choice of shops, making it an ideal place to browse in low gear. At the western end of Guozijian Jie stands a diminutive Fire God Temple (Huǒshén Miào), built in 1802 and now occupied by Běijīng residents. Only the first hall – the Mountain Gate (Shān Mén) – remains recognisable and the remaining temple halls have been greatly adapted.

West of the Confucius Temple stands the Imperial College (Guózǐjiàn), where the emperor expounded the Confucian classics to an audience of thousands of kneeling students, professors and court officials – an

GUANXI

If you want to locate or contact a tourist, entertainment, shopping or business venue in Běijīng (and 20 other cities in China) and you have a mobile phone, then text message the name of the venue to the wireless search engine GuanXi on ☎ 1066 9588 2929. The full name, address and directions, plus telephone number, will be immediately returned to you by SMS (Y1 to Y2 per enquiry). The information can also be relayed in Chinese, as long as your mobile phone can support Chinese text.

annual rite. Built by the grandson of Kublai Khan in 1306, the former college was the supreme academy during the Yuan, Ming and Qing dynasties. On the site is a marvellous glazed, three-gate, single-eaved decorative archway, called a *liúli páifāng* (glazed archway). The Biyong Hall beyond is a twin-roofed structure with yellow tiles surrounded by a moat and topped with a gold knob, its stupendous interior housing a vermillion and gold lectern.

Just east of the Confucius Temple is the relocated Songtangzhai Museum (Sōngtángzhái Bówùguǎn; 3 Guozijian Jie; 9am-6pm), where you can view a lovely collection of traditional carved gateways, drum stones, Buddhist effigies, ancient pillar bases and stone lions. It advertises itself as being free but that's only the front part; if you delve into the more interesting rear section, you get stung for Y30 (or Y100 for a tour with a guide – not worth it).

WORKERS CULTURAL PALACE
Map pp58-9
劳动人民文化宫 Láodòng Rénmín Wénhuà Gōng
adult Y2; 6.30am-7.30pm; Tiananmen Dong
Despite the prosaic name and epicentral location at the very heart of town, this reclusive park, northeast of the Gate of Heavenly Peace, is one of Běijīng's best-kept secrets, and a bargain to boot. Few visitors divert here from their course towards the main gate of the Forbidden City, but this was the emperor's premier place of worship and contains the Supreme Temple (太庙; Tài Miào). If you find the Forbidden City either too colossal or crowded, the temple halls here are a cheaper, much more tranquil and far more manageable alternative. The huge halls of the temple remain, their roofs enveloped in imperial yellow tiles, beyond a quiet grove of ancient cypresses and enclosed within the Glazed Gate (琉璃门; Liúli Mén). Rising up to the splendid Front Hall, the scene of imperial ceremonies of ancestor worship, are three flights of steps. Only gods could traverse the central plinth; the emperor was consigned to the left-hand flight. Note how the plaque above the Front Hall is inscribed in both Chinese and Manchu. Sadly this hall, as well as the Middle Hall (中殿; Zhōngdiàn) and Rear Hall (后殿; Hòu Diàn) behind, is inaccessible. The northern perimeter of the park abuts the

palace moat *(tǒngzi hé)*, where you can find a bench and park yourself in front of a fine view. For an offbeat experience, practise your backhand within earshot of the Forbidden City at the tennis court (6512 2856) in the park. Take the northwest exit from the park and find yourself just by the Forbidden City's Meridian Gate and point of entry to the palace, or pop out of the eastern gate to Nanchizi Dajie.

IMPERIAL ARCHIVES Map pp58-9
皇史宬 Huángshǐ Chéng
136 Nanchizi Dajie; admission free; 9am-7pm; Tiananmen Dong
Tucked away on the first road east of the Forbidden City is the former Imperial Archives, repository for the imperial records, decrees, the 'Jade Book' (the imperial genealogical record) and huge encyclopedic works, including the Yongle Dadian and the Daqing Huidian. With strong echoes of the splendid imperial palace, the courtyard contains well-preserved halls – peer through the closed door of the main hall and make out the chests in which the archives were stored.

IMPERIAL CITY EXHIBITION
Map pp58-9
皇城艺术馆 Huáng Chéng Yìshùguǎn
8511 5104; www.huangcheng.org; 9 Changpu Heyan; adult Y20, audio guide Y50; 10am-5.30pm; Tiananmen Dong
Substantial portions of Běijīng survive solely in a twilight world of fading nostalgia. This fascinating museum is devoted to the Imperial City (Huáng Chéng), which – beyond its fragmented constituent parts – exists largely in name alone. The museum is within the Changpu River Park (Chāngpú Hé Gōngyuán), a delightful, if contrived, formula of marble bridges, rock features, paths, a stream, willows, magnolias, scholar and walnut trees north of Dongchang'an Jie.

The museum functions as a memorial to the demolished imperial wall, gates and buildings of the Imperial City. A diorama in the museum reveals the full extent of the yellow-tiled Imperial City Wall, which encompassed a vast chunk of Běijīng nearly seven times the size of the Forbidden City. In its heyday, 28 large temples could be found in the Imperial City alone, along with many smaller shrines. Period photos of the

BEIJING MUSEUM PASS

The Beijing Museum Pass (博物馆通票; Bówùguǎn Tōngpiào) is a great investment that will save you both money and queuing for tickets. For Y80 you get either complimentary access or discounted admission (typically 50%) to almost 50 museums, temples or tourist sights in and around Bĕijīng. Attractions covered include the Confucius Temple and the Imperial College, the Bell Tower, the Imperial City Exhibition, Miaoying Temple White Dagoba, Dongyue Temple, Zhihua Temple, Fayuan Temple, Wanshou Temple, the Beijing Planetarium, the Beijing Natural History Museum, the Xu Beihong Museum and many others. Not all museums are worth visiting, but many are worthwhile and you only have to visit a small selection of museums to get your money back. The pass comes in the form of a booklet (Chinese with minimal English), valid from 1 January to 31 December in any one year. The pass can be picked up from participating museums and sights. It is sometimes hard to find (especially as the year progresses), so phone ☎ 6222 3793 or ☎ 8666 0651 (you may need a Chinese speaker) or consult www.bowuguan.bj.cn (in Chinese) to locate stocks.

old gates of Bĕijīng and images of the halls and pavilions in Zhōngnánhǎi are hung on the walls.

Further galleries have exhibits of imperial ornaments such as *ruyi* (sceptres), porcelain and enamelware, and the weapons and armour of the imperial guards.

ZHONGSHAN PARK Map pp58-9
中山公园 Zhōngshān Gōngyuán
adult Y3; ⏱ 6am-9pm; Ⓜ Tiananmen Xi
Named after Sun Zhongshan, the father of modern China, this peaceful park sits west of the Gate of Heavenly Peace, with a section hedging up against the Forbidden City moat. A refreshing prologue or conclusion to the magnificence of the imperial palace, the park was formerly the sacred Ming-style Altar to the God of the Land and the God of Grain (Shèjìtán), where the emperor offered sacrifices. The square altar *(wǔsè tǔ)* remains, bordered on all sides by walls tiled in various colours. Near the park entrance stands a towering dark-blue tiled *páilou* with triple eaves that originally commemorated the German Foreign Minister Baron von Ketteler, killed by Boxers in 1900. In the eastern section of the park is the Forbidden City Concert Hall (p192). Take the northeastern exit from the park and find yourself by the Forbidden City's Meridian Gate; from here you can reach the Supreme Temple and the Workers Cultural Palace.

MONUMENT TO THE PEOPLE'S HEROES Map pp58-9
人民英雄纪念碑 Rénmín Yīngxióng Jìniànbēi
Tiananmen Square; Ⓜ Tiananmen Xi, Tiananmen Dong or Qianmen
North of Mao's mausoleum, the Monument to the People's Heroes was completed in 1958. The 37.9m-high obelisk, made of Qīngdǎo granite, bears bas-relief carvings of key patriotic and revolutionary events (such as Taiping rebels and Lin Zexu destroying opium at Hǔmén), as well as calligraphy from communist bigwigs Mao Zedong and Zhou Enlai. Mao's eight-character flourish proclaims 'Eternal Glory to the People's Heroes'. The monument is illuminated at night.

DUAN GATE Map pp58-9
端门 Duān Mén
admission Y10; ⏱ 8.30am-4.30pm; Ⓜ Tiananmen Xi or Tiananmen Dong
Sandwiched between the Gate of Heavenly Peace and Meridian Gate, Duan Gate was stripped of its treasures by foreign forces quelling the Boxer Rebellion. The hall today is hung with photos of old Bĕijīng, but steer your eyes to the ceiling, wonderfully painted in its original colours and free of the cosmetic improvements so casually inflicted on so many of China's other historic monuments – including, it must be added, the slapdash red paintwork on the exterior walls of Duan Gate itself.

BELL TOWER Map pp58-9
钟楼 Zhōnglóu
9 Zhonglouwan Linzi; adult Y15; ⏱ 9am-5pm; 🚌 5, 58 or 107
At the north end of Di'anmenwai Dajie, and fronted by a Qing-dynasty stele, the Bell Tower – originally built in 1272 – sits along an alley directly north behind the Drum Tower. The tower burnt down during the reign of Yongle and was rebuilt in 1420, only to succumb once again to flames; the present tower dates to 1745. Clamber up the steep steps and marvel at its massive bell (Chinese bells have no clappers but are instead struck with a stout pole), weighing

63 tonnes and suspended within a pleasantly unrestored interior. Augment visits with rooftop drinks at the Drum & Bell (p181), located between its namesake towers.

DRUM TOWER Map pp58–9

鼓楼 Gŭlóu

Gulou Dongdajie; adult Y20; ☼ 9am–5.30pm; ☒ 5, 58 or 107

The Drum Tower was first built in 1272 and marked the centre of the old Mongol capital Dàdū. Originally constructed of wood, the structure went up in flames and was rebuilt in 1420, and since then it has been repeatedly destroyed and restored. Stagger up the incredibly steep steps for wide-ranging views over Běijīng's rooftops. The drums of this later Ming-dynasty version were beaten to mark the hours of the day – in effect the Big Ben of Běijīng. Time was kept with a water clock and an idiosyncratic system of time divisions. On view is a large collection of drums, including the large and dilapidated Night Watchman's Drum (更鼓; gēnggŭ; 'gēng' being one of the five two-hour divisions of the night) and a big array of reproduction drums. Originally there were 25 watch drums here, and damage to the drums is blamed on allied forces that quelled the Boxers back in 1900. There is also an analysis of the ancient Chinese seasonal divisions and an exhibition relating to old Běijīng. When ascending or descending the Drum Tower, watch out for slippery steps. The Drum Tower was the scene of a nasty and bizarre homicide just before the 2008 Olympics when an unemployed man from Zhèjiāng province slaughtered an American with a knife before throwing himself to his death from the tower.

NANLUOGU XIANG Map pp58–9

南锣鼓巷

⊙ Zhangzizhonglu/Beixinqiao

Once neglected and ramshackle, strewn with spent coal briquettes in winter and silent except for the hacking coughs of shuffling old-timers and the jangling of bicycle bells, the funky north–south alleyway of Nanluogu Xiang (literally 'South Gong and Drum Alley') has been undergoing evolution since around 2000 when the Passby Bar (p181) first threw open its doors. Today, the alley is an insatiably bubbly strip of bars, wi-fi cafes, restaurants, hotels and trendy shops. See the Sleeping chapter (p206) for recommendations on how to make Nanluogu Xiang your home while in Běijīng. In the mid-noughties, money was funnelled into a Nanluogu Xiang facelift: it is now the model for how an old hútòng haunt can satisfy those in need of decent breakfasts, good shopping, a fine lunch, tip-top sightseeing, a round of imported beers with dinner and funky hútòng accommodation (in that order). For more on the changing face of Nanluogu Xiang, see the boxed text, p48.

FOREIGN LEGATION QUARTER

Map pp58–9

租界区

⊙ Chongwenmen, Qianmen or Wangfujing

The former Foreign Legation Quarter, where the 19th-century foreign powers flung up their embassies, schools, post offices and banks, lay east of Tiananmen Square. Stroll around Taijichang Dajie and Zhengyi Lu, which still suggest its former European flavour (see the Tiananmen Square & Foreign Legation Quarter Walk, p135). On the northern corner of Taijichang Toutiao's intersection with Taijichang Dajie survives a brick in the wall engraved with the road's former foreign name: Rue Hart.

The district was turned into a war zone during the famous legation siege during the Boxer Rebellion (1899–1901). Probably the greatest cultural loss was the torching of the Hanlin Academy, the centre of Chinese learning and literature. Ricalton noted:

> The Classics of Confucius inscribed on tablets of marble were treasured there; these are gone; the 20,000 volumes of precious literature are gone; and this venerable institution, founded a thousand years before the Christian era…is a heap of ruins. The loss of thousands of volumes of ancient records recalls the destruction of the Alexandrian Library as an irreparable loss; not so many precious books, perhaps, yet the Hanlin College antedated the Alexandrian Library by nearly seven hundred years.

The library was burnt down by Huí (ethnic Chinese Muslims) troops in a disastrous bid to flush out besieged Westerners.

Don't forget to explore Legation Quarter (23 Qianmen Dongdajie), a classy cluster of

CULTURAL REVOLUTION SLOGANS TOUR

As a city in the constant throes of reinvention, Běijīng seems to change its guise almost daily. But it's all too easy to get carried away with the forward movement of Běijīng and ignore its equally relevant past. Unmarked by neither a memorial nor museum in Běijīng, the brutal Cultural Revolution (1966–76) is one period of history the authorities would rather just gloss over. Fortunately, faint echoes from that era still resonate in Běijīng's surviving brood of political slogans *(zhèngzhì kǒuhào)*.

Most slogans from the 1960s and 1970s have been either painted over or scrubbed clean, but some ghostly messages still haunt Běijīng. Other maxims have been exposed after layers of concrete have been stripped from walls, revealing hidden directives from the period of political fervour.

Daubed on the wall opposite 59 Nanluogu Xiang are the characters '工业学大庆 农业学大寨 全国学解放军', which mean 'For industry study Dàqìng, for agriculture study Dàzhài, for the whole nation study the People's Liberation Army'; left of this is a much earlier slogan from the 1950s, largely obscured with grey paint. The wall opposite the Guanyue Temple at 149 Gulou Xidajie is covered in faint, partially legible red slogans, including the characters '大立无产阶级' ('establish the proletariat') and the two characters '旧习' ('old habits').

The former Furen University (p92) has a magnificent slogan that can be seen from the road. Very indistinct characters can just be discerned under the windows of the former Banque de L'Indo-Chine at 34 Dongjiaomin Xiang in the Foreign Legation Quarter (opposite). The 798 Art District is heavily bedecked with slogans. One of the rarest and most enticing survives on the wall of the Cave Café (p133): a personal dedication written by Lin Biao, Mao Zedong's one-time chosen successor.

The village of Chuāndǐxià (p226) has a generous crop of slogans, as do some of the temples in Bādàchù (p134), most notably the exterior walls of the Great Treasure Hall at Dabei Temple. Maoist slogans can still be found in the Bailin Temple (p71), on the house at 27 Yingtao Xiejie (p140) and on the building at 65 Xidamo Changjie, opposite the Underground City (p85), where passers-by are again exhorted to 'study Dàqìng' (China's No 1 oilfield, whose workers were held up as exemplars of diligence) and to 'study Dàzhài' (China's model commune).

restored legation buildings at the west end of Dongjiaomin Xiang, the major east–west road driving through the quarter (renamed Anti-Imperialist Rd during the Cultural Revolution). The commercial quadrant – which opened straight into the jaws of the credit crunch – is home to several exclusive restaurants, shops and an art gallery.

At the junction of Taijichang Dajie and Dongjiaomin Xiang stands the gaunt twin-spired St Michael's Church (Dōngjiāomínxiàng Tiānzhǔ Jiàotáng), facing the buildings of the former Belgian Embassy. Along the western reaches of Dongjiaomin Xiang you'll pass the former French Legation (behind bright-red doors), the former French post office (now the Jingyuan Sichuan Restaurant), the fascinating Beijing Police Museum and the former Dutch Legation (undergoing splendid restoration).

POLY ART MUSEUM Map pp58-9
保利艺术博物馆 **Bǎolì Yìshù Bówùguǎn**
☎ 6500 8117; www.polymuseum.com; Poly Plaza, 14 Dongzhimen Nandajie; admission Y20; ⊚ Dongsishitiao
Recently rehoused in the new Poly Plaza and caressed with Chinese music (and occasional crackles from the security guards'

walkie-talkie), this excellent museum of antiquities has also mercifully dropped its stupendous admission prices. The first hall displays a glorious array of ancient bronzes from the Shang and Zhou dynasties, a magnificent high-water mark for bronze production. Check out the intricate scaling on the '*Zun* vessel in the shape of a Phoenix' (倗季凤鸟尊) or the '*You* with Divine Faces' (神面卣), with its elephant head on the side of the vessel. The detailed animist patterns on the *Gangbo You* (榈柏卣) are similarly vivid and fascinating. In an attached room are four of the Western-styled 12 bronze animals (see boxed text, p20) plundered with the sacking of the Old Summer Palace (p131) that have been acquired by the museum. The pig, monkey, tiger and ox peer out from glass cabinets – you can buy a model for Y12,000 if you want. The last room is populated with an exquisite collection of standing bodhisattva statues. Resembling a semidivine race of smiling humans, most of the statues are from the Northern Qi, Northern Wei and Tang dynasties. It's a sublime presentation and some of the statues have journeyed through the centuries with pigment still attached.

BEIJING POLICE MUSEUM Map pp58-9

北京警察博物馆 Běijīng Jǐngchá Bówùguǎn

☎ 8522 5018; 36 Dongjiaomin Xiang; adult
Y5, through ticket Y20; ⏰ 9am-4pm Tue-Sun;
⊜ Qianmen

Infested with propaganda perhaps, but
some riveting exhibits make this a fascinating exposé of Běijīng's *dà gài mào*
(local slang for the constabulary). Learn
how Běijīng's first Public Security Bureau
(PSB) college operated from the Dongyue
Temple (p109) in 1949 and find out how
officers tackled the 'stragglers, disbanded
soldiers, bandits, local ruffians, hoodlums
and despots…' planted in Běijīng by the
Kuomintang (KMT). There are also eye-
opening accounts of how KMT spies Li
Andong and Yamaguchi Takachi planned to
mortar the Gate of Heavenly Peace, and a welcome analysis of how the Běijīng PSB was
destroyed during the 'national catastrophe'
of the Cultural Revolution. Altogether 9685
policemen were dismissed from their posts
during the paroxysms of violence – spot
the yawning gap among portraits of PSB
directors from June 1966 to June 1977.
The museum covers grisly business: there's
Wang Zhigang's bombing of Beijing Train
Station on 29 October 1980, an explosion
at Xidan Plaza in 1968, while upstairs the
museum gets to grips with morbid crimes
and their investigations; for police weapons, head to the 4th floor. The through
ticket includes some shooting practise (plus
bullets) and a souvenir.

ST JOSEPH'S CHURCH Map pp58-9

东堂 Dōng Táng

74 Wangfujing Dajie; ⏰ 6.30-7am Mon-Sat, 6.30-
8am Sun; ⊜ Dengshikou

A crowning edifice on Wangfujing
Dajie, and one of Běijīng's four principal churches, St Joseph's Church is also
known locally as the East Cathedral. Originally built during the reign of Shunzhi in
1655, it was damaged by an earthquake
in 1720 and reconstructed. The luckless
church also caught fire in 1807, was destroyed again in 1900 during the Boxer
Rebellion and restored in 1904, only to
be shut in 1966. Now fully repaired, the
church is a testament to the long history
of Christianity in China (see boxed text,
p27). A large piazza in front swarms with
children playing; white doves photogeni-
cally flutter about and Chinese models in

bridal outfits wait for the sun to emerge
before posing for magazine shots. The
church is generally shut, but if you want to
see the interior, turn up for morning Mass.
You may want to avoid being pressganged
into buying tacky oils from the art museum behind the church.

BEIJING WANGFUJING PALEOLITHIC MUSEUM Map pp58-9

北京王府井古人类文化遗址博物
馆 Běijīng Wángfǔjǐng Gǔrénlèi Wénhuà Yízhǐ
Bówùguǎn

W1P3 Oriental Plaza, 1 Dongchang'an Jie; adult Y10;
⏰ 10am-4.30pm Mon-Fri, 10am-6.30pm Sat & Sun;
⊜ Wangfujing

Archaeologists and anthropologists will
be rewarded at this simple museum detailing the tools and relics (stone flakes,
bone scrapers, fragments of bone etc) of
Late Pleistocene Man who once inhabited
Běijīng. The discoveries on display were
unearthed during the excavation of the
foundations of Oriental Plaza in 1996. To
find the museum, take exit 'A' from Wangfujing Station.

ANCIENT OBSERVATORY Map pp58-9

古观象台 Gǔ Guānxiàngtái

☎ 6524 2202; adult Y10; ⏰ 9.30-4.30pm Tue-Sun;
⊜ Jianguomen

Stargazing is perhaps on the back foot in
today's Běijīng – it could take a supernova
to penetrate the haze that frequently blankets the nocturnal sky – but the Chinese
capital has a sparkling history of astronomical observation.

The observatory is mounted on the battlements of a watchtower lying along the
line of the old Ming City Wall and originally
dates back to Kublai Khan's days, when it
lay north of the present site. Khan, like later
Ming and Qing emperors, relied heavily on
astrologers to plan military endeavours. The
present observatory – the only surviving
example of several constructed during the
Jin, Yuan, Ming and Qing dynasties – was
built between 1437 and 1446 to facilitate
both astrological predictions and seafaring
navigation.

At ground level is a pleasant courtyard –
perfect for parking yourself on a bench
and recharging – flanked by halls housing
displays (with limited English captions).
Also within the courtyard is a reproduction-
looking armillary sphere supposedly dating

THE INTERPRETER

Rex Chen emigrated from China to Australia when he was a boy; he came to Běijīng several years ago, where he has established himself successfully as a freelance interpreter.

How long have you lived in Běijīng? About eight years.

What surprises you most about life in Beijing? After living in Běijīng for eight years, you become shock resistant.

What's the best thing about Běijīng? I can't decide between these two: 1 For someone more used to the climate of Shànghǎi and Sydney, laundry dries really fast here since it's so dry, and nothing goes mouldy; 2 Living in a dynamic cosmopolitan community means I meet really interesting people and get to do amazing things.

What's the worst thing about Běijīng? Can't decide: 1 Bad manners seen in public places; 2 It's so dry that it ruins your skin.

What's your favourite Běijīng experience? Spending a night in a country house sleeping on a fire-heated brick bed and having brunch in a restaurant called The Orchard – which is inside an orchard.

Do you miss Australia or not? I do. Every time I go back to see my parents and friends, I am awed by its beauty and peace.

---

to 1439, supported by four dragons. At the rear is an attractive garden with grass, sundials and a further armillary sphere.

Clamber the steps to the roof to admire a mind-boggling array of Jesuit-designed astronomical instruments, embellished with sculptured bronze dragons and other Chinese flourishes – a kind of East and West astronomical fusion. The Jesuits, scholars as well as proselytisers, arrived in 1601 when Matteo Ricci and his associates were permitted to work alongside Chinese scientists. Outdoing the resident calendar-setters, they were given control of the observatory and became the Chinese court's official advisers. Instruments on display include an Azimuth Theodolite (1715), an Altazimuth (1673) and an Ecliptic Armilla (1673); of the eight on view, six were designed and constructed under the supervision of the Belgian priest Ferdinand Verbiest. It's not clear which instruments on display are the originals.

During the Boxer Rebellion, the instruments disappeared into the hands of the French and Germans. Some were returned in 1902, and others were returned after WWI, under the provisions of the Treaty of Versailles (1919).

ZHIHUA TEMPLE Map pp58-9
智化寺 Zhìhuà Sì
5 Lumicang Hutong; adult Y20, audio guide Y10; ⏰ 8.30am-4.30pm; ⊕ Jianguomen or Chaoyangmen

Běijīng's surviving temple brood has endured a slapdash renewal that often buried authenticity beneath casual res-

toration work. This rickety shrine is thick with the flavours of old Peking though, having eluded the Dulux treatment that invariably precedes entrance fee inflation and stomping tour groups. You won't find the coffered ceiling of the third hall (it's in the USA), and the Four Heavenly Kings have vanished from Zhihua Gate (智化门; Zhìhuà Mén), but the Scriptures Hall encases a venerable Ming-dynasty wooden library topped with a seated Buddha and a magnificently unrestored ceiling. The highlight Ten Thousand Buddhas Hall (万佛殿; Wànfó Diàn) is an enticing two floors of miniature niche-borne Buddhist effigies and cabinets for the storage of sutras; its caisson ceiling currently resides in the Philadelphia Museum of Art. Creep up the steep wooden staircase (if it is open) at the back of the hall to visit the sympathetic effigy of the Vairocana Buddha seated upon a multipetalled lotus flower in the upper chamber, before wondering the fate of the 1000-Armed Guanyin that once presided over the Great Mercy Hall (大悲殿; Dàbēi Diàn) at the temple rear.

COURTYARD GALLERY Map pp58-9
四合院画廊 Sìhéyuàn Huàláng
☎ 6526 8882; www.courtyard-gallery.com; 319 Caochangdi, Cháoyáng; admission free; 🚍 735 or 402

Tucked discreetly away beneath its namesake restaurant (p162) perched overlooking prime views of the Forbidden City moat, this basement gallery is a crisp and trendy pocket-sized space of white painted bricks and contemporary paintings.

CON 'ARTISTS'

We receive an enormous amount of mail from those unfortunate enough to be scammed in Běijīng. By far the most notorious is the tea-ceremony scam, which exploits foreigners' ignorance of Chinese culture, unfamiliarity with the exchange rate and gullibility in a foreign setting; visitors are invited to drink tea at a tea house, after which the traveller is hit for a bill for hundreds of dollars. Many travellers pay up and only realise later that they have been massively conned. Foreigners at Tiananmen Square or wandering Wangfujing Dajie are also routinely hounded by pesky 'art students' either practising their English or roping visitors into going to exhibitions of overpriced art. They will try to strike up a conversation with you, but while some travellers enjoy their company, others find their attentions irritating and feel pressured into buying art. In all instances, be suspicious if you are approached by anyone who speaks good English on the street until you are sure all they want is to chat.

LAO SHE MUSEUM Map pp58-9
老舍纪念馆 Lǎo Shě Jìniànguǎn
☎ 6559 9218; 19 Fengfu Hutong; ⏱ 9am-4pm;
🚇 Tiananmen Dong

Brimful of uncomplicated charm, this courtyard house off Dengshikou Xijie was the home of Lao She (1899–1966), one of Běijīng's best-loved 20th-century writers. The life of Lao She – author of *Rickshaw Boy* and *Tea House*, and former teacher at London's School of Oriental and African Studies – is detailed in a modest collection of halls, via newspaper cuttings, first-edition books, photographs and personal effects. In typical Chinese fashion, the exhibition falls at the final hurdle, giving perfunctory mention to perhaps the most significant aspect of Lao She's life: his death by drowning in Taiping Lake on 24 August 1966 after a nasty beating by vituperative Red Guards the day before. Captions are largely in Chinese.

CHINA ART MUSEUM Map pp58-9
中国美术馆 Zhōngguó Měishùguǎn
☎ 6401 7076/2252; 1 Wusi Dajie; adult Y5;
⏱ 9am-5pm, last entry 4pm; 🚌 103, 104, 106 or 108 to Meishu Guan stop; ♿

This revamped museum has received a healthy shot of imagination and flair, with absorbing exhibitions from abroad promising doses of colour and vibrancy. Běijīng's art lovers have lapped up some top-notch presentations here, from the cream of Italian design to modern artworks from the Taipei Fine Arts Museum, the latter offering a chance to compare contemporary mainland Chinese art – with its burdensome political baggage and endlessly recurring themes – with the light-footed, invigorating and more universalist conceptions from the island across from Fújiàn. English captions can be sporadic, but this is a first-rate place to see modern art from China and abroad and, just as importantly, to watch the Chinese looking at art. Lifts allow for wheelchair access.

MAO DUN FORMER RESIDENCE
Map pp58-9
茅盾故居 Máo Dùn Gùjū
☎ 6404 4089; 13 Houyuan Ensi Hutong; adult Y5;
⏱ 9am-4pm Tue-Sun; 🚇 Beixinqiao

This small and unassuming museum off Jiaodaokou Nandajie is deep in the heart of the historic *hútòng* quadrant southeast of the Drum and Bell Towers. Mao Dun was the pen name of Shen Yanbing (1896–1981), who was born into an elite family in Zhèjiāng province but educated in Běijīng. In 1920 he helped found the Literary Study Society, an association promoting literary realism. Mao Dun joined the League of Left Wing Writers in 1930, becoming solidly entrenched in the bureaucracy after the communists came to power. He lay low during the Cultural Revolution, but briefly returned to writing in the 1970s. The museum is typically parsimonious and low-key.

DONGAN MEN REMAINS Map pp58-9
明皇城东安门遗址 Míng Huáng Chéng Dōng'ānmén Yízhǐ
Imperial Wall Foundation Ruins Park, cnr Donghuamen Dajie & Beiheyan Dajie; ⏱ 24hr; 🚇 Tiananmen Dong

In an excavated pit on Beiheyan Dajie sits a pitiful stump, all that remains of the magnificent Dōngān Mén, the east gate of the Imperial City. Before being razed, the gate was a single-eaved, seven-bay-wide building with a hip-and-gable roof capped with yellow tiles. The remnants of the gate – just two layers of 18 bricks – may make for dull viewing but of more interest are the accompanying bricks of the excavated Ming-dynasty road that used to run near

Dōngān Mén. The road is around 2m lower than the current road level, its expertly made bricks typical of precisely engineered Ming-dynasty brickwork. The remains are located in the Imperial Wall Foundation Ruins Park (皇城根遗址公园; Huángchéng Gēn Yízhǐ Gōngyuán), a thin strip of park that follows much of the course of the eastern side of the Imperial City Wall.

DITAN PARK Map pp58-9
地坛公园 Dìtán Gōngyuán
park admission Y2, altar Y5; ❉ 6am-9pm;
Ⓜ Yonghegong-Lama Temple

East of Andingmenwai Dajie, and cosmologically juxtaposed with the Temple of Heaven (Tiāntán), the Altar of the Moon (Yuètán), the Altar of the Sun (Rìtán; p114) and the Altar to the God of the Land and the God of Grain (Shèjìtán), Ditan is the Temple of the Earth. The park, site of imperial sacrifices to the Earth God, lacks the splendour of the Temple of Heaven Park but is worth a stroll if you've just been to nearby Lama Temple. During Chinese New Year

a temple fair is held here, and in winter a sparkling ice festival is staged. The park's large altar (fāngzé tán) is square in shape, symbolising the earth. Within the park, One Moon Art Gallery (Yíyuè Dāngdài Yìshù; ☎ 6427 7748; www.onemoonart.com; ❉ 11am-7pm Tue-Sun) displays thoughtful contemporary Chinese art from a 16th-century-dynasty temple hall, a funky meeting of the Ming and the modern. If you are just visiting the art gallery, the entrance fee for the park should be waived.

CHINA NATIONAL MUSEUM
Map pp58-9
中国国家博物馆 Zhōngguó Guójiā Bówùguǎn
❉ 8.30am-4.30pm; Ⓜ Tiananmen Dong

Housed in a sombre 1950s edifice on the eastern side of Tiananmen Square, this museum has become a permanent work in progress, shut for redesign for at least the last two editions of this book. The spotlight of public attention has swung instead to the more happening Capital Museum (p92) out in the west of town.

CHÓNGWÉN 崇文区

Eating p169; Shopping p147

Chóngwén ranges across the historic swathe of Běijīng south and southeast of the Forbidden City, largely enclosed within the long loop of the Hucheng River (Hùchénghé; City Moat) and the footprint of the now vanished Chinese City Wall. The territory north of Qianmen Xidajie and Qianmen Dongdajie and embraced within the Second Ring Rd was the Tartar City, the Manchu quarter of town where the Qing-dynasty imperial city belonged; to the south lay Chóngwén and Xuānwǔ (p116), more common districts historically known as the Chinese City. The two universes met at the mighty Qing-dynasty Tartar City Wall with their magnificent city gates – including Chongwen Gate (崇文门; Chóngwén Mén) itself – that towered above the mere mortals below. North was the Inner City but south was the Outer City (Wàichéng). The walls have been torn down, so the boundary line is more two-dimensional today, but a sense that Chóngwén is a shabbier, more everyday and 'outside' area survives to the present.

The subway stations of Qianmen, Chongwenmen and Jianguomen recall some of the Tartar City Wall's vast and imposing gates, of which only Front Gate (p69) and the Southeast Corner Watchtower (Dongbianmen) to the southeast, survive. The road looping south from Jianguomen Station, following the line of the city moat, marks the outline of the levelled Chinese City Wall, whose gates *(mén)* survive only in street names, such as Guangqumen Nanbinhe Lu, Zuo'anmen Xibinhe Lu and Yongdingmen Dongbinhe Lu. Vestiges of the wall can still be seen at the Ming City Wall Ruins Park.

Historically this was an enclave of the *lǎobǎixìng* (common people), and was far more down-at-heel than Dōngchéng or Xīchéng, threaded by small *hútòng* and home to the shops and bazaars of Dashilar and the *hóngdēngqū* (red-light district). Yet this district also belongs in the south, an aspect facing the sun and indicative of *yáng* (the male and positive principle). Blessed with such positive *fēngshuǐ* (geomancy; literally 'wind and water'), it is not surprising that the principal imperial shrine of Běijīng, the Temple of Heaven, is located in Chóngwén. The emperor would emerge from the Forbidden City in a splendid sedan to be conveyed south in a glorious imperial procession along the Imperial Way (along Qianmen Dajie) to the altar for sacrificial rites.

Even as late as the 1950s, north of the Temple of Heaven was a marshy area called the Goldfish Pond and Dragon's Whiskers Ditch, while to the east was a sparse expanse dotted with small temples through which the first Běijīng–Tiānjīn train line ran. The north section of Chóngwén was a region rich in *hútòng* – many of which survive, despite extensive development of this district. In the west, Qianmen Dajie splices Chóngwén from Xuānwǔ. In recent years the street has been lavishly restored in a bid to retrieve its early-20th-century character, at the expense of sacrificing its sense of community.

TEMPLE OF HEAVEN PARK Map p82
天坛公园 Tiāntán Gōngyuán

Tiantan Donglu; entrance/through ticket Y10/30, audio guide available at each gate Y40, deposit Y100; 🕑 park 6am-9pm, sights 8am-5pm; 🚇 Chongwenmen, Qianmen or Tiantandongmen

With soothing music emanating from speakers mixing with birdsong, Temple of Heaven Park is a relaxing oasis of peace in one of China's noisiest urban landscapes. Police whirr about in electric buggies as visitors stroll amid temple buildings and groves of ancient cypresses, planted in regular rows.

The temple originally served as a vast stage for the solemn rites that were performed by the emperor, the Son of

Heaven (天子; Tiānzǐ), as he sought good harvests, divine clearance and atonement

TRANSPORT: CHÓNGWÉN

Subway Line 2 stops at Qianmen Station, Chongwenmen Station and Beijing Train Station; and Line 5 intersects with Line 2 at Chongwenmen. For the Temple of Heaven take Line 5 direct to the Tiantandongmen stop; get off at Chongwenmen Station for the Ming City Wall Ruins Park and Southeast Corner Watchtower. Qianmen Station serves Qianmen Dajie, Dashilar and Tiananmen Square.

Bus Bus 20 journeys from Beijing South Train Station via the Temple of Heaven and Qianmen to Wangfujing, Dongdan and Beijing Train Station.

for the sins of the people. The complex of halls is set in a 267-hectare park with gates at each point of the compass and bounded by walls. The most perfect example of Ming architectural design, the Temple of Heaven is not so much a temple as an altar, so don't expect to see worshippers in prayer. As it's essentially Confucian and esoteric in function and cosmological purpose, don't expect to find any of the intriguing mystique of active Taoist temples or the incense-burning of Buddhist shrines here.

The Temple of Heaven's unique architectural features will, however, delight numerologists, necromancers and superstitious visitors – not to mention acoustic engineers and carpenters. Shape, colour and sound combine to take on symbolic significance. Seen from above the temples are round and the bases square, a pattern deriving from the ancient Chinese belief that heaven is round and earth is square. Thus the northern end of the park is semicircular and the southern end is square. The Temple of the Earth, also called Ditan (see Ditan Park, p79), in the north of Běijīng is on the northern compass point, and the Temple of Heaven is on the southern point.

The most important ceremony of the year was performed just before the winter solstice, when the emperor and his enormous entourage passed down Qianmen Dajie in total silence to the Imperial Vault of Heaven. Commoners were not permitted to view the ceremony and remained cloistered indoors. The procession included elephant and horse chariots and long lines of lancers, nobles, officials and musicians dressed in their finest, with flags fluttering. The imperial 12m-long sedan was almost 3m wide and employed 10 bearers; when the mood hit him, the emperor would turn to his golden spittoon to clear his throat. The next day the emperor waited in a yellow silk tent at the southern gate while officials moved the sacred tablets to the Round Altar, where the prayers and sacrificial rituals took place. It was thought that this ritual decided the nation's future; hence a hitch in any part of the proceedings was regarded as a bad omen. The last person to attempt the ritual was Yuan Shikai in 1914, who harboured unfulfilled ambitions of becoming emperor.

top picks

BĚIJĪNG PARKS

- Temple of Heaven Park (opposite) Explore the cosmic harmonies of Běijīng's principal altar.
- Beihai Park (p87) Spend half the day exploring temples and watching pavement calligraphers.
- Jingshan Park (p92) Clamber to the summit of Jingshan for matchless views over the Forbidden City.
- Fragrant Hills Park (p133) Autumn is the top season, but you can hike here any time of the year.
- Beijing Zoo (p95) Despite its furry menagerie, this was once a Qing imperial park.
- Olympic Forest Park (p114) Monumental, never-ending park in the north of town. Take food and water.

The parkland is typical of Chinese parks, with the imperfections and wild irregularity of nature largely eliminated and the harmonising hand of humans accentuated in its obsessively straight lines and regular arrangements. The resulting order, balance and harmony has an almost haunting but slightly claustrophobic beauty.

There are around 4000 ancient, knotted cypresses (some 800 years old, their branches propped up on poles) in the park. Get here at 6.30am (before the temple structures are open) to see *tàijíquán* (also known as taichi), dancing to Western music and various other games being played. This is how Běijīng awakens; by 9am it becomes just another Chinese park.

Although the park can be entered through any of the gates at the cardinal points, the imperial approach to the temple was via Zhaoheng Gate (昭亨门; Zhāohēng Mén) in the south, and that is reflected in our ordering of the principal sights below. You can either enter with just the basic ticket (Y10), then buy a Y20 ticket that includes each major sight later, or buy the through ticket (Y30) at the gate.

Round Altar 圜丘

The 5m-high Round Altar (Yuán Qiū) was constructed in 1530 and rebuilt in 1740. The altar once looked very different: its first incarnation was in deep-blue glazed stone before being redone in light green.

CHÓNGWÉN

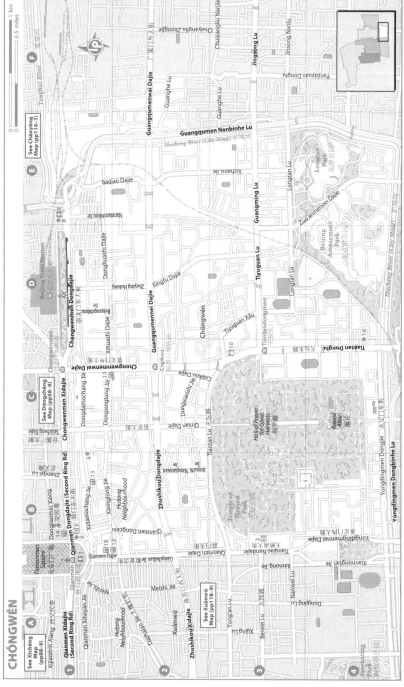

CHÓNGWÉN

The current white marble structure is arrayed in three tiers; its geometry revolves around the imperial number nine. Odd numbers were considered heavenly, and nine is the largest single-digit odd number. The top tier, thought to symbolise heaven, contains nine rings of stones. Each ring has multiples of nine stones, so that the ninth ring has 81 stones. The middle tier – earth – has the 10th to 18th rings. The bottom tier – humanity – has the 19th to 27th rings. The numbers of stairs and balustrades are also multiples of nine. If you stand in the centre of the upper terrace and say something, the sound bounces off the marble balustrades, making your voice sound louder (by nine times?).

Echo Wall 回音壁

Just north of the altar, surrounding the Imperial Vault of Heaven, is the Echo Wall (Huíyīn Bì), 65m in diameter. Its form has unusual acoustic properties, enabling a whisper to travel clearly from one end to the other – unless a tour group or a loudmouth with a mobile phone gets in the way. In the courtyard are the Triple-Sounds Stones (三音石; Sānyīn Shí). It is said that if you clap or shout standing on the stones, the sound is echoed once from the first stone, twice from the second stone and thrice from the third stone. Queues can get long at this one.

Imperial Vault of Heaven 皇穹宇

The octagonal Imperial Vault of Heaven (Huáng Qióng Yǔ) was built at the same time as the Round Altar, and is structured along the same lines as the older Hall of Prayer for Good Harvests. The vault once contained spirit tablets used in the winter solstice ceremony. Behind the Imperial Vault of Heaven stands the Nine Dragon Juniper, a hoary tree with a trunk of sinewy and coiling knots. Proceeding north from the Imperial Vault is a walkway called the Red Stairway Bridge (丹陛桥; Dānbì Qiáo), leading to the Hall of Prayer for Good Harvests.

Hall of Prayer for Good Harvests 祈年殿

The crowning structure of the whole complex is the recently restored Hall of Prayer for Good Harvests (Qínián Diàn; admission Y20), magnificently mounted on a three-tiered marble terrace and capped with a triple-eaved umbrella roof of purplish-blue tiles. Built in 1420, it was burnt to cinders in 1889 and heads rolled in apportioning blame (although lightning was the most likely cause). A faithful reproduction based on Ming architectural methods was erected the following year, the builders choosing Oregon fir for the support pillars, as explained by Lucian S Kirtland in *Finding the Worthwhile in the Orient* (1926):

> When it was desired to rebuild the temple, and the Manchus were determined to copy in detail the building which had been destroyed, it was found that China's forests were bereft of timbers which could uphold the heavy tiled roof. After much argument with themselves, the necromancers of the court finally decided that pine logs from the forests of Oregon would constitute proper feng-shui. This decision very happily corresponded with the best engineering advice, and the New World furnished the pillars which you now see.

The four central pillars symbolise the seasons, the 12 in the next ring denote the months of the year, and the 12 outer ones represent the day, broken into 12 'watches'. Embedded in the ceiling is a carved dragon, a symbol of royalty. The patterning, carving and gilt decoration of this ceiling and its swirl of colour is a dizzying sight.

All this is made more amazing by the fact that the wooden pillars ingeniously support the ceiling without nails or cement – quite an accomplishment for a building 38m high and 30m in diameter.

Other Buildings

With a green-tiled tow-tier roof, the Animal Killing Pavilion (Zǎishēng Tíng) was the venue for the slaughter of sacrifical oxen, sheep,

deer and other animals. Today it stands locked and passive but can be admired from the outside. Stretching out from here runs a Long Corridor (Chángláng) where Chinese crowds sit out and deal cards, listen to the radio, play keyboards, practise Beijing opera, dance moves and hacky-sack. Sacrificial music was rehearsed at the Divine Music Administration (Shényuè Shǔ) in the west of the park, while wild cats live in the dry moat of the green-tiled Fasting Palace (Zhāi Gōng).

QIANMEN DAJIE Map p82
前门大街
Ⓜ Qianmen

Recently reopened after a monumental and costly overhaul, this road – now pedestrianised and 'restored' to resemble a late-Qing-

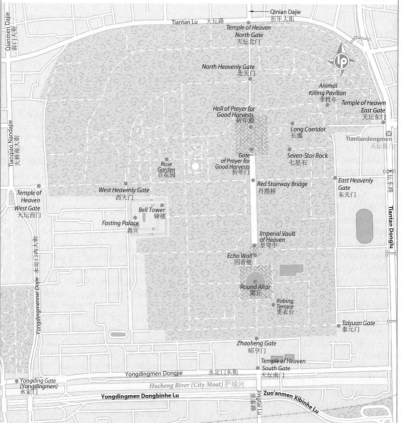

TEMPLE OF HEAVEN PARK

GOING UNDERGROUND

By 1969, as the USA landed on the moon, Mao had decided that the future for Běijīng's people lay underground. Alarmist predictions of nuclear war with Russia dispatched an army of Chinese beneath Běijīng's streets to burrow a huge warren of bombproof tunnels (p23). The task was completed Cultural Revolution–style – by hand – with the finishing touches made in 1979, just as Russia decided to bog down in Afghanistan instead.

Until recently, a damp section of tunnels enticingly known as the Beijing Underground City (Běijīng Dìxiàchéng; 62 Xidamochang Jie) could be explored. Combat-gear-clad guides would accompany you along parts of this mouldering warren, past rooms designated as battlefield hospitals, a cinema, arsenals, other anonymous vaults and portraits of Mao Zedong. Even a rudimentary elevator, floodproof doors and a ventilation system to expel poisonous gases could be seen. The guide would wave down dark and uninviting tunnels, announcing their end points: one led to the Hall of Preserving Harmony in the Forbidden City, another wound to the Summer Palace, while yet another reached Tiānjīn (a mere 130km away), or so the guide insisted. A tiresome detour to an underground silk factory concluded the trip.

At the time of research, the underground city was shut, and had been since a few months prior to the Olympics bonanza. An ageing and undated note was taped to the door, announcing: 'Welcome to our underground city. Since April we have a big construction inside until now so we don't open for the public. We're so sorry about this. Maybe it'll open next year.' A similar note in Chinese (dated April 2008) reveals more, explaining that an inspection of the underground city revealed problems with waterlogging (most of the tunnels are around 8m below ground, so it's cold and very damp, with the humidity increasing the deeper you go and sections at greater depths flooded) and structural defects. Deemed potentially hazardous to tourists, the tunnels have been shut, but there is no indication when or if they will reopen. Just east of the Underground City is Tongle Hutong, one of Běijīng's narrowest alleyways.

Other sections of tunnels have been redeployed as underground markets, for example at Xidan underground market, Ditan ice rink (p79) and the subterranean shopping arcade in Yuetan Park, while portions of the network are still employed by Běijīng top brass for clandestine manoeuvres around town.

dynasty street scene – was designed to funnel off visitors from Tiananmen Square trips and bring some nobility to a downwardly mobile area. As late as the 1950s, this road was called Zhengyangmen Dajie (Facing the Sun Gate St). At the time of writing, rents were clearly too high, as few of the shops had reopened and nearly all doors were shut, meaning visitors had little to do other than walk up and down the street, taking photographs of the rebuilt Qianmen Decorative Arch (the original was torn down in the 1950s) or hop on one of the two reproduction trams (Y20) gliding along the length of the street to Zhushikou. Dazhalan Xijie is next in developers' sights in their attempt to kick-start a 'Nanluogu Xiang effect' (p74), but it is unknown whether this kind of intervention will work. Embark on our Qianmen Dajie to Liulichang Xijie Walk (p139) to fully explore the area.

MING CITY WALL RUINS PARK Map p82
明城墙遗址公园 Míng Chéngqiáng Yízhǐ Gōngyuán
Chongwenmen Dongdajie; 24hr;
Chongwenmen

Levelled in the 1950s to facilitate transport and blot out the grandeur of earlier dynasties, the city wall is perhaps Běijīng's most conspicuous chunk of lost heritage. As modern-day Nánjīng in Jiāngsū province proves, modern Chinese cities can still grow without having to rip their city walls down. This last slice of the Ming Inner City Wall (originally 40km in length) has been restored and runs along the length of the northern flank of Chongwenmen Dongdajie, attached to a slender strip of park.

The wall stretches from the former site of Chóngwén Mén (崇文门; Chongwen Gate), one of the nine gates of the Inner City Wall, to the Southeast Corner Watchtower and then turns north for a short distance along Jianguomen Nandajie to Beijingzhan Dongjie. Chóngwén Mén was also called Shuì Mén (税门; Tax Gate) as the capital tax bureau lay just outside the gate. You can walk the park's length, taking in its higgledy-piggledy contours and the interior layers of stone in parts of the wall that have collapsed. The restored sections run for just over 2km, rising to a height of around 15m and interrupted every 80m with buttresses extending to a maximum depth of 39m. The most interesting sections of wall are those closer to their original and more dilapidated state and some of the bricks come complete with bullet holes.

SOUTHEAST CORNER WATCHTOWER & RED GATE GALLERY Map p82

东南角楼、红门画廊 Dōngnán Jiǎolóu & Hóngmén Huàláng

☎ 8512 1554; Dongbianmen; adult Y10; ⏱ 8am-5.30pm; ⊖ Jianguomen or Chongwenmen

This splendid fortification, with a green-tiled, twin-eaved roof rising up imperiously south of the Ancient Observatory, dates back to the Ming dynasty. Clamber up the steps for views alongside camera-wielding Chinese trainspotters eagerly awaiting rolling stock grinding in and out of Beijing Train Station. As you mount the battlements, two forlorn stumps of flag abutments and a cannon or two can be seen, but really worth hunting out are the signatures etched in the walls by allied forces during the Boxer Rebellion. You can make out the name of a certain P Foot; 'USA' is also scrawled on the brickwork. The international composition of the eight-nation force that relieved Běijīng in 1900 is noted in names such as André, Stickel and what appears to be a name in Cyrillic. One brick records the date 'Dec 16 1900'. Allied forces overwhelmed the redoubt after a lengthy engagement. Note the drainage channels poking out of the wall along its length. You can reach the watchtower from the west through the Railway Arch, which was built for the first railway that ran around Běijīng.

The watchtower is punctured with 144 archers' windows, and attached to it is a 100m section of the original Inner City Wall, beyond which stretches the restored Ming City Wall, extending all the way to Chongwenmen and north to Beijingzhan Dongjie. Inside the highly impressive interior is some staggering carpentry: huge red pillars that are topped with solid beams surge upwards. The 1st floor is the site of the Red Gate Gallery (☎ 6525 1005; www .redgategallery.com; admission free; ⏱ 10am-5pm), one of Běijīng's long-established modern art galleries; the 2nd-floor gallery has a fascinating photographic exhibition on the old gates of Běijīng, while the 3rd-floor gallery contains more paintings. Say

you're visiting the Red Gate Gallery and the Y10 entry fee to the watchtower will be waived.

BEIJING NATURAL HISTORY MUSEUM Map p82

北京自然博物馆 Běijīng Zìrán Bówùguǎn

☎ 6702 4431; 126 Tianqiao Nandajie; adult Y30; ⏱ 8.30am-4.30pm Tue-Sun, last entry 4pm; ⊖ Qianmen or Tiantandongmen

The main entrance to this overblown, creeper-laden museum, closed for refurbishment at the time of research, is hung with portraits of the great natural historians, including Darwin and Linnaeus. The contents range from dinosaur fossils and skeletons, including a *mamenchisaurus jingyanensis* – a vast sauropod that once roamed China – to creepy-crawlies, an aquarium with Nemo-esque clown fish and an exhibition on the origins of life on earth. Make sure your children don't wander unaccompanied into the creepy Hall of Human Bodies, where a ghoulish selection of spliced human cadavers and genitalia awaits.

BEIJING PLANNING EXHIBITION HALL Map p82

北京市规划展览馆 Běijīngshì Guīhuà Zhǎnlǎnguǎn

☎ 6701 7074; 20 Qianmen Dongdajie; admission Y30; ⏱ 9am-5pm Tue-Sun; ⊖ Qianmen

Clearly inspired by Shànghǎi's winning Urban Planning Construction Hall (which remains one of People's Square's top sights), this little-visited exhibition hall takes particular pains to present Běijīng's gut-wrenching, *hútòng*-felling metamorphosis in the best possible light. The detailed bronze map of 1949 Běijīng – ironically the very year that sealed the fate of old Peking – is worth scrutinising, and the huge, detailed diorama of the modern metropolis is a neat way to get the city's labyrinthine *hútòng* and enormous streets in perspective. The rest of the exhibition is a paean to modern city planning and the unstoppable advance of the concrete mixer and iffy modern architecture, while 3-D films trumpet 'The New Běijīng'.

Eating p171; Shopping p147; Sleeping p212

As equally impregnated with ancient temples and charming *hútòng* as Dōngchéng to the east, Xīchéng (literally 'West City') also belonged to the more exclusive Inner City, associated with the ruling Manchu dynasty. Although today it sprawls out west beyond the boundary of the old Tartar City Wall, most of Xīchéng is characterised by the *hútòng*-rich area within the Second Ring Rd to the west of Dōngchéng. Many of Xīchéng's underground station names recall its now-vanished city gates: Xizhimen, Fuchengmen, Fuxingmen, Xuanwumen and Hepingmen.

The majority of the Imperial City was in Xīchéng – lending it a regal grandeur that survives to this day – and the district is particularly notable for the long string of lakes that runs from Xīnhuá Mén at the southern extent of Zhōngnánhǎi, all the way to Jishuitan in the north. The lakes of Zhōnghǎi (literally 'Middle Sea') and Nánhǎi (literally 'South Sea') together make up Zhōngnánhǎi – once part of the emperor's sovereign domain, the fabulous Imperial City (p72) – which is now the centre of political power in China, inaccessible to everyone bar Communist Party VIPs, and visible on Google Earth and from the summit of Jingshan Park. The lake of Běihǎi (literally 'North Sea'; below) also belonged to the huge grounds of the Imperial City and before that served as the site of the Great Khan's Yuan-dynasty palace; it is open today to all and sundry as Beihai Park. North again, the elegant curve of lakes that make up Shíchàhǎi (literally 'Ten Buddhist Temple Lakes') takes in Qiánhǎi ('Front Lake'), Hòuhǎi ('Back Lake') and Xīhǎi ('West Lake').

The scenic areas around Qiánhǎi and Hòuhǎi are today littered with bars, cafes and restaurants, forming an accessible lakeside alternative to both Nanluogu Xiang (p74) and Sānlǐtún in Cháoyáng. Xīdān – named after the single *páilou* that once stood here (which has been rebuilt) – is a vast retail area to the west of Zhōngnánhǎi. Just west of Tiananmen Square and the Great Hall of the People is the silvery form of the National Grand Theatre, one of China's top 10 most controversial buildings. To the northwest, Xīchéng reaches out to ensnare Beijing Zoo before giving way to the colossal district of Hǎidiàn.

BEIHAI PARK Map pp88-9

北海公园 Běihǎi Gōngyuán

1 Wenjin Jie; standard ticket low/high season Y5/10, through ticket Y15/20; 6am-8pm, buildings to 4pm; Tiananmen Xi, then 5

Northwest of the Forbidden City, Beihai Park is largely lake, or more specifically the lake of Běihǎi (which literally means 'North Sea'). It offers a relaxing opportunity to amble about, grab a snack, sip a beer, rent a rowing boat, or admire calligraphers scribbling Chinese characters on paving slabs with water and fat brushes. The associated South and Middle Seas to the south together lend their name to the nerve centre of the Communist Party west of the Forbidden City, Zhōngnánhǎi.

The park, covering an area of 68 hectares, was the former playground of the Yuan emperors. Jade Islet in the lower middle is composed of the heaped earth scooped out to create the lake – some attribute this to Kublai Khan.

The site is associated with the Great Khan's palace, the navel of Běijīng before the Forbidden City replaced it. All that remains of the Khan's court is a large jar made of green jade dating from 1265 in the Round City (Tuán Chéng; admission Y1) near the park's southern entrance. Also within the Round City is the Chengguang Hall (Chéngguāng Diàn), where a white jade statue of Sakyamuni from Myanmar can be found, its arm wounded by the allied forces that entered Běijīng in 1900 to quash the Boxer Rebellion.

Dominating Jade Islet on the lake, the 36m-high White Dagoba was originally built in 1651 for a visit by the Dalai Lama, and was rebuilt in 1741. You can reach the dagoba through the Yongan Temple (included in the through ticket). Enter the temple through the Hall of the Heavenly Kings (Tiānwáng Diàn), past the Drum and Bell Towers to the Hall of the Wheel of the Law (Fǎlún Diàn), with its central effigy of Sakyamuni and flanked by bodhisattvas and 18 *luóhàn* (Buddhists, especially monks, who achieved enlightenment and passed to nirvana at death).

At the rear of the temple you will find a bamboo grove and quite a steep flight

XĪCHÉNG

Waigongcun 魏公村地铁站

Zhongguancun Nandajie

Dahuisi Lu

North Jiaotong University 北方交通大学

Gaoliangqiao Xiejie

Jiaoda Donglu

See Wǔdàokǒu Map (p125)

Xizhimen Beidajie

Wenhuiyuan Beilu

Hǎidiàn

Minzu Daxue Nanlu

Beijing North Train Station 北京北站地铁站

Deshengmen Xidajie (Second Ring Rd)

Zizhúyuàn Park 紫竹院公园

Zizhuyuan Lu 紫竹院路

Beijing Zoo 北京动物园

National Library 国家图书馆地铁站

Xizhimenwai Dajie 西直门外大街

Xizhimenwai Nanlu

Xizhimen 西直门地铁站

Xizhimennei Dajie

Xīchéng

Guanyuan Park 官园公园

Beilishi Lu

Xizhimen Nandajie

Chegongzhuang Xilu 车公庄西路

Chegongzhuang Dajie 车公庄大街

Chegongzhuang 车公庄地铁站

Ping'anli Xidajie

Sanlihe Lu

Zhanlanguan Lu

Fuxingmen Beidajie

34

Baiwanzhuang Xilu

Baiwanzhuang Dajie

See Hǎidiàn Map (p122)

14

16

Fucheng Lu 阜成路

Fuchengmenwai Dajie 阜成门外大街

Fuchengmen 阜成门地铁站

Fuchengmennei Dajie

Fuchengmen Nandajie (Second Ring Road)

Zhaodengyu Dajie

Yuyuántán Park 玉渊潭公园

Yuetan Beijie

Sanlihe Donglu

Yùyuan Tan 玉渊潭

Yuetan Nanjie

Yuetan Park 月坛公园

44

Guangningbo Jie 广宁街

Yongding River 永定河

Sanlihe Lu

Yuetan Nandajie (Second Ring Road)

Nanlishilu

Fuxingmen 复兴门地铁站

Jūnshìbówùguǎn 军事博物馆地铁站

Muxidi 木樨地地铁站

Yuyuan Tan

Fuxingmenwai Dajie

8

Fuxingmennei Dajie

Yangfangdian Lu

Xibianmennei Dajie

Naoshikou Dajie

Xinkai Chu

22

Guang'anmen Beibinhe Lu

23

Changchunjie 长椿街地铁站

See Xuānwǔ Map (pp118–9)

Lianhuachi Donglu

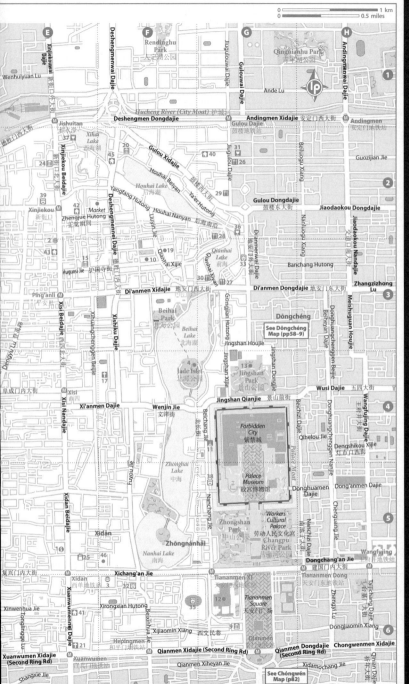

0 — 1 km
0 — 0.5 miles

E
Xinjiekouwai Dajie 新街口外大街
Wenhuiyuan Lu

F
Rendinghu Park 人定湖公园
Jiugulouwai Dajie

G
Qinghuahu Park 青年湖公园

H
Andingmenwai Dajie

Ande Lu

Hucheng River (City Moat) 护城河

Deshengmennei Dajie

Deshengmen Dongdajie

Andingmen Xidajie 安定门西街

Andingmen 安定门地铁站

Jishuitan 积水潭
Gulou Xidajie

Gulou Dajie 鼓楼地铁站

Beiluogu Xiang

Guozijian Jie

Xīhǎi Lake 西海湖

Xijinkou Beidajie

Houhai Beiyan

Jiugulouwai Dajie

Gulou Dongdajie 鼓楼东大街

Jiaodaokou Dongdajie

Houhai Lake 后海湖

Yangfang Hutong
Houhai Nanyan 后海南沿

Di'anmenwai Dajie 地安门外大街

Nanluogu Xiang

Jiaodaokou Nandajie

Xinjiekou 新街口
Zhengjue Hutong 正觉胡同
Market
Deshengmennei Dajie 德胜门内大街
Luyin Jie
Qiánhǎi Lake 前海
Banchang Hutong

Zhangzizhong Lu

Huguosi Jie 护国寺街
Di'anmen Xidajie

Qiánhǎi Xīyán

Di'anmen Dongdajie 地安门东大街

Meishuguan Houjie

Ping'anli 平安里

Xisi Beidajie
Xishiku Dajie
Xihuangchenggen Beijie

Beihai Park 北海公园

Gongjian Hutong

Beihai Lake 北海湖

Dōngchéng 东城

See Dōngchéng Map (pp58–9)

Donghuangchenggen Beijie

Beiheyan Dajie

Dengshikou Xidajie

Jade Islet 琼岛公园

Jingshan Houjie

Jingshan Xijie

Jingshan Park 景山公园

Jingshan Dongjie

Wusi Dajie 五四大街

Xi'anmen Dajie

Wenjin Jie 文津街

Jingshan Qianjie 景山前街

Donghuangchenggen Nanjie

Wangfujing Dajie 王府井大街

Xisi Nandajie

Beichang Jie

Qihelou Jie

Dengshikou Xijie 灯市口西街

Zhōnghǎi Lake 中海

Forbidden City 紫禁城

Palace Moat

Chenguang Lu

Xidan Beidajie

Palace Museum 故宫博物院

Donghuamen Dajie

Dong'anmen Dajie

Nanchang Jie

Xidan 西单

Nánhǎi Lake 南海

Zhōngnánhǎi 中南海

Zhongshan Park 中山公园

Workers Cultural Palace 劳动人民文化宫

Changpu River Park 菖蒲河公园

Wangfujing

Xichang'an Jie 西长安街

Xidan 西单地铁站

Xuanwumennei Dajie

Xirongxian Hutong

Dongchang'an Jie 建国门内大街

Tian'anmen Dong 天安门东地铁站

Xinwenhua Jie

Tongjinglou Lu

Tiananmen 天安门

Tiananmen Square 天安门广场

Zhengyi Lu

Taijichang Dajie 台基厂大街

Xuanwumen Xidajie (Second Ring Rd) 宣武门外西大街

Xuanwumen 宣武门地铁站

Hepingmen 和平门地铁站

Beixinhua Jie

Xijiaomin Xiang 西交民巷

Dongjiaomin Xiang

Shangxie Jie

Qianmen Xidajie (Second Ring Rd)

Qianmen Xiheyan Jie

Qianmen 前门地铁站

Qianmen Dongdajie (Second Ring Rd)

Xidamochang Jie

Chongwenmen Xidajie

See Chóngwén Map (p82)

XĪCHÉNG (pp88–9)

of steps up through a decorative archway, which is emblazoned with the characters 'Long Guang' (龙光) on one side and 'Zizhao' (紫照) on the other side. Head up more steps to the Zhengjue Hall (Zhèngjué Diàn), which contains a statue of Milefo and Weituo.

Pu'an Hall (Pǔ'ān Diàn) the next hall, houses a statue of Tsong Khapa, who was the founder of the Yellow Hat sect of Tibetan Buddhism, flanked by statues of the fifth Dalai Lama and the Panchen Lama. Eight golden effigies on either flank include tantric statues and the goddess Heinümu, adorned with a necklace of skulls. The final flight of steep steps brings you to the dagoba.

On the northeastern shore of the islet is the handsome, double-tiered Painted Gallery (Huàláng).

Xītiān Fànjìng, on the lake's northern shore, is one of the city's most interesting temples (admission is included in your park ticket). Taichi practitioners can frequently

be seen practising their artform outside the main entrance of the temple. The first hall, the Hall of the Heavenly Kings, takes you past Milefo, Weituo and the four Heavenly Kings.

The Dacizhenru Hall (Dàcízhēnrú Diàn) dates back to the Ming dynasty and contains three huge statues of Sakyamuni, the Amithaba Buddha and Yaoshi Fo (Medicine Buddha). Sadly, the golden statue of Guanyin at the rear is not approachable. The hall is supported by huge wooden pillars (which are called nánmù), and you can still make out where the original stone pillars once existed. At the very rear of the temple there is a glazed pavilion and a huge hall that are both unfortunately out of bounds.

The nearby Nine Dragon Screen (Jiǔlóng Bì; admission is included in the through ticket), a 5m-high and 27m-long spirit wall, is a glimmering stretch of coloured glazed tiles.

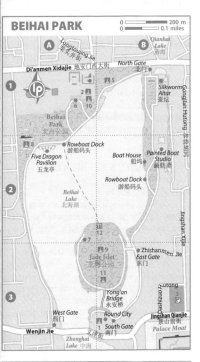

BEIHAI PARK

0 ———— 200 m
0 ———— 0.1 miles

NATIONAL GRAND THEATRE
Map pp88–9

国家大剧院 **Guójiā Dàjùyuàn**
admission Y30; 1.30-5pm Tue-Fri, 9.30am-5pm
Sat & Sun; Tiananmen Xi

Critics have compared it to an egg, but it looks more like a massive mercury bead, an ultramodern missile silo, a Bang and Olufsen–designed early-warning radar station or the futuristic lair of a James Bond villain. If aliens ever mustered above Běijīng, you can picture them speedily targeting the National Grand Theatre. As

out of place as a Starbucks in the Forbidden City (it happened), the unmistakable theatre building rises – if that is the word for it – immediately west of the Great Hall of the People. Like some huge reflective mushroom nosing up from the ground, the theatre's glass membrane is perennially cleaned by squads of roped daredevil cleaners fending off the Běijīng dust. Stand between the Great Hall of the People and the National Grand Theatre (home of the National Centre for the Performing Arts, p192) and measure, symbolically at least, how far China has come in the past 50 years. Despite protestations from designers that its round and square elements pay obeisance to traditional Chinese aesthetics, they're not fooling anyone: the theatre is designed to embody the transglobal (transgalactic perhaps) aspirations of contemporary China. While modernists love it to bits, traditionalists see it as a further kick in the teeth for 'old Peking'.

Examine the bulbous interior, including the titanic steel ribbing of interior bolsters (each of the 148 bolsters weighs eight tonnes). A fascinating exhibition inside reveals filtered-out competition entrants and the construction efforts that realised the building; note how many of the failed entrants (eg the proposal from Obermeyer & Deilmann) incorporated echoes of the Great Hall of the People into their design, something that the winning design (from Aeroports de Paris; ADP) avoided at all costs. A noticeboard in the foyer should inform you which of the three halls are open, as they are occasionally shut. It's all rounded off by an iffy modern art exhibition.

GREAT HALL OF THE PEOPLE
Map pp88–9

人民大会堂 **Rénmín Dàhuìtáng**
adult Y30, bag deposit Y2-5; usually 8.30am-3pm (times vary); Tiananmen Xi

On the western side of Tiananmen Square, on a site previously occupied by Taichang Temple, the Jinyiwei (Ming-dynasty secret service) and the Ministry of Justice, the Great Hall of the People is the venue of the legislature, the National People's Congress (NPC). The 1959 architecture is monolithic and intimidating, and a fitting symbol of China's remarkable political inertia. The

TRANSPORT: XĪCHÉNG

Subway Xīchéng is well served by Lines 1, 2 and 13. Line 4, due to open by the time this book is published, will make Beijing Zoo accessible by underground. Line 1 intersects with Line 2 at Fuxingmen, while Line 4 will intersect with Line 1 at Xidan and Xizhimen. The western section of east–west running Line 6 – which will run partially through Xīchéng – is due to open by 2012.

Bus Bus 1 runs along Xichang'an Jie, Fuxingmennei Dajie and Fuxingmenwai Dajie, taking you to Capital Museum. Bus 22 takes you from Tiananmen Xi to Xidan and then north to Xinjiekou.

tour parades visitors past a choice of 29 of its lifeless rooms named after the provinces of the Chinese universe. Also here is the banquet room where US President Richard Nixon dined in 1972, and the 10,000-seat auditorium with the familiar red star embedded in a galaxy of ceiling lights. The Great Hall of the People is closed to the public when the NPC is in session. The ticket office is down the south side of the building. Bags must be checked in but cameras are admitted.

JINGSHAN PARK Map pp88-9
景山公园 **Jǐngshān Gōngyuán**
Jingshan Qianjie; adult Y2; ⏱ 6am-9.30pm; ⊕ Tiananmen Xi, then 🚌 5
One of central Běijīng's few hills, this mound was created from earth excavated to make the Forbidden City moat. Called Coal Hill by Westerners during Legation days, Jinsghan Park also serves as a *fēngshuǐ* shield, protecting the palace from evil spirits – or dust storms – from the north. Clamber to the top for a magnificent panorama of the capital and princely views over the russet roofing of the Forbidden City. On the eastern side of the park a locust tree stands in the place where the last of the Ming emperors, Chongzhen, hung himself as rebels swarmed at the city walls.

CAPITAL MUSEUM Map pp88-9
首都博物馆 **Shǒudū Bówùguǎn**
☎ 6337 0491; www.capitalmuseum.org.cn; 16 Fuxingmenwai Dajie; admission Y15; ⏱ 9am-5pm Tue-Sun; ⊕ Muxidi
Behind the riveting good looks of the new Capital Museum are some first-rate gal-

leries, including a mesmerising collection of ancient Buddhist statues and a lavish exhibition of Chinese porcelain. There is also an interesting chronological history of Běijīng, an exhibition that is dedicated to cultural relics of Peking opera, a Běijīng Folk Customs exhibition, and displays of ancient bronzes, jade, calligraphy and paintings. There are seven daily screenings of 'Glorious Beijing' held in the Digital Theatre.

PRINCE GONG'S RESIDENCE Map pp88-9
恭王府 **Gōngwáng Fǔ**
☎ 6616 5005; 14 Liuyin Jie; adult Y20, tours incl opera performance & tea ceremony Y60; ⏱ 8.30am-4.30pm; ⊕ Gulou Dajie, then 🚌 60 or taxi
Reputed to be the model for the mansion in Cao Xueqin's 18th-century classic, *Dream of the Red Mansions,* the residence is one of Běijīng's largest private residential compounds. It remains one of Běijīng's more attractive retreats, decorated with rockeries, plants, pools, pavilions and elaborately carved gateways. Performances of Beijing opera are held in the Qing-dynasty Grand Opera House (☎ 6618 6628; adult Y80-120; ⏱ 7.30-8.40pm Mar-Oct) in the east of the grounds.

FORMER FUREN UNIVERSITY Map pp88-9
原辅仁大学 **Yuán Fǔrén Dàxué**
This grand building on Dingfu Jie just around the corner from Prince Gong's Residence once housed Furen University, founded by the Benedictine order in 1925. Today the magnificent building belongs to Beijing Normal University. On the wall to the west of the main door is a quality slogan from the Cultural Revolution, which poetically intones: 伟大的领袖毛主席是我们心中最红最红的红太阳 – 'The mighty leader Chairman Mao is the reddest, reddest of red suns in our heart'. On the wall on the other side of the door is another lengthy slogan that has been largely blotted out.

SONG QINGLING FORMER RESIDENCE Map pp88-9
宋庆龄故居 **Sòng Qìnglíng Gùjū**
☎ 6403 5858; 46 Beiheyan Lu; adult Y8; ⏱ 9am-4pm Tue-Sun; ⊕ Gulou Dajie or Jishuitan

Madam Song is lovingly venerated by the Chinese as the wife of Sun Yat-sen, founder of the Republic of China. Her house is rather dormant and moth-eaten; on display are personal items, pictures, clothing and books. You can find the museum on the northern side of Houhai Lake and within reach of Prince Gong's residence.

WHITE CLOUD TEMPLE Map pp88-9
白云观 Báiyún Guàn

☎ 6346 3887; 9 Baiyunguan Jie; adult Y10;
🕙 8.30am-4.30pm May-Sep, 8.30am-4pm Oct-Apr;
🚇 Muxidi, then 🚌 708

White Cloud Temple, once the Taoist centre of northern China, was founded in AD 739, although most of the temple halls date from the Qing dynasty. The temple is a lively, huge and fascinating complex of shrines and courtyards, tended by Taoist monks with their hair gathered into topknots.

Near the temple entrance, worshippers rub a polished stone carving for good fortune. The halls at the temple, centre of operations for the Taoist Quanzhen School and abode of the China Taoist Association, are dedicated to a host of Taoist officials and marshals. The Hall of the Jade Emperor celebrates this most famous of Taoist deities, while Taoist housewives cluster earnestly at the Hall to the God of Wealth to divine their financial future. Depictions of the Taoist Hell festoon the walls of the Shrine Hall for the Saviour Worthy.

Drop by White Cloud Temple during the Spring Festival (p12) and you will be rewarded with the spectacle of a magnificent temple fair (miàohuì). Worshippers funnel into the streets around the temple in their thousands, lured by artisans, street performers, wǔshù (martial arts) acts, craft workers, traders and a swarm of snack merchants.

To find the temple, walk south on Baiyun Lu from the Capital Museum and across the moat. Continue along Baiyun Lu and turn into a curving street on the left; follow it for 250m to the temple entrance.

SOUTH CATHEDRAL Map pp88-9
南堂 Nántáng

141 Qianmen Xidajie; 🕙 Mass in Latin 6am Sun-Fri, in English 10am Sun; 🚇 Xuanwumen

Běijīng's South Cathedral was built on the site of the house of Jesuit missionary Matteo Ricci, who brought Catholicism to China. Since being completed in 1703, the church has been destroyed three times, including being burnt down in 1775, and endured a trashing by anti-Christian forces during the Boxer Rebellion in 1900. The church is today decorated with modern stained glass, fake marbling, red carpets, portraits of the Stations of the Cross and cream-coloured confessionals, while black bibles in Chinese lie stacked about and the occasional local nun makes an appearance. All manner of crucifixes can be bought from the religious artefacts shop, near the statue of St Francis Xavier in the courtyard out the front.

THE RADIO PRODUCER

Christine Liu, originally from Sìchuān, has lived in Běijīng for over two decades. She has lived and studied in the UK and currently works for a radio station in Běijīng.

How long have you lived in Běijīng? Twenty-four years, since I was 10.

What has changed most in Běijīng in the last 10 years? I would have to say it's the landscape of the city. You might not be able to find your way home if you were away from Běijīng for a few years.

If you didn't live in Běijīng, where else in China would you want to live? Chéngdū, the provincial capital of Sìchuān.

What's the best thing about Běijīng? That's a hard question. I think the best thing about the capital is you can always be yourself, no matter where you are from or what your cultural background is. You are a Beijinger, but you can always be yourself, not like in Shànghǎi, where you have to change something to fit the standards of the Shanghainese.

What's the worst thing about Běijīng? It is too big now. And it is gradually losing its own characteristics, amid the process of being an international city. You can hardly ever hear a typical Běijīng accent – it is sad.

What's your favourite Běijīng experience? Local Beijingers' sense of humour!

How many times have you been to the Forbidden City? A dozen times. Not as many as I wish, but if I have time, it's always a place that is nice to visit.

top picks

FOR CHILDREN

Kids and the Forbidden City or tots and the Ming tombs just don't go together. Tiny heels will be dug in at every turn. Little lungs will be bellowing for freedom. China's one-child policy, however, means that Běijīng's sibling-less tykes are spoiled rotten by their parents, and the city is bursting with activities to keep the little emperors amused.

Events and attractions for children – from plays to arts-and-crafts events and seasonal parties – are listed in the monthly English-language culture magazine the *Beijinger* (www.thebeijinger.com). Many museums and attractions have a cheaper rate for children, usually applying to children shorter than 1.3m, so ask.

- Beijing Aquarium (opposite) Great for rainy or hazy days.
- Beijing Zoo (opposite) A fun-filled family outing.
- Beijing Planetarium (opposite) For the young stargazers.
- Beijing Natural History Museum (p86) Steer the children direct to the dinosaurs.
- Le Cool Ice Rink (p199) Put the kids on ice.
- China Puppet Theatre (p194) At weekends, this theatre casts a spell over its audience of little (and not-so-little) ones.
- New China Childrens Store (p147) When in doubt, take them shopping.
- Chaterhouse Booktrader (p148) The best kid's books section in Běijīng.
- Sanlitun Yashow Clothing Market (p149) The stalls on the 4th floor of this market also have toys.
- Kids Toys Market (p147) Toy bonanza in the building behind Hongqiao Market .

MEI LANFANG FORMER RESIDENCE
Map pp88-9

梅兰芳纪念馆 Méi Lánfāng Jìniàn Guǎn
☎ 6618 0351; 9 Huguosi Jie; adult Y10; 9am-4pm Tue-Sun Apr-Nov; Ⓜ Jishuitan
Place of pilgrimage for Beijing opera aficionados, this former *sìhéyuàn* (courtyard house) of actor Mei Lanfang is tucked away in a *hútòng* that's named after the nearby remains of Huguo Temple. Beijing opera (p37) was popularised in the West by Mei Lanfang (1894–1961), who played *dàn* (female roles) and is said to have influenced Charlie Chaplin. His former resi-

dence has been preserved as a museum, replete with costumes, furniture, opera programs and video presentations of his opera performances.

MIAOYING TEMPLE WHITE DAGOBA
Map pp88-9

妙应寺白塔 Miàoyīng Sì Báitǎ
☎ 6616 0211; 171 Fuchengmennei Dajie; adult Y20; 9am-4pm; Ⓜ Fuchengmen, then 🚌 13, 101, 102 or 103 to Baita Si
Stuffed away down a raggedy *hútòng*, the Miaoying Temple slumbers beneath its distinctive chalk-white Yuan-dynasty pagoda. The highlight of a visit here is its diverse collection of Buddhist statuary: pop into the Hall of the Great Enlightened One (大觉宝殿; Dàjué Bǎodiàn), which glitters splendidly with hundreds of Tibetan Buddhist effigies. In other halls resides a four-faced effigy of Guanyin (here called Parnashavari), as well as a trinity of the past, present and future Buddhas and a population of bronze *luóhàn* figures. After you finish here, exit the temple and wander the tangle of local alleyways for earthy shades of *hútòng* life.

NORTH CATHEDRAL Map pp88-9
北堂 Běitáng
☎ 6617 5198; Xishiku Dajie; Ⓜ Fuchengmen or 🚌 14 or 55 to Xi'anmen stop, then walk north
Also called the Cathedral of Our Saviour, this august cathedral is one of Běijīng's four main churches and the only one located within the former grounds of the Imperial City. Built in 1887, the cathedral served as a factory warehouse during the Cultural Revolution. Despite being covered in gaudy grey, flaking paint, the cathedral is worth visiting, especially for those keen to glimpse the growing stature of Christianity in China (see boxed text, p27).

XIBIANMEN WATCHTOWER Map pp88-9
西便门角楼 Xībiànmén Jiǎolóu
The counterpart of the Southeast Corner Watchtower (p86), the Xibianmen Watchtower is not as impressive as its robust and better-known sibling, but you can climb up onto a section of the old city wall amid the roaring traffic. The overlooked watchtower is simply shrieking to be converted into a boutique hotel (although parking could be a problem).

LU XUN MUSEUM Map pp88-9
鲁迅博物馆 Lǔ Xùn Bówùguǎn
19 Gongmenkou Ertiao; ☉ **9am-4pm Tue-Sun;**
⊖ **Fuchengmen**
Lu Xun (1881–1936) is often regarded as the father of modern Chinese literature. Born in Shàoxīng in Zhèjiāng province and buried in Shànghǎi, Lu Xun lived in Běijīng for over a decade. As a writer, Lu Xun, who first trained in medicine, articulated a deep yearning for reform by mercilessly exposing the foibles of the Chinese character in such tales as *Medicine* and *Diary of a Madman*. The exhibits range from photos and manuscripts to personal effects.

BEIJING ZOO & BEIJING AQUARIUM
Map pp88-9
北京动物园、北京海洋馆 Běijīng Dòngwùyuán & Běijīng Hǎiyángguǎn
www.bjzoo.com.cn; 137 Xizhimenwai Dajie; admission Y15 1 Apr–31 Oct, Y10 1 Nov–31 Mar, panda house Y5 extra, zoo & aquarium adult/child Y100/50, English audio guide Y40; ☉ **summer 7.30am-6pm, winter 7.30am-5pm;** ⊖ **Xizhimen, then** 🚌 **104, 205 or 106**
Although not as pleasant as Shànghǎi's green and wooded getaway, Beijing Zoo is a relaxing spot for a wander among the trees, grass and willow-fringed lakes, even if the creatures can be mere sideshows.

Zoologically speaking, the well-housed pandas are the prime diversions, especially if you are not en route to the Sìchuān wilds. The remaining menagerie remains cooped up in pitiful cages and enclosures, with the polar bears pinning their hopes on gaining admission to the excellent Beijing Aquarium (☎ 6217 6655; adult/child Y100/50; ☉ 9am-10pm high season, to 6pm low season) in the northeastern corner of the zoo. On view is an imaginative Amazon rainforest (complete with piranha), coral reefs, a shark aquarium (where you can dive with the flesh-eaters) and a marine mammal pavilion (which hosts lively aquatic animal displays). The ticket price to the aquarium includes entry to the zoo; you can buy this ticket at the zoo entrance.

The Popular Science Museum (Y5) within the grounds of the zoo has no English captions so is highly missable, but the small children's zoo (Y10; open 9am to 5pm) is fun for young zoologists.

From May to October, boats to the Summer Palace (p127) depart from the dock (☎ 8838 4476; one way Y40; ☉ hourly 10am-4pm).

East of the zoo is the distinctive Beijing Exhibition Center (Běijīng Zhǎnlǎn Guǎn; Map pp88–9), designed in the days when Chinese architects were party ideologues.

Getting to the zoo is easy enough: take the subway to Xizhimen Station, from where it's a 1.2km walk heading west or a short ride on any of the buses.

BEIJING PLANETARIUM Map pp88-9
北京天文馆 Běijīng Tiānwénguǎn
138 Xizhimenwai Dajie; old/new bldg Y15/10, Optical Planetarium Y15, 4-D Theatre Y30, Space Simulator Y30, Digital Space Theatre Y45; ☉ **10am-5pm Wed-Sun;** ⊖ **Xizhimen, then** 🚌 **104, 205 or 106**
Across from the zoo, children will find something to marvel at among the telescopes, models of the planets and the solar system, and the variety of shows in the new building, even though the typical absence of thorough English captions can make full comprehension an astronomical task.

XU BEIHONG MUSEUM Map pp88-9
徐悲鸿纪念馆 Xú Bēihóng Jìniàn Guǎn
☎ **6225 2042; 53 Xinjiekou Beidajie; adult Y5;** ☉ **9am-4pm Tue-Sun;** ⊖ **Jishuitan**
The Chinese artist Xu Beihong (1895–1953), best remembered for his galloping horses that injected dynamism into previously static forms of Chinese brushwork, is commemorated in this intriguing museum. Exposed to foreign (principally European) painting styles, Xu possessed one of 20th-century China's more fertile imaginations. The communists feted Xu, which partly explains the success and longevity of his name. His success is celebrated here in seven halls and remembered in a collection of oils, gouache, pen and ink sketches, and portraits.

PALEOZOOLOGICAL MUSEUM OF CHINA Map pp88-9
中国古动物馆 Zhōngguó Gǔdòngwùguǎn
142 Xizhimenwai Dajie; admission Y20; ☉ **9am-4.30pm Tue-Sun;** ⊖ **Xizhimen, then** 🚌 **104, 205 or 106**
A little bit cheesy, with an impressive tally of *zero* English captions, but young palaeontologists can scurry among the dinosaur remains and legions of Chinese schoolchildren, gawping at skeletons of *Tyrannosaurus*

Rex and *Tsingtaosaurus* and examining the parrot-like beak of *Psittacosaurus*.

CHINA NUMISMATIC MUSEUM
Map pp88-9

中国钱币博物馆 Zhōngguó Qiánbì Bówùguǎn
17 Xijiaomin Xiang; admission Y10; 9am-4pm Tue-Sun, closed when NPC in session; Tiananmen Xi

This intriguing three-floor museum follows the technology of money production in China from the spade-shaped coins of the Spring and Autumn period to the coinage and paper currency of the modern day. Of particular interest are the top-floor samples of modern Chinese paper renminbi, from the pragmatic illustrations of the first series to the far more idealistic third series (1962) and the fourth series dating from 1987, still adorned with Mao's head.

(Continued on page 109)

OURNEY TO THE GREAT WALL

Snowy peaks of the Great Wall of China, Jiànkòu

JOURNEY TO THE GREAT WALL

The most iconic monument in all China, the Great Wall (长城; Chángchéng) stands as an awe-inspiring symbol of the grandeur of China's ancient history. Dating back 2000-odd years, the Wall stretches from the border with North Korea in the east, to Lop Nur in the far western province of Xīnjiāng.

Known to the Chinese as the '10,000 Li Wall' (万里长城; Wànlǐ Chángchéng), which with one 'Li' equivalent to around 500m makes it the '5000km Wall', it is actually far longer than that. A report by China's State Administration of Cultural Heritage in April 2009 put its non-continuous length at 8851km, or about 5500 miles. Meandering its way through 17 provinces, principalities and autonomous regions, the Wall started out life as a line of defence against the Mongol hordes. But while it has had no real practical use for centuries, it retains its place in the imagination of both locals and foreigners.

HISTORY

The Wall has been adopted by the Chinese Communist Party (CCP), which likes to stress the unity of the Wall in its official histories. In fact, there are four distinct Walls, or five if you count the recently rebuilt sections, such as Bādálǐng. Work on the 'original' was begun during the Qin dynasty (221–207 BC), when China was unified for the first time under Emperor Qin Shihuang. Hundreds of thousands of workers, many political prisoners, laboured for 10 years to construct it. An estimated 180 million cu metres of rammed earth was used to form the core of this Wall, and legend has it that the bones of dead workers were used as building materials, too.

After the Qin fell, work on the Wall continued during the Han dynasty (206 BC–AD 220). Little more was done until almost a 1000 years later during the Jin dynasty (1115–1234) when the impending threat of Genghis Khan spurred further construction. The Wall's final incarnation, and the one most visitors see today, came during the Ming dynasty (1368–1644), when it was reinforced with stone, brick and battlements over a period of 100 years, and at great human cost to the two to three million people who toiled on it. During this period, it was home to around one million soldiers.

Watchtowers, Jinshanling Great Wall

The great irony of the Wall is that it rarely stopped China's enemies from invading. Never one continuous structure, there were inevitable gaps and it was through those that Genghis Khan rode in to take Běijīng in 1215. Perhaps the Wall's finest hour as a defensive bulwark came in 1644 at Shānhǎiguān, where the Wall meets the sea in the east and guarded the approach to Běijīng. The invading Manchus were unable to take this strip of Wall until the traitorous general Wu Sangui opened the gates, resulting in the fall of the Ming dynasty.

While the Wall was less than effective militarily, it was very useful as a kind of elevated highway, transporting people and equipment across mountainous terrain. Its beacon tower system, using smoke signals generated by burning wolves' dung, quickly transmitted news of enemy movements back to the capital. But with the Manchus installed in Běijīng as the Qing dynasty (1644–1911) and the Mongol threat long gone, there was little need to maintain the Wall and it fell into disrepair.

That degeneration accelerated during the war with Japan and then the civil war that preceded the founding of the new China in 1949. Compounding the problem, the communists didn't initially have much interest in the Wall. In fact, Mao Zedong encouraged people living near it to use it as a source of free building materials, something that still goes on unofficially today. It wasn't until 1984 that Mao's successor Deng Xiaoping ordered that the Wall be restored in places and placed under government protection.

Hikers scale Badaling Great Wall

RESTORATION OF THE WALL

Classic postcard images of the Wall – flawlessly clad in bricks and stoutly undulating over hills into the distance – do not reflect the truth of the bastion today. While the sections closest to Běijīng and a few elsewhere have been restored to something approaching their former glory, huge parts of the Wall are either rubble or, especially in the west, mounds of earth that could be anything.

Those sections that have been tarted up for tourist consumption now come complete with rapacious hawkers, souvenir shops, amusement park–style rides and, above all, big crowds, all of which can make it difficult to contemplate the true majesty of the Wall. Many travellers are now seeking out segments, such as Huánghuā and Jiànkòu, that are unrestored and remain in the hands of local communities (who charge far less than the official sites). The authorities try and discourage this with the threat of (rarely enforced) fines, while arguing that they are trying to prevent damage to the Wall. The reality is that they are keen to ensure the revenue from the official sites keeps flowing.

Nevertheless, the government does a much better job of protecting the Wall than it once did. The time when local authorities would blast sections of it into dust to make room for roads and new developments is thankfully gone. And so are the days when the Wall near Běijīng played host to raves that scandalised public opinion.

MYTHOLOGY

The Chinese were disappointed to lay to rest the myth that the Great Wall is the only man-made structure visible with the naked eye from the moon. China's first astronaut Yang Liwei failed to see the barrier when he went into space in 2003. According to US astronauts, it is possible to see the Wall (and other structures, such as motorways) from low orbit, but only if the weather is right. The claim originated in the 1930s and since it was refuted millions of textbooks across China have been corrected.

VISITING THE WALL

Bādálǐng is the most touristy part of the Wall, followed by Mùtiányù. Also renovated but less commercial are Sīmǎtái and Jīnshānlǐng. The Jiāo Shān (p225) section at Shānhǎiguān is also worth seeing, and a trip there can be combined with one to the Jiǔménkǒu p226) section in Liáonīng province.

When choosing a tour, check it visits the places you want to see. Tours to the Great Wall are often combined with trips to the Ming Tombs, so if you don't want to visit the tombs ensure they aren't on the itinerary. Some less-reputable tours make (sometimes expensive) diversions to gem exhibition halls and traditional Chinese medicine centres, which can be irritating if you are not interested. The tour organisers receive a commission from these businesses for every person they funnel through.

For a selection of outfits that can arrange tours to the Great Wall, see p249. The handiest tours to the Great Wall depart from the Beijing Sightseeing Bus Centre (Běijīng Lǚyóu Jísàn Zhōngxīn; Map pp58–9; ☎ 8353 1111), west of Front Gate at Qiánmén alongside Tiananmen Square. But

THE WALL THAT DISAPPEARED

It's hard to believe that a structure that runs for 8851km could go missing, but much of the Great Wall has. The most optimistic estimates are that just one-third of the Wall is still standing. The twin culprits for this are man and nature. The cavalier official attitude towards the Wall that existed until very recently saw it fall prey to both individual pilferers of bricks and stone, and unscrupulous developers.

For people living close to the Wall, some of whom claim descent from the soldiers who once manned it, the presence of all that raw building material was too tempting. Pass through villages in the Wall's vicinity and you will find everything from houses to pig pens built from stones, bricks and earth that were once part of it.

Developers and officials have done damage on a far bigger scale by destroying whole sections of the Wall to make room for roads, luxury villas and misguided tourism projects. Official restoration work in some places has not been done properly; in one notorious case in Shāndōng province, bathroom tiles were used to replace the original stone.

But it is nature that poses the greatest threat to the Wall. Desertification in China started centuries before the term 'climate change' was coined because imperial officials torched the forests within 95km of the Wall to deny the enemy a chance to launch surprise attacks. Now, with one million acres of grassland lost to the encroaching desert annually in China, what's left of the Wall, especially in the environmentally vulnerable northwestern provinces, faces being buried forever.

A dilapidated section of the Wall, Huánghuā

your hotel may run an equally convenient tour; many of the hostel trips to the Great Wall come recommended. For a distinctive voyage to the Great Wall, journey in a motorbike sidecar with Beijing Sideways (p249). Or if you really want to hit the Wall, then consider tackling the 3800 steps and brutal inclines of the Great Wall Marathon (www.great-wall-marathon.com) held every May. As with other popular destinations in China, avoid visiting the Wall at weekends and during the big national holiday periods in the first week of May and October.

BADALING GREAT WALL
八达岭长城

'This is a Great Wall and only a great people with a great past could have a great wall and such a great people with such a great wall will surely have a great future.'

President Richard Nixon

Majestic curve of the Badaling Great Wall

The mere mention of its name sending a shudder down the spine of hardcore wall walkers, Bādálǐng (Map p219; ☎ 010-6912 1737; admission adult/student Y45/25; ☺ summer 6am-8pm, winter 7am-6pm) is Běijīng's most-visited chunk of brick-clad bastion. Nixon, Thatcher, Reagan, Gorbachev and Queen Elizabeth have all stamped on Bādálǐng. It ticks all the iffy Great Wall boxes in one flourish: souvenir stalls, T-shirt flogging hawkers, restaurants, heavily restored brickwork, little authenticity, guardrails and mobs of sightseers. If you're curious to discover how many people can fit on the wall at any one time, the big holiday periods are a good time to find out. Some guidebooks trumpet that '130 million foreign and domestic tourists have visited Bādálǐng' as if it was a unique selling point. You may even pick up some Cantonese from the sheer number of Guǎngdōng folk storming the ramparts. On the plus side, the scenery is raw and striking and you get to see the Wall snaking off in classic fashion into the hills; but you can get both elsewhere.

TRANSPORT: BADALING GREAT WALL

Distance from Běijīng 70km

Direction Northwest

Tours All tour operators run tours to Bādálǐng. Youth hostels and hotels are often preferable and more convenient, running tours to Bādálǐng from around Y180, but some hotels charge astronomical prices so shop around.

Local bus The cheapest route to Bādálǐng is on bus 919 from just north of the Deshengmen gate tower, about 500m east of the Jishuitan subway stop. Buses leave regularly from 6.30am; ordinary buses take two hours and cost Y5, while faster, nonstop buses take one hour and cost Y12. The last bus leaves Bādálǐng for Běijīng at 6.30pm.

Tour bus Tour buses to Bādálǐng depart from the Beijing Sightseeing Bus Centre (Běijīng Lǚyóu Jísàn Zhōngxīn; Map pp58–9; ☎ 8353 1111), west of Front Gate, alongside Tiananmen Square. Line C runs to Bādálǐng (Y100 return, price includes entry to Great Wall, departs 7.30am to 11.30am); Line A runs to Bādálǐng and Dìng Líng at the Ming Tombs (Y160, includes entrance tickets and lunch, departs 6am to 10.30am). Plan about nine hours for the whole trip.

Taxi A taxi to Bādálǐng and back from Běijīng will cost a minimum of Y400 for the eight-hour hire (with a maximum of four passengers).

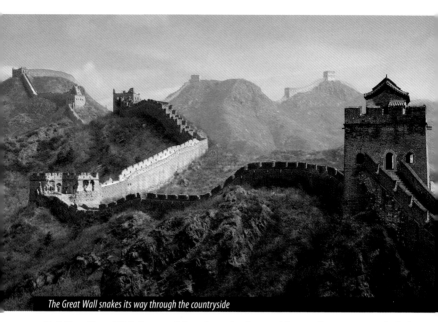
The Great Wall snakes its way through the countryside

Badaling Great Wall dates to Ming times (1368–1644) but underwent particularly heavy restoration work during the 1950s and 1980s, when it was essentially rebuilt. Punctuated with watchtowers *(dílóu)*, the 6m-wide wall is typical of the neat stonework of Ming engineers.

The frostbitten scenery of Bādálǐng in winter sees precious few visitors, but you may need to dress like an Eskimo if you visit then, especially if it's windy. Due to elevation and exposure, Bādálǐng is much colder than urban Běijīng. Snow on the walls is a very popular photographic attraction – but watch your footing.

Two sections of wall trail off to the left and right of the main entrance. The restored sections crawl for some distance before nobly disintegrating into ruins; unfortunately you cannot realistically explore these more authentic fragments. Cable cars are there if you need them (Y50 return trip). Many tours from Běijīng to Bādálǐng also include the Ming Tombs (十三陵; Shísān Líng; p229).

The admission fee also gets you into the China Great Wall Museum (中国长城博物馆; Zhōngguó Chángchéng Bówùguǎn; 🕑 9am-4pm).

MUTIANYU GREAT WALL 慕田峪长城

'The Great Wall here is very beautiful, very grand, more beautiful and grander than what I imagined.'

President Bill Clinton

TRANSPORT: MUTIANYU GREAT WALL

Distance from Běijīng 90km

Direction Northeast

Local bus From Dongzhimen Transport Hub Station (Dōngzhímén Shūniǔzhàn; Map pp58–9) take bus 916 to Huáiróu (Y6 to Y12, one hour 40 minutes, departs 6.30am to 7.30pm). There are also fast 916 buses (Y12, one hour, departs 6.30am to 7.30pm). Then change for a minibus to Mùtiányù (Y25).

Tour bus Youth hostels and hotels run tours to Mùtiányù from around Y200; such tours are very convenient, but some hotels charge sky-high prices. During the summer months, weekend tour bus 6 departs between 7am and 8.30am for Mùtiányù (Y50) from outside the South Cathedral (Nántáng; Map pp88–9) on Qianmen Xidajie.

Famed for its Ming-era guard towers and excellent views, the 3km-long section of wall at Mùtiányù (Map p219; ☎ 010-6162 6022; admission Y45; ☻ summer 7am-6.30pm, winter 7.30am-5.30pm), northeast of Běijīng in Huairou County, is largely a recently restored Ming dynasty structure that was built upon an earlier Northern Qi dynasty edifice. US President Bill Clinton came here (Reagan went to Bādálǐng), if that's anything to go by. With 26 watchtowers, the wall is impressive and manageable, with most hawking reserved to the lower levels (hawkers go down to around Y15 for cotton 'I climbed the Great Wall' T-shirts): the further you get away from Mùtiányù central the better. It's actually possible to hike from Mùtiányù all the way west to Huánghuā (p107) and the front section of Jiànkòu (below).

If time is tight, take the four-minute cable car (single/return Y35/50; ☻ 8.30am-4.30pm) ride up and trot down or sweep down on a toboggan (single/return Y40/55). October is the best month to visit, with the countryside drenched in autumn hues.

If you want to overnight near Mùtiányù, book a room at the Mutianyu Great Wall Guesthouse (☎ 010-6962 6867), scenically located in a restored watchtower on the wall, or at the Schoolhouse at Mutianyu Great Wall (小园; Xiǎoyuán; ☎ 010-6162 6505; www.theschoolhouseatmutianyu.com).

JIANKOU GREAT WALL 箭扣长城

For stupefying hikes along perhaps Běijīng's most incomparable section of wall, head to the rear section of the Jiankou Great Wall (后箭扣长城; Hòu Jiànkòu Chángchéng; Map p219; admission Y20), accessible from Huáiróu. It's a 40-minute walk uphill from the drop off at Xizhazi Village (西栅子村; Xīzhàzi Cūn) to a fork in the path among the trees that leads you to either side of a collapsed section of wall, one heading off to the east, the other heading west. Tantalising panoramic views spread out in either direction as the brickwork meanders dramatically along a mountain ridge; the setting is truly sublime.

Tread carefully – sections are badly collapsing and the whole edifice is overgrown with plants and saplings – but its unadulterated state conveys an awe-inspiring and raw beauty. If you are ambitious and want to continue along the wall, you will need to dismount the wall at several places to skirt brickwork that has either completely disintegrated or plunges almost vertically down mountain sides like a roller coaster. One of these sections is called Heaven's Ladder (天梯; Tiāntī) – a precipitous section of crumbling bricks. Clamber up to the Nine Eye Tower (九眼楼; Jiǔyǎn Lóu) for fantastic views.

TRANSPORT: JIANKOU GREAT WALL

Distance from Běijīng 100km
Distance Northeast
Local bus Take bus 916 from Dongzhimen Transport Hub Station (Dōngzhímén Shūniǔzhàn; Map pp58–9) to Huáiróu (Y12, one hour, departs 6.30am to 7.30pm). Try to get the fast 916 that takes the Jingcheng Expressway, as the regular buses are slower (Y6 to Y12, one hour 40 minutes, departs 6.30am to 7.30pm). At Huáiróu you will need to hire a minivan to the rear Jiànkòu section; this should cost around Y200 return (one hour each way) as it's a fair distance. Alternatively, hire a van and driver either in Huáiróu (or Běijīng) for around Y400 for a day-long Great Wall tour, including Jiànkòu, Huánghuā, Mùtiányù, Xiǎngshuǐhú and other sections of wall.

Ming-dynasty design, Mutianyu Great Wall

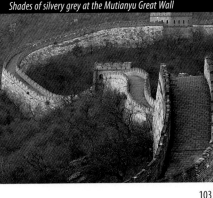
Shades of silvery grey at the Mutianyu Great Wall

On top of the world, Simatai Great Wall

Panoramic views from the Jiankou Great Wall

Xizhazi Village is rudimentary, but if you want to overnight, ask around and a household may put you up very cheaply for a night or more. Some visitors spend weeks here, making a thorough exploration of the surrounding landscape.

XIANGSHUIHU GREAT WALL
响水湖长城

Xiàngshuǐhú (Map p219; ☎ 010-6314 0663; admission Y25) means 'loud water lake', which may suggest tempting visions of the Great Wall reflected in turbulent waters. The name actually derives from a nearby spring and the surrounding area can be quite dry, especially in winter and spring. Nonetheless, the restored Ming-era wall here has some staggeringly steep gradients, which make for quite a Great Wall StairMaster workout. Sections of the fortification, which divides into two at the road, come with 1m-high steps that make you feel totally Lilliputian. Take shoes with good grip. Located to the west of Mùtiányù and about 30km from Huáiróu.

TRANSPORT: XIANGSHUIHU GREAT WALL

Distance from Běijīng 78km
Direction Northeast
Local bus From Dongzhimen Transport Hub Station (Dōngzhímén Shūniǔzhàn; Map pp58–9) take bus 916 to Huáiróu (Y6 to Y12, one hour 40 minutes, departs 6.30am to 7.30pm) – try to get one of the fast 916 buses (Y12, one hour, departs 6.30am to 7.30pm). Minibuses run from Bei Dajie in Huáiróu to Xiangshuihu Great Wall, leaving at 6.30am, 10.30am, 2pm and 4pm. If you miss the bus, then grab a minitaxi.

JUYONGGUAN GREAT WALL 居庸关长城

First constructed in the 5th century, rebuilt by the Ming and more recently restored, **Jūyōngguān** (Juyong Pass; Map p219; ☎ 010-6977 1665; admission Y45; 🕑 6am-4pm) was considered one of the most strategically significant parts of the Wall. This is the closest section of wall to Běijīng, but it has been over-renovated, so little authenticity remains. Usually quiet, the steep and somewhat strenuous circuit can be done in under two hours.

TRANSPORT: JUYONGGUAN GREAT WALL

Distance from Běijīng 50km
Direction Northwest
Local bus Jūyōngguān is on the road to Bādálǐng so public buses heading to Bādálǐng will get you to there. Take the slow bus 919 to Yánqìng (Y5, 90 minutes, first bus 6.30am) from Deshengmen gate tower, about 500m east of the Jishuitan subway stop. Do not take the express bus to Bādálǐng.

SIMATAI GREAT WALL
司马台长城

'He who has not climbed the Great Wall is not a true man.'

Mao Zedong

In Miyun County near the far-flung town of Gŭběikŏu near the Héběi border, the stirring remains at Sīmǎtái (Map p219; ☎ 010-6903 1051; admission Y40; ☺ 8am-5pm) make for an exhilarating Great Wall experience. Built during the reign of Ming-dynasty emperor Hongwu, the 19km stretch is characterised by watchtowers, steep plunges and scrambling ascents.

This rugged section of wall can be heart-thumpingly steep and the scenery is dramatic. Following the crowds to the wall, you have a choice: either head west for the hike (four hours one way) to Jīnshānlíng (below) or walk east as far as you can. The hike to Jīnshānlíng makes the long journey out here worth it, but you will need to set off early in the morning; you can do the hike in either direction, but it's usually more convenient transport-wise to return to Běijīng from Sīmǎtái. The Sīmǎtái section destined for Jīnshānlíng consists of 18 watchtowers ranging north of the old vestiges of wall dating to the Northern Qi.

Heading east, after around the twelfth watchtower (called Jiāngjūn Lóu or General Watchtower) things start getting rather precarious and the fourteenth, fifteenth and sixteenth watchtowers (Cat's Eye Watchtower, Fairy Watchtower and Capital View Watchtower) are largely inaccessible or tricky to get to. A few slopes have 70-degree inclines and you need both hands free, so bring a day-pack to hold your camera and other essentials. One narrow section of footpath has a 500m drop, so it's no place for acrophobics. The cable car (return trip Y50) saves time and could be an alternative to a sprained ankle. Take strong shoes with a good grip.

Sīmǎtái has some unusual features, such as 'obstacle-walls' – walls within walls used for defending against enemies who had already scaled the Great Wall. Small cannons have been discovered in this area, as well as evidence of rocket-type weapons, such as flying knives and flying swords.

TRANSPORT: SIMATAI GREAT WALL

Distance from Běijīng 110km

Direction Northeast

Local bus Take bus 980 from Dongzhimen Transport Hub Station (Dōngzhímén Shūniǔzhàn; Map pp58–9) to Mìyún (Y15) and change to a minibus for Sīmǎtái (Y15, one hour) or a taxi (return trip Y120).

Tour bus In summer, early morning tour bus 12 (Y60) leaves on Saturdays and Sundays for Sīmǎtái from outside the South Cathedral (Nántáng; Map pp88–9) on Qianmen Xidajie.

Hotel tours Youth hostels and other hotels often run early morning trips by minibus (excluding/including ticket Y180/260) to Jīnshānlíng for the four-hour hike to Sīmǎtái – this is the best way to visit Sīmǎtái. Buses usually leave at around 6am or 7am and the entire journey from Běijīng and back can take up to 12 hours. If you are interested in a hiking trip to Sīmǎtái, enquire at Beijing Downtown Backpackers Accommodation (☎ 8400 2429) or Red Lantern House West Yard (☎ 6656 2181).

Taxi Hiring a taxi from Beijing for the day costs about Y400.

JINSHANLING GREAT WALL 金山岭长城

The Jinshanling Great Wall (Jīnshānlíng Chángchéng; Map p219; ☎ 0314-883 0222; admission Y40), near the town of Gŭběikŏu, marks the starting point of an exhilarating 10km hike to Sīmǎtái (above). The adventure – winding through stunning mountainous terrain – takes around four hours as the trail is steep and parts of the wall have collapsed, but it can be traversed without too much difficulty. Note that the watchtowers are in various states of preservation and some have been stripped of their bricks.

Autumn is the best season for the hike; in summer you'll be sweating gallons so load up with water before you go (ever-present hawkers on the wall sell pricey water for around Y10 a bottle, or more depending on how thirsty you appear).

To commence the hike, turn left when you reach the wall and keep going. The cable car at the start of Jīnshānlíng is for the indolent or infirm (one way/return trip Y30/50). Arriving at Sīmǎtái you have to buy another ticket to cross a rope bridge (Y5).

Stairway to heaven, Sīmǎtái

TRANSPORT: JINSHANLING GREAT WALL

Distance from Běijīng 110km
Direction Northeast
Local bus Grab any Chéngdé-bound bus and get off at Jīnshānlíng. Buses (Y56 to Y74, four hours) to Chéngdé depart hourly from the Liuliqiao and Sihui Long-Distance Bus Stations in Běijīng.
Hotel tours Youth hostels and other hotels often run early morning trips by minibus (excluding/including ticket Y180/260) to Jīnshānlíng for the four-hour hike to Sīmǎtái. Buses usually leave at around 6am or 7am and the entire journey from Běijīng and back can take up to 12 hours. If you are interested in a hiking trip to Sīmǎtái, enquire at Beijing Downtown Backpackers Accommodation (☎ 8400 2429) or Red Lantern House West Yard (☎ 6656 2181).

You can do the walk in the opposite direction, but getting a ride back to Běijīng from Sīmǎtái is easier than from Jīnshānlíng. Of course, getting a ride should be no problem if you've made arrangements with your driver to pick you up (and didn't pay in advance).

HUANGHUA GREAT WALL 黄花长城

Far less touristy than the other sections of the Great Wall close to Běijīng, Huánghuā (Map p219) is genuine wild Wall. Undulating across the hillsides east and west of a small reservoir and offering spectacular views of the surrounding countryside, it has undergone only partial restoration and is refreshingly free of the hawkers who can make visits to other sections a trying experience. That's mostly because this strip of Wall remains under the control of the people who live here, despite the best efforts of the tourist authorities to wrest it off them.

During the week especially, it is strikingly free of crowds, which means visitors can admire this classic and well-preserved example of Ming defence, with high and wide ramparts, intact parapets and sturdy beacon towers, in relative isolation. The patchy and periodic restoration work on the Wall here has left its crumbling nobility and striking authenticity largely intact, with the ramparts occasionally dissolving into rubble and some of the steps in ruins.

It is believed that the renowned general Cai Kai masterminded the construction of this section, employing meticulous quality control. Each *cùn* (inch) of the masonry represented one labourer's whole day's work. When the Ministry of War got wind of the extravagance, Cai was beheaded for his efforts. In spite of the trauma, his decapitated body stood erect for three days before toppling. Years later, his work was judged to be exemplary and he was posthumously pardoned by the emperor.

Huánghuā's unofficial status means visitors are greeted by a large sign saying it is closed. Ignore that, as the locals will encourage you to do, even though in theory you risk a possible fine.

From the road, you can go either east or west. The eastern route is the more popular. There are two approaches to the eastern section. One takes you across a small dam, built with stone from the Wall, and up a path that clings to the side of the Wall until it reaches the second watchtower. Then you clamber up a metal ladder to the watchtower and you're on the Wall proper. The second approach is less hair-raising: you cross a wooden bridge 100m south of the dam (look for the sign pointing the way to Mr Li's Tavern), go through an outdoor restaurant and then scramble up through someone's back garden until you get to the second watchtower. Whichever way you go, the price (Y2) is the same.

TRANSPORT: HUANGHUA GREAT WALL

Distance from Běijīng 60km
Direction North
Local bus From the new Dongzhimen Transport Hub Station (Dōngzhímén Shūniǔzhàn; Map pp58–9), by exit B of Dongzhimen subway stop, take bus 916 to Huáiróu (Y6 to Y12, one hour 40 minutes, departs 6.30am to 7.30pm) and get off at Míngzhū Guǎngchǎng. There are also fast 916 buses (Y12, one hour, departs 6.30am to 7.30pm) that make fewer stops but run less frequently. At Míngzhū Guǎngchǎng, minivan drivers wait on both sides of the road. Ask for Huánghuāchéng (40 minutes). If the van is full, expect to pay Y10 for the one-way journey. Otherwise, depending on the number of people, the price can be as high as Y80 to Y100 for the return trip.
Tour bus Huánghuā's relative anonymity means there are no official tours there, although some hotels and hostels will organise one if there is enough demand.

Sunrise at Jinshanling Great Wall

From the second watchtower, the Wall climbs abruptly uphill through a series of further watchtowers before going over and dipping down the hill to continue meandering on. It is steep and, in places, the stone has been worn smooth, making it very slippery. You need shoes with a good grip and to exercise caution going downhill and in wet weather. There are also no guard rails here. If you don't want to turn back and have a couple of spare days, it is possible to make it all the way to the Mùtiányù (p102) section of the Wall.

To head west, climb the steps opposite the wooden bridge. After paying the ticket collector Y2 you can head up this very steep parapet. The reward for aching knees and leg muscles is the magnificent sight of the Wall stretching off into the distance. This section, though, is in worse condition than the eastern one and most people loop back to the road after the third watchtower. You can keep going, but it is very hard going and hairy in places. If you walk for four days, then theoretically you should reach Bādálǐng (p101).

You can spend the night at Huánghuā, with prices ranging from Y50 to Y150. At the entrance to the western part of the wall, the Ténglóng Fàndiàn (腾龙饭店; ☎ 010-6165 1929; summer dm Y50-80) has clean and simple rooms. The more expensive rooms have private showers and toilets. There are a number of restaurants on both sides of the road.

About 5km from Huánghuā (Y15 by taxi van) is the Huanghuacheng Great Wall Lakeside Reserve (黄花城水长城旅游区; Huánghuāchéng Shuǐchángchéng Lǚyóuqū; ☎ 010-6165 1111; admission Y25; ☼ 8am-5.30pm). You can't access the Wall here, but there are splendid vistas of crumbling sections of the Wall clinging to the surrounding hillsides. The reservoir itself is a pleasant, if unremarkable, body of water. You can get a speedboat to whisk you across it (Y15), or hire your own more-sedate boat (Y10) and paddle yourself. It takes about three hours to walk around the reservoir.

lonelyplanet.com

CHÁOYÁNG 朝阳区

Eating p172; Shopping p148; Sleeping p213

This district – which literally means 'Facing the Sun', in tribute to its easterly aspect – covers a vast swathe of Běijīng east and northeast of the Second Ring Rd. Cháoyáng extends east of Dōngchéng, Chóngwén and Hǎidiàn and is named after Cháoyáng Mén (朝阳门) – Chaoyang Gate – one of the principal gates in the Tartar City Wall that enveloped the centre of town. Chaoyang Gate was colloquially also called Liáng Mén (粮门) – Grain Gate – as it was the principal conduit for grain and other merchandise entering the city.

Look at old maps of Běijīng and you'll see that Cháoyáng hardly features at all. On the *Beijing City Street Map* from 1950 the only mention of the area is a small settlement called Chaoyangmen Waishi (朝阳门外市), directly east of Chaoyang Gate and beyond the city moat and the railway that ran around the city walls. Several of Běijīng's main altars lay outside the city walls, and the Temple to the Sun (日坛; Rìtán) could be found in Cháoyáng, as it lay to the east of town (the Altar to the Moon was on the west side of Běijīng). Also on the map is Beijing's Tapwater Works, located where today's Dongzhimenwai Xijie begins the run to Capital Airport.

As Cháoyáng lay beyond the old city walls, it is not a historic district, so there is a limited collection of notable sights and little if any sense of old Běijīng. However, it is a lively, youthful and vivacious area, home to Sānlǐtún – one of Běijīng's major drinking and shopping hubs – and Liàngmǎ Qiáo, where a bottleneck of top-end hotels and department stores converge. Cháoyáng also contains the Jianguomenwai embassy area, its associated restaurants and hotels and the grid-like pattern of roads of the Sānlǐtún embassy district. Most travellers find themselves coming to Cháoyáng at night for its excellent nightlife, leaving other districts of Běijīng for daylight exploration. Note that Cháoyáng is far bigger than our map suggests and extends north to the Bird's Nest, Water Cube and Olympic Forest Park and beyond. However, for the purposes of this book we have focused the map on one section of the neighbourhood.

NEIGHBOURHOODS CHÁOYÁNG

DONGYUE TEMPLE Map pp110–11

东岳庙 Dōngyuè Miào

☎ 6553 4148; 141 Chaoyangmenwai Dajie; adult Y10, with guide Y40; ☻ 8.30am-4.30pm Tue-Sun; Ⓜ Chaoyangmen

Dedicated to the Eastern Peak (Tài Shān) of China's five Taoist mountains, the morbid Taoist shrine of Dongyue Temple is an unsettling albeit fascinating experience. With its roots poking deep into the Yuan dynasty, what's above ground level has

been revived with care and investment. Dongyue Temple is an active place of worship where Taoist monks attend to a world entirely at odds with the surrounding glass and steel high-rises. Note the temple's fabulous *páifāng* (memorial archway) lying to the south, divorced from its shrine by the intervention of Chaoyangmenwai Dajie.

Stepping through the entrance pops you into a Taoist Hades, where tormented spirits reflect on their wrongdoing and

TRANSPORT: CHÁOYÁNG

Subway Line 2: Dongyue Temple is a 10-minute walk east of Chaoyangmen Station; Dongsishitiao is the closest subway stop to the bars and restaurants of Sānlǐtún – exit and hop on bus 115. Line 10: part of this line blazes through the eastern part of Cháoyáng: the most useful stations are Tuanjiehu (for Sānlǐtún and Chaoyang Park), Agricultural Exhibition Center (also for Sānlǐtún and Chaoyang Park), Liangmaqiao (for the Lufthansa Center) and Sanyuanqiao (for the Airport Express). Line 10 can also connect you with Line 1 at Guomao, Line 5 at Huixinxijie Nankou, the Airport Express and Line 13. Line 8: the Olympic Green and Olympic Sports Center Stations serve the Olympic sights; exit South Gate of Forest Park Station for the Olympic Forest Park. Line 8 intersects with Line 10 at Beitucheng.

Bus Double-decker bus 3 takes you from the Jingguang New World Hotel, past Tuanjiehu Park and the Agricultural Exhibition Center to the Lufthansa Center; bus 110 runs from Chaoyangmen Station along Chaoyangmenwai Dajie, past the Dongyue Temple and then north along Gongrentiyuchang Donglu via the Workers Stadium and up Xin Donglu; bus 115 runs east along Gongrentiyuchang Beilu from the Dongsishitiao subway stop to Sānlǐtún.

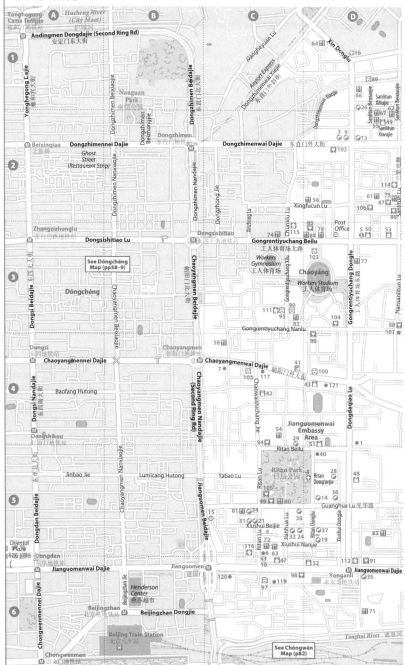

Yonghegong-
Lama Temple
雍和宫地铁站

Andingmen Dongdajie (Second Ring Rd)
安定门东大街

Hucheng River
(City Moat)
护城河

Xin Donglu
新东路

Airport Express

Aiangheyuan Lu

Dongzhimenwai Xiejie 东直门斜街

Sanlitun
Xilujie

Sanlitun
Beixiaojie

Sanlitun
Xiwujie

Yonghegong Cajie

Dongzhimen Beixiaojie

Dongzhimen Beidajie
东直门北大街

Dongzhimenwai Xiejie

Nanguan
Park
南馆公园

Beixinqiao
北新桥

Dongzhimennei Dajie

Dongzhimen Dajie 东直门内大街

Dongzhimen
东直门

Dongzhimenwai Dajie 东直门外大街

Ghost
Street
(Restaurant Strip)

Dongzhimen Nanxiaojie

Dongzhimen Nandajie

Dongzhimen Nandajie

Dongzhimen Beizhongjie

Xingfucun Lu

Zhangzizhonglu
张自忠路地铁站

Dongsishitiao Lu

Dongsishitiao
东四十条地铁站

Gongrentiyuchang Beilu
工人体育场北路

Post
Office

Dongsi Beidajie 东四北大街

See Dōngchéng
Map (pp58–9)

Chaoyangmen Beidajie

Workers
Gymnasium
工人体育场

Cháoyáng

Gongrentiyuchang Donglu

Dōngchéng

Workers Stadium
工人体育场

Gongrentiyuchang Zhonglu

Nansanlitun

Dongsi
东四地铁站

Chaoyangmennei Dajie

Chaoyangmen
朝阳门地铁站

Gongrentiyuchang Nanlu

Dongsi Nandajie

Baofang Hutong

Chaoyangmen Nandajie
(Second Ring Rd)

Chaoyangmenwai Dajie
朝阳门外大街

Dengshikou
灯市口地铁站

Jinbao Jie

Lumicang Hutong

Jianguomenwai
Embassy
Area

Dongdajie

Dongdan Beidajie

Chaoyangmen Nanxiaojie

Jianguomen Beidajie

Yabao Lu

Ritan Beilu

Ritan Park
日坛公园

Ritan
Dong'erjie

Ritan Lu

Guanghua Lu 光华路

Oriental
Plaza
东方广场

Dongdan
东单地铁站

Jianguomenwai Dajie

Jianguomen
建国门

Xiushui Beijie

Xiushui Nanjie

Xiushui Dongjie

Xiushui Dongjie

Chongwenmennei Dajie

Jianguomenwai Dajie

Yonganli
永安里地铁站

Jianguomenwai Dajie

Jingzhan Jie

Henderson
Center
恒基中心

Beijingzhan
北京站地铁站

Beijingzhan Dongjie

Beijing Train Station
北京火车站

Tonghui River 通惠河

Chongwenmen
崇文门地铁站

See Chóngwén
Map (p82)

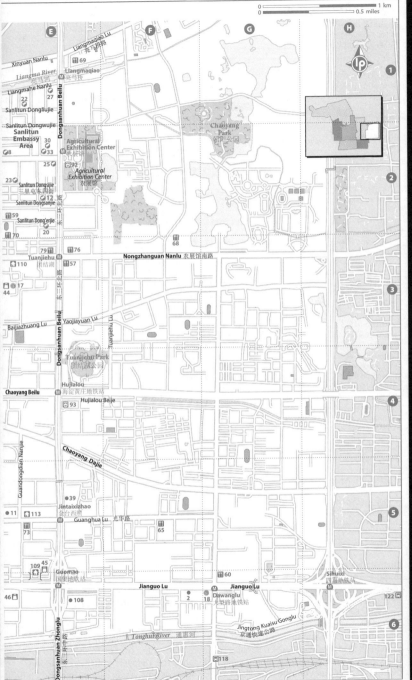

0 ———————— 1 km
0 ———————— 0.5 miles

Xinyuan Nanlu

Liangmaqiao Lu 亮马桥路

E 69

Liangma River 亮马河

Liangmaqiao 亮马桥

Liangmahe Nanlu 22 27

Sanlitun Dongliujie

Sanlitun Dongwujie

Sanlitun Embassy Area 30
8 33
25

23 Sanlitun Dongsijie 三里屯东四街

Sanlitun Dongsanjie 12

59 Sanlitun Dong'erjie

70 20

79 76

Tuanjiehu 团结湖 57

110

17 44

Baijiazhuang Beilu Yaojiayuan Lu

Tuanjiehu Park 团结湖公园

Hujialou

Chaoyang Beilu

Hujialou Beijie 93

Chaoyang Dajie

Guandongdian Nanjie

Jintaixizhao 金台西照 39

11 113

Guanghua Lu 光华路 65

73

109 45

Guomao 国贸

46 108

Jianguo Lu 63 60

2 Jianguo Lu

18 Dawanglu 大望路

Sihuixi 四惠西

122

Jingtong Kuaisu Gonglu 京通快速公路

Tonghui River 通惠河 118

Dongsanhuan Zhonglu

Dongsanhuan Beilu

Chaoyang Park 朝阳公园

Agricultural Exhibition Center 农展馆 92
Agricultural Exhibition Center 农展馆

Nongzhanguan Nanlu 农展馆南路 68

Grid references: E F G H 1 2 3 4 5 6

111

CHÁOYÁNG (pp110–1)

elusive atonement. You can muse on life's finalities in the Life and Death Department or the Final Indictment Department. Otherwise get spooked at the Department for Wandering Ghosts or the Department for Implementing 15 Kinds of Violent Death.

It's not all doom and gloom: the luckless can check in at the Department for Increasing Good Fortune and Longevity. Ornithologists will be birds of a feather with the Flying Birds Department, while the infirm can seek cures at the Deep-Rooted Disease Department. The Animal Department has colourful and lively fauna. English explanations detail department functions.

Other halls are no less fascinating. The huge Daiyue Hall (Dàiyuè Diàn) is consecrated to the God of Tàishān, who manages the 18 layers of hell. Visit during festival time, especially during the Chinese

CHÁOYÁNG (pp110–1)

New Year and the Mid-Autumn Festival
(p14), and you'll see the temple at its most
vibrant.

CCTV BUILDING Map pp110–11
央视大楼 Yāngshì Dàlóu
32 Dongsanhuan Zhonglu; 🚇 Jintaixizhao
The astonishingly complex 234m-high form
of the CCTV Building is probably central
Běijīng's most distinctive chunk of modern

architecture, if you can somehow ignore the
outlandish National Grand Theatre (p91). From
an engineering point of view, the CCTV
Building's construction – a continuous loop
running through horizontal and vertical
planes, creating a quite unique addition to
the Běijīng skyline – is boldly ambitious. Designed by Rem Koolhaas and Ole Scheeren
of OMA, the building is an audacious statement of modernity despite being dubbed

MONKEY OFFERS PEACH IN RITAN PARK

An excellent place for a breather from sightseeing, Ritan Park, Běijīng's former Altar to the Sun, is one of many altars where imperial sacrifices were performed. It's also a great place to immerse yourself in training with English-speaking *tàijíquán* (taichi) or *bāguà zhǎng* ('eight trigram palm') instructors who can introduce you to Monkey Offers Peach (designed to land a crippling blow to an opponent's neck) and other handy techniques. Mornings and evenings are good times to come and follow the movements of these ancient martial arts in a tranquil setting that inspires an affinity for Běijīng that weeks of sightseeing cannot. To find a teacher, check the classified pages under Martial Arts of free expat magazines the *Beijinger* (www.thebeijinger.com; p249) or *Time Out* (p249), call the Běijīng Milun School of Traditional Kung Fu (☎ 136 2113 3764; www.kungfuinchina.com), which gives lessons near the west gate of Ritan Park, or turn to the Martial Arts section (p199) in the Sports & Activities chapter. Most schools and teachers accept students at all levels, including total novices.

'Big Underpants' by Beijingers. Sadly, occupiers CCTV (China Central Television) are the very paragon of mediocrity, a state-controlled outfit with a passion for censorship. In February 2008, stray fireworks from CCTV's own Lantern Festival fireworks display sent the costly Television Cultural Center in the north of the complex up in flames, burning for five hours with spectacular ferocity. CCTV famously censored its own reporting of the huge conflagration (Běijīng netizens dryly noting that CCTV created one of the year's biggest stories only to not cover it). Along with the Beijing Mandarin Oriental, a visitor's centre and theatre were also destroyed in the blaze. Big Underpants escaped unsinged.

RITAN PARK Map pp110–11
日坛公园 **Rìtán Gōngyuán**
☎ 8563 5038; Ritan Lu; ☼ 6am–9pm;
◉ **Chaoyangmen**
Dating from 1530, this park in Běijīng's diplomatic quarter is one of Běijīng's oldest, established as an altar for ritual sacrifice to the sun. The square altar, typically surrounded by kite-flyers and children playing, is ringed by a circular wall, while the rest of the park is given over to pines and quietude. It's also an excellent place for a soirée, as there's a host of popular bars and restaurants within the park or on its fringes.

BIRD'S NEST & WATER CUBE
Map pp128–9
国家体育场、国家游泳中心 **Guójiā Tǐyùchǎng & Guójiā Yóuyǒng Zhōngxīn**
Bird's Nest Y50; ☼ 9am–5.30pm; Water Cube Y30;
☼ 9am–6.30pm; ◉ **Olympic Sports Center**
After the event, walking around the Olympic Sports Center midweek is rather

like being stuck in a district of Brazilia or a soul-destroying intersection in *Gattica* or *Alphaville*. Traffic lights go red and there are no cars to stop; the green man flashes and there's no one to cross the brand-spanking-new roads. It's now hard to imagine that this was the scene of great sporting exultation in August 2008, but such is the fate of most Olympics projects. Squinting in the sun, guards in ill-fitting black combat gear point the occasional group of map-clutching tourists to the Water Cube and the signature National Stadium, which is more colloquially known as the Bird's Nest. Enter the Bird's Nest stadium in an attempt to recapture the euphoria of '08 and even ascend the medals podium (for a further Y200). Patrol the nearby Water Cube and recall Michael Phelps' astonishing haul of eight swimming golds. When all's said and done, however, the Olympic Sports Center has 'costly white elephant' written all over it (the Bird's Nest is largely unused and needs rebranding), a condition amplified by the grandiosity of the adjacent 'seven-star' Pangu Hotel.

OLYMPIC FOREST PARK Map pp128–9
奥林匹克森林公园 **Àolínpǐkè Sēnlín Gōngyuán**
admission free; ☼ 9am–5pm; ◉ **South Gate of Forest Park**
Dry as a pack of instant noodles and hay-coloured in winter, this humungous 680-hectare grassy expanse may seem like a blessed release from the concrete quagmire of the nearby Olympics sights, but it may be too colossal for its own good, unless you've the heart and lungs of a decathlete. The park is predictably washed over with therapeutic music of the 'harmonious society' variety, so the quasi-

military guards clad in black combat gear at the gate come as little surprise. The blurb is defiantly upbeat, though, intoning that the park is 'the ideal recreation place for the public'. In summer you can hop on a boat across the lake, which seethes with fat and well-fed fish, or hike along brick and concrete paths, or simply make a break for the hills. Considering the epic dimensions of the park, it's a great way to shed a kilo or two, but you may end up flagging down a passing electric buggy (Y20, 9am to 5pm) when your shuddering legs start folding at the knee.

CREATION ART GALLERY Map pp110-11
可创铭佳艺苑 Kěchuàng Míngjiā Yìyuàn
☎ 8561 7570; www.creationgallery.com.cn; cnr Ritan Donglu & Ritan Beilu; admission free; ☼ 10am-7pm Tue-Sun; ◉ Yonganli
This well-lit, intimate space off the northeast corner of Ritan Park presents an enjoyable array of paintings and sculptures, with a small area for sedentary contemplation of what's on view. Of the 20 or 30 artworks – many contemporary landscapes – several are composed by the gallery owner, Li Xiaoke. Prices start at around US$800.

XUĀNWǓ 宣武区

Shopping p151; Sleeping p214

Like Chōngwén, Xuānwǔ is part of the ancient Outer City, an historic district that belonged to the Chinese City, as distinct from the Tartar City to the north. Cleaved from the Inner City by the intervention of the Tartar City Wall, Xuānwǔ today is a low-key district that can make for an excellent base for exploring town. The northeast corner of Xuānwǔ nudges up against Qiánmén and Tiananmen Square and embraces the historic shopping streets of Dashilar and Liulichang.

Unlike Cháoyáng district, which existed outside the old city walls, Xuānwǔ is clearly incorporated into old maps of town. The district owes its name to the grand old gate of Xuānwǔ Mén (宣武门), sadly now demolished. Locals used to call it by its more nefarious nickname, the Gate of Punishment (刑门; Xíng Mén), as it rose up near the execution ground at Càishì Kǒu (菜市口).

As well as Xuānwǔ Mén and Hépíng Mén (和平门), Xuānwǔ has quite a few other vanished landmarks. The old West Train Station (西车站; Xī Chēzhàn) stood just to the west of Qiánmén, but is no more (the large Kentucky Fried Chicken outlet – China's first of over a thousand branches – stands roughly where it once was). The railway used to head west all the way along Qianmen Xidajie. A long river, running just south of the railway near the border between Xuānwǔ district and Xīchéng, is also marked on 1950s maps of Běijīng, but is no more. The river survives in some street names, such as Qianmen Xiheyan Jie (前门西河沿街) – literally Qianmen West River Bank St.

The historic area around Dashilar has seen considerable destruction over the past few years and Dashilar itself is reportedly due for a huge makeover to try to repeat the success of Nanluogu Xiang (p74). If so, the kind of shabby grittiness of the area will vanish; others say it's best to let these things occur by themselves, rather than forcing them. The long road of Meishi Jie was widened several years ago, leading to considerable destruction of surrounding *hútòng*.

Travellers will enjoy shopping along Dashilar (p151) and rummaging for curios in the stalls and shops of Liulichang (p151). The district around the Niujie Mosque is distinctive for its Huí (Chinese Muslim) character, while the recently restored shopping strech of Qianmen Dajie (p84) divides Xuānwǔ district from Chóngwén.

DASHILAR Map pp118-19

大栅栏 **Dàzhàlan**

🚇 Qianmen

Just west of Qianmen Dajie runs this historic shopping street; walking along Dashilar (Dàzhàlan) is a fascinating way to reach the antique shop street of Liulichang (p139). Standout shops with history include Ruifuxiang (p152), Tóngréntáng (p152), Neiliansheng Shoe Shop (p152) and Liubiju. The word is that Dashilar is to be converted in the vein of Nanluogu Xiang (p74); how successful this will be is open to question (considering that the sense of community along Qianmen Dajie has been destroyed in its revamp). For more information on Dashilar, see p151.

FAYUAN TEMPLE Map pp118-19

法源寺 **Fǎyuán Sì**

7 Fayuansi Qianjie; adult Y5; ⏰ 8.30-11am & 1.30-3.30pm Thu-Tue; 🚌 6 to Niu Jie or 10 to Libaisi stop

Infused with an air of reverence and devotion and set within an area of recently destroyed *hútòng*, this lovely temple originally dates back to the 7th century. Now the China Buddhism College, the active temple was originally built to honour Tang soldiers who had fallen during com-

TRANSPORT: XUĀNWǓ

Subway For Qianmen Dajie and Dashilar, get off at the Qianmen stop on Line 2. You can reach the South Cathedral at the Xuanwumen stop on Line 2. Get off at the Junshibowuguan stop on Line 1 for the Military Museum and the Muxidi stop for the Capital Museum. Line 4 (due to open late 2009) will connect with Line 1 at Xidan and with Line 2 at Xuanwumen, heading south to Beijing South Train Station.

Bus Bus 10 connects Niu Jie with Wangfujing Dajie, running through Tiananmen, Xidan and Changchun Jie.

HONG KONG SUPERSTAR SHOT DEAD (AGAIN) Damian Harper

'Andy Lau killed in Hong Kong!' bellows the newspaper vendor on Běijīng's Meishi Jie, and a small gaggle of pedestrians stops to read the news in the hot midday haze. The front page of the Chinese-language *Hainan News Journal* has a pensive photo of Andy Lau and graphic descriptions of how the heartthrob actor/crooner – star of *Infernal Affairs* and countless chart-topping Hong Kong hits – has been gunned down by gangsters in Kowloon. China's best-loved male superstar is dead, slaughtered by the Triads.

Most Běijīng folk ignore the newspaper and don't give it a second glance. Some *wàidìrén* – those from outside Běijīng – are keen to know more and hand over Y2 for a copy. They have been conned: Andy Lau has not been shot. Welcome to the world of fake Chinese newspapers.

Fake news is one of the latest manifestations of China's unrivalled ability to counterfeit all things. Fake sports goods, designer labels, luxury watches, bags, baby milk powder, DVDs, liquor and even fake Lonely Planet guides have all been peddled wholesale across China, but fabricating news stories for profit may seem like an original departure.

In fact, the newspapers have been sold for a few years to unsuspecting commuters by vendors near Běijīng's underground exits. The front page – without a date so any day will do for sales – grapples with Andy Lau's tragic murder on the night of his birthday party, while the first few inside pages detail miscellaneous celebrity gossip. The rest of the tabloid is bulked out with dated pages from another paper, so at first glance it looks and feels like a real newspaper.

Perhaps most incredibly, the story does not appear to change and the unfortunate Andy Lau has been repeatedly shot dead since at least 2006.

A nearby policeman appeared unmoved by the revelation. Scratching the back of his head under his cap, he explained that the vendors have been arrested before, but they just move on and start all over again. The only advice another policeman in front of Tiananmen Gate had was to 'avoid buying such papers again', before turning to the task of checking the bag of an old man who shuffled past.

The vendor was still there the next day with a huge pile of papers draped over his arm. 'Andy Lau shot dead!', he shouted. A mass of Běijīng folk walked past and ignored the man, but every now and then an out-of-towner was snared by the earth-shattering story, digging into his pocket for change and walking off with a copy of the fake news.

bat against the northern tribes. The temple follows the typical Buddhist layout, with drum and bell towers, but do hunt out the unusual copper-cast Buddha seated atop four further Buddhas, themselves ensconced atop a huge bulb of myriad effigies in the Pilu Hall (the fourth hall). Within the Guanyin Hall is a Ming-dynasty Thousand Hand and Thousand Eye Guanyin, while a huge supine Buddha reclines in the rear hall. From the entrance of Niujie Mosque, walk left 100m then turn left into the first *hútòng*. Follow the *hútòng* for about 10 minutes, and you'll arrive at Fayuan Temple.

NIUJIE MOSQUE Map pp118-19
牛街礼拜寺 Niújiē Lǐbài Sì
☎ 6353 2564; 88 Niu Jie; adult Y10, admission free for Muslims; ☷ 8am-sunset; ☒ 6 to Niu Jie or 10 to Libaisi stop

Dating back to the 10th century and lively with worshippers on Fridays, Běijīng's largest mosque was the burial site for several Islamic clerics. Surrounded by residential high-rises, the Chinese-styled mosque is pleasantly decorated with plants and flourishes of Arabic – look out for the main prayer hall (note that only Muslims can enter), women's quarters and the Building for Observing the Moon (望月楼; Wàngyuèlóu), from where the lunar calendar was calculated. Remember to dress appropriately for a mosque (no shorts or short skirts).

XIANNONG ALTAR & BEIJING ANCIENT ARCHITECTURE MUSEUM
Map pp118-19
先农坛、北京古代建筑博物馆 Xiānnóng Tán & Běijīng Gǔdài Jiànzhù Bówùguǎn
21 Dongjing Lu; admission Y15; ☷ 9am-4pm; ☒ Qianmen

Dating to 1420, this altar – to the west of the Temple of Heaven – was the site of solemn imperial ceremonies and sacrificial offerings. Glance at any pre-1949 map of Běijīng and you can gauge the massive

lonelyplanet.com

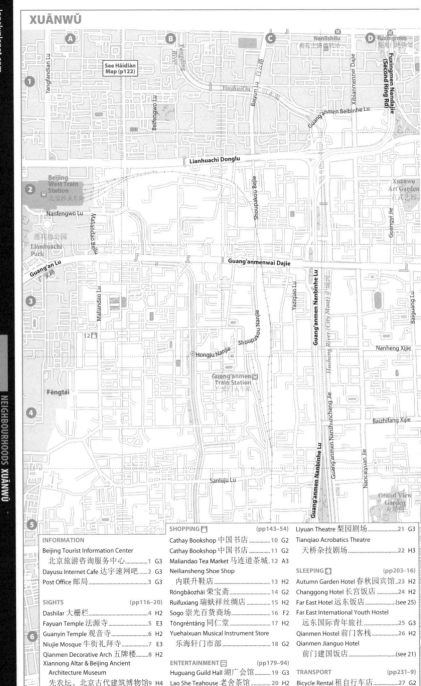

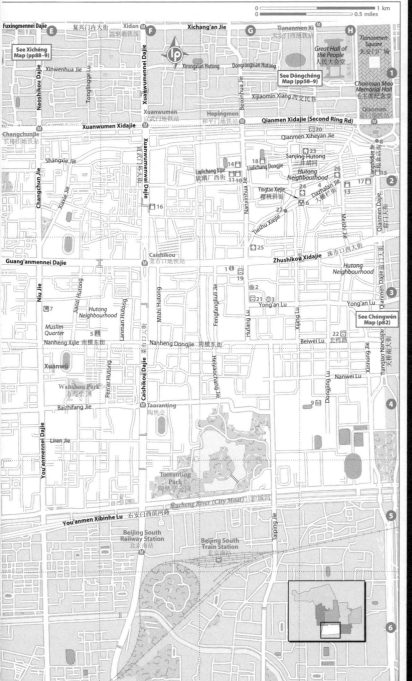

Fuxingmennei Dajie 复兴门内大街 **E** Xidan 西单 **F** Xichang'an Jie 西长安街 **G** Tiananmen Xi 天安门西地铁站 **H**

Tiananmen Square 天安门广场

See Xichéng Map (pp88–9)

Xinwenhua Jie 新文化街

Yirongxian Hutong

Dongrongxian Hutong

Great Hall of the People 人民大会堂

Chairman Mao Memorial Hall 毛主席纪念堂

Xijiaomin Xiang 西交民巷

See Dōngchéng Map (pp58–9)

Qianmen 前门地铁站

Xuanwumen 宣武门地铁站

Hepingmen 和平门地铁站

Qianmen Xidajie (Second Ring Rd)

1

Xuanwumen Xidajie

Changchunjie 长椿街地铁站

Qianmen Xiheyan Jie

Shangxie Jie

20

Sanjing Hutong 三井胡同

23

Xuanwumenwai Dajie

18 Liulichang Xijie 琉璃厂西街 **14**

Liulichang Dongjie 琉璃厂东街

Hutong Neighbourhood

26

17

2

11

10

Nanxinhua Jie

Yingtao Xiejie 樱桃斜街

Dazhalan Jie 大栅栏街

24

6

13

Xiajie Jie

16

Jieshu Xiejie 结束斜街

27

Meishi Jie

Qianmen Dajie 前门大街

Changchun Jie 长椿街

15

Guang'anmennei Dajie

Caishikou 菜市口地铁站

Zhushikou Xidajie 珠市口西大街

Hutong Neighbourhood

3

Niu Jie 牛街

7

Jiaozi Hutong

Hutong Neighbourhood

1

19

Yong'an Lu

Hutong

Yong'an Lu

See Chóngwén Map (p82)

Muslim Quarter

5

Lanman Hutong

Mishi Hutong

Caishikou Dajie 菜市口大街

Fengzangliulu

2

3

Yong'an Lu

Beiwei Lu 北纬路

22

Nanheng Xijie 南横东街

Nanheng Dongjie 南横东街

Heiyaochang Jie

Xinnong Jie

Xuānwǔ

Wanshou Park 万寿公园

Pen'er Hutong

Nanwei Lu

Beiwei Lu 北纬路

Mangqao Nandalie 天桥南大街

Baizhifang Jie

Taoranting 陶然亭

4

Liren Jie

9

Dongjing

You'anmen Dajie 右安门大街

Taoranting Park 陶然亭公园

Hucheng River (City Moat) 护城河

5

You'anmen Xibinhe Lu 右安门西滨河路

Taiping Jie

Beijing South Railway Station 北京南站

Beijing South Train Station 北京南站

6

NEIGHBOURHOODS XUĀNWŬ

119

THE GREAT PALL OF CHINA

Visible from space (and perhaps even the moon), the Great Pall of China may still become one of the nation's most enduring legacies. It is certainly one of the great challenges facing the current Běijīng leadership. In 2005 Běijīng was identified by the European Space Agency as having the world's highest levels of nitrogen dioxide, a pollutant that contributes to the city's famous haze.

It's all part of China's nationwide environmental emergency: cancer due to pollution has become China's leading cause of death, and air pollution is annually responsible for hundreds of thousands of deaths. Come winter, coal is liberally burnt in the capital, and spent cylindrical honeycomb briquettes of *fēngwōméi* (coal) lie heaped along *hútòng* in wintertime. The airborne miasma is, however, cyclical and you can spend a week in Běijīng without seeing much pollution, especially if there is wind; on bad days, however, visibility is much reduced as a curtain of thick haze descends over town.

Běijīng introduced a series of extreme measures to cut down on pollutants in the run-up to the 2008 Olympic Games and some of these initiatives (eg restricting car use on certain days) were kept in place after the games, generating more 'blue sky days', but Běijīng air quality remains dicey.

scale of the altar; today, many of its original structures survive, but what remains is a tranquil and little-visited constellation of relics. Located within what is called the Hall of Jupiter (太岁殿; Tàisuì Diàn) – the most magnificent surviving hall – is the excellent Běijīng Ancient Architecture Museum (⊙ 9am-4pm), which informatively narrates the elements of traditional Chinese building techniques. Brush up on your *dǒugǒng* brackets and *sǔnmǎo* joints, get the lowdown on Běijīng's courtyard houses, while eyeballing detailed models of standout temple halls and pagodas from across the land. There are English captions throughout the museum.

HĂIDIÀN 海淀区

Eating p177; Sleeping p215

Hăidiàn district occupies a huge, unruly mass of west and northwest Běijīng, an area noted for its historic and prestigious universities and the Zhōngguāncūn high-tech district, which has rapidly expanded over the past few decades in line with the frenzied development of the Chinese computer industry.

Hăidiàn sprawls unremittingly from the flat lands of the district just east of Xīchéng to the dramatic outline of the Western Hills (西山; Xī Shān), where you can discover excellent rambling territory. Not travellers' first port of call in Běijīng perhaps, but the district contains several notable temples, including the Indian-style Wǔtǎ Sì, a very distinctive Buddhist shrine just to the north of Beijing Zoo that abuts the district, and the outstanding collection of Buddhist effigies at the Wanshou Temple & Beijing Art Museum. You can also climb aboard a boat in summer and float all the way to the picturesque Summer Palace from the dock at Beijing Zoo, outside the Wanshou Temple & Beijing Art Museum or from Yuyuantan Park. The Military Museum is a handy primer to China's nationalist interpretations of its own history and the obsession Chinese have for their armed forces. Ironically, the museum stands only a kilometre or so to the west of Mùxīdì, where a major part of the People's Liberation Army's civilian bloodletting of 3 and 4 June 1989 took place. Otherwise, Hăidiàn also encloses the neighbourhood of Wǔdàokǒu, largely on the map for its glut of popular student-set bars and clubs.

WANSHOU TEMPLE & BEIJING ART MUSEUM Map p122
万寿寺、北京艺术博物馆
Wànshòu Sì & Běijīng Yìshù Bówùguǎn
Suzhou Jie; adult Y15; 9am-4pm;
 Gongzhufen, then 944

Ringed by a red wall on the southeastern corner of Suzhou Jie (off the Third Ring Rd), the Ming-dynasty Wanshou Temple was originally consecrated for the storage of Buddhist texts. The temple's name echoes the Summer Palace's Longevity Hill (Wànshòu Shān; p127); in fact, from Qing times the imperial entourage would put their feet up here and quaff tea en route to the palace. Wanshou Temple fell into disrepair during the Republic, with the Wanshou Hall burning down in 1937. Things went from bad to worse and during the Cultural Revolution the temple served as an army barracks.

The highlight of a visit to this restored temple is its prized collection of bronze Buddhist statuary in the 'Buddhist Art Exhibition of Ming and Qing Dynasties'. The displays guide you through the Buddhist pantheon with statues of Sakyamuni, Manjusri, Amitabha, Guanyin (in bronze and déhuà, or blanc-de-Chine porcelain) and exotic tantric pieces. Also look out for the kapala bowl made from a human skull, dorje and purbhas (Tibetan ritual daggers). Further halls are devoted to Ming and Qing porcelain. Also worth noting is the decidedly masculine-looking Guanyin at the rear of the Mahavira Hall (she is usually, but not exclusively, female). The pavilion at the rear once housed a 5m-high gold-lacquered brass statue now long gone; in its place is a miniature pagoda alloyed from gold, silver, zinc and lead. Some of China's holy mountains (including Pǔtuó Shān and Éméi Shān) in the form of small rockeries can also be found here.

WUTA TEMPLE Map p122
五塔寺 Wǔtǎ Sì
24 Wutasi Cun; adult Y20, audio guide Y5; 9am-4pm Tue-Sun; Xizhimen, then 104, 205 or 106

Known also as Zhenjue Temple (真觉寺; Zhēnjué Sì), the distinctive Indian-styled Wuta Temple (Five Pagoda Temple) is topped by its five magnificent namesake pagodas. The exterior of the main hall is

TRANSPORT: HĂIDIÀN

Subway Line 1 travels from Xizhimen to Dongzhimen in Dōngchéng, via several stops in Hăidiàn, including Wǔdàokǒu. Line 10 intersects with Line 13 at Zhichunlu and connects eastern and southeastern Běijīng with stations in Hăidiàn, including Bagou. The new Line 4 will connect with Line 2 at Xizhimen before running on to Beijing Zoo, the Old Summer Palace and the Summer Palace.

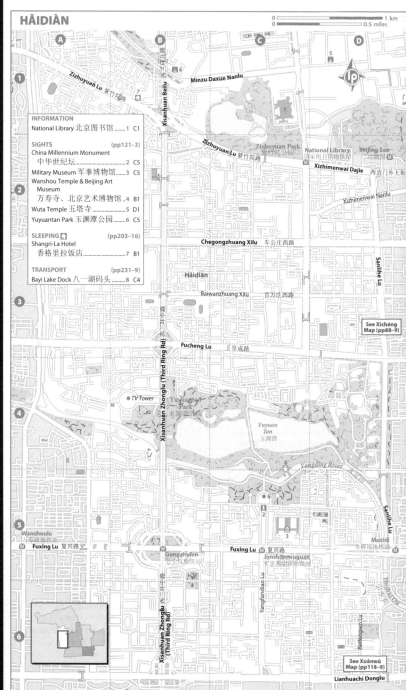

0 ———————— 1 km
0 ———————— 0.5 miles

INFORMATION
National Library 北京图书馆 1 C1

SIGHTS (pp121–3)
China Millennium Monument
中华世纪坛 2 C5
Military Museum 军事博物馆 3 C5
Wanshou Temple & Beijing Art
Museum
万寿寺、北京艺术博物馆 .. 4 B1
Wuta Temple 五塔寺 5 D1
Yuyuantan Park 玉渊潭公园 6 C5

SLEEPING (pp203–16)
Shangri-La Hotel
香格里拉饭店 7 B1

TRANSPORT (pp231–9)
Bayi Lake Dock 八一湖码头 8 C4

Zizhuyuan Lu 紫竹院路

Xisanhuan Beilu 西三环北路

Minzu Daxue Nanlu

Zizhuyuan Lu 紫竹院路

Zizhuyuan Park
紫竹院公园

National Library
国家图书馆地铁站

Beijing Zoo

Xizhimenwai Dajie 西直门外大街

Xizhimenwai Nanlu

Sanlihe Lu

Chegongzhuang Xilu 车公庄西路

See Xichéng
Map (pp88–9)

Hăidiàn

Baiwanzhuang Xilu 百万庄西路

Fucheng Lu 阜成路

Xisanhuan Zhonglu (Third Ring Rd) 西三环中路

● TV Tower

Yuyuantan
Park
玉渊潭公园

Yuyuan
Tan
玉渊潭

Yongding River

Wanshoulu
万寿路地铁站
Ⓜ **Fuxing Lu** 复兴路

Gongzhufen
公主坟地铁站

Fuxing Lu Ⓜ 复兴路

Junshibowuguan
军事博物馆地铁站

Muxidi
木樨地地铁站

Sanlihe Lu

Yangfandian

Xisanhuan Zhonglu
(Third Ring Rd)
西三环中路

Baibanyao

See Xuânwú
Map (pp118–9)

Lianhuachi Donglu

NEIGHBOURHOODS HĂIDIÀN

decorated with dorje, hundreds of images of Buddha and legions of beasts, amid traces of red pigment. Facing you as you climb the steps to the five pagodas – themselves carved with a galaxy of Buddhist images – are wall carvings of the feet of Buddha. During Ming times, the temple ranged to at least six halls, all later tiled in yellow during Qing times; the terrace where the Big Treasure Hall once stood can still be seen. The temple, dating from 1473, is reached by the canal bridge directly opposite the rear exit of Beijing Zoo; it also houses the Carved Stone Museum (Shíkē Bówùguǎn), with clusters of stone stelae, statues and *bìxì* – mythical tortoise-like dragons often seen in Confucian temples (see p71).

MILITARY MUSEUM Map p122
军事博物馆 Jūnshì Bówùguǎn
9 Fuxing Lu; adult Y20; ☽ **8am-5pm, last entry 4.30pm;** ⊚ **Junshibowuguan**
Military enthusiasts may get a rush at this hulking monolith of a building topped with a communist star. Cold War–era F-5 fighters, the much larger F-7 and F-8, tanks, and HQ-2 (Red Flag-2) surface-to-air missiles muster below, while upstairs bristles with more weaponry. For the full-on revolutionary version of China's wars, the Hall of Agrarian Revolutionary War and the Hall of the War to Resist US Aggression and Aid Korea is a tour de force of communist spin.

CHINA MILLENNIUM MONUMENT
Map p122
中华世纪坛 Zhōnghuá Shìjì Tán
9a Fuxing Lu; admission Y30; ☽ **8.30am-5.30pm;** ⊚ **Junshibowuguan**
Vaguely resembling a vast sundial pointing directly south to Beijing West Train Station, this cumbersome monument solidifies Běijīng's triumphant 21st-century aspirations in stone. For such a momentous statement, the design is devoid of imagination or artistry, while examination of the stone cladding shows it already requires repair. The art gallery, however, is worth perusing (included in the ticket price) and you can pick up boats from the dock (世纪坛码头; Shìjìtán Mǎtou; adult one way Y70) to the Summer Palace, leaving daily at 10am, 11am, 2pm and 5pm, or go for a stroll in Yuyuantan Park (Yùyuāntán Gōngyuán; Map p122; admission Y2) to the north, where you can also board boats (one way/return Y60/80; departing at 10.10am, 11.10am, 2.10pm and 3.10pm) to the Summer Palace from the Bayi Lake dock (Bāyī Hú Mǎtou; Map p122).

WŬDÀOKŎU 五道口

Eating p177; Shopping p152

A chunk of Hǎidiàn district in northwest Běijīng, Wǔdàokǒu is a vibrant and thriving student hang-out with an out-and-out concentration of top-tier universities and colleges. The Chinese equivalents of Oxford and Cambridge, China's two premier institutions of higher learning – Peking University and Qinghua University – can be found here, along with a prestigious gathering of other specialist colleges. Responsible for churning out the cream of Běijīng's political bigwigs, bankers, financiers, linguists, aeronautical specialists and experts in other fields, this is a young area.

The name Wǔdàokǒu ('Five Rail Crossings') only goes back around a hundred years, signifying the rail intersections on the Jingzhang Railway Line that runs through it – the first ever railway designed and constructed by the Chinese. The railway attracted an influx of residents to the once-neglected district, and the local population, once very thin on the ground, began to swell. The neighbourhood only really crept onto the *lǎowài* (foreigner) tourists' radars when Sānlǐtún (p183) dropped a few pegs after the southern section was bulldozed and bar proprietors were sent packing. The exodus of Sānlǐtún bartenders, the emergence of other bar districts (such as Hòuhǎi and Nanluogu Xiang; p74) and a simultaneous interest in Wǔdàokǒu's thirsty student population prompted a mushrooming bar scene, bringing splashes of neon and live music to the district.

Today Wǔdàokǒu is one of the principal arms of Běijīng's ever-shifting drinking axis and bars are nine to the dozen. Low local-student incomes dictate reasonable bar prices, drawing in mobile crowds of budget drinkers from across town. Wǔdàokǒu is also well known for its Korean and Japanese populace, served by a plethora of Korean and Japanese restaurants (p177). You won't be tripping over many Ming relics or marvelling at much *hútòng* charm, but Wǔdàokǒu is pinched between the Old Summer Palace and the Yuan-Dynasty Walls Relics Park, while the Great Bell Temple is one of Běijīng's most notable Buddhist shrines. There's hardly classic sightseeing material here, but you're likely to find yourself pitching up in Wǔdàokǒu for its *shāokǎo* (barbecue) restaurants, cafes, bars, clubs and full-on student vibe.

GREAT BELL TEMPLE Map p125
大钟寺 Dàzhōng Sì
☎ 6255 0819; 31a Beisanhuan Xilu; adult Y10; ⏱ 8.30am-4.30pm; ⓜ Dazhongsi, 🚌 361, 367 or 422

Originally called Juesheng Temple, this famous shrine was once a pit stop for Qing emperors who came here to pray for rain. Today the temple is named after its massive Ming-dynasty bell: 6.75m tall and weighing a hefty 46.5 tonnes, the gargantuan bell is inscribed with Buddhist sutras, comprising more than 227,000 Chinese characters and decorated with Sanskrit incantations. The bell was cast during the reign of Emperor Yongle in 1406, with the tower built in 1733. To get the bell from the foundry to the temple, a shallow canal was dug, and when it froze over in winter, the bell was shunted across the ice by sled.

If you're bell crazy, you'll be spellbound by the exhibitions on bell casting, and the collection of bells from France, Russia, Japan, Korea and other nations. Also on view are copies of the bells and chimes of the Marquis of Zeng and a collection of Buddhist and Taoist bells, including vajra bells and the wind chimes hung from temple roofs and pagodas.

ARTHUR M SACKLER MUSEUM OF ART & ARCHAEOLOGY Map p125
赛克勒考古与艺术博物馆 Sàikèlè Kǎoguv Yǔ Yìshù Bówùguǎn
Peking University; admission Y5; ⏱ 9am to 4.30pm; ⓜ East Gate of Peking University

TRANSPORT: WŬDÀOKŎU

Subway Trains run along Line 13 of the Beijing underground (linking Dongzhimen and Xizhimen) through Wǔdàokǒu, stopping at Dazhongsi, Zhichun Lu and Wudaokou. Underground Line 10 also runs through the district, with stations at Xitucheng, Zhichun Lu, Zhichun Li and Haidian Huangzhuang. Several stations of underground Line 4 will be located in the west of the district when the line opens in 2009.

Bus Bus 331 links Wǔdàokǒu with the Old Summer Palace and the Summer Palace, the Beijing Botanic Gardens, the Sleeping Buddha Temple and Fragrant Hills Park. Bus 375 links Wǔdàokǒu with Xizhimen.

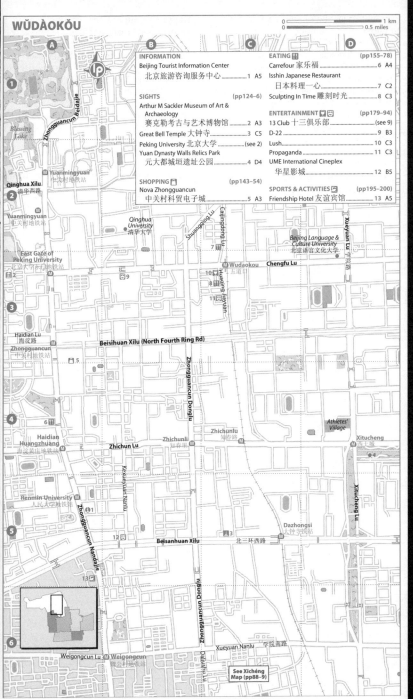

INFORMATION

Beijing Tourist Information Center
北京旅游咨询服务中心 1 A5

SIGHTS (pp124–6)

Arthur M Sackler Museum of Art &
Archaeology
赛克勒考古与艺术博物馆 2 A3
Great Bell Temple 大钟寺 3 C5
Peking University 北京大学 ....(see 2)
Yuan Dynasty Walls Relics Park
元大都城垣遗址公园 4 D4

SHOPPING (pp143–54)

Nova Zhongguancun
中关村科贸电子城 5 A3

EATING (pp155–78)

Carrefour 家乐福 6 A4
Isshin Japanese Restaurant
日本料理一心 7 C2
Sculpting In Time 雕刻时光 8 C3

ENTERTAINMENT (pp179–94)

13 Club 十三俱乐部 ....(see 9)
D-22 ....9 B3
Lush 10 C3
Propaganda 11 C3
UME International Cineplex
华星影城 12 B5

SPORTS & ACTIVITIES (pp195–200)

Friendship Hotel 友谊宾馆 13 A5

Excellent collection of relics collected together on the campus of Peking University (enter via west gate). Exhibits include the Jinniushan Man, a 280,000-year-old skeleton, bronze artefacts, jade pieces and a host of other relics from primordial China. Don't overlook wandering around the leafy university campus and tuning out from central Běijīng's frantic mayhem.

YUAN-DYNASTY WALLS RELICS PARK Map p125
元大都城垣遗址公园
Yuán Dàdū Chéngyuán Yízhǐ Gōngyuán
admission free; ⊛ **Xitucheng**

The name is rather an ambitious misnomer as there aren't many genuine Yuan-dynasty relics here, but this slender strip of parkland, running alongside the Little Moon River (Xiǎoyuè Hé), commemorates a strip of the long-vanished Mongol city wall that it is built upon. At 9km in length, this is Běijīng's longest parkland, beginning in Hǎidiàn district and charting a course east into Cháoyáng. The original wall was made of tamped earth, and not clad in brick like the later Ming- and Qing-dynasty city walls. It's a relaxing place for a stroll and you can check out the Beijing Hundred-Bird Garden (Běijīng Bǎiniǎo Yuán), a sanctuary for thousands of fowl.

Eating p178; Shopping p153; Sleeping p215

Greater Beijing describes the city's outlying regions sandwiched between the city proper and the colossal territory beyond that makes up the remaining rural Great Wall–studded sprawl of the municipality, investigated in the Excursions chapter (p218). Much of this region is in Hǎidiàn, which ranges off in a great cartographic splodge to the west and northwest, while large chunks of Cháoyáng – a similarly extensive district – extend off into the east and northeast. Transport begins to get sketchier and bus rides get longer in Greater Beijing – a prelude to the more epic journeys further out – so you may expect less traveller volume around here. Yet the region boasts some of Běijīng's premier sights and a completely different take on China's swiftly modernising capital. There's little of the flavour or charm of old central Běijīng, whose *hútòng* remit expires beyond the Second Ring Rd, but there's certainly no deficit of history. Temple hunters will have their hands full rummaging around in Fragrant Hills Park, the Sleeping Buddha Temple, shrine-studded Bādàchù, the Summer Palace and Fahai Temple. The ruined European buildings of the Old Summer Palace create a melancholic vignette of late-Qing-dynasty China, when the weakened nation lived under the constant threat of foreign incursion. The district undeniably reaches for its gold-plated trump card with the Summer Palace, an epic and beautiful swathe of imperial territory dedicated to ceremonial hubris and luxury. Greater Beijing is also where urban Běijīng's monotonous flatland begins to get dramatic comeuppance in the dramatic peaks to the west. The Western Hills create excellent rambling opportunities for travellers who simply can't handle another inch of level pavement and all-smothering traffic emissions. Both Fragrant Hills Park and Bādàchù offer invigorating uphill hikes in a wild and temple-rich setting; pack food and water and make a day of it. And art lovers won't feel short-changed: Běijīng's foremost constellation of art galleries, 798 Art District, in a converted East German–built factory district, puts the northeast firmly and squarely on the cultural map.

SUMMER PALACE Map pp128-9
颐和园 Yíhé Yuán

☎ 6288 1144; ticket Y20, through ticket Y50, audio guide Y40; ⏰ 8.30am-5pm; Ⓜ Wudaokou, then 🚌 375, or 332 from zoo; Ⓜ Xiyuan

The splendid regal encampment of the Summer Palace in the northwest of town is one of Běijīng's must-see sights. Once a playground for the imperial court fleeing the insufferable summer torpor of the Forbidden City, today the palace grounds, its temples, gardens, pavilions, lakes, bridges, gate-towers and corridors are a marvel of imperial landscaping. Despite its size, half of China may seem to be visiting the palace grounds with you, so shun weekends and especially China's 'Gold Week' holiday periods (p245).

The site had long been a royal garden and was considerably enlarged and embellished by Qing emperor Qianlong in the 18th century. Enlisting 100,000 labourers, he deepened and expanded Kunming Lake (Kūnmíng Hú) and reputedly surveyed imperial naval drills from a hilltop perch.

Anglo-French troops badly damaged the buildings during the Second Opium War in 1860. Empress Dowager Cixi began a refit in 1888 with money flagged for a modern navy, indulging herself with the extrava-

gant marble boat on the northern edge of the lake.

Foreign troops, victorious over the Boxers, again rampaged through the palace grounds in 1900, prompting further restoration work. The palace fell into disrepair during the years of the Republic, and a major overhaul began in 1949.

Three-quarters of the park is water – Kunming Lake – and the most notable structures are near the east gates and on Longevity Hill (Wànshòu Shān). The main building is the Hall of Benevolence & Longevity (Rénshòu Diàn) by the east gate; it houses a hardwood throne and is fronted by a courtyard decorated with bronze animals, including the mythical *qílín* (a hybrid animal that appeared on earth only at times of harmony).

Perennially seething with visitors, along the lake's northern shore stretches the Long Corridor (Cháng Láng), trimmed with paintings. The slopes and crest of Longevity Hill behind are decorated with temples and fantastic views await at the peak. Slung out uphill on a north–south axis are Buddhist Fragrance Pavilion (Fóxiāng Gé; admission Y10) and Cloud Dispelling Hall (Páiyún Diàn), which are connected by corridors. At the crest sits the Buddhist Temple of the Sea of Wisdom (Zhìhuì Hǎi),

GREATER BEIJING

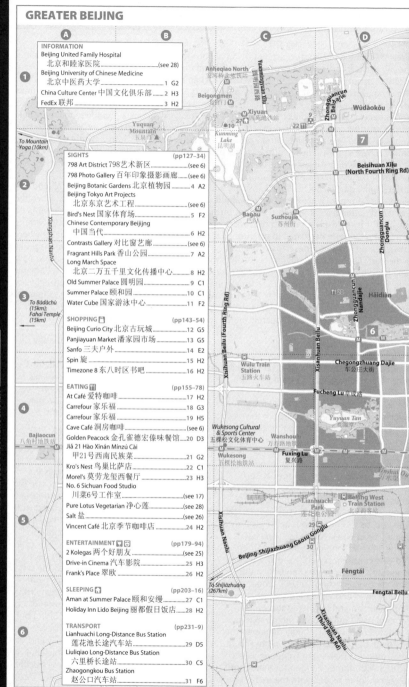

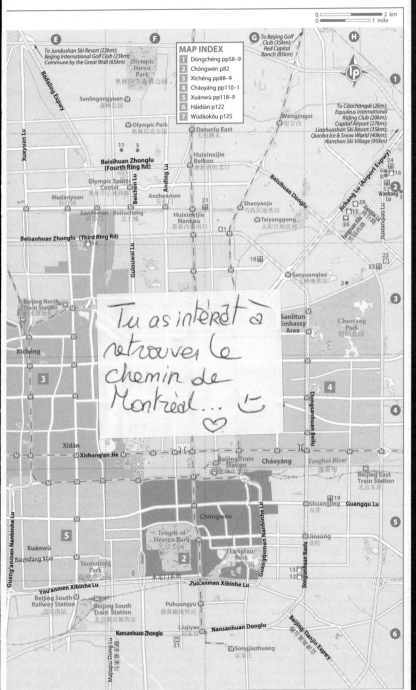

MAP INDEX
1 Dōngchéng pp58–9
2 Chóngwén p82
3 Xīchéng pp88–9
4 Cháoyáng pp110–1
5 Xuānwǔ pp118–9
6 Hǎidiàn p122
7 Wǔdàokǒu p125

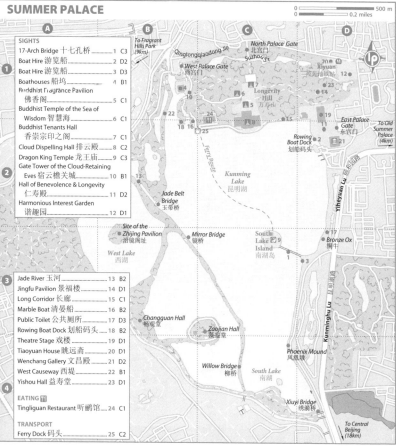

SUMMER PALACE

with glazed tiles depicting Buddha. Sadly, on many tiles Buddha's head has been obliterated. You can traverse Kunming Lake by boat (Y8; only in summer) to South Lake Island from the northern shore where Cixi's marble boat idles. North of her stone vessel stand some fine Qing boathouses and the Gate Tower of the Cloud-Retaining Eaves (Sùyúnyán Guānchéng), which once contained an ancient silver statue of Guanyu (the God of War), carted off by Anglo-French forces.

If you have time, do a circuit of the lake along the West Causeway (Xīdī) and then up the east shore (or in the other direction). It gets you away from the crowds, the views are gorgeous and it's a great cardiovascular workout. Based on the Su Causeway in Hángzhōu and lined with willow and mulberry trees, the causeway kicks off just west

of the Ming boathouses. With its delightful hump, the grey and white marble Jade Belt Bridge (Yùdài Qiáo) dates from the reign of emperor Qianlong and crosses the point where the Jade River (Yùhé) flows into the lake (when it flows).

The graceful 17-arch bridge spans 150m to South Lake Island (Nánhú Dǎo) from the eastern shore of the lake. Cixi visited the island's Dragon King Temple (Lóngwáng Miào) to beseech the temple's statue for rain in times of drought. Peek through the door to meet the gaze of the terrifying Dragon King himself. On clear days, photographers muster at sunset on the east shore of the lake for spectacular images of the sun disappearing over the hills.

Set in a clean and engaging pocket of reproduction Qing architecture, the Wenchang

Gallery (Wénchāng Yuàn; ☎ 6256 5886, ext 224; adult Y20; ✎ 8.30am-5pm) to the south of the entrance comprises a porcelain exhibition, a jade gallery and an unusual selection of Qing artefacts (including some of Cixi's calligraphy), plus some decent bronzes. In the north of the grounds is Suzhou Street (Sūzhōu Jiē; admission Y10) a fun diversion of riverside walkways, shops and eateries. Purchases are made with antique Chinese coins; exchange your renminbi at the top of the street.

Pedal boats are available from the dock (four-person boat Y40 per hour, six-person boat Y60 per hour, minimum one hour; from 8.30am to 4.30pm in summer) on the shore of Kunming Lake.

The Summer Palace is about 12km northwest of central Běijīng. The nearest light-rail station is Wudaokou (then take bus 331 or a taxi). The Summer Palace will be accessible by metro with the new Line 4. In summer, boats head along the canal, departing from the dock behind the Beijing Exhibition Center (Map pp88–9; ☎ 6823 2179, 6821 3366; one way/return incl Summer Palace admission Y45/75) near the zoo or from the dock behind the China Millennium Monument. Cycling (1½ to two hours) from the centre of town is feasible and taking the road following the Beijing–Miyun Diversion Canal is pleasant.

OLD SUMMER PALACE Map pp128-9
圆明园 Yuánmíng Yuán

☎ 6262 8501; 28 Qinghua Xilu; adult Y10, through ticket Y25, map Y6; ✎ 7am-7pm; ◉ Yuanmingyuan, ◉ Wudaokou, then ➔ 375 or 726, or minibus from Summer Palace

Located northwest of the city centre, the original Summer Palace was laid out in the 12th century. The ever-capable Jesuits were later employed by Emperor Qianlong to fashion European-style palaces for the gardens, incorporating elaborate fountains

and baroque statuary. During the Second Opium War, British and French troops torched and looted the palace, an event forever inscribed in Chinese history books as a nadir in China's humiliation by foreign powers. Most of the wooden palace buildings were burned down in the process and little remains, but the hardier Jesuit-designed European Palace buildings were made of stone, and a melancholic tangle of broken columns and marble chunks survives.

The subdued marble ruins of the Palace Buildings Scenic Area (Xīyánglóu Jǐngqū) can be mulled over in the Eternal Spring Garden (Chángchūn Yuán) in the northeast of the park, near the east gate. There were once more than 10 buildings here, designed by Giuseppe Castiglione and Michael Benoist. The buildings were only partially destroyed during the 1860 Anglo-French looting and the structures apparently remained usable for quite some time afterwards. However, the ruins were gradually picked over and carted away by local people all the way up to the 1970s (see boxed text, p20).

The Great Fountain Ruins (Dàshuǐfǎ) themselves are considered the best-preserved relics. Built in 1759, the main building was fronted by a lion-head fountain. Standing opposite is the Guānshuǐfǎ, five large stone screens embellished with European carvings of military flags, armour, swords and guns. The screens were discovered in the grounds of Peking University in the 1970s and later restored to their original positions. Just east of the Great Fountain Ruins stood a four-pillar archway, chunks of which remain.

West of the Great Fountain Ruins are the vestiges of the Haiyantang Reservoir (Hǎiyàntáng Xùshuǐchí Táijī), where the water for the impressive fountains was stored in a tower and huge water-lifting devices were employed. The metal reservoir was commonly called the Tin Sea

TRANSPORT: GREATER BEIJING

Subway Greater Beijing is increasingly well covered by the underground, and is served by Line 1, Line 5, Line 10, Line 13, the Batong Line, the Airport Express and Line 4 (when it opens in late 2009). Line 4 will be particularly useful for reaching the Summer Palace and the Old Summer Palace, previously an effort to reach by public transport.

Bus Greater Beijing is a huge area, so using buses alone to navigate its sights is a challenge. However, useful lines include bus 375 from Wudaokou Station to the Summer Palace, bus 332 from Beijing Zoo to the Old Summer Palace and the Summer Palace, bus 375 from Wudaokou Station to the Old Summer Palace, bus 331 from the Old Summer Palace to Fragrant Hills Park, bus 360 from Xizhimen to Fragrant Hills Park, and bus 958 or 389 from Pingguoyuan Station to Bādàchù. For the 798 Art District, hop on bus 909 from Dongzhimen.

OLD SUMMER PALACE

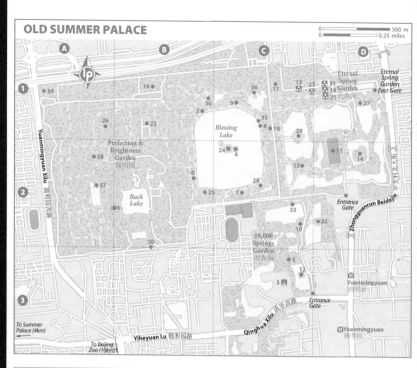

(Xīhǎi). Also known as the Water Clock, the Hǎiyàntáng, where 12 bronze human statues with animal heads jetted water for two hours in a 12-hour sequence, was constructed in 1759. The 12 animal heads from this apparatus ended up in collections abroad (see boxed text, p20) and Běijīng is attempting to retrieve them (four

of the animal heads can be seen at the Poly Art Museum, p75). Just west of here is the Fāngwàiguàn, a building turned into a mosque for an imperial concubine; an artful reproduction of a former labyrinth called the Garden of Yellow Flowers is also nearby.

The palace gardens cover a huge area – 2.5km from east to west – so be prepared for some walking. Besides the ruins, there's the western section, the Perfection & Brightness Garden (Yuánmíng Yuán) and in the southern compound, the 10,000 Springs Garden (Wànchūn Yuán). Electric buggies can whizz you around for Y5.

You can take some pleasant trips in the area by public transport. Take bus 332 from the zoo to both the old and new Summer Palaces; change to bus 333 for Fragrant Hills Park; from Fragrant Hills Park change to bus 360 to go directly back to Beijing Zoo.

Another route is to take the subway to Pingguoyuan (the last stop in the west), and from there take bus 318 to Fragrant Hills Park; change to bus 331 for the Summer Palace and then bus 332 for the zoo. When Line 4 of the Běijīng underground is completed, the Old Summer Palace will be accessible by train.

FRAGRANT HILLS PARK Map pp128-9
香山公园 Xiāng Shān Gōngyuán
☎ 6259 1283; adult Y10; ⏱ 8am-6pm; ⓖ Pingguoyuan, then 🚌 318, or 331 from Summer Palace, or 360 from Xizhimen (via Beijing Zoo)

Easily within striking distance of the Summer Palace are the Xī Shān (Western Hills), another former villa-resort of the emperors. The part of Xī Shān closest to Běijīng is known as Fragrant Hills (Xiāng Shān). Scramble up the slopes to the top of Incense-Burner Peak (Xiānglú Fēng), or take the chairlift (one way/return Y30/50; ⏱ 8.30am-5pm). From the peak you get an all-embracing view of the countryside, and you can leave the crowds behind by hiking further into the Western Hills. Beijingers flock here in autumn when the maple leaves saturate the hillsides in great splashes of red.

Near the north gate of Fragrant Hills Park is the excellent Azure Clouds Temple (Biyún Si; adult Y10; ⏱ 8am-5pm), which dates back to the Yuan dynasty. The Mountain Gate Hall contains two vast protective deities: Heng and Ha, beyond which is a small courtyard and the drum and bell towers, leading to a hall with a wonderful statue of Milefo – it's bronze, but coal-black with age. Only his big toe shines from numerous inquisitive fingers.

The Sun Yat-sen Memorial Hall contains a statue and a glass coffin donated by the USSR on the death of Mr Sun in 1925. At the very back is the marble Vajra Throne Pagoda, where Sun Yat-sen was interred after he died, before his body was moved to its final resting place in Nánjīng. The Hall of Arhats is well worth visiting; it contains 500 luóhàn statues, each crafted with an individual personality.

Southwest of the Azure Clouds Temple is the Tibetan-style Temple of Brilliance (Zhāo Miào), and not far away is a glazed-tile pagoda. Both survived visits by foreign troops intent on sacking the area in 1860 and 1900.

798 ART DISTRICT Map pp128-9
798 艺术新区 Yishù Xīnqū
☎ 6438 4862; 2 & 4 Jiuxianqiao Lu; admission free; ⏱ galleries 10am-6pm, some closed Mon, bars & bistros open longer; 🚌 403 or 909

A disused and converted electronics factory built by the East Germans, 798 Art District is Běijīng's leading concentration of contemporary art galleries. The industrial complex celebrates its proletarian roots in the communist heyday of the 1950s via retouched red Maoist slogans decorating gallery interiors and statues of burly, lantern-jawed workers. The voluminous factory workshops are ideally suited to art galleries that require space for multimedia installations and other ambitious projects. You could easily spend a day visiting the complex and its cafes and restaurants, making 798's noncentral inaccessibility less of an inconvenience and more of an opportunity for an outing. Some galleries are more innovative than others; there is challenging and cutting-edge work, but prepare also for hackneyed and technically unaccomplished material. Worth browsing are Long March Space (☎ 6438 7107; www.longmarchspace.com; ⏱ 11am-7pm Tue-Sun), with paintings, photos, installations and videos, and the well-known Chinese Contemporary Beijing (Zhōngguó Dāngdài; ☎ 8456 2421; www.chinesecontemporary.com; 4 Jiuxianqiao Lu; ⏱ 11am-7pm). Other worthwhile galleries include Contrasts Gallery (☎ 6432 1369; ⏱ 10am-6pm Tue-Sun) and Běijīng Tokyo Art Projects (Běijīng Dōngjīng Yishù Gōngchéng; ☎ 8457 3245; www.tokyo-gallery.com; 4 Jiuxianqiao Lu) – a huge space exhibiting conceptual art – and the excellent 798 Photo Gallery (Bǎinián Yinxiàng; ☎ 6438 1784; www.798photogallery.cn; 4 Jiuxianqiao Lu), with its intriguing prints from the Cultural Revolution and thematic photographic exhibitions. Timezone 8 (p154) is the place for art and design books. There are several cafes when your legs tire. Cave Café (Dòngfáng Kāfēi; ☎ 5978 9516) does a fine cuppa and has a unique diversion on its foyer wall – a hand-inscribed dedication from Lin

Biao, Mao's chosen successor who mysteriously died in a plane crash. A further extensive colony of art galleries can be found around 3km northeast of 798 Art District at Cáochǎngdi (草场地).

BEIJING BOTANIC GARDENS
Map pp128-9

北京植物园 Běijīng Zhíwùyuán

☎ 6259 1283; adult Y5; ⏰ 7am-5pm; ⓜ Pingguoyuan, then ☐ 318, or 331 from Summer Palace, or 360 from Xizhimen (via Beijing Zoo)

Exploding with blossom in spring, these well-tended gardens, set against the backdrop of the Western Hills and about 1km northeast of Fragrant Hills Park, make for a pleasant outing among bamboo fronds, pines, orchids, lilacs and China's most extensive botanic collection. Containing a rainforest house, the standout Beijing Botanical Gardens Conservatory (admission Y50; ⏰ 8.30am-4pm) bursts with 3000 different varieties of plants.

About a 15-minute walk from the front gate (follow the signs) within the grounds is Sleeping Buddha Temple (Wòfó Sì; adult Y5; ⏰ 8am-5pm). The temple, first built during the Tang dynasty, houses a huge reclining effigy of Sakyamuni weighing 54 tonnes; it's said to have 'enslaved 7000 people' in its casting. Sakyamuni is depicted on the cusp of death, before his entry into nirvana. On each side of Buddha are arrayed some sets of gargantuan shoes, gifts to Sakyamuni from various emperors in case he went for a stroll.

On the eastern side of the gardens is the Cao Xueqin Memorial (Cáo Xuěqín Jìniànguǎn; ☎ 6259 5904; 39 Zhengbaiqi; admission Y10; ⏰ 8.30am-4.15pm), where Cao Xueqin lived in his latter years. Cao (1715–63) is credited with penning the classic *Dream of the Red Mansions*, a vast and prolix family saga set in the Qing period. Making a small buzz in the west of the gardens is the little China Honey Bee Museum (☎ 8.30am-4.30pm Mar-Oct).

BĀDÀCHÙ off Map pp128-9
八大处

admission Y10; ⏰ 6am-6pm, later in summer; ☐ 622, 958 or 389

With a profusion of monks and pilgrims and named after the eight nunneries and monasteries scattered through its attractive wooded valleys, Bādàchù (Eight Great Sites) is an attractive and invigorating hilly area. Topped with a glittering golden spire, the 13-eaved green-tiled brick Lingguang

Temple Pagoda (Língguāng Sì Tǎ) is also called the Buddha's Tooth Relic Pagoda; it was built to house a sacred tooth accidentally discovered when the allied powers demolished the place in 1900.

Follow the path past the small Sanshan Nunnery (Sānshān Ān) to the Dabei Temple (大悲寺; Dàbēi Sì), famed for its 18 *arhats* in the Great Treasure Hall (Dàxióngbǎo Bǎodiàn), which were carved by Liu Yuan, a Yuan-dynasty sculptor. Made from a composite of sand and sandalwood, the effigies are over 700 years old. The hall itself is coated in slogans from the Cultural Revolution glorifying the supremacy of the Communist Party and commenting on how studying Marxism should not only be done from books but also by way of class struggle and in proximity to the workers and peasants etc etc.

Further slogans adorn the gate to Longquan Nunnery (龙泉庵; Lóngquán Ān); such additions perhaps survive as some of these temples have been less well restored than other sights in Běijīng. Peek into the Longwang Hall (Lóngwáng Táng), where the Dragon King sits with huge, round, black eyes.

The largest of all the temples is Xiangjie Temple (Xiāngjiè Sì). The mountain has plentiful apricot trees, which makes for some cheerful and sweet-smelling scenery around April when the trees briefly bloom. As with other sights, it is inadvisable to visit at weekends, which are busy. A cable car (Y20) exists for trips to the top of the hill and a toboggan (Y40) can sweep you down again. A fast way to reach Bādàchù is to take the underground to Pingguoyuan Station and then jump on bus 958 or 389.

FAHAI TEMPLE off Map pp128-9
法海寺

ⓜ Pingguoyuan, then taxi

The peaceful Fahai (Sea of the Law) Temple (Fǎhǎi Sì) on the western edge of Běijīng is unremarkable apart from the Ming-dynasty murals on the walls of the Mahavira Hall (Dàxióng Bǎodiàn). Painted in their original colours (a rarity in today's Běijīng), the frescos are shrouded in darkness to protect their 500-year-old pigments, so pack a torch (a mobile phone may work). A taxi to the temple from Pingguoyuan Station costs Y10. Fahai Temple can be tied in with a trip to Bādàchù. Not far away is the peaceful tomb of Tian Yi, a Ming-dynasty eunuch.

WALKING & CYCLING TOURS

Běijīng is thankfully as flat as a mah-jong table but walking around town can be an Olympic challenge, as unrelenting kilometres of pavement, shocking traffic manoeuvres, vehicle fumes, the stifling heat of summer or bone-chilling cold of winter drain the wind from your sails. The following walks are short and easy to manage, lassoing in some of Běijīng's most fascinating and charming central areas.

TIANANMEN SQUARE & FOREIGN LEGATION QUARTER WALK

1 Gate of Heavenly Peace From the stately Gate of Heavenly Peace (p67), pop across to the immense flatland of Tiananmen Square (p66) via the underground tunnel beneath Dongchang'an Jie.

2 Great Hall of the People To your west rises the communist pomp of the Great Hall of the People (p91), obscuring the extraterrestrial lines of the National Grand Theatre beyond.

3 Chairman Mao Memorial Hall Beyond the Monument to the People's Heroes (p73) sits the dumpy Chairman Mao Memorial Hall (p68), resting place of Mao Zedong. Walk to the east side of the square and if you're peckish, fortify yourself with Peking duck at Quanjude Roast Duck Restaurant (☎ 6512 2265; 44 Dongjiaomin Xiang; whole duck Y168; ☿ lunch & dinner).

4 Dongjiaomin Xiang Climb the 16 steps into Dongjiaomin Xiang (东交民巷; once known as Legation St) and the Foreign Legation Quarter (p74): the red-brick building next to the Tian'an Hotel at No 39 was the former French Hospital.

5 Legation Quarter (p74) Through a grey-brick archway stands this elegant quadrant of ash-grey legation architecture and sharp, modern glass lines, a zone of trendy and smart restaurants facing onto a grass quadrangle.

6 Dutch Legation Behind a wall a short walk east rises a green-roofed, orange-brick building at No 40, which was once the Dutch Legation (p75).

7 Beijing Police Museum Further along on your right stands a building with massive pillars, the erstwhile address of the First

WALK FACTS

Start Gate of Heavenly Peace
End Raffles Beijing Hotel, Wangfujing Dajie
Distance 2.5km
Time 2 hours
Fuel stop Quanjude Roast Duck Restaurant

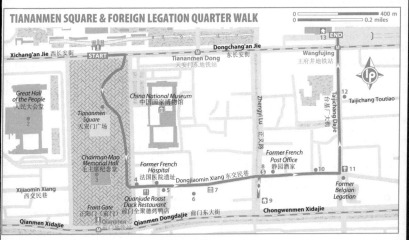

TIANANMEN SQUARE & FOREIGN LEGATION QUARTER WALK

National City Bank of New York (花旗银行; Huāqí Yínháng), now the riveting Beijing Police Museum (p76).

8 Yokohama Specie Bank Keep walking east to the domed building at 4a Zhengyi Lu on the corner of Zhengyi Lu (正义路) and Dongjiaomin Xiang, once the Yokohama Specie Bank. North on the right-hand side of Zhengyi Lu was the former Japanese Legation, opposite the old British Legation to the west.

9 Huafeng Hotel South down Zhengyi Lu near the corner with Qianmen Dongdajie is the Huafeng Hotel (5 Qianmen Dongdajie), once the Grand Hotel des Wagon-Lits (六国饭店; Liùguó Fàndiàn).

10 French Legation Backtrack along Dongjiaomin Xiang to the grey building at No 19, formerly the French post office, now Jingyuan Sichuan Restaurant, before reaching the former French Legation. The main gate, at No 15, is a large red entrance guarded by a pair of stone lions and impassive security guards. The Capital Hotel on the other side is built in the former German Legation.

11 St Michael's Church Backing onto a small school courtyard, the twin spires of the Gothic St Michael's Church (东交民巷天主教堂; Dongjiaominxiang Catholic Church) rise ahead at No 11, facing the green roofs and ornate red brickwork of the old Belgian Legation.

12 Rue Hart Stroll north along Taijichang Dajie and hunt down the brick street sign embedded in the northern wall of Taijichang Toutiao (台基厂头条), carved with the old name of the road, Rue Hart. Located along the north side of Rue Hart was the Austro-Hungarian Legation, south of which stood the Peking Club.

13 Raffles Beijing Hotel Reaching the north end of Taijichang Dajie, across busy Dongchang'an Jie is the Raffles Beijing Hotel (p206), in a building that dates to 1900.

WANGFUJING DAJIE TO THE FORBIDDEN CITY WALK

1 Oriental Plaza Facing north up Wangfujing Dajie, a short walk to your left is the Raffles Beijing Hotel (p206), while dazzling Oriental Plaza (p146), a gargantuan shopping mall spanning the entire block to Dongdan Beidajie, sparkles off to your east.

2 Wangfujing Snack Street Behind a colourful *páilou* is Wangfujing Snack Street (p169), a bustling melee of open-air food stalls, snack vendors, restaurants and thronging diners. Adventurous diners can opt for scorpions, seahorses or cicadas on a stick, or tuck into a starfish. Delve further along the street to scoop up souvenirs, collectables and odds and ends from alleyside vendors at the Haoyuan Market (p146).

3 Quanjude Roast Duck Restaurant Buried along Shuaifuyuan Hutong (帅府园胡同) is a popular branch of the celebrated Quanjude Roast Duck Restaurant (☎ 6525 3310; 9 Shuaifuyuan Hutong; whole roast duck Y168).

4 Dong An Plaza & Sundongan Plaza Further ahead on the east side of Wangfujing Dajie stretches the long shopping mass of Dong An Plaza and Sundongan Plaza, all the way to Jinyu Hutong (金鱼胡同; Goldfish Alley), typical of an old Běijīng alleyway that has been widened into a main road.

5 St Joseph's Church A short foray north along Wangfujing Dajie is rewarded by the abrupt appearance of St Joseph's Church (p76), with lovingly tended rose bushes along its flank.

6 Donghuamen Night Market Backtrack south and walk west along Dong'anmen Dajie (东安门大街) past the vocal stallholders of Donghuamen Night Market (p169) plying their snacks and culinary exotica from the four corners of China (from midafternoon onwards).

7 Imperial Wall Foundation Ruins Park At the junction of Dong'anmen Dajie and Donghuangchenggen Nanjie runs the thin strip of the Imperial Wall Foundation Ruins Park (皇城根遗址公园; Huáng Chéng Gēn Yízhǐ Gōngyuán; p79), following the course of the former Imperial City Wall all the way north to Di'anmen Dongdajie.

8 Dōngān Mén Cross the road and examine the pitiful remains of Dōngān Mén, the razed east gate of the Imperial City.

9 Courtyard Traverse the road and continue west along Donghuamen Dajie, past several traditional-style tea houses and gift shops.

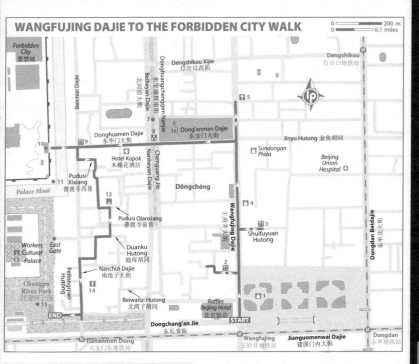

WANGFUJING DAJIE TO THE FORBIDDEN CITY WALK

WALK FACTS

Start Oriental Plaza
End Forbidden City
Distance 3.2km
Time 2 to 3 hours
Fuel stop Wangfujing Snack Street, Quanjude Roast Duck Restaurant, Donghuamen Night Market

Cross Beichizi Dajie and pop into Courtyard (p162), a restaurant hidden behind bamboo fronds, with a minimalist basement art gallery (p77).

10 Dōnghuá Mén Just west over the bridge that straddles the Forbidden City moat rises the twin-eaved Dōnghuá Mén, the east gate of the Forbidden City (p56). Note: you cannot enter the palace via this gate.

11 Decorative corner towers It's tempting to follow the delightful moat-side road to the Meridian Gate of the palace; on the way you'll pass one of the intricate decorative corner towers of the Forbidden City wall. The lethargic can take one of the buggies (Y1) that run from here to the Meridian Gate and back.

12 Pudu Temple Alternatively, head south down Nanchizi Dajie and take the first left into Pudusi Xixiang (普渡寺西巷; Pudu Temple West Alley), a restored *hútòng* with exclusive, red-painted *sìhéyuàn* doors. Follow the alley south till you reach Pudusi Qianxiang (普渡寺前巷), which heads east to Pudu Temple (普度寺; Pǔdù Sì), a charmingly restored temple. Continue due south along Pudusi Qianxiang for about 130m, then turn right onto Duanku Hutong (缎库胡同) or 'Satin Storehouse Alley'. Follow the *hútòng* to its end and find yourself once more on Nanchizi Dajie.

13 Supreme Temple With its graceful rooftops, regularly spaced trees and narrow *hútòng* openings, Nanchizi Dajie is thick with the flavours of traditional Běijīng. The yellow-tiled halls of the Supreme Temple lie splendidly just to the east in the Workers Cultural Palace (p72), which can be reached through the east gate that's on the other side of the road.

14 Imperial Archives Further down the road are the historic Imperial Archives (p72). The small *hútòng* opening just opposite the south

137

gate of the Imperial Archives opens onto the splendidly named Feilongqiao Hutong (飞龙桥胡同; Flying Dragon Bridge Alley).

15 Forbidden City Running east and west along Dongchang'an Jie are pleasant walks along delightful Changpu River Park (菖莆河公园; Chāngpú Hé Gōngyuán), leading to the imperial palace.

QIANHAI LAKE TO NANLUOGU XIANG

1 Beihai Park This walk is best undertaken after visiting Beihai Park (p87).

2 Lotus Lane Exit the park from the north gate to cross Di'anmen Xidajie (地安门西大街) to Lotus Lane (天荷坊; Tiānhé Fāng), running along Qianhai Xiyan (前海西沿) skirting the western shore of Qianhai Lake. Take your pick from one of the waterfront restaurants or cafes. Walking north, exit Lotus Lane onto Qianhai Beiyan (前海北沿).

3 Houhai Lake Continue along Qianhai Beiyan to a long concentration of bars and cafes wrapping around Houhai Lake's southern shore to the north. A shorter strip of bars faces you along Houhai Beiyan (后海北沿), while further bars and restaurants cluster in pockets elsewhere around the lake. There are boats that can be hired at several spots in the area.

4 Silver Ingot Bridge Cross Silver Ingot Bridge and hang a right onto Yandai Xiejie

(烟袋斜街) – a narrow jumble of shops, bars and cafes that have quickly dislodged the dilapidated businesses that once operated here.

5 Guangfuguan Taoist Temple The ancient Guangfuguan Taoist Temple is on your left at Nos 37 and 51 as you walk east along Yandai Xijie – look out for the rounded archway. The alley is a snapshot of the new Běijīng economy, with Tibetan and ethnic jewellery shops and cafes cheek by jowl with dazed-looking local residents. A branch of Plastered T-Shirts (p147) is at No 9.

6 Drum Tower Exit onto the bustling Di'anmenwai Dajie to find Drum Tower (p74) rising massively northwards, obscuring the Bell Tower (p73) behind; both worth a visit. For a breather and premier views, the rooftop terrace of the Drum & Bell (p181) bar is romantically slung between the namesake towers.

7 Huangwa God of Wealth Temple Walk east along Gulou Dongdajie for around 600m to this small temple sitting just north of the opening to Běijīng's most famous alley: Nanluogu Xiang (p74).

WALK FACTS

Start Beihai Park
End Nanluogu Xiang
Distance 3.5km
Time 2 hours
Fuel stop Drum & Bell

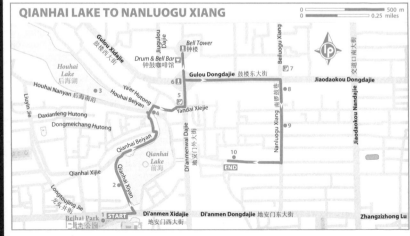

QIANHAI LAKE TO NANLUOGU XIANG

8 Nanluogu Xiang Head due south down this fantastic alley, crowded with shops, cafes, bars, restaurants and all the vibrant paraphernalia of a revitalised *hútòng* world.

9 Maoist Slogan Track down Plastered T-Shirts (p147) at No 61 and size up the grey-brick wall opposite, where a slogan from the Cultural Revolution has been exposed (see boxed text, p75).

10 Mao'er Hutong Further down Nanluogu Xiang is Mao'er Hutong, one of Běijīng's most historic alleys. Take time to explore this lane and any of the other *hútòng* that fork off east and west from the main drag – they are stuffed with some of the city's most archetypal scenes.

QIANMEN TO LIULICHANG WALK

1 Qian Men Railway Station Building Set to open as the Beijing Railway Museum at the time of writing, the old station building distinctively stands to the east of the imposing Zhengyang Gate Arrow Tower, itself immediately south of Zhengyang Gate and Tiananmen Square.

2 Qianmen Decorative Arch Walk south to the rebuilt Five-Bay Decorative Arch (Wǔpáilóu) an ornamental arch that was originally felled in the 1950s and was reconstructed prior to the Olympic Games in 2008.

3 Qianmen Dajie Emblazoned in green, gold, red and blue, the arch stands at the head of Qianmen Dajie (p84), a street completely revamped in the style of old Peking and decorated with birdcages and drums. If you want, hop on a tram in a straight line all the way down to Zhushi Kou (珠市口).

4 Restored Old Shop Buildings Take time to look at some of the renovated old shops along Qianmen Dajie. The buildings at No 3 and No 12 have both been restored; the overdone exterior of the Quanjude Roast Duck Restaurant (p170) stands next to an impressive building at No 34, ornamented with three bas-relief maps of the world.

5 Dashilar Turn right through the metal arch onto Dashilar (p116), where the complexion of the area immediately changes to something

shabbier and busier; it's a riot of colour and noise, although plans to prettify the street are in the pipeline. Down the first alley on the left is Liubiju, a traditional Běijīng *lǎozìhào* (old, established shop) famous for its pickled condiments.

6 Ruifuxiang Push on through the crowds a bit further and on your right at No 5 is Ruifuxiang (p152), a famous old Běijīng silk store dating to 1893. Pop in and look at the entrance hall, in grey brickwork and carved decorative flourishes. Further ahead is a historic branch of Tóngréntáng (p152), the celebrated Chinese pharmacy.

7 Guanyin Temple St (Guanyinsi Jie) This rather threadbare street, named after the small and now anonymous Guanyin Temple,

WALK FACTS

Start Qian Men Railway Station Building
End Liulichang Xijie
Distance 2.5km
Time 1 hour
Fuel stop Quanjude Roast Duck Restaurant

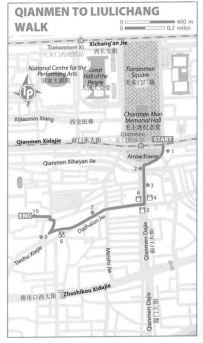

commences on the other side of Meishi Jie, a *hútòng* that was widened several years ago, resulting in the loss of many historical buildings. The official name of Guanyin Temple St street is Dashilan Xijie.

8 Guanyin Temple If you're peckish, stop at any of the vendors of noodles, pancakes, corn cakes or stinky tofu, then turn right at the fork with Yingtao Xiejie (櫻桃斜街) to find the small Guanyin Temple (Nos 6 to 8 Yingtao Xiejie) on the left opposite the Changgong Hotel (p215). There are plans to restore the temple halls – standing in a row with grass sprouting from their roofs – to their former function.

9 Cultural Revolution Slogan Continue along Yingtao Xiejie past the narrow and pinched Taitou Xiang (抬头巷; Raise Head Alley) for around 100m and examine the house at 27 Yingtao Xiejie. Once belonging to an official and then an opera singer, the wall of the building is still daubed with a largely indecipherable slogan, although the half-vanished red characters 'Long Live the Revolution' (革命万岁) can be seen.

10 Liulichang Dongjie Loop round to the right and continue along Yingtao Xiejie (also called Yingtao Hutong) and at the end turn sharp left and the road will bend round to Liulichang Dongjie (p151). Browse at will among the shops selling calligraphy brushes, paintings, antiques and knickknacks from the Cultural Revolution and continue on to Liulichang Xijie further ahead.

BĚIJĪNG BIKE RIDE

Běijīng's sprawling distances and scattered sights can make for blistering sightseeing on foot, but voyaging the city's streets and alleyways by bike allows you to take it all in at just the right velocity. Hop on a pair of wheels (p234), get that bell jangling and tour past some of the city's finest monuments and rarely visited off-the-beaten-track spots. Many of Běijīng's *hútòng* have red-painted signs in Pinyin and Chinese characters, so following the route should not be too difficult, but *hútòng* names (and other sights) have been added in Chinese characters below to aid navigation.

1 Southeast Corner Watchtower Pedal off from Dōnghuá Mén (东华门), the Forbidden City's east gate (exit only, no admission). Cycle south between the moat and the palace

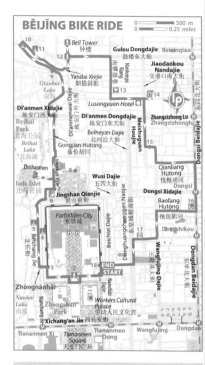

BĚIJĪNG BIKE RIDE

0 ___ 500 m
0 ___ 0.25 miles

BIKE RIDE FACTS

Start Southeast Corner Watchtower
End Dōnghuá Mén
Distance 11km
Time 2 to 3 hours
Fuel stop Passby Bar

walls and admire the Southeast Corner Watchtower (p86). Defending the palace, the 10m-high walls are assembled from 12 million bricks with a highly elaborate three-eaved tower (角楼; *jiǎolóu*) at each corner.

2 Meridian Gate The journey around the moat is one of Běijīng's most stunning, whatever the season. At the large gate of Quezuo Men (阙左门), you may have to dismount, but you can wheel your bike through and past Meridian Gate (午门; Wǔ Mén; p62), the dwarfing three-gated 'n'-shaped entrance to the palace. Prepare for a swarm of tour guides and phalanxes of Cantonese tourists.

3 Xīhuá Mén Traversing the busy courtyard, take your bike through the gate of Queyou Men (阙右门) to continue along the moat.

Reaching Xīhuá Mén (西华门; no admission or exit), the palace's West Gate, look directly west along Xihuamen Dajie (西华门大街) and all the way to the eastern gates of Zhōngnánhǎi, the out-of-bounds nerve centre of Běijīng's political power.

4 Fuyou Temple Cycle north onto Beichang Jie (北长街) past Fuyou Temple (福佑寺; Fúyòu Sì), locked away to your right behind the palace wall. Dating to the start of the Qing dynasty, the temple once served as a Lama temple and was also called the Rain God Temple (Yǔshén Miào).

5 Wanshouxinglong Temple Further north at No 39 on your left are the crumbling remains of the Wanshouxinglong Temple (万寿兴隆寺; Wànshòuxīnglóng Sì). Its band of monks long gone and now occupied by Běijīng residents, the former Qing-dynasty temple served as the residence for surviving imperial eunuchs after 1949.

6 Dagaoxuan Temple Reaching the T-junction with Jingshan Qianjie (景山前街) and Wenjin Jie (文津街), bear right onto Jingshan Qianjie and push your bike across the zebra crossing to the other side of the road. A short distance east at No 23 Jingshan Xijie (景山西街) are the remains of the vast Taoist Dagaoxuan Temple (大高玄殿). Dating to 1542, the temple is now a restricted zone and cannot be entered.

7 Dagaoxuan Temple Rear Hall Backtrack west to the slender opening of Dashizuo Hutong (大石作胡同; Big Stonemason's Alley), which wiggles north. Follow the alley – where the stone for the Forbidden City was carved – as it bends right, then left. As you exit, spot the Dagaoxuan Temple to your right; a graceful cylindrical building capped with a gold-knob-topped, blue-tiled umbrella roof, the rear hall is visible through the gate around the corner at No 21 Jingshan Xijie (entry not allowed).

8 Jingshan Park If you head west along Zhishanmen Jie (陟山门街) you will find the east gate to Beihai Park (p87), while to your east is the west gate of Jingshan Park (p92). Park your bike if you want and clamber up the hill for unparalleled views over the Forbidden City.

9 Yinding Bridge Cycle north along Jingshan Xijie and at the northern tip of the street head up Gongjian Hutong (恭俭胡同); its entrance

is virtually straight ahead of you. You will exit the alley on Di'anmen Xidajie (地安门西大街). Beihai Park can also be accessed here through the north gate, a short distance to your west. Push your bike over the zebra crossing and cycle north along Qianhai Nanyan (前海南沿) on the east shore of Qianhai Lake. Pass quaint Yinding Bridge (银锭桥) to your west.

10 Dazanglonghua Temple Continue up along Houhai Beiyan (后海北沿) past a strip of bars until you reach the small Dazanglonghua Temple (大藏龙华寺) at No 23, a modest temple dating from 1719 and now a kindergarten. The lakes here are called Shíchàhǎi (literally 'Ten Buddhist Temple Lakes'). If you reach the rebuilt Sea-Overlooking Pavilion (望海楼; Wànghǎi Lóu), you have overshot.

11 Guanghua Temple Take the first right about 10m after the Dazanglonghua Temple and work your way through this minute, 1.5m-wide alley, which leads to Ya'er Hutong (鸦儿胡同). Turn right onto Ya'er Hutong and cycle back in the direction of Silver Ingot Bridge, passing the Buddhist Guanghua Temple (广化寺) on the way.

12 Drum Tower & Bell Tower At the end of Ya'er Hutong you will meet Yandai Xiejie (烟袋斜街; Pipe Cross-St), with Silver Ingot

top picks

IT'S FREE

Poorly off in Peking? The following are complimentary:

- Chairman Mao Memorial Hall (p68) Costs not a single *máo* to see Mao.
- Tiananmen Square (p66) The square is on the house.
- 798 Art District (p133) Totally free (but only serious skinflints will actually walk there).
- Hútòng (p46) One of the best ways to walk your shoes off in Běijīng.
- Wangfujing Dajie (p145) You don't have to buy anything wandering along Wangfujing Dajie.
- Ming City Wall Ruins Park (p85) One of the city's most priceless remains – at zero cost.
- Bike riding (opposite) OK, so the bicycle won't come free, but the views will.
- Shopping Arcade, Peninsula Beijing Hotel (p146) One of the quietest places in town (just don't open your wallet).

Bridge to your right. Cycle along Yandai Xie-jie – stuffed with name *chop* vendors, Tibetan silver trinket sellers, bars and cafes – and exit onto Di'anmenwai Dajie (地安门外大街). Head north towards the Drum Tower (p74) and the Bell Tower (p73) before heading east along Gulou Dongdajie (鼓楼东大街).

13 Passby Bar After cycling about 600m along Gulou Dongdajie, turn right and immediately duck into Nanluogu Xiang (南锣鼓巷; p74), a splendid north–south alley in a constant state of renovation and with wi-fi bars, cafes and trinket shops, and a healthy crop of fully restored *sìhéyuàn*. If you want to rest your feet, take in a coffee in relaxed, snug surrounds by popping into the Passby Bar (p181), delightfully installed in an old courtyard home.

14 Wen Tianxiang Temple Take the first left just beyond the Passby Bar, and cycle along Banchang Hutong (板厂胡同), a charming stretch of old *sìhéyuàn*. You'll pass Lusongyuan Hotel (p209) at No 22, an old courtyard house now serving as a hotel. As Banchang Hutong meets Jiaodaokou Nandajie (交道口南大街), take a small detour north and into the first *hútòng* on your right – Fuxue Hutong (府学胡同). A short way along on the left-hand side is the Wen Tianxiang Temple (文天祥祠; 63 Fuxue Hutong; adult Y10; 9am-5pm Tue-Sun), a shrine fronted by a huge *páilou*.

15 Dafosi Dongjie Head south along Jiaodaokou Nandajie, cross the junction with Di'anmen Dongdajie (地安门东大街) and continue south down Meishuguan Houjie (美术馆后街). Take the fourth street on your left and follow the promisingly named Dafosi Dongjie (大佛寺东街; Big Buddha Temple East St). Spot the residence on your left at No 6 with a

spirit wall (*yǐngbì*) facing the gate and a pair of stepping-on stones (*shàngmǎ shí*) by the door that the owner would have once used for clambering onto his horse. Follow the road as it turns the corner and heads south. The Big Buddha Temple in question was once located at No 76 Meishuguan Houjie. The temple was torn down during the Cultural Revolution.

16 Dongsi Mosque Turn east just before Dafosi Dongdajie opens onto Meishuguan Houjie and cycle along the courtyard-studded alley of Qianliang Hutong (钱粮胡同). Exiting Qianliang Hutong, go right onto Dongsi Beidajie (东四北大街), a lively stretch of shops and restaurants. Heading south, cross the intersection with Dongsi Xidajie (东四南大街) and continue along Dongsi Nandajie (东四南大街), to the Dongsi Mosque, one of Běijīng's few historic mosques, on your right. The guardians at the door may be fickle about admitting non-Muslims.

17 Lao She Museum Take the first right past the mosque into Baofang Hutong (报房胡同), at the end of which, turn left onto Wangfujing Dajie (王府井大街) and cycle past the Capital Theatre on your left.At the first main intersection, turn right onto Dengshikou Xijie (灯市口西街); if you haven't yet seen St Joseph's Church continue south along Wangfujing Dajie and then double back, looking out for the second *hútòng* on your right, which leads into Fengfu Hutong (丰富胡同), home of the Lao She Museum (p78) at No 19.

18 Dōnghuá Mén Continuing west, turn left onto Donghuangchenggen Nanjie (东皇城根南街) and at the next major right turn right onto Donghuamen Dajie, which returns you to Dōnghuá Mén, the east gate of the Forbidden City.

SHOPPING

top picks

SHOPPING

It's not just the Chinese government that dreams of the day when China becomes a genuine consumer economy, enabling it to become less dependent on exports. The prospect of 1.3 billion potential customers gets foreign companies drooling and is one of the reasons why they invest huge amounts of money in the country. But persuading the Chinese to spend, spend, spend is easier said than done. China is a nation of savers and people are careful with money. The high cost of education and health care, as well as the fact that most of the population still lacks the cash to splash out on fancy consumer items, means the Chinese tend to keep their money in their pockets.

Běijīng, though, is something of an exception to this. With much of the nation's wealth concentrated in the capital, shopping has become a favourite pastime of the rising middle class, especially the 20-somethings with white-collar jobs. Catering for them is an ever-growing selection of shops. They range from vast malls, which have sprung up across the city in recent years and are home to both local and Western brands, to department stores, markets, street-side vendors and itinerant hawkers.

There are several notable shopping districts offering all sorts of clothes and goods, including Wangfujing Dajie, Xidan Beidajie and Qiánmén (including Dashilar). More luxurious shopping areas can be found in Sānlǐtún and the CBD around Jianguomenwai Dajie. For visitors, Běijīng's most popular markets are the Silk Market (p149), Panjiayuan Market (p153), Hongqiao Market (p147) and Sanlitun Yashow Clothing Market (p149). There are many other specialist shops that sell everything from computers to fishing gear.

Souvenir hunters will not go home disappointed. Běijīng is a great place to pick up curios such as embroidered purses, paper cuttings, wooden and bronze Buddhas, paper lanterns and kites. Hit specialised shopping districts such as Liúlìchǎng and the area around Panjiayuan Market for Mao memorabilia, *chops* (carved name seals), brushes, inks, scrolls, handicrafts and antiques. Běijīng is also a good place to source silks, jade and pearls. And while home-grown contemporary fashion designers are still a rare breed, there are a few quality ones around.

Prices vary enormously. In the Western-style shopping malls you'll be paying much the same as you would in the West. But the city's markets and smaller vendors offer both bargains and the chance to test out your haggling skills – diehard shopaholics and the canny will love the experience. For the less choosy, there are fakes galore here, too (p150), and you won't have to travel far to encounter someone selling them. For pharmacies, see p247.

SHOPPING TIPS

Generally, shops in Běijīng open earlier than in the West and close later; they usually open between 8am and 8.30am and close between 9pm and 10pm. The opening hours of the shops listed in this chapter are included in each review. Open-air markets are generally open from dawn to around sunset, but might open later and close earlier.

Always remember that foreigners are likely to be quoted an inflated price for goods and services in Běijīng. Prices at department stores are generally fixed (although a 10% discount might be possible if you ask), but bargaining is very much standard practice elsewhere and vendors expect it. In markets such as Panjiayuan, Hongqiao and Sanlitun Yashow, haggling is essential. It's always best to bargain with a smile on your face. Remember: the point of the process is to achieve a

top picks

SHOPPING HAUNTS

- Wangfujing Dajie (opposite) Běijīng's showpiece shopping drag, east of the Forbidden City.
- Liulichang Xijie (p151) Curios and souvenirs in a quaint, old-style Běijīng street in Xuānwǔ district.
- Dashilar (p151) Bustling street of historic Qing dynasty–era shops not far from Tiananmen Square.
- Village (p151) Běijīng's mall of the moment in the heart of Sānlǐtún.
- Maliandao Tea Market (p152) All the tea in China can be found south of Beijing West Train Station.

mutually acceptable price, not to screw the vendor into the ground, and no stall holder is going to lose money, or face, just to get a ale. Unless you really want the item in question and can't find it anywhere else, simply walking away from the seller often results in a price reduction.

Most large department stores take credit cards, but make sure that your card type is accepted. Smaller stores might only take Chinese credit cards and markets deal in cash, so come with plenty of it. Large department stores and shopping malls will have ATMs that take international plastic.

It's worth noting that in many shops you can't pay for your goods at the counter where you find them. The salesperson will give you a ticket for your goods, you then go to a till and hand over your ticket and pay. The stamped ticket is then given back to you and you return to the salesperson, who takes the stamped ticket and hands you your purchase. It can be a tiresome, time-consuming process.

Many tourist shops can arrange shipping overseas, but it is always best to check the costs and charges with the vendor before proceeding.

DŌNGCHÉNG 东城

Locals, out-of-towners and tourists haunt Wangfujing Dajie, a prestigious, partly pedestrianised shopping street heading north just west of Oriental Plaza, which boasts a solid strip of stores selling midrange brands. For more eclectic clothes and gifts, the hútòng (alleyway) of Nanluogu Xiang is now home to a rash of small boutiques and jewellery stores, while nearby Gulou Dongdajie has become a popular place for young Beijingers to shop for vintage gear and skater fashion.

BEIJING ARTS & CRAFTS CENTRAL STORE

Map pp58-9   Art, Crafts & Jade

工艺美术服务部 Gōngyì Měishù Fúwùbù

☎ 6523 8747; 200 Wangfujing Dajie; 王府井大街200号; ⏰ 9.30am-9.30pm; ⑩ Wangfujing

It's a bit of a tourist trap, for both Chinese and Westerners, but this centrally located store (with a sign outside saying 'Artistic Mansion') does have a huge selection of potential purchases for anyone hunting for gifts or souvenirs. It's well known for its jade (with certificates of authenticity), deite, cloisonné vases, carpets and other

CLOTHING SIZES

Women's clothing

Aus/UK	8	10	12	14	16	18
Europe	36	38	40	42	44	46
Japan	5	7	9	11	13	15
USA	6	8	10	12	14	16

Women's shoes

Aus/USA	5	6	7	8	9	10
Europe	35	36	37	38	39	40
France	35	36	38	39	40	42
Japan	22	23	24	25	26	27
UK	3½	4½	5½	6½	7½	8½

Men's clothing

Aus	92	96	100	104	108	112
Europe	46	48	50	52	54	56
Japan	S		M	M		L
UK/USA	35	36	37	38	39	40

Men's shirts (collar sizes)

Aus/Japan	38	39	40	41	42	43
Europe	38	39	40	41	42	43
UK/USA	15	15½	16	16½	17	17½

Men's shoes

Aus/UK	7	8	9	10	11	12
Europe	41	42	43	44½	46	47
Japan	26	27	27½	28	29	30
USA	7½	8½	9½	10½	11½	12½

Measurements approximate only; try before you buy

Chinese arts and crafts. There's also jewellery (gold, silver, jade and pearl) on the first two floors. You'll find calligraphy, lacquerware, paintings, seals and woodcarvings on the 3rd floor. Head to the 4th floor for jade carvings.

FOREIGN LANGUAGES BOOKSTORE

Map pp58-9   Books

外文书店 Wàiwén Shūdiàn

☎ 6512 6911; 235 Wangfujing Dajie; 王府井大街235号; ⏰ 9.30am-9.30pm; ⑩ Wangfujing

You will find a reasonable selection of English-language novels (a range which seems to be improving all the time) here, as well as lots of nonfiction and art, architecture and design books. The kid's section is good and it stocks Lonely Planet guides. English-language books are on the ground floor; head upstairs for foreign languages. This is a good place to pick up maps of Běijīng (Y8).

JINGDEZHEN CERAMIC CITY

Map pp58-9   Ceramics

景德镇陶瓷城 Jǐngdézhèn Táocí Chéng

☎ 6512 4925/4867; www.jdtcc.com.cn; 277 Wangfujing Dajie; 王府井大街277号; ⏰ 10.30am-9pm; ◉ Wangfujing

Just off Wangfujing Dajie, displays of well-lit ceramics from the Jingdezhen kilns are spread over several floors here. Pieces are modern, but many works on view employ traditional decorative styles and glazes, such as dòucǎi (blue and white and coloured), fěncǎi (famille rose or 'soft colours') and qīnghuā (blue and white).

LU PING TRENDSETTERS

Map pp58-9   Clothing

北京贵人私服高级成衣定制 Běijīng Guìrén Sīfú Gāojí Chéngyī Dìngzhì

☎ 6402 6769; 198 Gulou Dongdajie; 鼓楼东大街198号; ⏰ 9.30am-5.30pm; ◉ Andingmen

Exquisite, hand-embroidered qípáo (traditional Chinese dresses) are the order of the day at this tiny shop. They're not cheap but the quality is superb and Lu Ping is one of the few Chinese designers who specialises in making them. The shop does traditional menswear. It's best to call ahead to arrange an appointment.

MEGA MEGA VINTAGE

Map pp58-9   Clothing

☎ 8404 5637; 241 Gulou Dongdajie; 鼓楼东大街241号; ⏰ 2-10pm; ◉ Andingmen

Gulou Dongdajie, which runs east of the Drum Tower, has been overrun with vintage clothing shops, many of which are more akin to second-hand clothing stores than boutiques. But with a mock-up of an old British red phone box as its fitting room and a decent range of leather jackets (from Y400), cute summer skirts and dresses (from Y99), as well as T-shirts and accessories, Mega Mega is the real deal for anyone looking to dress back in time.

ZHĀOYUÁNGÉ Map pp58-9   Kites

昭元阁

☎ 6512 1937; 41-3a Nanheyan Dajie; 南河沿大街甲41-3号; ⏰ 10am-5pm; ◉ Tiananmen Dong

Cute cubbyhole of a shop that sells handmade, traditional Chinese paper kites of all shapes and sizes (from Y18), as well as a range of fans and opera masks. The owner doesn't speak much English, but is friendly and eager to help.

ORIENTAL PLAZA

Map pp58-9   Shopping Ma

东方广场 Dōngfāng Guǎngchǎng

☎ 8518 6363; 1 Dongchang'an Jie; 东长安街1号; ⏰ 9.30am-10pm; ◉ Wangfujing

A busy, mega-mall at the foot of Wangfujing Dajie that's a favourite with Beijingers, Oriental Plaza has high-end brands (Burberry, DKNY, Paul Smith and Valentino), as well as more reasonably-priced midrange ones, such as Columbia, MNG and Nike. The food court in the basement, Megabite (p168), is a good place to grab a cheap meal when you're in the area. There's also Star City (p193) cinema and Olé (p162), one of Běijīng's best supermarkets.

SHOPPING ARCADE, PENINSULA BEIJING

Map pp58-9   Shopping Ma

王府饭店 Wángfǔ Fàndiàn

☎ 6559 2888; 8 Jinyu Hutong; 金鱼胡同8号; ⏰ 11am-9.30pm; ◉ Dengshikou

The big boys of fashion: Chanel, Dior, Gaultier, Gucci, Hermès, Louis Vuitton, Prada and Versace can be found in this exclusive and very hushed basement-level shopping haunt beneath the Peninsula Beijing (p207) hotel. There are also Cartier and Tiffany outlets, so you can pick up the diamonds you'll need to go with your new outfit.

GRIFTED Map pp58-9   Souveni

贵福天地 Guìfú Tiāndì

☎ 135 5286 0077; 32 Nanluogu Xiang; 南锣鼓巷32号; ⏰ 10am-10pm; ◉ Andingmen

A plethora of tongue-in-cheek gift options is available at this friendly shop in the heart of trendy Nanluogu Xiang. Check out the dolls of communist icons: Che Guevara, Fidel Castro, Mao, Marx and Lenin re-imagined as soft toys, and the Mao-print cushions. There are also lanterns made from recycled candy wrapping, quirky umbrellas and T-shirts. Most of the products here are made locally.

HAOYUAN MARKET

Map pp58-9   Souveni

豪园市场 Háoyuán Shìchǎng

West off Wangfujing Dajie; 王府井大街西侧; ◉ Wangfujing

Branching off from Wangfujing Snack St is this small, bustling souvenir market. There's lots of Mao memorabilia, pandas and Buddhas, as well as other tacky tourist tat, but if you're pushed for time and need a last-minute present you might find something. Haggling is imperative.

PLASTERED T-SHIRTS

Map pp58-9   T-shirts

创可贴T-恤 Chuàngkětiē Tìxù

☎ 139 1020 5721; www.plasteredtshirts.com; 1 Nanluogu Xiang; 南锣鼓巷61号; ☻ 10am-10pm; ⊖ Andingmen

Surveyors of ironic T-shirts that are good to give or keep as mementos of Běijīng. The cotton T-shirts, from Y98, incorporate iconic Běijīng logos and signs: Yanjing beer, old taxi rate stickers, the Běijīng subway map, or you can go for the ones that portray the capital as a Hawaii-like haven of palm trees and sunsets. Opposite the entrance to the shop is a rare surviving slogan from the Cultural Revolution era, which exhorts the people to put their trust in the People's Liberation Army (PLA; China's armed forces). To find more Cultural Revolution slogans around town, see p75.

TEN FU'S TEA Map pp58-9   Tea

天福茗茶 Tiānfú Míngchá

☎ 6524 0958; www.tenfu.com; 88 Wangfujing Dajie; 王府井大街88号; ☻ 10am-9pm; ⊖ Wangfujing

With branches all across Běijīng, this Taiwanese chain is the easiest place to pick up tea, even if the prices are higher than at the tea shops in Maliandao Lu. It stocks top-quality loose tea from all over the country; prices start at Y20 for a one *jīn* (500g). The staff can line you up with a free tea tasting.

DANNERMAN TANG'S TOYS & CRAFTS Map pp58-9   Toys

盛唐轩 Shèng Táng Xuān

☎ 8404 7179; 38 Guozijian Jie; 国子监街38号; ☻ 10am-7pm; ⊖ Andingmen

The family that own this shop west of the Confucius Temple have been making toys for over 150 years. The miniature scenes of old (old) Běijīng street life, stuffed toys and different-sized opera masks work better as souvenirs than as toys and they're marvellously intricate. Look for the giant toy statue that stands guard outside the shop.

NEW CHINA CHILDRENS STORE

Map pp58-9   Toys & Kids Clothing

新中国儿童用品商店 Xīn Zhōngguó Értóng Yòngpǐn Shāngdiàn

☎ 6528 1774; 168 Wangfujing Dajie; 王府井大街168号; ☻ 10am-9.30pm; ⊖ Wangfujing

If you need to find somewhere to occupy kids, bring them to this maze of toys, model cars and trains, gadgets, puzzles, flashing lights and electronic noises, overseen by helpful staff. On the 2nd floor, you can find nappies (diapers) and lots of clothing for babies and kids.

CHÓNGWÉN 崇文

Chóngwén's Qianmen Dajie (p84) was given an extensive facelift for the 2008 Olympics and is now something of a tourist theme park, complete with a tram that runs up and down it. The shops were not all occupied at the time of writing. In this area beware of scam artists who offer to guide you, or take you to see a traditional tea ceremony. Some visitors have been stung for a lot of money in these scenarios.

HONGQIAO (PEARL) MARKET

Map p82   Market

红桥市场 Hóngqiáo Shìchǎng

☎ 6711 7429; 36 Hongqiao Lu; 红桥路36号; ☻ 9am-7pm; ⊖ Tiantandongmen

Besides a cosmos of clutter (shoes, clothing, electronics and lots and lots of handbags), Hongqiao is home to more pearls than the South Sea. The range is huge – freshwater, seawater, white and black pearls – and prices vary incredibly depending on quality. The 3rd floor has the cheaper ones, mostly sourced from Zhèjiāng province, as well as standard jewellery. The better-quality, more pricy pearls can be found on the 4th and 5th floors, where there's a roof terrace that offers a view of the Temple of Heaven. Prices are generally high, while the vendors, who often speak some English, are canny bargainers. If you have kids, don't miss the Kids Toys Market (Hóngqiáo Tiānlè Wánjù Shìchǎng; 红桥天乐玩具市场; Map p82; ☻ 8.30am-7pm) in the building behind, stuffed to the gills with soft toys, cars, model kits, Wii sets, Playstations and computer games.

XĪCHÉNG 西城

Xidan Beidajie is where the masses come to shop. The street, which runs north from the intersection with Xi'changan Jie, is lined with malls featuring few Western brands and prices lower than you'll find in Sānlǐtún. Absolutely rammed at weekends, come here to watch the local shopaholics in action. It's also a good spot to pick up a mobile phone.

77TH STREET Map pp88-9 · Shopping Mall
77街 Qīshíqī Jiē
☎ 6608 7177; B2-3F, 180 Xidan Beidajie; 西单北大街180号地下2-3层; ☗ 9.30am-10pm; ◉ Xidan
Descend the stairs into this unique underground mall and see where ordinary teen and 20-something Beijingers go for their clothes and accessories. It opens out into a huge, circular, three-storey collection of hundreds of stores. As well as funky T-shirts, belts and bags, there are shoe shops galore and a food court. It's lots of fun, but a madhouse at weekends. To get there walk north on Xidan Beidajie from the subway and take the first right, then look for the 77th Street sign.

CHÁOYÁNG 朝阳

The Cháoyáng district has some of the swankiest malls in town, as well as many of the most popular markets for visitors, including the Silk Market. The market is heaving at weekends, so visit during the week for a more serene shopping experience. Key areas for purchases are Sānlǐtún and Guómào, but there are shops of all descriptions spread across the district. Panjiayuan Market (p153) is on the edge of the Cháoyáng district.

BOOKWORM Map pp110-11 · Book
书虫 Shūchóng
☎ 6586 9507; Bldg 4, Nansanlitun Lu; 南三里屯路4号楼; ☗ 9am-1am; ◉ Tuanjiehu
Apart from its lending library of over 14,000 books, the 'worm has a small but interesting selection of new English-language fiction and nonfiction, especially China-related, for sale. You can also find UK and US magazines here. There is a cafe and bar on the premises; see p173.

CHATERHOUSE BOOKTRADER
Map pp110-11 · Book
☎ 6587 1328; B-107, Basement, Place, 9a Guanghua Lu; 光华路9号世贸天阶中心地库B107; ☗ 10am-10pm; ◉ Yonganli
Home to by far the best kid's books section in Běijīng, as well as the widest range of new fiction, Chaterhouse is an invaluable

---

BEST BUYS IN BĚIJĪNG

Arts, crafts and antiques are tempting buys in Běijīng, but it takes an expert eye to sort the wheat from the chaff, and even connoisseurs get fleeced sometimes. It's not just DVDs that are pirated; ceramics, oils and carvings regularly get the facsimile treatment. If you're after real treasures, look for the special certificate that's required to take a genuine antique out of China (see Customs Regulations, p241) and check for the red-wax seal that allows the owner to export it. Technically, items dating from before 1795 cannot be exported from China, but you would be very lucky to find anything that old. Don't expect to unearth anything of significant value; China has largely been sieved of nuggets. If you are buying a convincing reproduction or fake, ask the vendor to provide paperwork proving it does not infringe export regulations.

Silk (sīchóu) is an important commodity in Běijīng and excellent prices for both silk fabrics and clothing can be found. The top places for silk in Běijīng include the Silk Market (p149) and Ruifuxiang (p152).

Carpets (dìtǎn) can be found at several stores and Běijīng is an excellent place to shop for rugs, both antique and new, from all over China – from Xīnjiāng and Níngxià to Gānsù and Tibet. Antique carpets are often preferred for their richness in colour, attained through the use of natural dyes, and because they are handmade. As well as specialist stores, carpet vendors can be found at Panjiayuan Market (p153) and Beijing Curio City (p153). Some rugs advertised as Tibetan are actually made in factories in mainland China, so try to visit a reputable dealer rather than hunting out the cheapest item. Other carpets are woven from imported Australian wool, the fibres of which are not particularly suitable for rugs. A carpet should be woven from a durable wool, rather than a soft one. The quality of the dye is something else to ask about.

Tailor-made clothes are excellent if you have the time to have them made, and made-to-measure clothing, including traditional Chinese gowns (qípáo, or cheongsam in Cantonese) and Mao suits, can be a bargain in Běijīng. Most tailors supply material, or you can bring your own. Beware of tailors who offer to run up a suit in 24 hours. It takes a lot longer than that to make a quality item of clothing. Cashmere (yángróngshān) from Inner Mongolia is also a good buy in Běijīng. The 2nd floor of the Silk Market (p149) is a great place to hunt for cashmere bargains; however, as with other items here, eye it up carefully as synthetics sometimes pose as the real thing.

resource for reading material, even if the prices are higher than elsewhere. Western magazines are sold here, too.

FIVE COLOURS EARTH

Map pp110-11   Clothing

五色土 Wǔsètǔ

☎ 5869 2923; 2505, 25th fl, Bldg 14, Jianwai Soho, 39 Dongsanhuan Zhonglu; 东三环中路39号 建外SOHO 14号楼25层2505室; ⏱ 9am-6pm; Ⓜ Guomao

Stylish, unique clothing with a traditional Chinese twist can be found at this store located in the swish Jianwai Soho development. The designs are from a local designer and include sexy tops, jackets and skirts that incorporate embroidery made by the Miao minority in Guìzhōu province. It's good for coats, too. Much of Five Colours Earth's stock is sold overseas, in the US and Italy, but you can pick it up far cheaper here.

ROUGE BAISER ELISE

Map pp110-11   Clothing & Linen

☎ 6464 3530; Sanlitun Xiwujie; 三里屯西五街; ⏱ 11am-7pm Mon, 10am-7pm Tue-Sun; Ⓜ Agricultural Exhibition Center

Posh pyjamas, kimonos, cute clothes for toddlers, as well as bed linen, table cloths and curtains are on offer here. Designed by a Shànghǎi-based Frenchwoman, the clothes and linen feature embroidered patterns that incorporate traditional Chinese motifs.

SANLITUN YASHOW CLOTHING MARKET

Map pp110-11   Clothing Market

三里屯雅秀服装市场 Sānlǐtún Yǎxiù Fúzhuāng Shìchǎng

☎ 6416 8945; 58 Gongrentiyuchang Beilu; 工体北路58号; ⏱ 10am-9pm; Ⓜ Tuanjiehu

Five floors of virtually anything you might need and a favourite with expats and visitors. Basement: shoes, handbags and suitcases. Big Shoes (☎ 137 0113 9838) is useful if you're struggling to find suitably sized footwear. First floor: coats and jackets. Second floor: shirts, suits and ladies wear. Third floor: silk, clothes, carpets, fabrics and tailors to fashion your raw material into something wearable. Fourth floor: jewellery, souvenirs, toys and a beauty salon. Bargain hard here.

top picks

CLOTHING STOPS

- **Sanlitun Yashow Clothing Market** (left) Běijīng's most comprehensive multifloor clothing emporium.
- **Oriental Plaza** (p146) Upscale labels in window-shopping heaven.
- **Silk Market** (p149) Haggle, haggle, haggle.
- **Place** (p150) Midrange brands and all the more popular for it.
- **77th Street** (opposite) Where young Beijingers go to shop.

ALIEN'S STREET MARKET

Map pp110-11   Clothing Market

老番街市场 Lǎo Fān Jiē Shìchǎng

Chaowaishichang Jie; 朝外市场街; ⏱ 9.30am-7pm; Ⓜ Chaoyangmen

This market, just north of Ritan Park, is packed with a huge variety of clothing, as well as tonnes of accessories. You can find most things here and it's popular with visiting Russian traders, which means the clothes come in bigger sizes than usual and the vendors will greet you in Russian. Haggling is essential.

SILK MARKET Map pp110-11   Clothing & Silk

秀水市场 Xiùshuǐ Shìchǎng

☎ 6501 8811; 14 Dongdaqiao Lu; 东大桥路14号; ⏱ 10am-8.30pm; Ⓜ Yonganli

The six-storey Silk Market continues to thrive despite some vendors being hit by lawsuits from top-name brands tired of being counterfeited on such a huge scale. Not that the legal action has stopped the coach loads of tourists who descend on this place every day. Their presence makes effective bargaining difficult. But this is a good place for cashmere, T-shirts, jeans, shirts, skirts and, of course, silk, which is one of the few genuine items you will find here.

BAINAOHUI COMPUTER SHOPPING MALL Map pp110-11   Computers & Electronics

百脑汇电脑市场 Bǎinǎohuì Diànnǎo Shìchǎng

☎ 6599 5912; 10 Chaoyangmenwai Dajie; 朝阳门外大街10号; ⏱ 9am-8pm; Ⓜ Chaoyangmen or Hujialou

Four floors of gadgetry, including computers, iPods, MP3 players, blank CDs and

DVDs, gaming gear, software and other accessories. The prices are fairly competitive and you can bargain here, but don't expect too much of a reduction. Next to this mall there are a number of shops that are good places to pick up mobile phones and local SIM cards.

FRIENDSHIP STORE

Map pp110-11   Department Store

友谊商店 Yǒuyì Shāngdiàn

☎ 6500 3311; 17 Jianguomenwai Dajie; 建国门外大街17号; ⏰ 9.30am-8.30pm; ⓔ Jianguomen or Yonganli

The Friendship Store is overpriced, and the service is notoriously offhand, but the books and magazines section is worth a look (you can pick up overseas newspapers here) and the supermarket has a fair selection of wine and foreign food.

SHARD BOX STORE Map pp110-11   Jewellery

慎德阁 Shèndégé

☎ 8561 3712; 1 Ritan Beilu; 日坛北路1号; ⏰ 9am-7pm; ⓔ Yonganli

Using porcelain fragments from Ming and Qing dynasty vases that were destroyed during the Cultural Revolution, this family-run store creates beautiful and unique shard boxes. The boxes range from the tiny (Y20), for storing rings or cufflinks, to the very large

(Y2000). It also repairs and sells jewellery, mostly sourced from Tibet and Mongolia.

3.3 SHOPPING CENTRE

Map pp110-11   Shopping Mall

服饰大厦 Fúshì Dàshà

☎ 6417 3333; 33 Sanlitun Beijie; 三里屯北街33号; ⏰ 11am-11pm; ⓔ Tuanjiehu

With its collection of trendy boutiques and accessories stores, this mall in the heart of Sānlǐtún caters for Běijīng's bright young things. Prices are accordingly high. But with 300 shops here, it's good window-shopping territory.

CHINA WORLD SHOPPING MALL

Map pp110-11   Shopping Mall

国贸商城 Guómào Shāngchéng

☎ 6505 2288; 1 Jianguomenwai Dajie; 建国门外大街1号; ⏰ 10am-9.30pm; ⓔ Guomao

Adjacent to the first-rate China World Hotel, this is a popular, if soulless, mall packed with top-name brands, including Burberry, Marc Jacobs and Prada, as well as boutiques, jewellery stores and fast-food restaurants. The Le Cool Ice Rink (p199) is in the basement.

PLACE Map pp110-11   Shopping Mall

世贸天阶 Shìmào Tiānjiē

☎ 8595 1755; 9a Guanghua Lu; 光华路甲9号; ⏰ 10am-10pm; ⓔ Yonganli

THE PIRATES OF PEKING

In May 2009, the US Congress listed China as one of the world's worst five offenders when it came to violating intellectual property rights (IPR). That won't come as a surprise to anyone who has wandered the streets of Běijīng. Despite regular raids on such high-profile shopping areas as the Silk Market (p149), the piracy of everything from DVDs to software and top-name clothing brands remains endemic in the capital. In fact, unless you're buying a Western brand name from a reputable outlet, it's safe to assume it's fake.

That presents an ethical conundrum for visitors. On the one hand, some people come to Běijīng aware of its reputation as a haven of high-quality knock-off goods and are keen to take advantage of that. Many of the principal clothes markets, where almost everything is fake, are regular stops for tour groups. Indeed, until a few years ago, the Silk Market was listed as Běijīng's third-most popular tourist attraction, after the Forbidden City and the Great Wall. Even if you would never buy fakes in your own country, the temptation can be strong once you compare the price of the real thing with a very good imitation.

But customs officials can take a dim view of people who return home with suitcases stuffed with the latest pirated goods. US and Australian customs in particular are increasingly intolerant of DVD piracy and some people have received hefty fines for having an ersatz version of the latest Hollywood blockbuster in their baggage. And don't even think about shipping a crate of them home, unless you're keen to see the inside of a prison cell.

For China, too, being known as a pirate's paradise is becoming more embarrassing, especially as the country assumes ever-greater importance in the world economy. Crackdowns are more frequent than ever, although they're often timed to coincide with events like the 2008 Olympics when the world's eyes are on China. Some global labels have started testing the Chinese courts by bringing IPR lawsuits against the sellers of fakes. Despite that, the pirates continue to prosper in Běijīng. Just remember, though, that not everything you buy will necessarily last long or work. And you won't get a receipt.

DASHILAR

Shops were barred from the city centre in imperial Běijīng, so the *hútòng* (alleyways) south of Qiánmén served as early versions of modern-day malls. Dashilar (Dàzhàlan; Map pp118–19), a *hútòng* running west from the top end of Qianmen Dajie, was a particularly popular shopping spot and many of Běijīng's oldest shops, including Ruifuxiang (p152) and Tóngréntáng (p152), can be found along or near this crowded street. It's a heady jumble of silk shops, tea shops, department stores, theatres, herbal medicine stores, food and clothing specialists and some unusual architecture.

Dashilar sees a lot of tourists, both domestic and foreign, but there's still an echo of the days when bustling markets plying specialised products thronged the surrounding *hútòng* – lace in one, lanterns in the other, jade in the next. Dashilar was Silk St, but its official name referred to a wicket gate that was closed at night to keep prowlers out. The *hútòng* south of Dashilar retain some of the area's old, medieval flavour and are good for a wander.

Dominated by its spectacular giant outdoor video screen, the Place has an object of fascination for kids, the Place has an extremely popular branch of Zara, as well as French Connection and Miss Sixty, and one of Běijīng's best book stores in Chaterhouse Booktrader (p148). There's a good food court in the basement, too.

VILLAGE Map pp110-11   Shopping Mall
☎ 6419 8900; 19 Sanlitun Lu; 三里屯路19号;
🕙 10am-10pm; ◉ Tuanjiehu
Strategically located at the junction of Sanlitun Lu and Gongrentiyuchang Beilu, this new, eye-catching mall looms over Sānlǐtún and has become a hotspot very quickly, as much for the restaurants on the 3rd floor as for its shops. It is home to China's first Apple store, as well as the world's largest branch of Adidas and midrange Western brands such as Benetton, Columbia, Levi's and Quiksilver. This is the south village; the nearby north village is set to open in late 2009.

XUĀNWǓ 宣武

Xuānwǔ's Liulichang (meaning 'glazed-tile factory') is Běijīng's premier antique street, even if the goods on sale are largely fake. Split in two halves by the busy Nanxinhua Jie, the street is something of an oasis in the area and worth delving into for its quaint, albeit dressed-up, village-like atmosphere. Alongside ersatz Qing monochrome bowls and Cultural Revolution kitsch, you can rummage through old Chinese books, paintings, brushes, ink and paper. Prepare yourself for pushy sales staff and overly optimistic prices. If you want a name *chop* made, this is a good place to do it.

At the western end of Liulichang Xijie, a collection of more informal shops flog bric-a-brac, Buddhist statuary, Cultural Revolution pamphlets and posters, shoes for bound feet, silks, handicrafts and so on. Xuānwǔ is also home to the Maliandao Tea Market, an essential stop for tea lovers and buyers.

CATHAY BOOKSHOP
Map pp118-19   Books & Chinese Artwork
中国书店 Zhōngguó Shūdiàn
☎ 6303 2104; 34 Liulichang Xijie; 琉璃厂西街 34号; 🕙 9am-6.30pm; ◉ Hepingmen
There are two branches of the Cathay Bookshop on Liulichang. This branch (Gǔjí Shūdiàn), on the south side of Liulichang Xijie opposite Róngbǎozhāi, is worth checking out for its wide variety of colour art books on Chinese painting, ceramics and furniture, and its books on religion (most books are in Chinese). Upstairs has more art books, stone rubbings and antiquarian books. The store takes MasterCard and Visa. There's another, smaller branch close by on Liulichang (Map pp118–19; 18 Liulichang Xijie; 琉璃厂西街18号) that sells paper cuts and bookmarks, some of which feature photographs of the old Qing imperial household, including snapshots of Reginald Johnson (last emperor Henry Puyi's English tutor), Puyi practising shadow boxing, eunuchs and Cixi dressed as Avalokiteshvara (Guanyin).

RÓNGBǍOZHĀI Map pp118-19   Chinese Artwork
荣宝斋
☎ 6303 6090; 19 Liulichang Xijie; 琉璃厂西街 19号; 🕙 9am-5.30pm; ◉ Hepingmen
Spread over two floors and sprawling down quite a length of the road, the scroll paintings, woodblock prints, paper, ink and brushes here are presented in a rather flat, uninspired way by bored staff – a consequence of it being state run. But it has plenty of goods on offer. Prices are generally fixed, although you can usually get 10% off.

TÓNGRÉNTÁNG

Map pp118-19   Chinese Medicine

同仁堂

☎ 6303 1155; 24 Dazhalan Jie; 大栅栏街24号;
🕑 8am-7.30pm; 🚇 Qianmen

This famous, now international, herbal medicine shop has been peddling pills and potions since 1669. It was a royal dispensary in the Qing dynasty and its medicines are based on secret prescriptions used by royalty. You can be cured of anything from fright to encephalitis, or so the shop claims. Traditional doctors are available on the spot for consultations. You can find the three-storey shop just west of the Zhang Yiyuan Teastore, with a pair of *qílín* (hybrid animals that appear on earth in times of harmony) standing outside.

YUEHAIXUAN MUSICAL INSTRUMENT STORE

Map pp118-19   Musical Instruments

乐海轩门市部 **Yuèhǎixuān Ménshìbù**

☎ 6303 1472; 97 Liliuchang Dongjie; 琉璃厂东街97号; 🕑 9.30am-6.30pm; 🚇 Hepingmen

Fantastic, friendly emporium that specialises in traditional Chinese musical instruments, such as the zither-like *gǔzhēng* (some of which come with elaborate carvings on them), the *èrhú* and *bǎnhú* (two-string Chinese violins), and *gǔ* (drums). It does great gongs and has many esoteric instruments from Tibet and Mongolia, too. It's on the eastern side of Liliuchang.

NEILIANSHENG SHOE SHOP

Map pp118-19   Shoes

内联升鞋店 **Nèiliánshēng Xiédiàn**

☎ 6301 4863; 34 Dazhalan Jie; 大栅栏街34号;
🕑 9.30am-9pm; 🚇 Qianmen

They say this is the oldest existing cloth shoe shop in China (it opened in 1853) and it has a factory that still employs more than 100 workers. Mao Zedong and other luminaries had their footgear made here and you too can pick up ornately embroidered shoes, or the simply styled cloth slippers frequently modelled by Běijīng's senior citizens. It does cute, patterned kid's slippers and shoes (from Y42), too.

SOGO

Map pp118-19   Shopping Mall

崇光百货商场 **Chóngguāng Bǎihuò Shāngchǎng**

☎ 6310 3388; 8 Xuanwenmenwai Dajie; 宣武门外大街8号; 🕑 10am-10pm; 🚇 Xuanwumen

Sogo is one of Běijīng's most pleasant mall experiences. The mix of hip Japanese (Sogo is a Japanese company) and European boutiques, the convenient layout and an excellent, cheap food court on the 6th floor makes Sogo more fun than you'd expect a shopping centre to be. Add espresso bars on each floor, the impressive basement supermarket (with pharmacy) and the 6th-floor games arcade, where you can deposit kids while shopping, and you're in mall heaven.

RUIFUXIANG

Map pp118-19   Silk

瑞蚨祥丝绸店 **Ruìfúxiáng Sīchóudiàn**

☎ 6303 5313; 5 Dazhalan Jie; 大栅栏街5号;
🕑 9.30am-9pm; 🚇 Qianmen

Housed in a historic building on Dashilar, this is one of the best places in town to browse for silk. There's an incredible selection of Shāndōng silk, brocade and satin-silk. The silk starts at Y38 a metre, although most of the fabric is more expensive. On the 2nd floor, it sells ready-made, traditional Chinese clothing. Ruifuxiang also has an outlet at Wangfujing Dajie (Map pp58-9; ☎ 6525 0764; 190 Wangfujing Dajie; 王府井大街190号).

MALIANDAO TEA MARKET

Map pp118-19   Tea

马连道茶城 **Mǎliándào Cháchéng**

☎ 6334 3963; 6 Maliandao Lu; 马连道路6号;
🕑 9am-7pm; 🚇 Junshibowuguan

South of Beijing West Train Station is Maliandao, the largest tea market in northern China. The four-storey building is home to if not all the tea in China, then an awful lot of it. There are brews from all over the country here, including pu'er and oolong. Although it's mostly for wholesalers, the market is a great place to wander for anyone interested in tea and the vendors are normally happy to let you sample some. Maliandao Lu itself has hundreds of tea shops, where prices for tea and tea sets are lower than in the tea shops in tourist areas. To find the tea market, look for the statue of Lu Yu, the 8th-century sage who wrote the first book on growing, preparing and drinking tea, which stands outside it.

WǓDÀOKǑU 五道口

On the edge of the student-dominated Wǔdàokǒu neighbourhood in the northwest of the city, the Zhōngguāncūn area has the widest and cheapest range of computers and electronic gear in Běijīng. It's also the place to head to when your laptop is on the blink.

ART CLASS

The contemporary Chinese art bubble of the last few years has deflated somewhat, which is good news for those visitors to Běijīng searching for affordable artwork to take home with them. Buying a piece that is going to be of lasting value, as opposed to something that is useful only for covering up that damp patch on your living room wall, is not as simple as it sounds though. But there are a few guidelines you can follow that will increase your chances of walking off with a future masterpiece.

Spend some time researching the art scene before you arrive. Visit galleries at home and check out magazines like *Art Forum* (artforum.com), *Art News* (www.artnews.com) and *Flash Art* (www.flashartonline.com) to find out about current trends and artists attracting attention. Once you're in Běijīng visit as many galleries as you can. By seeing a lot of art, you'll develop a sense of what is good or bad and, more importantly, what appeals to you.

The staff in reputable galleries will help you, too. Galleries depend on word of mouth for their reputations and the established ones won't just try and sell you any old piece, they'll try to find something that fits with what you want. Rely on your gut instinct when dealing with the galleries; if you think you're being taken for a ride, walk away. Once you do find something you want to buy, you should be able to bargain a little. Unless the gallery is under strict instructions from the artist not to negotiate, or they feel the artist is truly exceptional, they will be flexible over the price.

Ultimately, how much you're prepared to spend will depend on your bank balance and how much you like the piece you're interested in. But the days when Chinese artists let their work go for knockdown prices are long gone. Realistically, you'll need to spend at least US$1000 for something from an up-and-coming artist that will subsequently increase in value.

NOVA ZHONGGUANCUN

Map p125   Computers & Electronics

中关村科贸电子城 Zhōngguāncūn Kēmào Diànzìchéng

8253 6688; 18 Zhongguancun Dajie; 中关村大街18号; 9am-7pm; Zhongguancun

Zhongguancun is China's Silicon Valley and Zhongguancun Dajie and the streets around it are home to computer companies and many malls selling digital and electronic products. Nova is the biggest of them, a huge space full of vendors selling reasonably priced computer software and hardware, games, cell phones, MP3 players and iPods; just about any IT product you could want. Not all of it is the genuine article, but you can bargain here.

GREATER BEIJING

Some of Běijīng's most intriguing shopping destinations can be found away from the city centre. In particular, the 798 Art District and Panjiayuan Market are essential stops for anyone interested in purchasing art or antiques.

BEIJING CURIO CITY

Map pp128-9   Antiques, Art & Crafts

北京古玩城 Běijīng Gǔwán Chéng

6774 7711; 21 Dongsanhuan Nanlu; 东三环南路21号; 10am-6pm; Jinsong

South of Panjiayuan and next to the Antique City Hotel, Curio City is four floors of antiques, scrolls, ceramics, carpets and furniture. The ground floor has jade and pearls, the 2nd and 3rd floors offer antiques and carpets, and the 4th has antique clocks and watches. Popular with tour groups, this is a good place to find knick-knacks and souvenirs, but prices are high and don't assume the antiques are the real deal.

PANJIAYUAN MARKET

Map pp128-9   Antiques, Art & Crafts

潘家园古玩市场 Pānjiāyuán Gǔwán Shìchǎng

6775 2405; West of Panjiayuan Qiao; 潘家园桥西侧; 4.30am-6pm Sat & Sun; Jinsong

Hands down the best place to shop for arts (*yìshù*), crafts (*gōngyì*) and antiques (*gǔwán*) in Běijīng is Panjiayuan (aka the Dirt or Sunday Market). The market takes place on weekends and has everything from calligraphy, Cultural Revolution memorabilia and cigarette ad posters to Buddha heads, ceramics, Qing dynasty–style furniture and Tibetan carpets.

Panjiayuan hosts 3000 dealers and up to 50,000 visitors a day, all scoping for treasures. The serious collectors are early birds, swooping here at dawn to snare precious relics. If you want to join them, an early start is essential. You might not find that rare Qianlong *dòucǎi* stem cup or late Yuan dynasty *qīnghuā* vase, but what's on view is no less than a compendium of Chinese curios and an A to Z of Middle kingdom knick-knacks. This market is chaotic and can be difficult if you find crowds or hard bargaining intimidating. Also,

SHOPPING GREATER BEIJING

153

ignore the 'don't pay more than half' rule here – some vendors might start at 10 times the real price. Make a few rounds to compare prices and weigh it up before forking out for something. It's off Dongsanhuan Nanlu (Third Ring Rd).

TIMEZONE 8 Map pp128-9   Books
东八时区书吧 **Dōngbā Bāshíqū Shūbā**
☎ 5978 9072; 4 Jiuxianqiao Lu; 酒仙桥路4号;
⏱ 11am-7.30pm; ⊖ Sanyuanqiao

The *only* bookshop in Běijīng for anyone interested in art, architecture, design, film and fashion, Timezone 8 has a wonderful selection of books. It's especially strong on Chinese contemporary art, but the books cover global subjects. Located in the 798 Art District (p133), this is also the one place in the city where you'll find design and fashion mags like *i-D*, *Frieze* and *Wallpaper*. There's an attached cafe next door.

SPIN Map pp128-9   Ceramics
旋 **Xuán**
☎ 6437 8649; 6 Fangyuan Xilu; 芳园西路6号;
⏱ 11am-9.30pm; ⊖ Sanyuanqiao

On a road just off Fangyuan Xilu and close to the rear exit of the Holiday Inn Lido, Spin keeps the ancient art of Chinese ceramics alive, while giving it a decidedly 21st-century twist. The cool, long plates, oddly shaped but gorgeous vases, tea sets and all manner of striking household items are the product of Jǐngdézhèn craftsmen and young Shànghǎi designers. Look for the long, single-storey brick building.

SANFO Map pp128-9   Climbing & Hiking Gear
三夫户外 **Sānfū Hùwài**
☎ 6236 8090; 2-3 Madian Nancun, Beisanhuan Zhonglu; 北三环中路马甸南村2楼3号;
⏱ 10am-8pm; ⊖ Jiandemen

With no less than three shops grouped together, Sanfo is the place to come for outdoor wear, climbing and camping gear, as well as surfboards, mountain bikes and anything you might need if you're into adventure sports. It's something of a nexus for Beijing's hikers and climbers – Sanfo organises weekend trips – and is a good place to pick up information, as well as the supplies you'll need if you're thinking of walking the Great Wall for a few days.

EATING

top picks

EATING

'Two pointed sticks of ivory or ebony, do the office of knife and fork; their meats are cut into small square pieces, and served up in bowls; their soups are excellent, but they use no spoons; so that after sipping the thin, the grosser parts of it are directed to mouth by their chopsticks.'

Sir George Staunton, An Historical Account of the Embassy to the Emperor of China (1797

No other city in China can match the sheer range of eating options on offer in Běijīng. From food stalls and hole-in-the-wall establishments, to fancy fusion places and five-star gourmet palaces, Běijīng's restaurants compete to serve up not just the best of the local specialities, but cuisines from every corner of China and the rest of the world. If you think that eating out in Běijīng just means the obligatory visit to a Peking duck restaurant, then you're in for a very pleasant surprise.

The dazzling array of dishes available reflects the sheer joy the Chinese take in eating, and the way food is an absolute obsession. Famines have been an unpleasant reality throughout much of China's history and, as late as the 1980s, food shortages were common. Now, the Chinese are making up for all those meagre meals of the past. Dining out is the main social activity in China and it's in restaurants that the Chinese hang out with friends, romance each other, hold family reunions and do business.

People are at their most relaxed and convivial around a restaurant table, which makes meals out unrestrained, raucous affairs, where voices are raised along with glasses and no one stands on ceremony. Diners sit around circular tables, the communal dishes arrive in waves and everyone digs in straightaway. At times, Běijīng's restaurants can seem like organised chaos as the waiters (服务员; *fúwùyuán*) weave around packed tables, the decibel level goes through the roof and stray debris from the meal ends up on the floor.

Běijīng's native cuisine (京菜; *jīngcài*) is one of the four major styles of cooking in China (opposite). Apart from Peking duck (p158), which originated in the kitchens of the Forbidden City, many popular dishes, such as hotpot (火锅; *huǒguō*), have their origins in Mongol cuisine and arrived in the wake of Genghis Khan. Běijīng's bitter winters mean that warm, filling dishes are essential, with noodles, buns and dumplings preferred over rice. There's also a wide range of street snacks (p160) unique to the capital.

But there is far more to Běijīng's dining scene than just the local food. Rising incomes and increased curiosity about the outside world, along with an influx of foreigners, have transformed the city into a haven of fine dining. The top Chinese chefs gravitate to Běijīng, making the capital the best place in the country to sample the huge variety of China's cuisines. In recent years their foreign counterparts – Michelin-starred legends and the young and ambitious alike – have descended on the city in droves, too. Whether you're pining for burritos or bouillabaisse, it's being served somewhere in Běijīng.

Běijīng is a magnificent place for culinary adventures and even the most picky or jaded diner will find something to satisfy them here. So do as the locals do – pick up those chopsticks and dive in. Some of your most memorable Běijīng experiences will happen when you're sitting around a dining table.

ETIQUETTE

Strict rules of etiquette don't really apply to Chinese dining, with the notable exception of formal banquets. Table manners are relaxed and get more so as the meal unfolds and the drinks flow. Meals can commence in Confucian fashion – with good intentions, a harmonic arrangement of chopsticks and a clean tablecloth – before spiralling into Taoist mayhem, fuelled by never-ending glasses of *píjiǔ* (啤酒; beer) or *báijiǔ* (白酒; white spirits) and a procession of dishes. At the end of a meal, the table can resemble a battlefield, with empty bottles, stray bones and other debris strewn across it.

A typical dining scenario sees a group seated at a round table. Often, one person will order for everyone and the dishes will be shared; group diners never order dishes just for themselves. Many foreigners get asked if they mind dishes that are *là* (辣; spicy); if you don't, then say 'bú yào tài là' (not too spicy). The Chinese believe that a mix of tastes, textures and temperatures is the key to a good meal, so they start with cold dishes and titbits and follow them with a selection of hot meat, fish and vegetable dishes. Bear in mind that waiters will expect you to order straightaway after sitting down and will hover at your shoulder until you do. If you want more time, say 'wǒ huì jiào nǐ' (I'll call you).

At big tables, the dishes are placed on a lazy Susan, which revolves so everyone can access the food. Rice often arrives at the end of the meal but if you want it before, just ask. The mainland Chinese dig their chopsticks into communal dishes, or spoons will be used to ladle out the food, but don't root around for a piece of food. Instead, identify it first and go directly to it without touching what's around it. Bones can be deposited in your side dish, or even on the table itself. If you're in doubt about what to do, just follow the example of the people around you.

Don't worry too much about your chopsticks technique. While chopsticks are tricky to wield at first, most people get to grips with them quickly out of necessity (it's either that or go on an involuntary crash diet). Remember, many Chinese find eating with knives and forks equally daunting and no one will scorn you for your shortcomings; there's no shame in dropping a dumpling, or being bamboozled by broccoli.

Until recently, only posh places handed out their own, reusable chopsticks, while cheap joints relied on disposable wooden ones. The disposable ones are more hygienic, but with China getting through 63 billion pairs of them a year, which is an awful lot of bamboo, they're not environmentally friendly. Since 2007 the government has imposed a tax on disposable chopsticks in an effort to cut their use. If you don't want to use them but are worried about hygiene, then consider carrying your own pair of chopsticks.

Always remember to fill your neighbours' glasses up when they are empty, as they will do the same for you. You can thank the pourer by gently tapping your middle finger on the table. It's regarded as bad manners to serve yourself any drink without serving others first. With alcohol, the Chinese toast each other much more than people do in the West, often each time they take a drink. A formal toast involves raising the glass in both hands in the direction of the toastee and crying out 'gānbēi', literally 'dry the glass' and the Chi-

nese equivalent of 'cheers'. That's the cue to drain the glass in one hit. If that's too much for you, or you're getting legless too quickly, then say 'gān bànbēi', which indicates that you'll only sink half the glass.

Although there is talk of imposing a ban on smoking in public places in Běijīng, nothing has happened as yet. While many international restaurants have nonsmoking areas, that's not the case in most Chinese ones, even if they have no-smoking signs on prominent display. Indeed, smoking while you eat is perfectly acceptable in China, which can be a trial for nonsmokers. If you do smoke, then make sure you offer your ciggies around, as Chinese fans of the weed are generous to the last. As in other neighbouring Asian countries, toothpick (牙签; yáqiān) etiquette is for one hand to shield the mouth while the other gets to work on the teeth.

The arrival of the bill is an excuse for selfless histrionics. The Chinese pride themselves on unwavering generosity in public. Unless you are the host, you should at least make an attempt – however feeble and futile – to pay, but you will be thrust aside by the gaggle of hands gesturing for the bill. If you insist on paying, you could cause the host to lose face, so don't push it too far before raising your hands in mock surrender. Going Dutch is not as common as it is in the West, so if you invite someone out for dinner, be prepared to foot the bill.

DESSERTS & SWEETS 甜点

The Chinese do not generally eat dessert, but fruit is considered to be an appropriate end to a good meal. Western influence has added ice cream to the menu in some restaurants, but in general sweet stuff is consumed as snacks and is seldom available in restaurants.

One exception to the rule is caramelised fruits, including apples (拔丝苹果; básī píngguǒ) and bananas (拔丝香蕉; básī xiāngjiāo), which you can find in a few restaurants. Other sweeties include shaved ice and syrup (冰沙; bīngshā); a sweet, sticky rice pudding known as Eight Treasure Rice (八宝饭; Bābǎofàn); and various types of steamed bun filled with sweet bean paste.

REGIONAL CUISINES

All of China's cuisines converge on Běijīng, from far-flung Tibet to the hardy northeast, the arid northwest and the fecund south. The most popular cooking styles are from Sìchuān, Shànghǎi, Hong Kong, Guǎngdōng

(Cantonese) and Běijīng, but if you want to explore China's full compendium of cooking styles, the capital is *the* place to start.

Běijīng 京菜

Běijīng cuisine is classified as a 'northern cuisine' and typical dishes are made with wheat or millet, whose common incarnations are as dumplings (饺子; *jiǎozi*) or noodles, while arguably the most famous Chinese dish of all is Peking duck. Vegetables are more limited, so there is a heavy reliance on freshwater fish and chicken; cabbage and turnips, as well as yams and potatoes, are some of the most ubiquitous vegetables found on menus.

Not surprisingly, the influence of the Mongols is felt most strongly in Běijīng, and two of the region's most famous culinary exports – Mongolian barbecue and Mongolian hotpot – are adaptations from Mongol field kitchens. Animals that were hunted on horseback could be dismembered and cooked with wild vegetables and onions using soldiers' iron shields on top of hot coals as primitive barbecues. Alternatively, each soldier could use his helmet as a pot, filling it with water, meat, condiments and vegetables to taste. Mutton is now the main ingredient in Mongolian hotpot.

Roasting was once considered rather barbaric in other parts of China and is still more common in the northern areas. The main methods of cooking in the northern style though, are steaming, baking and 'explode frying' (爆炒; *bàochǎo*), a rapid method o cooking in which the wok is superheated ove a flame and the contents tossed in for a swif stir-frying. The last of these is the most common, historically because of the scarcity o fuel and, more recently, due to the introduction of the peanut, which thrives in the nortl and produces an abundance of oil. Althougl northern-style food has a reputation for being salty and unsophisticated, it has the benefit o being filling and therefore well suited to the region's punishing winters.

Sìchuān 川菜

Sìchuān is famed as China's fieriest cuisine - approach the menu with caution and lot of chilled H2O and/or beer. A concoctior of searing red chillis (introduced by Span ish traders in the early Qing dynasty), sta anise, peppercorns and pungent 'flowe pepper' (花椒; *huājiāo*), a numbing herl peculiar to Sìchuān cooking, Sìchuān dishe are simmered to allow the chilli pepper time to seep into the food. Meats are ofter marinated, pickled or otherwise processe before cooking, which is generally by stir- o explode-frying.

STORY OF THE DUCK

You'd have to be quackers to leave Běijīng without trying Peking duck. Undoubtedly the capital's most iconic dish, Peking (or Běijīng) duck's fame has spread around the world. But nothing beats sampling it in the city where it comes from.

Its origins go back as far as the Yuan dynasty, where it was listed in royal cookbooks as an imperial dish. The Qing poet Yuan Mei once wrote, 'roast duck is prepared by revolving a young duckling on a spit in an oven. The chief inspector Fang's family excel in preparing this dish'. It wasn't until the Qing dynasty fell in 1911 and imperial rule in China came to an end, though, that most ordinary people got the chance to try it, as the former palace cooks set up roast duck restaurants around Běijīng.

Chefs go through a lengthy process to prepare the duck, which is reared on special farms outside Běijīng. First the birds are inflated by blowing air between the skin and body. The skin is then pricked and boiling water poured all over the duck. Sometimes the skin is rubbed with malt sugar to give it an amber colour, before being hung up to air dry and then roasted in the oven. When roasted, the flesh becomes crispy on the outside and juicy on the inside. The bird is meticulously cut into slices and served with fermented bean paste, light pancakes, sliced cucumbers and green onions.

Prices for duck vary widely, as does the quality, but in most restaurants expect to pay from Y60 for a half bird. The most famous restaurant in Běijīng for Peking duck is the Quanjude Roast Duck Restaurant (p170), which first opened in 1864. There are now six branches around town, but the flagship of the empire is at Qianmen Dajie. Hordes of tourists, both local and foreign, make the trip there for ducks that are roasted with fruit-tree wood, giving the dish a special fragrance.

True duck devotees prefer the Beijing Dadong Roast Duck Restaurant (p164) – where the duck is much leaner and comes with the skin infused with sugar, the way the emperors used to eat it – and the ramshackle Liqun Roast Duck Restaurant (p170), where the duck is so popular that you need to call in advance to order one.

Another quality roast duck restaurant is Bianyifang (p170), founded in 1855. The duck here is slow-cooked in a straw-fuelled oven, instead of with fruit-tree wood, and prior to being put in the oven, the duck is filled with soup.

Landlocked Sìchuān is a long way from the coast, so pork, poultry, legumes and *dòufu* (豆腐; bean curd) are commonly used, and supplemented by a variety of wild condiments and mountain products, such as mushrooms and other fungi, as well as bamboo shoots. Seasonings are heavy: the red chilli is often used in conjunction with Sìchuān peppercorns, garlic, ginger and onions. Hallmark dishes include camphor-smoked duck, Granny Ma's bean curd (Mápó dòufu) and spicy chicken with peanuts (*gōng bǎo jī dīng*).

Cantonese 粤菜

Cantonese cuisine is what non-Chinese consider to be 'Chinese' food, largely because most émigré restaurateurs originate from Guǎngdōng (Canton) or Hong Kong. Cantonese flavours are generally more subtle than other Chinese styles – almost sweet – and there are very few spicy dishes. Sweet-and-sour and oyster sauces are common. The Cantonese are almost religious about the importance of fresh ingredients, which is why so many restaurants are lined with tanks full of finned and shelled creatures. Stir-frying is by far the most favoured method of cooking, closely followed by steaming. Dim sum (点心; *diǎnxīn*), now a worldwide Sunday institution, originated in this region; to go *yám cha* (饮茶; Cantonese for 'drink tea') still provides most overseas Chinese communities with the opportunity to get together at the weekend. Dim sum can be found in restaurants around Běijīng.

Expensive dishes – some that are truly tasty, others that appeal more for their 'face' value – include abalone, shark's fin and bird's nest. Pigeon is a Cantonese speciality served in various ways but most commonly roasted.

Shànghǎi 上海菜

Shànghǎi cuisine is generally sweeter and oilier than China's other cuisines. Unsurprisingly, Shànghǎi cuisine features plenty of fish and seafood, especially cod, river eel and shrimp.

Fish is usually *qīngzhēng* (清蒸; steamed) but can be stir-fried, pan-fried or grilled. Crab-roe dumplings (*xièròu jiǎozi*) are another Shanghainese luxury.

Several restaurants specialise in cold salty chicken, while drunken chicken gets its name from being marinated in Shàoxīng rice wine. *Bāo* (煲; clay pot) dishes are braised for a long time in their own casserole dish. Shànghǎi's

EATING DOS & DON'TS

- Don't wave your chopsticks around or point them at people; this is considered rude.
- Don't drum your chopsticks on the side of your bowl – only beggars do this.
- Never stick your chopsticks vertically into your rice as they will resemble incense sticks in a bowl of ashes and will be considered an omen of death.
- Wait to be seated when entering a restaurant.
- Steer clear of politics and other controversial topics at dinner.
- Do try to sample all dishes, if possible.
- Don't let the spout of a teapot face towards anyone; make sure it is directed outward from the table or to where nobody is sitting.

most famous snack is *xiǎolóngbāo* (小笼包), small dumplings containing a meaty interior bathed in a scalding juice.

Vegetarian dishes include *dòufu*, cabbage in cream sauce, *mèn* (焖; braised) *dòufu* and various types of mushrooms, including *xiānggū báicài* (香菇白菜; mushrooms surrounded by baby bok choy). Tiger-skin chillies are a delicious dish of stir-fried green peppers seared in a wok and served in a sweet chilli sauce. Fried pine nuts and sweet corn (*sōngzǐ chǎo yùmi*) is another common Shanghainese dish.

Dàzháxiè (大闸蟹; hairy crabs) are a Shànghǎi speciality between October and December. They are eaten with soy, ginger and vinegar and downed with warm Shàoxīng rice wine. They are delicious but can be fiddly to eat. The body opens via a little tab on the underside (don't eat the gills or the stomach).

Uighur 新疆菜

The Uighur style of cooking reflects the influences of Xīnjiāng's chequered past. Yet, despite centuries of sporadic Chinese and Mongol rule, the strongest influence on ingredients and methods is still Turkic or Middle Eastern, which is evident in the reliance on mutton for protein and wheat for the staple grain. When rice is eaten, it is often in the central-Asian version of pilau (*plov*). Nevertheless, the infusion of Chinese culinary styles and ingredients makes it probably the most enjoyable region of central Asia in which to eat.

Uighur bread resembles Arabic *khoubz* (Indian naan) and is baked in ovens based on the *tanour* (Indian tandoor) model. It is

STREET FOOD BĚIJĪNG STYLE

Off the main roads and in Běijīng's alleys is a world of steaming food stalls and eateries teeming with activity. Be adventurous and eat this way and you will be dining as most Beijingers do.

Breakfast can be easily catered for with a *yóutiáo* (油条; deep-fried dough stick), a sip of *dòuzhī* (豆汁; bean curd drink) or a bowl of *zhōu* (粥; rice porridge). Other snacks include the crunchy, pancake-like and filling *jiānbǐng* (煎饼); *jiānbǐng* vendors are easily spotted, as they cook from tricycle-mounted white painted wooden stalls where pancakes are fried on a large circular griddle. The heavy meat-filled *ròubǐng* (肉饼; cooked bread filled with finely chopped pork) are lifesavers and very cheap. A handy vegetarian option is *jiǔcài bǐng* (韭菜饼; bread stuffed with cabbage, chives, leek or fennel and egg). *Dàbǐng* (大饼; a chunk of round, unleavened bread sprinkled with sesame seeds) can be found everywhere, and of course there's *mántou* (馒头; steamed bread). *Málà tàng* (麻辣烫) is a spicy noodle soup (very warming in winter) with chunks of *dòufu* (豆腐; bean curd), cabbage and other veggies – choose your own ingredients from the trays. Also look out for *ròu jiāmó* (肉夹馍), a scrumptious open-your-mouth-wide bun filled with diced lamb, chilli and garlic shoots. Another must are *kǎo yángròu chuàn* (烤羊肉串; lamb kebabs). They're a staple at the Donghuamen Night Market (p169) and the Wangfujing Snack Street (p169), but are more expensive at these places. They're cheaper on the streets and down Běijīng's alleyways (look for the billowing plumes of smoke), where you can pick up a skewer for Y1. If you want your kebabs spicy, ask for *là* (辣; spicy); if you don't, ask for *bùlà* (不辣; not spicy).

Hóngshǔ (红薯; baked sweet potatoes) are cheap (Y3), filling snacks sold at street stalls throughout the city during winter. Vendors attach oil drums to their bikes, which have been converted into mobile ovens. Choose a nice soft sweet potato and the vendor will weigh it and tell you how much it costs.

often eaten straight from the oven and sprinkled with poppy seeds, sesame seeds or fennel. Uighur bakers also make excellent *girde nan* (bagels). Wheat is also used for a variety of noodles. *Laghman* are the most common: noodles cooked al dente, thick and topped with a combination of spicy mutton, peppers, tomatoes, eggplant, green beans and garlic. *Suoman* are noodle squares fried with tomatoes, peppers, garlic and meat, sometimes quite spicy. *Suoman goshsiz* is the vegetarian variety.

Kebabs, both shashlik and tandoori styles, are common, as they are throughout the Middle East and central Asia. *Samsas* or *samsis* are the Uighur version of samosas: baked envelopes of meat. Meat often makes an appearance inside *chuchura* (dumplings), which can be steamed or fried.

WHERE TO EAT

With upwards of 60,000 restaurants in the city, you won't have to travel too far to find one that interests you: the most popular are concentrated within the Second Ring Rd, with Dōngchéng, Chóngwén and Xīchéng the main restaurant neighbourhoods, and in the Sānlǐtún and embassy neighbourhoods of Cháoyáng. Nor will eating out break the bank; Běijīng's restaurants are not as cheap as they once were, but there are still plenty of places where you can find a bowl of noodles or portion of dumplings for under Y10.

In contrast, there are also establishment where the bill will be eye-popping. Foreig food is generally more expensive than the local cuisine, but it's always a good idea to clarify prices, especially for seafood, before you order to avoid a nasty shock at the end of the meal.

Ordering is much easier these days, a most restaurants now have some kind of English menu, or a picture one, even if the translations can be so literal to make the dishes sound less than appetising (anyon for lamb cartilage?). If a place has only Chinese menu, then check out the Food Glossary (p260) in the Language chapter. Failing that, no one will mind if you take a walk around the restaurant and point out dishe that other people are eating. The best option, of course, is to eat with Chinese friend who can order for you. Dining in a group also enables you to sample a much wide variety of dishes.

While Běijīng's restaurants are great fun with a crowd, they are not so good if you are looking for a romantic evening out. Big bustling and bright, they put quality of food ahead of ambience and are designed for over sometimes ostentatious, dining displays rather than for privacy. Service, too, can b erratic and/or lackadaisical. If you want to whisper sweet nothings to your loved one in a candlelit corner, or are on a mission to ge intimate with someone, go for an international restaurant.

VEGETARIANS & VEGANS
素菜

China has a long history of Taoist and Buddhist philosophers who abstained from eating animals, and vegetarianism can be traced back over 1000 years. The Tang-dynasty physician Sun Simiao extolled the virtues of vegetarianism in his 60-volume classic, *Prescriptions Worth a Thousand Pieces of Gold*. Legend has it that Sun lived to the ripe old age of 101. But try telling that to your waiter when he brings out a supposedly pristine veggie or tofu dish decorated with strips of pork or chicken. The majority of Chinese have little understanding of vegetarianism and many consider it a strange Western concept.

Because of China's history of poverty and famine, eating meat is a sign of status and symbolic of health and wealth. Vegetables are often fried in animal-based oils, and soups are most commonly made with chicken or beef stock. Saying you don't eat meat confuses many Chinese, who may interpret this to mean that seafood, or even chicken or pork, is OK. Trying to explain why you don't eat meat brings even more confusion. Male vegetarians especially are looked down upon because not eating meat is thought to decrease sexual virility.

However, in larger cities such as Běijīng, Shànghǎi and Guǎngzhōu, vegetarianism is slowly catching on and there are new chic vegetarian eateries appearing in fashionable restaurant districts. Buddhist temples also often have vegetarian restaurants.

Buddhist vegetarian food often consists of mock meat' dishes made from tofu, wheat gluten and vegetables. Some of the dishes are almost works of art, with vegetarian ingredients sculpted to look like spare ribs or fried chicken. Sometimes the chefs go to great lengths to create 'bones' from carrots and lotus roots. Some of the more famous vegetarian dishes include vegetarian 'ham', braised vegetarian 'shrimp' and sweet-and-sour 'fish'.

PRACTICALITIES

There are food-related Chinese words and phrases in this chapter and an extensive list in the Language chapter, p256.

Opening Hours

Běijīng restaurants are mostly open from around 10am to 11pm, although there are quite a few that run 24/7. Some establishments shut after lunch and reopen at 5pm or 6pm. Generally, the Chinese eat much earlier than Westerners, lunching from 11am and having dinner about 6pm. Cafes open and sometimes shut earlier. All the cafes in this chapter have wi-fi access.

How Much?

Despite the rich aromas around town, you won't pay through the nose for it all. One of the joys of Běijīng is that eating out is a relatively inexpensive experience. But if you want to spend more, then there are plenty of upmarket places that will be happy to take your cash.

The restaurants listed in this chapter cater to all budgets. At cheap eateries, meals (for one) will cost less than Y50; midrange dining options will cost between Y50 and Y100; and top-end choices more than Y100.

Credit cards are accepted mostly at hotel restaurants and the most expensive eateries. If you're dining anywhere else, make sure you have enough cash on you.

Be warned that some (but by no means all) restaurants in tourist areas still fob off foreigners with an English menu (英文菜单; *yīngwén càidān*) at higher prices than the Chinese menu (中文菜单; *zhōngwén càidān*). Unfortunately, deciphering the Chinese menu will require either assistance or Chinese reading skills. But most places have picture and/or English menus now. All restaurants serving foreign food have English menus. Generally, very few waiting staff will be able to speak any English, no matter how expensive the restaurant is.

If your preferred tipple is wine, then restaurants in Běijīng can be a financial challenge. The Chinese tend to drink beer or *báijiǔ*, a super-strong white spirit, with their meals. Some restaurants will stock domestic wines, such as Great Wall, but many won't. In places that do have foreign wines, you can expect to pay well over the odds for a bottle.

If you speak Chinese, it's good to call ahead and see if it's OK to bring your own booze. If it is, then visit one of the supermarkets or Western delis listed in this chapter (p162) and buy wine, which will be a far cheaper option. You may have to pay a corkage charge.

PRICE GUIDE

The following guide is for one person:

YYY	over Y100
YY	Y50-100
Y	up to Y50

Tipping

Tipping is not standard practice in Běijīng. If you do leave a tip in a local restaurant, you're likely to find a waiter running after you because they think you've forgotten your change. A small minority of upmarket Western places, though, do tack on a service charge to the bill, while high-end hotel restaurants automatically add on a 15% service charge.

Self-Catering

Eating outside of restaurants in Běijīng is easy and even the most selective chef will be able to find just about any ingredient they might want. But if you're staying in an apartment, you might be stumped by the lack of an oven in the kitchen; Chinese cooking doesn't call for them.

The best supermarket in Běijīng is the French hypermarket chain Carrefour (www.carrefour.com.cn; 8.30am-10.30pm), which moved into China early on. There are currently seven branches in Běijīng and they stock just about everything you need, as well as providing ATMs and taking credit cards. They're open every day and are always crowded. You can find three branches in Cháoyáng (Beisanhuan Donglu Map pp128–9; ☎ 8460 1043; 6b Beisanhuan Donglu; Guangqu Lu Map pp128–9; ☎ 5190 9500; 31 Guangqu Lu; Guangshun Beidajie ☎ 5912 4033; 16 Guangshun Beidajie), one each in Xuānwǔ (☎ 6332 2155; 11 Malian Dao) and Fēngtái (☎ 6790 9911; 15, Zone 2 Fangchengyuan Fangzhuang), and two in Hǎidiàn (Zhongguancun Dajie Map p125; ☎ 8836 2729; 56a Zhongguancun Dajie; Zhongguancun Plaza ☎ 5172 1516/17; Zhongguancun Plaza).

Another reliable supermarket is Olé, which has a number of branches around town. The most convenient are the ones at the China World Shopping Mall in Guómào (Map pp110–11; 1 Jianguomenwai Dajie; 9.30am-9.30pm; Guomao), the Oriental Plaza Mall in Wángfǔjǐng (Map pp58–9; Basement, 1 Dongchang'an Jie; 8.30am-10.30pm; Wangfujing) and the Ginza Mall in Dōngzhímén (Map pp58–9; Basement, 48 Dongzhimenwai Dajie; 10am-10pm; Dongzhimen).

Then there are the two branches of the redoubtable Friendship Supermarket (Jianguomenwai Dajie Map pp110–11; ☎ 6500 3311; 17 Jianguomenwai Dajie; 9.30am-8.30pm; Jianguomen; Sanlitun Lu Map pp110–11; ☎ 6532 1871; 7 Sanlitun Lu; 8.30am-8.30pm; Dongzhimen), once the only place in Běijīng to go for a taste of home.

For everyday needs such as milk and bread, as well as for more-esoteric necessities such as Australian and French wine, English tea,

imported cheese and peanut butter, Jenny Lou's (p177) and April Gourmet (p177) are expat favourites. They also stock many of the products available at the above supermarkets.

Many restaurants will deliver food free of charge, as does the Cháoyáng branch of Carrefour on Beisanhuan Donglu (Map pp128–9). The minimum order is Y500; you can order via email: customer@carrefour.com.

DŌNGCHÉNG 东城

This historic part of Běijīng has a huge range of dining options covering every type of Chinese cuisine, as well as plenty of international places. It's also home to some of the capital's most atmospheric restaurants, from beautifully converted courtyards, to the many hole-in-the-wall establishments scattered throughout the local hútòng (narrow alleyways). The Donghuamen Night Market (p169) draws in tourists with its exotic insect and lizard snacks, while locals head to the very popular Ghost Street (鬼街; Gui Jie; opposite) for hotpot and seafood at all hours.

YÙ SHÀN TÁNG

Map pp58-9   Chinese Imperial YYY

御膳堂

☎ 8402 5588; 20 Qinlao Hutong; 南锣鼓巷秦老胡同20号; set menus from Y500; dinner; Andingmen

Located off Nanluogu Xiang, inside Han's Royal Garden, Běijīng's biggest courtyard hotel, the spectacular setting – individual dining rooms with intricately painted ceiling panels, hanging lanterns and rosewood wall panels – is a suitable backdrop to sample imperial cuisine, in one of the few places that carry on the tradition of the eight restaurants sanctioned by the Qing to serve up food fit for emperors. The dishes come carved in extraordinary shapes, such as dragons, and look so good it seems wrong to eat them. The set menus start at Y500 (maximum 16 people) but go as high as you like, depending on your tastes – you can't dine like an emperor on the cheap. Book ahead to customise your menu.

COURTYARD   Map pp58-9   Fusion YY

四合院 Sìhéyuàn

☎ 6526 8883; 95 Donghuamen Dajie; 东华门大街95号; meals Y400; dinner; Tiananmen Dong;

GHOST STREET

For a close-up look at how Beijingers treat their restaurants as party venues and not just places for a meal, take a trip to Ghost Street (鬼街; Gui Jie; Map pp58–9).

This 1.4km strip of Dongzhimennei Dajie is home to over 150 restaurants that attract everyone from hipsters to office workers, man-bag-toting businessmen and families, as well as the odd celebrity. It never closes, making it one of Běijīng's most buzzing streets, and it's especially fun on Friday and Saturday nights. From sundown to sunrise, it's lit by hundreds of red lanterns, and traffic slows to a crawl as the restaurant workers line the side of the road trying to entice passing cars to stop at their joint. Crowds of people spill out onto the pavement waiting for a free table, while inside the packed restaurants the sweating staff rush around delivering food and beers to people celebrating the end of the week.

Most styles of Chinese cuisine are represented on Ghost Street, which gets its name from an eerie night market that was once located here. It's best known, though, for its hotpot and spicy seafood restaurants.

The giant Xiao Yu Shan (Map pp58–9; ☎ 6401 9899; 195 Dongzhimennei Dajie; 东直门内大街195号; ⏱ 10am-6am) is always jammed with people cracking open crayfish and shrimp. For classic Mongolian hotpot, try Little Sheep (Map pp58–9; ☎ 8400 1669; 209 Dongzhimennei Dajie; 东直门内大街209号; ⏱ 9.30am-3am), which sources its mutton from Inner Mongolia. Head to Ming Hui Fu (Map pp58–9; ☎ 6401 3636; 199-201 Dongzhimennei Dajie; 东直门内大街199-201号; ⏱ 10am-4.30am) for superb grilled fish (kǎoyú).

Ghost Street begins just west of the Dongzhimen bridge (Ⓜ Dongzhimen) and ends where Dongzhimennei Dajie meets Jiaodaokou Dongdajie (Ⓜ Beixinqiao). It's at its most atmospheric at the western end.

The Courtyard enjoys a peerless location perched by the side of the moat surrounding the Forbidden City. Romantics will need to book ahead to ensure they have one of the cosy window tables that offer the best views. Forage to find the entrance (up the steps curtained by fronds of bamboo). Inside, the menu has a vague southern-hemisphere theme – think grilled Polynesian pork with a ginger rice pilaf (Y205) – and is particularly strong on seafood such as Maine diver scallops or wild king prawns with a baked clam ratatouille (Y235). The wine list starts at Y200. There's a 15% service charge here, too.

TIĀNDÌ YĪJIĀ Map pp58-9   Chinese Mixed YYY
天地一家

☎ 8511 5556; 140 Nanchizi Dajie; 南池子大街140号; meals Y300; ⏱ lunch & dinner; Ⓜ Tiananmen Dong; ✕

Doing business from a restored building alongside Changpu River Park (Chāngpú Hé Gōngyuán; p72), this refined, Chinese courtyard–style restaurant is notable for the water feature with multicoloured fish that dominates the elegant dining room. There's also a balcony overlooking the Imperial Archives (Huángshǐ Chéng; p72). The menu, which spans a number of provinces and styles, is strong on seafood with snob appeal – shark's fin, abalone and lobster – as well as traditional delicacies such as bird's-nest soup and local faves such as

Peking duck. It also does dim sum. But the black-clad waitresses are not a bundle of laughs and there's a slightly stiff feel to the whole establishment.

HUÁNG TÍNG
Map pp58-9   Chinese Cantonese YYY
凰庭

☎ 8516 2888, ext 6707; Peninsula Beijing, 8 Jinyu Hutong; 金鱼胡同8号王府半岛酒店; meals from Y230; ⏱ lunch & dinner; Ⓜ Dongdan; ✕

Faux old Peking is taken to an extreme in the courtyard setting of Huáng Tíng. Enter though a sìhéyuàn (courtyard house) entrance with carved lintels and a wooden portal to an interior fashioned from grey bricks with stone lions, water features, birdcages, stone floor flagging, decorated lanterns, and Ming and Qing dynasty–style mahogany and sandalwood furniture – it's like a Fifth Generation film set. Despite its artificiality and location (in the bowels of a five-star hotel), the setting is impressive, caressed by the sounds of zhēng (13- or 14-stringed harp), pípa (lute) and other traditional Chinese instruments. Even the loos have their own wooden door and brass courtyard-style handles. Despite the quintessentially Běijīng look, come here for Cantonese dishes, especially the dim sum (set lunch Y198). But there's also Peking duck (Y280) and dishes from all over China. A 15% service charge is automatically added to the bill.

BEIJING DADONG ROAST DUCK RESTAURANT

Map pp58-9   Peking Duck YYY

北京大董烤鸭店 **Běijīng Dàdǒng Kǎoyādiàn**

☎ 5169 0328/29; 1st fl, Nanxincang International Plaza, 22 Dongsishitiao Lu; 东四十条22号(南新仓国际大厦); roast duck Y198; ◷ lunch & dinner; ◉ Dongsishitiao

The opening of the second branch of this long-time favourite in Nánxīncāng, an entertainment complex located in the former Imperial Granary (which dates back to the 15th century), has really upped the ante in the ongoing battle between Běijīng's rival duck restaurants. Its hallmark bird, a crispy, lean duck without the usual high fat content (trimmings are Y8 per person), is now served up in a big, light dining room, split into two sections, with comfy booths and staff running everywhere. There's also a bar for the inevitable wait for a table (book ahead). The huge menu has plenty of non-duck options, but this is perhaps the best place in town, if not the cheapest (a half duck is Y99), to try the capital's signature dish. It's always packed. Nánxīncāng is just off Dongsishitiao. The original branch is further east in Cháoyáng (Map pp110–11; ☎ 6582 2892/4003; Bldg 3, Tuanjiehu Beikou; 团结湖北口三号楼; ◷ lunch & dinner).

SOURCE Map pp58-9   Chinese Sìchuān YYY

都江园 **Dūjiāngyuán**

☎ 6400 3736; 14 Banchang Hutong; 板厂胡同14号; meals Y188; ◷ lunch & dinner; ◉ Andingmen

Swish Sìchuān with a twist, served up in a courtyard that was once the home of a famous Qing-dynasty general. Source is an amenable place to sample the delights of some of China's hottest dishes, as the chefs here tend to go easy on the chillis; they'll also adjust the temperature of the food on request. You choose from a selection of set menus (Y188), which change every month and include a couple of main courses, as well as cold dishes, soup, rice and noodles and a dessert. The garden is a lovely spot in summer and the service is pleasant; it's a good place to bring a date. There's a set lunch for Y108.

DOMUS Map pp58-9   French/Italian YYY

☎ 8511 8015; 115 Nanchizi Dajie; 南池子大街115号; mains from Y128; ◷ lunch & dinner; ◉ Tiananmen Dong; ☒

Directly opposite Tiāndì Yījiā, and owned by the same people, this new restaurant couldn't be more different, in everything from the food, contemporary Italian and French, to the gorgeous design – think Minotti furniture, grey-brick walls, a huge, open kitchen and a lovely, central bar in which to lounge around – and the pleasant service. Upstairs, you can sip a martini (Y70) and try the Italian antipasti menu, or proper bar snacks such as oysters. Downstairs is the restaurant (dinner only, closed Sundays), which riffs on a French theme with dishes such as pigeon roasted in tobacco leaves (Y168). The wine list is substantial and pricey (from Y450 a bottle).

DALI COURTYARD

Map pp58-9   Chinese Yúnnán YYY

大理 **Dàlǐ**

☎ 8404 1430; 67 Xiaojingchang Hutong, Gulou Dongdajie; 鼓楼东大街小经厂胡同67号; set menus from Y100; ◷ lunch & dinner; ◉ Andingmen

The beautiful setting in a restored courtyard house in a hútòng makes this one of Běijīng's more idyllic places to eat, especially in summer. Specialising in the subtle flavours of the cuisine of southwestern Yúnnán province, it's also one of the more creative. You have to book in advance and there's no menu. Instead, you pay Y100 a head (drinks are extra) and the chef decides what to give you, depending on what inspires him and what ingredients are fresh. Normally, that means five or six dishes, with an emphasis on fish and pork flavoured with Yúnnán herbs. Specify your dietary requirements when booking. It's the first left down Xiaojingchang Hutong; look for the red lantern to guide you there.

DĪNG DĪNG XIĀNG

Map pp58-9   Chinese Hotpot YY

鼎鼎香

☎ 6417 9289; 2nd fl, Yuan Jia International Mansion, 40 Dongzhong Jie; 东直门外东中街40号元嘉国际公寓二层; meals for 2 Y150; ◷ lunch & dinner; ◉ Dongsishitiao

Hotpot restaurants are a favourite with Beijingers. You sit around a bowl of boiling water (the hotpot) flavoured to your specifications and cook the raw ingredients yourself. It's a fun, sociable way of eating and the staff is always on hand to help you out. Dǐng Dǐng Xiāng is very much at the posh end of hotpot dining; with its waiters dressed in tails or black tie, and hotpot bowls polished to within an inch of their lives, it's the complete opposite of the more rowdy and chaotic hotpot restaurants on Ghost Street (p163). It's rather more expensive, too, but the food makes up for it, with excellent fish balls, superior cuts of beef and mutton, and plenty of veggie options. Don't forget to order the excellent dipping sauces; the Dǐng Dǐng Xiāng special sauce (Y16) is an essential accompaniment to a meal here. English menu. There's another branch (Map pp58–9; ☎ 6417 2546; 1st fl, 14 Dongzhong Jie; 东直门外东中街14号楼一层; ⏱ lunch & dinner) just down the road.

CAFÉ DE LA POSTE Map pp58-9   French YY
云游驿 Yúnyóu Yì

☎ 6402 7047; 58 Yonghegong Dajie; 雍和宫大街58号; mains from Y45; ⏱ lunch & dinner; ◉ Yonghegong-Lama Temple

Just down the street from the Lama Temple, this is the closest Běijīng gets to an authentic French bistro. With its relaxed vibe and friendly service, it's a key meeting point for French expats. A small bar area where you can sip a glass of wine or a pastis opens into an intimate, nicely lit dining area. The food is unpretentious and hearty; the steaks (from Y82) are impressive cuts of meat. But it does a decent Salade Lyonnais (Y38), too, while the desserts include the renowned Death by Chocolate (Y48). There's a three-course set lunch (Y78) during the week and brunch at weekends (Y120). The wine list starts at Y138 a bottle.

VINEYARD CAFÉ Map pp58-9   Western YY
葡萄院儿 Pútáo Yuànr

☎ 6402 7961; 31 Wudaoying Hutong; 五道营胡同31号; set lunches Y55-60; ⏱ lunch & dinner, closed Mon; ◉ Yonghegong-Lama Temple; ✕

A few minutes' walk from the Lama Temple down a hútòng that, like many in the area, has become increasingly trendy, this hip cafe-restaurant is ideal for brunch or lunch, or for a meal and drinks in the evening. The British owner does an excellent full English breakfast, while the set lunch – a salad and pizza or quiche – is terrific value. There's a nice conservatory, a nonsmoking area and lots of sofas to sink into. In the evening, it's a restaurant that serves up Western standards such as mussels in white wine (Y45), as well as being a laid-back spot for a drink.

FÀNQIÁN FÀNHÒU
Map pp58-9   Taiwanese YY
饭前饭后

☎ 6405 9598; A13 Gucangqun Nanxincang International Plaza, 22 Dongsishitiao Lu; 东四十条22号南新仓国际大厦古仓群A13; dishes from Y30; ⏱ lunch & dinner; ◉ Dongsishitiao

Taiwanese cuisine is influenced by Fújiàn and Hakka food, with dishes that are lighter and less spicy than most mainland ones. This hectic, large restaurant is one of a number of Taiwanese places that have opened in Běijīng recently. It specialises in home-style food, with some dishes named after Taiwanese pop stars, as well as staples such as stir-fried vermicelli (Y32), beef in cream sauce and spinach (Y36), and fine homemade tofu (which looks like mashed potato) and Taiwanese sausage. Make sure to try the luóhànsùlāo (Y38), a mix of fruit and vegetables in a cold, soup-like sauce.

GRANDMA'S KITCHEN
Map pp58-9   American YY
祖母的厨房 Zǔmǔ De Chúfáng

☎ 8403 9452; 28 Shique Hutong, Beixinqiao; 北新桥石雀胡同28号; dishes from Y28; ⏱ 7.30am-11pm; ◉ Beixinqiao; ✕

The perfect place for Americans pining for a taste of home, Grandma's Kitchen could have been transported from the midwest – only the white picket fence is missing. There's a great conservatory for outside dining and it offers a simple but well-cooked take on classics such as meat loaf, steaks, burgers, pancakes and apple pie. The all-day breakfasts, either the vegetarian option (Y30) or the hefty Grandma's Skillet (Y45), are justifiably popular. It's nonsmoking and almost opposite exit C of the Beixinqiao subway stop. There's another branch (Map pp110–11; ☎ 6503 2893; 11 Xiushui South St; 秀水南街11号) next door to Makye Ame (p175), as well as one close to the Forbidden City (☎ 6528 2790; 47-2 Nanchizi Dajie; 南池子大街47-2号).

BAIHE VEGETARIAN RESTAURANT
Map pp58-9   Chinese Vegetarian YY
百合素食 Bǎihé Sùshí

☎ 6405 2082; A23 Caoyuan Hutong; 东直门内北小街草胡同23号; dishes from Y26; ⏱ lunch & dinner; ◉ Dongzhimen or Beixinqiao; ✕

Don't be fooled by the anonymous entrance to this hidden gem, off Dongzhimen Beixiaojie; once inside, you walk past a shrine to Confucius to enter a large courtyard that's divided into a shop selling organic coffee and tea, and a spacious dining room. As in all Běijīng's vegetarian restaurants, the dishes masquerade as meat or fish. Here, though, they're more imaginative – think lamb kebabs, sizzling shrimp and Peking duck (Y68). With courteous service, this is one of Běijīng's more soothing dining experiences; and it's nonsmoking throughout. English menu. To get here, walk north on Dongzhimen Beixiaojie from the junction with Ghost Street for 100m, then turn left into the first *hútòng*. The restaurant is on the right.

LYDIA'S MANOR CAFÉ

Map pp58–9   Western YY

大牛比萨 **Dàniú Bǐsà**

☎ 6400 8173; 70 Beixinqiao Santiao; 北新桥三条70号; dishes from Y22; ☻ noon-midnight; ◉ Beixinqiao

In a *hútòng* just around the corner from Café de la Poste and very close to the Lama Temple, this is a great place for cheap and tasty Western comfort food such as pizza, pasta and burgers, or for an afternoon coffee or evening drink. The friendly owner speaks excellent English. The prices for foreign beers such as Budweiser, Guinness and Tiger are just about the lowest in town. Local draught beer is Y10 a pint.

HUĀ JIĀ YÍ YUÁN

Map pp58–9   Chinese Mixed YY

花家怡园

☎ 6405 1908; 235 Dongzhimennei Dajie; 东直门内大街235号; dishes from Y20; ☻ 24hr; ◉ Beixinqiao; ✕

The menu at this landmark Běijīng restaurant is vast, taking in various Chinese styles, from Cantonese to Běijīng cuisine via Shāndōng. The seafood is particularly good, perhaps because the fish and various crustaceans get to await their death in nice, clean tanks, unlike some Běijīng restaurants where the fish float in murky water in distinctly dubious receptacles. Otherwise, you can take your pick from Peking duck, hotpot, dumplings, ribs – whatever you want, really. The Cantonese-style desserts are justly popular. With its atmospheric setting in a restored courtyard house, topped by a greenhouse-like glass roof, and a house band that plays traditional Chinese music, this place gets busy at peak times (it's a popular spot for wedding receptions) and

service can be erratic. But it never closes, so it's particularly useful for nightbirds. English menu. Nonsmoking area upstairs.

FISH NATION Map pp58–9   Western YY

鱼邦 **Yúbāng**

☎ 6401 3249; 31 Nanluogu Xiang; 南锣鼓巷31号; fish & chips Y35; ☻ lunch & dinner; ◉ Andingmen

A home from home for those who miss eating fish and chips, whether standing on a street corner in the rain in England, or sitting on the beach at Bondi. There's no sand at Fish Nation, nor does it rain very often in Běijīng, but there is a pleasant roof terrace with a view over the surrounding *hútòng*. As well as obvious choices such as cod and chips (Y35) and calamari in beer batter (Y20), it does good salads and serves the Big British Breakfast (Y50) until 4pm. There's a wide range of foreign beers. It's very kid friendly, too. There's a more basic branch that caters for the late-night drinking crowd in Sānlǐtún (Map pp110–11; ☎ 6415 0119; Sanlitun Beijie).

KŌNG YǏJǏ Map pp58–9   Chinese Zhèjiāng YY

孔乙己酒店

☎ 6404 0507; 322 Dongsi Beidajie; 东四北大街322号; dishes from Y18; ☻ lunch & dinner; ◉ Zhangzizhonglu or Dongsi

Shàoxīng in Zhèjiāng province is famous for being the birthplace of Lu Xun, the man who invented modern Chinese literature, and for its eponymous sherry-like wine. So it's entirely appropriate that this restaurant, which takes its name from an alcoholic character in one of Lu's stories, serves some dishes – such as drunken shrimp (*zuìxiā*) and drunken chicken – swimming in Shàoxīng wine. Rest assured that it tastes better than *báijiǔ*. Also popular at this wooden-floored, old-school place are the many pork and fish dishes, such as the very addictive *dōngpō ròu*, which are alcohol-free. If you want to try Shàoxīng wine, which is also known as *huángjiǔ* (yellow wine), it's served warm in silver jugs (Y38). There's a limited English menu, but this is a restaurant where it's better to take a look at what other people are eating before ordering. Opposite a Bank of Beijing.

XIAO Map pp58–9   Chinese Guizhōu YY

晶馆 **Xiǎo Guǎn**

☎ 6401 8004; 130 Gulou Dongdajie; 鼓楼东大街130号; dishes from Y18; ☻ lunch & dinner; ◉ Andingmen

This cool restaurant located in the front section of a cleverly converted courtyard house maximises its limited space by being built in tiers, so you eat on different levels on either side of the stairs. It specialises in the sour and spicy cuisine of southwestern Guìzhōu province. Make sure to try the superb Miao-style spare ribs (Y48), the spicy tofu stuffed with pork balls (Y26) and the sizzling eggplant (Y26), but all the dishes are consistently good here. Rice wine is Y10 per person. English menu.

HOME SWEET HOME
Map pp58-9   Taiwanese YY

小城故事 Xiǎo Chéng Gùshì

☎ 6522 9889; 235 Chaoyangmen Nanxiaojie; 朝阳门内南小街235号; dishes from Y18; ☟ lunch & dinner; ◉ Dengshikou; ✖

It doesn't look like much from the outside, and the interior is simple, but this friendly restaurant serves up some of the most authentic Taiwanese cuisine in town. The emphasis is on traditional Taiwanese dishes such as three cup chicken (Y38), which comes in a clay pot, spiced with garlic and basil, as well as deep-fried, pepper salt shrimp or frog (Y42) and ǒ-á-chian, an oyster omelette topped with a sweet sauce that's the most popular snack in Taiwan. Nonsmoking throughout. English menu.

TRAKTIRR PUSHKIN
Map pp58-9   Russian YY

彼得堡俄餐厅 Bǐdébǎo Écāntīng

☎ 8407 8158; 5-15 Dongzhimennei Dajie; 东直门内大街5-15号; dishes from Y18; ☟ 11am-midnight; ◉ Dongzhimen

Russian restaurants were the first foreign eateries to appear in Běijīng and have remained popular, mostly because Russian cuisine's emphasis on meat, potatoes and cream means it's perfect for anyone looking for an extra layer of fat to help them survive Běijīng's freezing winters. This one's location near the Russian embassy guarantees it a loyal stream of customers drawn in by classic dishes such as borscht (Y18), Russian-style dumplings (Y20), chicken Kiev (Y38) and trout in sour cream (Y58). As it's a Russian restaurant, there's a sterling selection of alcohol to choose from. If you need a change from weak Chinese beer, go for the Russian Baltika (Y25), or try one of the many vodkas available (from Y15 a shot).

BĀGUÓ BÙYĪ
Map pp58-9   Chinese Sichuān YY

巴国布衣

☎ 6400 8888; 89-3 Di'anmen Dongdajie; 地安门东大街89-3号; dishes from Y16; ☟ lunch & dinner; ◉ Andingmen

This Chéngdū restaurant chain has spread around China in recent years, thanks to its formula of solid Sìchuān dishes served up in a retro Chinese inn setting, with balconies, a central stairway and dolled-up waiting staff. It feels like you've strolled into a period Chinese TV drama, with the added bonus of food and nightly performances of opera snippets, and it's popular with domestic tourists. Dishes include Chóngqìng làzi jī (Chongqing hot pepper chicken; Y48), Mápó dòufu (Y16) and xiānjiāo yúpiàn (chilli fish slices). Walk through the red doors on Dianmen Dongdajie, just past the southern end of Nanluogu Xiang, to reach the restaurant.

CRESCENT MOON MUSLIM RESTAURANT
Map pp58-9   Chinese Xinjiāng YY

新疆弯弯月亮维吾尔穆斯林餐厅 Xīnjiāng Wānwānyuèliàng Wéiwú'ěr Mùsīlín Cāntīng

☎ 6400 5281; 16 Dongsi Liutiao Hutong; 东四六条胡同16号(东四北大街); dishes from Y18; ☟ lunch & dinner; ◉ Dongsishitiao

You can find a Chinese Muslim restaurant on almost every street in Běijīng. Most are run by Huí Muslims, who are Han Chinese, rather than ethnic-minority Uighurs from the remote western province of Xīnjiāng. The Crescent Moon, tucked away down a hútòng off Dongsi Beidajie, is the real deal – owned and staffed by Uighurs, it attracts many Běijīng-based Uighurs and people from central Asia. The yáng'ròu chuàn (lamb skewers; Y6) are succulent and the best in town, or try the dàpánjī (Y50), a dish of chicken, potato, peppers and vegetables served over thick, pasta-like noodles. Picture menu. Xīnjiāng black beer is Y15 a bottle.

LÓNG YUÁN TÁNG
Map pp58-9   Chinese Guǎngxī YY

龙元堂

☎ 8404 9502; 6 Xiang Er Hutong; 东四北大街香饵胡同6号; dishes from Y18; ☟ lunch & dinner; ◉ Beixinqiao

This cosy courtyard restaurant off Dongsi Beidajie specialises in Guǎngxī dishes, specifically those of the Zhuang people, China's largest ethnic minority group. Pickled vegetables are often used; try the suānsǔn chǎo

top picks

JIĂOZI JOINTS

Dine on dumplings just like real Beijingers do.

- **Din Tai Fung (p174)** Legendary, world-famous *xiǎolóngbāo*, small dumplings containing a meaty interior bathed in a scalding juice.
- **Dūyìchù (p171)** Purveyors of dumplings since the mid-Qing dynasty, and *shāomài* (delicate dumplings that originated in eastern China) specialists.
- **Manchurian Special Flavour Jiǎozi Restaurant (p176)** Hearty dumplings in a fun, raucous atmosphere.
- **Niúgē Jiǎozi (below)** Fantastic range of dumplings that you can watch being made at this old-school establishment.

ròupiàn, pickled bamboo shoots stir-fried with pork. There's a picture menu, but it's worth checking out what the other diners are eating before you order.

CHUĀN BÀN   Map pp58-9   Chinese Sìchuān YY
川办餐厅
☎ 6512 2277, ext 6101; 5 Gongyuan Toutiao, Jianguomennei Dajie; 建国门内贡院头条5号; dishes from Y12; ☺ lunch & dinner; ◉ Jianguomen
Every Chinese province has its own official building in Běijīng, complete with a restaurant for cadres and locals working in the capital who are pining for a taste of home. Often they're the most authentic places for regional cuisines. This restaurant in the Sìchuān Government Offices is always crowded and serves up just about every variety of Sìchuān food you could want. It's very much a place for fire fiends: almost every dish comes loaded with chilli, whether it's bamboo shoots, Sìchuān specials such as *làzi jī* (spicy chicken), or the steamed fish with pepper and taro (Y58). But there's an English menu, and the staff, surprisingly helpful given that this is a government-run restaurant, can help you avoid choosing anything too extreme. Beers are Y10; you'll need them to restore feeling to your tongue.

NIÚGĒ JIĂOZI
Map pp58-9   Chinese Dumplings Y
牛哥饺子
☎ 6525 7472; 85 Nanheyan Dajie; 南河沿大街85号; dumplings from Y10; ☺ 6am-10.30pm; ◉ Tiananmen Dong

East of the Forbidden City, this cute dumpling joint dishes up dozens of varieties of *jiǎozi*, including beef (*niúròu*), lamb (*yángròu*), pork (*zhūròu*), duck (*yāròu*) and donkey (*lǘròu*), as well as a wide range of veggie ones such as mushroom and cabbage (*xiānggū báicài*). The limited English menu lists the basic range of dumplings, but there are many further mixed options, such as chicken and leek or celery, and pork or shrimp and eggplant, on the Chinese menu. A standard portion of *jiǎozi* is called a *liǎng* and the staff will do their best to help you out, or you can watch the chefs at work in the open kitchen and point out the ingredients you want. The restaurant is opposite the building with the sign on the roof saying 'Hualong St'.

MEGABITE   Map pp58-9   Chinese Mixed Y
大食代 Dàshídài
Basement, Oriental Plaza, 1 Dongchang'an Jie; 东长安街1号东方广场地下; dishes from Y10; ◉ Wangfujing
This hygienic fast-food emporium puts Cantonese, Yúnnán, Sìchuān, teppan-yaki, clay pot, Korean and porridge (*zhōu*) outlets all under one roof and is a reliable place for a lunchstop if you're shopping in the area. Look out for decent dumplings (*jiǎozi*) and *xiǎolóngbāo*, the steamed buns that are Shànghǎi's favourite street snack. There are also solid noodle sets available here, as well as Indian samosas and *roti prata*. Portions are generous and good value – you can eat very well for around Y20. You don't pay in cash for your dish; instead, buy a card (Y5 deposit; cards come in denominations of Y30, Y50, Y100, Y200, Y500 and Y1000 units) at the kiosk at the entrance and credits are deducted with each dish ordered.

JĪN DĬNG XUĀN
Map pp58-9   Chinese Cantonese Y
金鼎轩
☎ 6429 6888; 77 Hepingli Xijie; 地坛南门和平里西街77号; dim sum from Y8; ☺ 24hr; ◉ Yonghegong-Lama Temple
By the south gate of Ditan Park, this giant, busy, neon-lit restaurant on three floors serves up cheap dim sum, as well as expensive seafood and a wide range of cakes and sweet things, around the clock. There's another branch in Cháoyáng (☎ 8596 8881; 15 Tuanjiehu Nanlu; 团结湖南路15号; ☺ lunch &

dinner). There are two menus (in English): one for dim sum, as well as a separate one for children.

QÍN TÁNG FǓ Map pp58-9   Chinese Shǎnxī Y
秦唐府

☎ 6559 8135; 69 Chaoyangmen Nanxiaojie; 朝阳门南小街69号; dishes from Y7; ☻ lunch & dinner; ◉ Dongsi

Shǎnxī province is great for filling, cheap eats such as the delicious *yángròu pàomó* (Y18), a mutton, noodle and bread soup, and Xī'ān sausage (Y22), as well as fried pork in bread (*ròujiāmó*; Y7), the Shǎnxī version of the hamburger. There's an English menu and the only drawbacks here are the seriously eccentric chairs and tables, which are so low they're like something out of a kid's playroom. It's so popular that there's another branch (☎ 6525 4639; 53 Chaoyangmennei Nanxiaojie; 朝阳门内南小街53号) a few doors down the road.

DONGHUAMEN NIGHT MARKET
Map pp58-9   Snacks Y

东华门夜市 Dōnghuámén Yèshì

Dong'anmen Dajie; 东安门大街; snacks from Y5; ☻ 6-10pm, closed Chinese New Year; ◉ Wangfujing

A sight in itself, the bustling night market near Wangfujing Dajie is a veritable food zoo: lamb, beef and chicken skewers, corn on the cob, smelly *dòufu*, cicadas, grasshoppers, kidneys, quail's eggs, snake, squid, fruit, porridge, fried pancakes, strawberry kebabs, bananas, Inner Mongolian cheese, stuffed eggplants, chicken hearts, pitta bread stuffed with meat, shrimps – and that's just the start. It's not a very authentic Běijīng experience, but the vendors take great glee in persuading foreigners to try such delicacies as scorpion on a stick. Expect to pay around Y5 for a lamb skewer, far more than you would pay for the same snack from a *hútòng* vendor.

WANGFUJING SNACK STREET
Map pp58-9   Chinese Mixed Y

王府井小吃街 Wángfǔjǐng Xiǎochījiē

West off Wangfujing Dajie; 王府井大街西侧; dishes from Y5; ☻ lunch & dinner; ◉ Wangfujing

Fronted by an ornate archway, this quadrant is lined with cheap-and-cheerful food stalls that are always busy. It's a good place to pick up Xīnjiāng or Muslim Uighur cuisine such as lamb skewers and flat

bread. Also on offer are other dishes from all over China, including *mlà tàng* (a spicy soup from Sìchuān), *zhájiàngmiàn* (noodles in fried bean sauce) and noodles in peppery sauce. Also being scoffed by the bowl here are Lánzhōu *lāmiàn* (Lánzhōu noodles), Shāndōng *jiānbǐng* (Shāndōng pancake), Yúnnán *guòqiáo mǐxiàn* (Yúnnán cross-the-bridge noodles) and oodles of Sìchuān food. At most outlets you have to sit outside elbow-to-elbow with other diners.

CHÓNGWÉN 崇文

Busy with shoppers and tourists alike, Chóngwén may not be as hip as Cháoyáng, but it is home to some of Běijīng's oldest restaurants. Many of the best-known Peking duck restaurants are located in the historic Qiánmén district, while the Legation Quarter, an oasis of high-class foreign eateries and bars close to Tiananmen Square, is a vivid illustration of just how much Běijīng, and China, has changed since the Chairman was running things.

MAISON BOULUD Map p82   French YYY
布鲁宫 Bùlǔ Gōng

☎ 6559 9200; 23 Qianmen Dongdajie; 前门东大街23号; mains from Y205; ☻ lunch & dinner; ◉ Qianmen; ✗

Nothing symbolises the dramatic changes that Běijīng's dining scene has undergone in recent years more than the opening of this outpost of chef Daniel Boulud's empire. Acclaimed as one of the top 100 restaurants in the world, it is located in the newly restored Legation Quarter, which was the home of embassies in pre-Revolution days. The imposing facade gives way to a spacious, smoke-free dining room that allows for real privacy – a rarity in Běijīng restaurants – while the service is as good as it gets in the capital. The French-inspired food is predictably fine, with the menu and ingredients changing every couple of months to reflect the season. If you are feeling flush, try the eight-course dégustation menu (Y800), which is a galaxy of flavours. But if you're not on the company credit card, or if you're celebrating a special occasion, the three-course lunch menu (Y165) is a very decent deal for food of this quality. Alternatively, the bar is a good place for

DUCK DEVOTION

Zhang Liqun, owner of the Liqun Roast Duck Restaurant (below), is 60 years old and has spent 27 years of his life serving up duck in Běijīng.

How did you come to be a roast duck chef? Even though I'm a third-generation Beijinger, my first job was as a farmer. I left school in 1968, during the Cultural Revolution, and was sent to work on a farm in Shānxī. After I came back to Běijīng, I just felt an urge to cook delicious food. I had a friend who worked at Quanjude Roast Duck Restaurant and he helped me get a job there in 1982.

Does it take a long time to learn how to cook Peking duck? I started at the bottom in the kitchen. First you study everything about ducks: how they should be fed and slaughtered, although cooks don't kill the ducks themselves anymore. Then you learn about all the ingredients that go into making it taste so good. Finally, you learn how to cook the bird. It takes about three years to learn how to cook it properly. It's difficult to be a good roast duck chef. You have to be very nimble with your fingers.

Why did you open your own place? By 1992 I was in charge of opening new branches of Quanjude and wasn't cooking anymore, so I had a lot of free time and decided to open my own restaurant. Quanjude didn't mind; it's a much bigger company. Back then, we sold the duck for Y30 each and it was the same quality as it is now.

What's the secret of your restaurant's success? It's because we cook the duck in the traditional way and after 17 years we won't change that. Normally, we cook 50 ducks a day. On public holidays and at Chinese New Year, we'll go through 100 ducks in a day.

Do you still cook the duck yourself? Not unless it's a very busy time. I sometimes cook at home, but not roast duck because I see enough of that in the restaurant.

a cocktail (from Y70) if you just want to sample the ambience.

QIANMEN QUANJUDE ROAST DUCK RESTAURANT Map p82   Peking Duck YYY

前门全聚德烤鸭店 Qiánmén Quánjùdé Kǎoyādiàn

☎ 6701 1379, 6511 2418; 30 Qianmen Dajie; 前门大街30号; roast duck Y198; ⏰ lunch & dinner; Ⓜ Qianmen

As fundamental as a visit to the Great Wall, the sampling of Peking duck is an absolute must for any visitor to the capital. The most popular branch of Běijīng's most famous destination for duck – check out the photos of everyone from Fidel Castro to Zhang Yimou – this place is geared to the tourist hordes (both domestic and foreign). A consequence of the crowds is that service can be peremptory, while the huge, two-floor venue lacks atmosphere. But the duck, while not the best in town, is pretty good, and roasted in ovens fired by fruit-tree wood. That means the birds have a unique fragrance, as well as being juicy, if slightly fatty. Remember that you'll pay extra for all the trimmings. There's a slightly less frenetic branch (Map pp58–9; ☎ 6525 3310; 9 Shuaifuyuan Hutong; 帅府园胡同 9号) just off Wangfujing Dajie. Book ahead, or get your duck to go at the booth outside (vacuum-packed duck Y108; vacuum-packed pancakes Y15; sauce Y1).

BIANYIFANG Map p82   Peking Duck YYY

便宜坊烤鸭店 Biànyìfáng Kǎoyādiàn

☎ 6712 0505; 3rd fl, China New World Shopping Mall, 5 Chongwenmenwai Dajie; 崇文门外大街5号新世界商场二期三层; roast duck Y188; ⏰ lunch & dinner; Ⓜ Chongwenmen; ✕

Despite having shifted location to a shopping mall that sees few foreign faces, Bianyifang remains a solid duck option. Claiming to be the original Peking duck restaurant – it cites a heritage that dates back to the reign of the Qing emperor Xianfeng – Bianyifang roasts its duck in the *mènlú* style – in a closed oven, as opposed to a half-open one where the duck hangs to cook – and the meat is nice and tender. A half bird is Y94 with all the trimmings and the menu also offers duck liver, heart and feet dishes. In fact, just about any part of the duck that is edible is available here. Nonsmoking throughout. English menu.

LIQUN ROAST DUCK RESTAURANT Map p82   Peking Duck YYY

利群烤鸭店 Lìqún Kǎoyādiàn

☎ 6702 5681, 6705 5578; 11 Beixiangfeng Hutong; 前门东大街正义路南口北翔凤胡同11号; roast duck Y168; ⏰ lunch & dinner; Ⓜ Qianmen

Buried away in east Qianmen, the approach to this compact courtyard restaurant is through a maze of crumbling *hútòng* that have somehow survived total demolition; look for the signs pointing the way. If that doesn't inspire confidence, reassure yourself with the thought that the delectable duck on offer here is so in demand that it's essential to call ahead to reserve both a bird and a table (otherwise, turn up off-peak and be prepared to wait an hour). Inside, it's a little tatty (no prizes for the toilets) and chaotic, but walk by the ovens with their rows of ducks on hooks, squeeze past the scurrying, harried waiters and then sit back and enjoy some of the finest duck in town. English menu.

DŪYĪCHÙ Map p82   Chinese Dumplings YY
都一处

☎ 6702 1671; 38 Qianmen Dajie; 前门大街38号; dishes from Y26; ✆ 7.30am-9pm; ⊕ Qianmen

Now back on the newly spiffy street where it started business during the mid-Qing dynasty, Dūyīchù specialises in the delicate dumplings called *shāomài*. The shrimp-and-leek (Y36) and crabmeat (Y86) ones are especially good – and are presented very nicely – but there are plenty of other options available on the English menu, as well as a selection of Shāndōng-style dishes. Be prepared to queue at weekends, or book ahead.

XĪCHÉNG 西城

With the lakes of Qianhai and Houhai as a focal point, Xīchéng is one of the more popular and picturesque dining areas in town, especially in summer. Many places offer views across the lakes, which are rammed with pedalos in summer and ice-skaters in winter. Other restaurants are tucked away in the *hútòng* that surround the lakes, or the ones behind the Drum Tower.

CAFÉ SAMBAL Map pp88-9   Malaysian YY

☎ 6400 4875; 43 Doufuchi Hutong; 旧鼓楼大街豆腐池胡同43号; set lunches Y80, dishes from Y60; ✆ lunch & dinner; ⊕ Gulou Dajie

This cool Malaysian restaurant located off Jiugulou Dajie is in a cleverly converted courtyard house at the entrance to Doufuchi Hutong. The minimalist bar opens into a narrow dining area that has a temporary roof during winter, but is open in summer so you can dine under the stars and satellites. It's a popular spot for dates. The food is classic Malaysian. Try the beef rendang (Y60), or the various sambals (from Y70). The wine list is decent, while the barman here mixes what many claim to be the best mojito (Y45) in town.

HUTONG PIZZA Map pp88-9   Pizza YY
胡同比萨 **Hútòng Bǐsà**

☎ 8322 8916; 9 Yindingqiao Hutong; 什刹海银锭桥胡同9号院; pizzas from Y57; ✆ lunch & dinner; ⊕ Gulou Dajie

Nestling in a *hútòng* that was one of the locations for the movie *Beijing Bicycle*, Hutong Pizza's trademark square pizzas are perhaps the best in town. There's a wide selection to choose from, including veggie options, or you can build your own, and they're big: the large pizzas (Y98) will easily satisfy two hungry people. Salads, burgers and pasta options are available, too, as well as local and foreign beers. It gets busy, so it's advisable to book at peak times; it does deliver, though. Watch out for the mini-pond just inside the entrance; put one step wrong and you'll be swimming with the fish.

LE PETIT SAIGON
Map pp88-9   French/Vietnamese YY
西贡在巴黎 **Xīgòng Zài Bālí**

☎ 6401 8465; 141 Jiugulou Dajie; 旧鼓楼大街141号; mains from Y48; ✆ 11.30am-midnight; ⊕ Gulou Dajie

The menu at this stylish bistro – with a nice roof terrace in summer – is a mix of classic Vietnamese, *pho* and lemon chicken, and French, beef bourguignon and foie gras. The desserts are especially good. The decor and wine list are decidedly Gallic, making it popular with French expats and anyone in search of a proper cup of coffee (Y23), whether it's the European or Vietnamese variety.

YUELU SHANWU
Map pp88-9   Chinese Húnán YY
岳麓山屋

☎ 6617 2696; 19a Qianhai Xiyan; 什刹海前海西沿甲19号(荷花市场内); dishes from Y28; ✆ lunch & dinner; ⊕ Gulou Dajie

With a marvellous view over Qianhai Lake, this pretty and civilised Húnán restaurant – the name means 'house at the foot of the mountain' – serves a range of hot and mild dishes from the province renowned for its searing flavours and for being the birthplace of Mao Zedong. It's appropriate then to try Mao's home-style pork (Y48), but it does a good boiled frog (Y68), too, as well as excellent, country-style *dòufu*. The stewed snake with ginger is especially fiery. A bottle of *huángjiǔ* will ease it down. English menu.

HÀN CĀNG Map pp88-9 Chinese Hakka YY
汉仓

☎ 6404 2259; 12 Qianhai Nanyan; 什刹海前海南沿12号; dishes from Y22; ☷ lunch & dinner; ◉ Gulou Dajie

In summer, when the large outside terrace comes into its own, this is one of Běijīng's hot restaurant destinations. It's still good in winter, too, especially if you get one of the upstairs rooms that have a great view over the frozen lake. Hakka cuisine uses a lot of fresh fish. Go for the whole fried fish with pine nuts (Y58), or the prawns in a bucket of salt, a Hakka classic. But there's also plenty here for meat lovers: the roast beef fillet with garlic and wrapped in a lotus leaf (Y38) is a favourite of many. It gets loud here, and it's always crowded, so book, or be prepared for a wait, if you want an outside table in the evenings. English menu.

CHÁOYÁNG 朝阳

This giant district has every conceivable type of cuisine and the presence of embassies and many foreign companies, as well as the Sānlǐtún bar and entertainment district, means it has the greatest concentration of international restaurants. There are some popular Chinese places around the Workers Stadium, while further afield the Lìdū area and the 798 Art District (p133) in Dàshānzi are home to many cafes and restaurants.

LA MARÉE Map pp110-11 French YYY
海潮餐厅 Hǎi Cháo Cāntīng

☎ 8521 9585; 2nd fl, 16 Yong'an Dongli; 永安东里16号2层(CBD国际大厦内); meals Y300; ☷ lunch & dinner; ◉ Yonganli

Hard to find (it's inside CBD International Mansions, down a road off Jianguomenwai Dajie very close to exit C of Yonganli Station), this southern-French seafood restaurant is one of the nicest international restaurants in town. The dining room is decorated in maritime blue, with fishing nets strung across the ceiling, while the French chef gives a modern spin to traditional seafood dishes using both local and imported ingredients (there are also meat dishes that use beef from Australia). The splendid seafood platter for two (Y498) is a good introduction. Otherwise, mains start at Y125. Thankfully, it also does a more affordable lunch deal, where you pay Y48 for a soup and salad bar and then up to Y50 for

a main course. There are 200 French wines available, starting at Y198 a bottle and going up to Y56,000 for really big spenders.

MOSTO Map pp110-11 Western YYY
摸石头 Mōshítou

☎ 5208 6030; 3rd fl, Nali Patio, 81 Sanlitun Beilu; 三里屯北路81号那里花园3层; mains from Y120; ☷ lunch & dinner; ◉ Tuanjiehu; ✕

Another of the increasing number of contemporary restaurants working on a Mediterranean theme, and something of a clone of Salt (p178), Mosto offers up solid, well-presented, if not truly exciting, food in an attractive setting. The local business/embassy crowd, as well as ladies who lunch, pack it out at lunchtime (two- /three-course set lunch Y70/85), but it's also busy at night. Good wine list (from Y200 a bottle) and excellent desserts. There's a small outside area and it's nonsmoking inside. Book ahead.

MOREL'S Map pp110-11 Belgian YY
莫劳龙玺西餐厅 Mòláo Lóngxǐ

☎ 6416 8802; Gongrentiyuchang Beilu; 工体北路工人体育馆北门对面; mains from Y78; ☷ lunch & dinner, closed Mon; ◉ Dongsishitiao

Top-notch steaks and fine fresh fish are the trademark of this homely Belgian eatery, opposite the north gate of the Workers Gymnasium. The Brussels pepper steak (Y125), Flemish beer beef stew (Y78) and the pot of mussels (Y118) are deservedly popular. Good desserts and a vast selection of Belgian beers (from Y40). During the week, there's a three-course set lunch (Y88). Book for evenings. There's another branch (Map pp128-9; ☎ 6437 3939; 27 Liangmaqiao Lu; 亮马桥路27号东座一层) near the Lufthansa Center.

HATSUNE Map pp110-11 Japanese YY
隐泉日本料理 Yǐn Quán Rìběn Liào Lǐ

☎ 6581 3939; 2nd fl, Heqiao Bldg C, 8a Guanghua Lu; 光华路甲8号和乔大厦C座二层; sushi from Y25, set lunch Y75; ☷ lunch & dinner; ◉ Jintaixizhao or Dawanglu; ✕

A favourite with expats and increasing numbers of locals, this stylish and efficient eatery has a sense of humour – its house-speciality hand rolls have names like Ninja (Y60), featuring shrimp tempura, crab, maguro and a very spicy sauce, and the aptly named King Kong (Y78) is a true monster of a roll. More like a Californian sushi joint than a traditional Japanese place, it's fun and the food is delicious. There's a generous set lunch deal, which has bento box, sushi and sashimi options. Sit at the sushi bar, or in the dining room, which has a nonsmoking section and an interesting, if distracting, water feature. There's a more casual branch in Sānlǐtún, opposite Element Fresh.

BOOKWORM Map pp110-11   Western YY
书虫 Shūchóng

☎ 6586 9507; Bldg 4, Nansanlitun Lu; 南三里屯路4号楼; mains from Y72; ⏰ 9am-2am; ◉ Tuanjiehu; ✕

A combination of a bar, cafe, restaurant and library, the Bookworm is a Běijīng institution. Perhaps it's the 14,000-plus books you can browse while sipping your coffee, or working your way through the extensive wine list. The food maintains the bookish theme, with sandwiches (Y42) and dishes named after famous authors, even if it, and the alcohol, is overpriced. The Bookworm is much more than just an upmarket cafe, however. It's one of the epicentres of Běijīng cultural life and hosts lectures, poetry readings, a Monday-night quiz and an annual book festival. Any author of note passing through town gives a talk here. The local listings mags will tell you what events are coming up. There's a roof terrace in summer, and a nonsmoking area.

RUMI Map pp110-11   Persian YY
入迷

☎ 8454 3838; 1a Gongrentiyuchang Beilu; 工体北路1-1号; mains from Y69; ⏰ lunch & dinner; ◉ Tuanjiehu

Located in a strip of Middle Eastern restaurants, this is Běijīng's only Persian place. Inside, it's all cool white walls and furniture, but the food is authentic, with dishes such as ghormeh sabzi (Y69), a beef or vegetarian stew, fine shish kebabs (including a vegetarian option) and decent hummus. It doesn't serve alcohol, but you can bring your own and there's no corkage charge. It's opposite the Zhaolong Hotel.

LA MARE Map pp110-11   Spanish YY
古老海西餐厅 Gǔlǎohǎi Xīcāntīng

☎ 6595 4178/2890; 1st fl, e-Tower, 12c Guanghua Lu; 光华路丙12号数码01大厦一层; 2-/3-course set lunches Y68/88; ⏰ lunch & dinner; ◉ Guomao

Incongruously located on the ground floor of an office building just off Guanghua Lu, this popular Spanish restaurant offers 30 different authentic tapas (from Y35), including sizzling

top picks

FOREIGN FAVOURITES

For a taste of home or something different.
- **Café Sambal** (p171) Cool courtyard restaurant with spicy Malaysian dishes and top-notch mojitos.
- **Domus** (p164) Gorgeous interior design and a choice of French or Italian cuisine.
- **Element Fresh** (below) MSG-free dishes and imaginative salads for when you need a dose of healthy eating.
- **Hatsune** (opposite) Stylish, California-meets-Japan sushi joint with a huge selection of hand rolls
- **Hutong Pizza** (p171) The trademark square pizzas here are the tastiest in town.
- **La Marée** (opposite) Superb French-style seafood in a maritime-themed setting.
- **Salt** (p178) Fine, unfussy contemporary cuisine with a Mediterranean twist, in a relaxed setting.
- **Vineyard Café** (p165) Laid-back hútòng establishment that's perfect for a lazy brunch.

EATING CHÁOYÁNG

garlic prawns, stir-fried chorizo, baby squid and salty cod, as well as justly popular paella (Y90 per person). There's an extensive, but expensive, wine list (from Y288 a bottle).

ELEMENT FRESH Map pp110-11   Western YY
北京新元素餐厅 Běijīng Xīn Yuánsù Cāntīng

☎ 6417 1318; 8-3-3, Bldg 8, Village, 19 Sanlitun Lu; 三里屯路19号三里屯Village南区8号楼8-3-3单元; pastas from Y58; ⏰ 11am-11pm Mon-Fri, 8am-11pm Sat & Sun; ◉ Tuanjiehu; ✕

The arrival of this perennially popular Shànghǎi chain in Běijīng was much anticipated and it's packed out with Western families at the weekends, even if the locals seem a tad less enthused by its mix of healthy and hefty salads, sandwiches (Y39), smoothies (Y28) and the MSG-free mains (from Y98). There's a large outside terrace and wi-fi access. Be prepared to queue at busy times, but it delivers in the area, too.

PURE LOTUS VEGETARIAN
Map pp110-11   Chinese Vegetarian YY
净心莲 Jìngxīnlián

☎ 6592 3627; Zhongguo Wenlianyuan, 12 Nongzhanguan Nanlu; 农展馆南路12号中国文联院; mains from Y58; ⏰ lunch & dinner; ◉ Tuanjiehu; ✕

At this very smart, monk-run establishment, diners are greeted by umbrella-wielding staff who will shield you from the elements as you walk past the statues of monks clutching their alms bowls that line the small outside area to a hushed dining room in which the waiters seem to glide around. Best of all are the private rooms – with cave-like entrances and individual Buddhas looming over the tables – which can be booked by groups. The dishes are a mix of soybean, tofu and vegetables, and have wonderful names such as 'The ordinary one with virtue holds lightning'. But don't expect any charity when it comes to the bill. The restaurant is adjacent to a Hanting Express hotel, in a forecourt just off Nongzhanguan Nanlu. There's another branch (Map pp128–9; ☎ 6437 6288; 3rd fl, Holiday Inn Lido, Jiangtai Lu; 蒋台路丽都假日饭店三层; ⏱ lunch & dinner) inside the Holiday Inn complex at the Lido. Nonsmoking throughout.

DIN TAI FUNG
Map pp110-11   Chinese Dumplings YY
鼎泰丰
☎ 6553 1536; 6f, Shin Kong Place, 87 Jianguo Lu; 建国路87号新光天地店6楼; dumplings from Y45; ⏱ 11.30am-9.30pm Mon-Fri, 11am-10pm Sat & Sun; Ⓜ Dawanglu; ☒

Over 20 years ago, the New York Times picked the original Taipei branch of this upmarket dumpling chain as one of the 10 best restaurants in the world. That's no longer true, but the dumplings here are certainly special. The xiǎolóngbāo – thin-skinned packages with meat or veggie fillings that are surrounded by a superb, scalding soup – are especially fine. It also does Shànghǎi hairy crabmeat jiǎozi and shāomài, as well as excellent soups and noodle dishes. Completely nonsmoking, it prides itself on being kid friendly and it's packed out with families at weekends. It's on the top floor of the posh Shin Kong Place Mall, where there are also branches of Dīng Dīng Xiāng (p164) and Bellagio (opposite).

LE PETIT GOURMAND
Map pp110-11   French YY
小美食家 Xiǎo Měishíjiā
☎ 6417 6095; 3rd fl, Tongli Studios, Sanlitun Beijie; 三里屯北酒吧街同里三层; mains from Y43; ⏱ 9am-midnight; Ⓜ Tuanjiehu
Located off Sanlitun Lu, this is an excellent place to while away a few hours, either on the laptop (there's wi-fi), immersed in one of the 9000-odd books in the library, or over a coffee or crêpe (from Y22), there's also a spacious, enclosed terrace. The menu offers a selection of traditional French clas-

sics, including good salads and couscous, but the crêpes are the real draw here: try the banana and chocolate (Y30) or the apple and calvados (Y40). There's also a set lunch deal (Y65). The books, which include a reasonable selection of French-language tomes as well as a kid's section, are available for loan to members (Y300 a year).

PURPLE HAZE
Map pp110-11   Thai YY
紫苏庭 Zǐsū Tíng
☎ 6413 0899; Down a small alley opposite the north gate of the Workers Stadium (first alley east of Xinjiang Red Rose Restaurant); 工人体育场北门对面胡同; dishes from Y42; ⏱ 10am-midnight; Ⓜ Dongsishitiao; ☒
The trendiest and most congenial Thai restaurant in town, Purple Haze offers Thai standards such as tom yum soup (Y58), red and green curry (Y46), and tangy, spicy salads – a house speciality – in a mellow, if slightly alarming purple-hued environment. The small, nonsmoking area at the front of the restaurant makes a good coffee stop (with wi-fi) during the day. There's another branch (Map pp110–11; ☎ 6501 9345; 201, Bldg 3, China View, Gongrentiyuchang Donglu; ⏱ 10am-midnight) further east. Book ahead at weekends.

INDIAN KITCHEN
Map pp110-11   Indian Y
北京印度小厨餐厅 Běijīng Yìndù Xiǎo Chú Cāntīng
☎ 6462 7255; 2f, 2 Sanlitun Beixiaojie; 三里屯北小街2号二楼; dishes from Y38; ⏱ lunch & dinner; Ⓜ Agricultural Exhibition Center
Always busy with expat Indians, this simple, comfortable place has authentic dishes and attentive staff. The wide-ranging menu covers the classics: masalas, kormas, tikkas, but if you want something not on the menu, or you like your dishes more fiery (all China-based Indian restaurants err on the tame side when it comes to spices), staff will prepare it. Beers start at Y10. The set lunch buffet (Y42) is one of the better deals in town.

ANNIE'S
Map pp110-11   Italian Y
安妮意大利餐厅 Ānnī Yìdàlì Cāntīng
☎ 6503 3871; 16 East 3rd Ring Rd; 农展馆正门南侧东三环路16号; dishes from Y38; ⏱ lunch & dinner; Ⓜ Agricultural Exhibition Center; ☒
Immediately south of the Agricultural Exhibition Center, and next door to the CD Jazz Café (p188), this two-floor, home-style Italian place does the little things right – good service and a welcoming atmosphere (it's very child friendly) – while sticking to a tried-and-tested menu of Italian standards. No

surprises, but the food is well prepared and it's popular. There are other branches around town, including Ritan Park (Map pp110–11; ☎ 8569 3031; 39 Shenlujie, Ritan High Life 2-3-93; 神路街39号日坛上街2-3-93; ❂ lunch & dinner).

THREE GUIZHOU MEN
Map pp110-11   Chinese Guìzhōu YY

三个贵州人 Sāngè Guìzhōu Rén

☎ 6551 8517; Gongrentiyuchang Xilu; 工体西路8号楼(工体小南门旁); dishes from Y35; ❂ 24hr; ❂ Chaoyangmen

Inside the west gate of the Workers Stadium (around the corner from Bellagio), this hip but relaxed restaurant specialises in the spicy cuisine of southwestern Guìzhōu province. The food is delicious, some of the best in Běijīng. The fried pork ribs (Y68) are a must, but almost everything is good. Try the stir-fried grass roots with Guìzhōu bacon (Y35), or the superb salads. The Guìzhōu smashed potato (Y28), a regional version of mashed potato, is tremendous. The spacious dining room is decorated with Chinese contemporary art and the only drawback is that it doesn't do wine by the glass. English menu. There's another branch in Jianwai Soho (Map pp110–11; ☎ 5869 0598; Jianwai Soho, Bldg 7, Dongsanhuan Lu; 东三环路建外SOHO7号楼; ❂ 10am-10pm).

SCHINDLER'S TANKSTELLE
Map pp110-11   German YY

申德勒加油站 Shēndélè Jiāyóuzhàn

☎ 8562 6439; 15a Guanghua Lu; 光华路甲15号; dishes from Y35; ❂ 11am-midnight; ❂ Jianguomen

Sausages, sauerkraut and a strong selection of German beers make this place a reliable option for anyone seeking a taste of central Europe in Běijīng. The German-style breakfast (Y45) will set you up for the day, although the cholesterol-heavy black pudding may also induce cardiac arrest. There's an outside terrace at the back in summer. You can walk off the meal afterwards in nearby Ritan Park.

MAKYE AME
Map pp110-11   Tibetan YY

玛吉阿米 Mǎjí Āmǐ

☎ 6506 9616; 2nd fl, 11a Xiushui Nanjie; 秀水南街甲11号二层; dishes from Y30; ❂ 11am-midnight; ❂ Yonganli or Jianguomen

Tucked behind the Friendship Store (p150), this is one of Běijīng's few Tibetan restaurants. The dining room has a nice atmosphere, with walls lined with Tibetan art and ornaments, sofas to sink into and a prayer wheel to spin. Some might say that the nightly floor show (8pm), which consists of Tibetan dancers and singers in traditional costume, is a little over

the top, but we like it. The menu is long on Tibetan staples such as yak meat, including ribs and boiled yak with chilli, and tsampa (roasted barley meal). There are also salads and Tibetan barley beer (Y25). Book ahead.

BELLAGIO
Map pp110-11   Taiwanese YY

鹿港小镇 Lùgǎng Xiǎozhèn

☎ 6551 3533; 6 Gongrentiyuchang Xilu; 工体西路6号; dishes from Y28; ❂ 11am-5am; ❂ Chaoyangmen

Despite the Italian name, this is a slick, late-opening Taiwanese restaurant conveniently located next to the strip of nightclubs on Gongrentiyuchang Xilu (Gongti Xilu). During the day and the evening, it attracts cashed-up locals and foreigners. After midnight, the club crowd moves in. The large menu includes Taiwanese favourites such as three cup chicken (Y46) and spicy vermicelli with pork and mushrooms (Y32), as well as a wide range of vegetarian options. But the real reason to come here is for the wonderful puddings. The shaved–ice cream desserts are rightly renowned. Try the red beans with condensed milk on shaved ice (Y26) and the fresh mango cubes on shaved ice (Y34). The coffee is top-notch, too. English menu. There's another branch in East Chaoyang (☎ 8451 9988; 35 Xiaoyun Lu; 霄云路35号; ❂ 11am-5am).

XIAO WANG'S HOME RESTAURANT
Map pp110-11   Chinese Běijīng YY

小王府 Xiǎo Wángfǔ

☎ 6594 3602, 6591 3255; 2 Guanghua Dongli; 光华东里2号; dishes from Y26; ❂ lunch & dinner; ❂ Guomao or Yonganli

Treat yourself to home-style Běijīng cuisine at this bustling restaurant and go for one of Xiao Wang's specials. The deep-fried spare ribs with pepper salt (piāoxiāng páigǔ; Y68) are excellent, as are Xiao Wang's fried hot and spicy Xīnjiāng-style chicken wings (zīrán jīchì; Y45). The crispy and lean Peking duck (Y128 per duck) is also a good option here. There's a swankier, more expensive branch inside the north gate of Ritan Park (☎ 8561 7859; Ritan Beilu; ❂ lunch & dinner). English menu.

HERBAL CAFÉ
Map pp110-11   Chinese Cantonese YY

泰和草本工坊 Tàihé Cǎoběn Gōngfáng

☎ 6416 0618; S6-33, 3f, Village, 19 Sanlitun Lu; 三里屯路19号院3层S6-33; dishes from Y26; ❂ lunch & dinner; ❂ Tuanjiehu

At this MSG-free, Hong Kong–style eatery you can eat in a booth that's a mock-up of the inside of one of Hong Kong's famous trams, or sit on the white sofas in the main dining area and watch 1930's Shanghai movies. It's a great spot for cheap dim sum, as well as for noodle dishes and delicate Cantonese desserts such as the Portuguese egg tarts. The soups, which change daily, come in cool canisters and are popular. There's a good selection of teas, too.

HAITANGHUA PYONGYANG COLD NOODLE RESTAURANT

Map pp110-11   North Korean YY

平壤海棠花冷面馆 Píngrǎng Hǎitánghuā Lěngmiàn Guǎn

☎ 6461 6295/6298; 8 Xinyuanxili Zhongjie; 新源西里中街8号; cold noodles Y20; ☽ lunch & dinner; ◉ Dongzhimen

There aren't many North Korean restaurants around the world, but then there aren't that many in the DPRK itself. A night at this kitsch hangover from the Cold War is rather more fun than an evening out in Pyongyang, though, thanks to the accomplished singing waitresses who take it in turns to serenade the diners with a selection of Korean pop tunes. There's not much difference between North Korean and South Korean cuisine; apart from the cold noodles, it's kimchi (Y19) and barbecue all the way.

XINJIANG RED ROSE RESTAURANT

Map pp110-11   Chinese Xinjiāng Y

新疆红玫瑰餐厅 Xīnjiāng Hóngméiguī Cāntīng

☎ 6415 5741; Gongrentiyuchang Beilu, Xingfuyi-cun; 工人体育场北路幸福一村七巷; dishes from Y14; ☽ lunch & dinner; ◉ Dongsishitiao

This is a touristy but fun restaurant that serves up reliable Xīnjiāng classics against a backdrop of live Uighur music and dancing (from 7.30pm to 9pm every night); you may find yourself dragged up on stage to throw a few shapes with the performers. It gets loud, so avoid sitting next to the speakers and prepare to shout. You can pass on the whole roast lamb (Y1080) unless you're a crowd, but with its long, canteen-like communal tables, this is definitely a place for groups rather than for a tête-à-tête. Down an alley opposite the Workers Stadium north gate.

SEQUOIA BAKERY & CAFÉ

Map pp110-11   Cafe Y

美洲杉咖啡屋 Měizhōushān Kāfēiwū

☎ 6501 5503; 44 Guanghua Lu; 光华路44号; sandwiches from Y28; ☽ 8am-8pm; ◉ Jianguomen

Deservedly popular with diplomats from the neighbouring embassies, this friendly

cafe is a good place to pick up a caffeine fix (coffee Y19) if you're chasing visas in the area. Decent pastries and deli-style sandwiches, too. There's another branch in Sānlǐtún (☎ 6415 6512; Bldg 15, North Sanlitun Beijie; ☽ 8am-8pm).

KIOSK Map pp110-11   Western Y

南斯拉夫烤肉屋 Nánsīlāfū Kǎoròuwū

☎ 6413 2461; Nali Mall, Sanlitun Beijie; 三里屯北街那里服装市场; hamburgers/sandwiches from Y26; ☽ lunch & dinner, closed Mon; ◉ Tuanjiehu

A good place for a quick lunchtime snack, or for early-evening, predrinking sustenance, Kiosk serves up burgers, chips and sandwiches from a tiny hut just off Sānlǐtún's bar street. The big bite burger is a classic, as is the grilled Serbian-style sausage sandwich (Y28). You can get a salad and a beer here, too. There's a little outside area where you can also eat.

BOCATA Map pp110-11   Cafe Y

☎ 6417 5291; 3 Sanlitun Lu; 三里屯北路3号; sandwiches from Y23; ☽ 11am-midnight; ◉ Tuanjiehu

Great spot for lunch, especially in summer, located slap-bang in the middle of Sānlǐtún's bar street. As the name suggests, there's a vague Mediterranean/Middle Eastern theme to the food, with decent hummus, but the sandwiches on ciabatta, and top-class chips (Y14) are decidedly Western in flavour. The coffee (Y18), juices and smoothies (from Y25) go down a treat, too. The large outside terrace gets busy if the weather's nice.

MANCHURIAN SPECIAL FLAVOUR JIĂOZI RESTAURANT

Map pp58-9   Chinese Dōngběi Y

东北人

☎ 6415 2855; 1a Xinzhong Jie; 东直门外新中街1号; jiǎozi from Y10; ☽ lunch & dinner; ◉ Dongzhimen

With its singing waitresses in their colourful qípáo (traditional Chinese dress) and a menu that proclaims, 'We all love you', this friendly, noisy restaurant specialises in the cuisine of northeastern China, a region of icy winds and biting cold. That means lots of hearty meat dishes such as stewed chicken (Y28) and shredded pork with wild vegetables (Y25). But the real deal here are the delicious jiǎozi. There's a whole range to pick from, but the green pepper and pork, Chinese cabbage and pork, and pumpkin and egg are particularly addictive. Try a few bottles of Hapi, Harbin's very own beer (Y12), to make it the perfect Dōngběi experience. English menu.

KEMPINSKI DELI   Map pp110-11   Deli Y
凯宾美食廊 **Kǎibīn Měishíláng**
☎ 6465 3388, ext 5741; 1st fl, Kempinski Hotel, Lufthansa Center, 50 Liangmaqiao Lu; 亮马桥路50号凯宾斯基饭店1层; deli items from Y5; ◷ 7am-10pm; ◉ Dongsishitiao, then 🚌 701 heading east

Just off the shuddering Third Ring Rd, the deli in the Kempinski Hotel continues to produce some of the best desserts, breads and cakes (discounted after 8pm) in town. Tables are available for patrons to park themselves for coffee and a chat in a smart environment.

JENNY LOU'S   Map pp110-11   Deli Y
婕妮璐
☎ 6461 6928; 6 Sanlitun Beixiaojie; 三里屯北小街6号; bread from Y8; ◷ 8am-10pm; ◉ Agricul-ural Exhibition Center

The most popular deli for expats and well-heeled locals alike, thanks to the fresh meat and fish and the array of cheeses, along with an impressive selection of wine. It stocks all the usual staples as well. Not cheap, but it caters to a captive market. There are six branches. The most convenient branches are this one and the one by the west gate of Chaoyang Park (Map pp110–11; ◷ 6501 6249; Chaoyang Park; 朝阳公园西门; ◷ 8am-10pm).

APRIL GOURMET   Map pp110-11   Deli Y
绿叶子食品店 **Lǜyèzi Shípǐndiàn**
☎ 8460 1030; 1 Sanlitun Beixiaojie; 三里屯北小街1号; bread from Y8; ◷ 8am-9pm; ◉ Agricul-ural Exhibition Center

A rival with Jenny Lou's (above) for the affections of home cooking–starved Westerners, April Gourmet operates three stores in Běijīng. Its selection isn't quite as extensive as Jenny Lou's, but the prices are similar. Cheese, fresh bread, butter, wine, sauces, Western soups, coffee, milk, meats and frozen food are all available. Another branch (Map pp110–11; ☎ 6417 770; 1f Jiezuo Mansion, Xingfucun Zhonglu; 幸福村中路杰座大厦一层) stays open till midnight.

HǍIDIÀN 海淀
With the majority of Běijīng's universities located in Hǎidiàn, there's no shortage of places to eat in this vast, northwestern district. The area around Wèigōngcūn and the Central University for the Nationalities is a great area for ethnic-minority – especially Dǎi, Xīnjiāng and Mongolian – restaurants.

GOLDEN PEACOCK
Map pp128-9   Chinese Dǎi YY
金孔雀德宏傣味餐馆 **Jīnkǒngquè Déhóng Dǎi Wèi Cānguǎn**
☎ 6893 2030; Wèigōngcūn; 魏公村韦伯豪家园西南门对面; dishes from Y22; ◷ lunch & dinner; ◉ Weigongcun

Located opposite the southwest gate of Weibohao Jiayuan in Wèigōngcūn, this un-pretentious, Dǎi-run restaurant may be out of the way but it is very popular (expect to wait for a table). The Dǎi, an ethnic minority from southern Yúnnán, use many of the flavourings common to Southeast Asian cuisine, such as lemongrass, as well as a lot of pre-served vegetables. Try the steamed fish in a banana leaf (Y38). The rice wine (Y16) and the pineapple rice (Y22) are the best in town.

WǓDÀOKǑU 五道口
This district in Hǎidiàn is Běijīng's student heartland and has a surfeit of busy cafes, as well as many cheap Japanese and Korean-barbecue joints.

ISSHIN JAPANESE RESTAURANT
Map p125   Japanese Y
日本料理一心 **Rìběn Liàolǐ Yī Xīn**
☎ 8261 0136; Room 403, West Bldg, 35 Chengfu Lu; 成府路35号院内西楼403室; sushi from Y12; ◷ lunch & dinner; ◉ Wudaokou

Just off an unpromising looking road, about 50 metres north of the traffic lights at the intersection of Chengfu Lu and Wudaokou Station, Isshin is well worth tracking down if you're in the area. With its thoughtful design, laid-back atmosphere and reasonable prices, it's a place where business types, expat Japanese and students can all feel at home. The set lunch (Y28), sushi, salad and noodles, is a great deal and there are set meals (Y58) in the evenings. The menu includes hotpots, Udon noodles and teriyaki dishes.

SCULPTING IN TIME   Map p125   Cafe Y
雕刻时光 **Diāokè Shíguāng**
☎ 8259 8296; 1f, Bldg 12, 1 Huaqing Jiayuan, Chengfu Lu; 成府路华清嘉园12号楼1层; pasta dishes from Y30; ◷ breakfast, lunch & dinner; ◉ Wudaokou

Taking its name from a book by the late Russian film director Andrei Tarkovsky, this is a fashionable hang-out for the Wǔdàokǒu laptop crowd, as well as for lunch, or coffee (Y20) at any time. There are books and maga-zines to browse through, as well as sand-wiches and pasta for when you get peckish.

GREATER BEIJING

The Lìdū area is home to some fine eateries, while there are a smattering of decent places to eat in the 798 Art District.

SALT Map pp128-9 Western YYY
盐 Yán
☎ 6437 8457; 1st fl, 9 Jiangtai Xilu; 蒋台西路 9号1层珀丽酒店西侧; 2-/3-course set dinners Y178/198; ☑ lunch & dinner; ◉ Sanyuanqiao; ✄

West of the Rosedale Hotel, this stylish but friendly restaurant – dominated by its big, open kitchen, which gives diners a bird's-eye view of the chefs at work – is perhaps the most popular place in town for contemporary Western cuisine. The menu changes weekly, but the food has a Mediterranean flavour, with a hint of South America in the excellent steaks. Salt nods its head to current gastronomic trends, such as foam dishes, but it's not just for serious foodies. It's about fine dining in a casual, relaxed atmosphere. Service is efficient and discreet and the restaurant is lit with candles at night, transforming the modern dining room into a magical place. The set lunch (two/three courses Y88/98) and the extremely popular Sunday brunch (two/three courses Y138/158) are a cheaper way to sample the delights of this consistently impressive restaurant. There's an extensive wine list and it's nonsmoking throughout, apart from the bar, where you can try the potent cocktails. It's essential to reserve.

JIǍ 21 HÀO XĪNÁN MÍNZÚ CÀI
Map pp128-9 Chinese Fusion YY
甲21号西南民族菜
☎ 6489 5066; 21 Beitucheng Donglu; 北土城东路21号; meals Y60; ☑ lunch & dinner; ◉ Huixinxijienankou; ✄

It's slightly off the beaten track, but diners who come here are rewarded with imaginative dishes that take their inspiration from the southwestern cuisine of Yúnnán and Guìzhōu, with a dash of Sìchuān spice. The suān tāng yú (sour fish soup) is worth the trip. The decor, palm trees and concrete walls, as well as the huge ceilings and giant dining area (with a nonsmoking section), is a little bizarre, but don't let that put you off.

KRO'S NEST Map pp128-9 Pizza YY
鸟巢比萨店 Niǎo Cháo Bǐsà Diàn
☎ 6252 8057; 1 Fuyuanmen, Yiheyuan Lu; 颐和园路福缘门1号, 101中学西边; pizzas from Y55; ☑ lunch & dinner; ◉ Suzhoujie

Huge pizzas, onion rings, chips and chicken wings draw in the student crowd (both local and foreign) from the surrounding colleges. The grungy decor, wooden tables and floors, as well as the free beer nights, give the place a frat-boy feel that's authentically American. It's on the west side of 101 Middle School. There's a daily set lunch deal (Y55) and another branch (Map pp110–11; ☎ 6553 5253) inside Workers Stadium north gate.

VINCENT CAFÉ Map pp128-9 Cafe Crêperie
北京季节咖啡店 Běijīng Jìjié Kāfēi Diàn
☎ 8456 4823; 2 Jiuxianqiao Lu; 酒仙桥路2号; crêpes from Y20; ☑ 11am-8pm; ◉ Sanyuanqiao

A cornucopia of crêpes is available at this French-run, country-style cafe in the 798 Art District (p133). The 'fisherman', made with shrimps, leeks and white wine (Y45), has an authentic Breton flavour. Steaks, salads, pizzas, French onion soup, coffee and juice are also on the menu. Good chips, and an outside area in summer.

AT CAFÉ Map pp128-9 Cafe
爱特咖啡 Àitè Kāfēi
☎ 5978 9942; 4 Jiuxianqiao Lu; 酒仙桥路4号; dishes from Y16; ☑ 11am-midnight; ◉ Sanyuanqiao

The first cafe to open in the 798 Art District (p133), this is no longer the hipster hang-out it was when artists could actually afford to live in the area. But the clever design (check out the holes in the interior walls), the fact that it stays open later than nearby places, and the cheap coffee (Y22) and alcohol mean it's still busy. The menu has standard pasta, pizza and sandwiches options, but the desserts, especially the tiramisu (Y30), are better.

NO. 6 SICHUAN FOOD STUDIO
Map pp128-9 Chinese Sichuan
川菜6号工作室 Chuān Cài Liù Hào Gōngzuòshì
☎ 5978 9623; 4 Jiuxianqiao Lu; 酒仙桥路4号; dishes from Y16; ☑ lunch & dinner; ◉ Sanyuanqiao

Most cafes and restaurants in 798 stick to a tried-and-tested formula of Western staples. Not this place; it's a Sìchuān shrine, with home-style dishes such as double-fried pork slices with chilli (Y22) and Mápó dòufu (Y16), as well as a selection of hotpots from Y60. It's a fabulous space, too, with its walls covered in Cultural Revolution–era propaganda posters and a lurid, pink statue of Mao Zedong overlooking the ground-floor dining area.

ENTERTAINMENT

top picks

ENTERTAINMENT

Just as China's economy started roaring to life in the late 1980s, before becoming the behemoth it is now, so Běijīng's entertainment scene has made such rapid strides in the last few years that visitors to the city are often amazed at the options available. It's staggering to contemplate a you sip a martini in the latest hotspot, or dance while a big-name European DJ is spinning, bu until 20 years ago there weren't any bars or nightclubs, outside of a few in hotels, anywhere in Běijīng. That strait-laced past is long gone and with increasing numbers of locals acquiring taste for Western-style fun once the sun goes down, new bars and clubs open every week.

Some bars would not look out of place in London or New York – Běijīng can now match Shànghǎi's traditionally more sophisticated nightlife. Thankfully, though, prices have yet to catch up with Hong Kong. Best of all, Běijīng is now developing a distinct nightlife identity of its own, whether it's *hútòng* (alleyway) bars, or clubs and live-music venues that promote local DJs and bands, instead of simply aping what goes on elsewhere. Nevertheless, foreigner continue to drive the nightlife scene, a reflection of the fact that bar and club culture is sti very new here.

But there's far more than just drinking dens and nightclubs on offer. Běijīng is the cultura capital of China, as well as the political one, making it the place to be if you're interested i seeing ballet and contemporary dance, or want to listen to classical music and opera. It's a obligatory stop for the top orchestras and dance companies from around the world when the are on tour; often Běijīng is the only place on the mainland they'll come to.

Běijīng is the centre of China's film industry (more movies get shown here than anywhere els in the country) and the home of the most vibrant live-music circuit on the mainland. Whethe it's jazz or punk you're after, you'll find it here. The theatre is a far less popular medium i China than it is in the West, but Běijīng has a more active scene than any other city. Then ther are traditional pastimes such as Beijing opera (*jīngjù*) and acrobatic shows, which are fixture on the tourist circuit.

Finding out what is going on is easy. The monthly expat magazines (p249), which can be picke up around town, list events and track new openings.

DRINKING

The Chinese down around 40 billion litres of beer (*píjiǔ*) a year, making China the biggest beer market in the world, as well as vast quantities of *báijiǔ*, a pungent, potent white spirit, the drinking of which inevitably ends in the loss of limb control and an evil hangover. But most of that alcohol is consumed in restaurants or at home. Bars are a new-fangled invention in China and only started appearing in Běijīng at the end of the 1980s.

Until a few years ago, they were mostly concentrated in the Sānlǐtún area of Cháoyáng district. Now, though, they have mushroomed across the city, a result of both the rising incomes of Beijingers and the influx of foreigners.

Dōngchéng district is now full of cool *hútòng* bars, ranging from the big and swanky to hole-in-the-wall operations, with the *hútòng* of Nanluogu Xiang the focus of the scene. Further west, the lakes of Qianhai and Houhai have become a magnet for bars.

Otherwise, slick cocktail lounges abound i the CBD, drawing in the expat business cre and those out to impress, while students cor gregate in the bars in Wǔdàokǒu.

Remember this is China, where change constant, so bars open and close as quick as you can down a drink. Prices, too, var enormously (p184). Above all, don't judg Běijīng's bars by their exterior appearance There are plenty of swish-looking place that are dire, while many of the finest e tablishments look less than enticing fro the outside.

Practicalities
OPENING HOURS
Most bars in Běijīng open their doors in th late afternoon and close them at 2am. B many stay open longer, especially on wee ends, while others shut up shop around mi night. Cafes open much earlier and sometim close early, too. All the cafes in this chapt have wi-fi access.

DŌNGCHÉNG 东城

The ancient and once quiet *hútòng* of Nanluogu Xiang, which runs north–south between Gulou Dongdajie and Di'anmen Dongdajie, has become one of Běijīng's nightlife hubs in the last couple of years. While the character of the *hútòng* has changed irrevocably – most of the residents have rented out their homes for bars, restaurants and shops and decamped to the suburbs – it does now feature a wide range of bars that cater to both locals and Westerners. For a less-hectic time, especially at weekends, there are bars on and off Gulou Dongdajie and Andingmennei Dajie and around the Drum Tower that are relaxing places for a drink.

12SQM Map pp58-9 Bar

12平米 Shí'èr Píngmǐ

☎ 6402 1554; cnr Nanluogu Xiang & Fuxiang Hutong; 南锣鼓巷福祥胡同1号; beers from Y15, cocktails from Y35; noon-midnight; Zhangzizhonglu;

Běijīng's smallest bar – the clue is in the name – this cosy establishment is run by an Aussie-Chinese couple. Despite the lack of space, they have found room for a proper, old-school wooden bar top, a great selection of malt whiskies and exotic brews, such as Coopers. They can whip up mean mixed drinks, too. On special occasions, hot meat pies (Y35) are available.

DRUM & BELL Map pp58-9 Bar

鼓钟咖啡馆 Gǔzhōng Kāfēiguǎn

☎ 8403 3600; 41 Zhonglouwan Hutong; 钟楼湾胡同41号; beers from Y15, cocktails from Y35; 1pm-2am; Gulou Dajie

Located in between the Drum and Bell Towers, from whom it takes its name, the main attraction of this bar is its splendid roof terrace. It's a great spot to catch some rays on lazy Sunday afternoons, or to wile away a summer evening. In winter, retreat downstairs, where there are comfy sofas to sink into. There are bar snacks, too.

PALACE VIEW BAR Map pp58-9 Bar

观景酒吧 Guānjǐng Jiǔbā

☎ 6513 7788; 10th fl, Grand Hotel Beijing, 35 Dongchang'an Jie; 东长安街35号 贵宾楼饭店10层; cocktails from Y70; 6pm-midnight May-September; Tiananmen Dong or Wangfujing

For refined refreshment with a top-notch panorama, the Palace View is in a league of its own. Outdoor tables graced by a string of palm trees make this a wonderful, if rarefied, place to escape the city and size up the view overlooking Dongchang'an Jie, the Forbidden City and Tiananmen Square.

PASSBY BAR Map pp58-9 Bar

过客 Guòkè

☎ 8403 8004; 108 Nanluogu Xiang; 南锣鼓巷108号四合院; beers from Y18; 9.30am-2am; Andingmen

The first bar to open on Nanluogu Xiang and now something of an institution, the Passby attracts a diverse crowd of locals, expats and travellers looking for a less manic experience than that provided by some of the nearby bars. It operates from a courtyard house that has polished beams, a low ceiling and a useful library of books that are available for loan; you need to donate three books to join the library. The

NONALCOHOLIC DRINKS

A fundamental part of Chinese existence, tea is celebrated by an ancient saying as one of the seven basic necessities of life, alongside fuel, oil, rice, salt, soy sauce and vinegar. The Chinese were the first to cultivate tea *(chá)*, and the art of brewing and drinking tea – popular since the Tang dynasty (AD 618–907) – shows few signs of losing steam.

China has three main types of tea: green *(lǜchá)* or unfermented; black tea *(hóng chá)*, which is fermented; and wulong *(wūlóngchá)*, or semi-fermented. But there are numerous varieties, from jasmine *(mòlìhuāchá)* and chrysanthemum *(júhuā chá)* to pu'er *(pǔ'ěrchá)*, Iron Guanyin *(tiěguānyīn)* and beyond. Cheap restaurants often serve on-the-house pots of weak jasmine or green tea. Higher quality brands of tea are available in tea shops and supermarkets. Traditionally, Chinese would never put milk or sugar in their tea but things are changing. Now 'milk tea' *(nǎi chá)* is available everywhere in Běijīng, often served cold with a whopping amount of sugar. Thirst-quenching bubble tea *(zhēnzhū nǎichá)*, a hot or cold concoction sold in a variety of sweet flavours, is also widely available.

Coffee *(kāfēi)* long ago took Běijīng by storm and cafes of wildly varying quality have covered town like a rash. Prices are on a par with the West, with a cup of coffee costing from Y20 up.

Soft drinks *(qìshuǐ)* can be found at every turn, along with bottled water. Milk *(niúnǎi)* and yoghurt *(suānnǎi)* are available from supermarkets and convenience stores, along with powdered milk *(nǎifěn)*.

pleasant outside area is normally over-subscribed in summer. There's a fair selection of foreign beers and wine, as well as a menu offering a range of Italian, Western and Chinese dishes (from Y38).

RED MOON BAR Map pp58-9 Bar
东方亮 Dōngfāng Liàng

☎ 6510 9366; Grand Hyatt Beijing, 1 Dongchang'an Jie; 东长安街1号, 北京东方君悦大酒店; cocktails from Y75; ☽ 5pm-1am; ◉ Wangfujing

This very sleek and seductive lounge bar in the heart of Wángfǔjīng is the perfect place to recover with a chilled cocktail after an afternoon's shopping in the area. Super service, a sushi bar and a fine wine list, as well as a cigar selection, add to its high-toned delights. There is a 15% service charge here, though.

REEF BAR Map pp58-9 Bar
触礁 Chùjiāo

☎ 6403 2736; 14-1 Nanluogu Xiang; 南锣鼓巷14-1号; beers from Y10, cocktails from Y25; ☽ 2pm-late; ◉ Andingmen

Much more of a bar for locals than many others in the area, the Reef has a friendly vibe that makes it an easy place to hang out. Located in a converted *hútòng* house, there's a small bar area, a few sofas and tables, and a wide selection of foreign beers. Run by a cheerful husband-and-wife team, it stays open into the wee hours on busy nights.

SALUD Map pp58-9 Bar
老伍 lǎowǔ

☎ 6402 5086; 66 Nanluogu Xiang; 南锣鼓巷66号; beers from Y20, cocktails from Y30; ☽ 3pm-late; ◉ Andingmen

The biggest and most happening bar on Nanluogu Xiang, Salud gets very busy on weekends with a young-ish, mixed crowd of locals and expats who party well into the early hours. Its house-special flavoured rums (Y20) come in test-tube-like vessels and are lethal. There's live music and bar snacks are available, but watch out for the very low ceiling on the 2nd floor.

YĪN Map pp58-9 Bar
饮

☎ 6523 6877; Emperor Hotel, 33 Qihelou Jie; 骑河楼街33号; cocktails from Y57; ☽ 11am-2am Apr-Nov; ◉ Dongsi

Ascend the stairs of the orange-themed Emperor Hotel (p208) to reach this terrace bar, and then climb the wooden steps to its highest point for a stunning view over the rooftops of the Forbidden City. Lovely at sunset, the drinks aren't as special as the setting: try the Emperor's Martini – a vodka, sake, peach and cranberry concoction. There's a DJ on weekends, a happy hour (4pm to 10pm) on Thursdays, and a hot tub for exhibitionists and the sort of people who go out drinking in their swimsuits.

GINGKO Map pp58-9 Bar-Cafe
银杏西餐酒吧 Yínxíng Xīcān Jiǔbā

☎ 6402 7532; 199 Andingmennei Dajie; 安定门内大街199号; beers from Y15, cocktails from Y35; ☽ 11am-late; ◉ Andingmen

A slightly schizophrenic blend of a bar, cafe, restaurant and live-music venue, this place is clearly anxious to cover all the bases. It works best as a bar and cafe – the coffee is good – but it's also a nice, intimate location to hear the bands and musicians of all varieties that take to the small stage a couple of times a week. There's Guinness and a reasonable selection of wine, as well as a far more impressive range of snacks – from croquettes to mussels, paninis and pizzas – than is usual in a Běijīng bar.

WAITING FOR GODOT Map pp58-9 Cafe
等待戈多 Děngdài Gēduō

☎ 6407 3093; 24 Jiaodaokou Dongdajie; 交道口东大街24号; coffee & beers from Y20; ☽ 10am-2am; ◉ Beixinqiao

Cool and charming cafe that takes it name from Samuel Beckett's best-known play. Local bohemians and Westerners who live in the area are drawn in by the moody lighting and the arthouse movies that play on the big screen TV, as much as they are by the coffee, tea and good selection of foreign beers. The friendly staff can rustle up basic pasta dishes and salads, too. It's an easy place to wile away a few hours. A few doors down the road, its equally chilled sister establishment, the Sea (☎ 8401 1893; Bldg 4, 30 Jiaodaokou Dongdajie; 交道口东大街30号四号楼), is tucked behind a flower shop.

XĪCHÉNG 西城

In recent years, the lakes of Houhai and Qianhai have become a backdrop for a huge number of bars, which are very popular with local drinkers. Sadly, most are overpriced cookie cutter imitations of each other and come complete with lame live music and annoyin

ENTERTAINMENT DRINKING

bar touts. There are still a few fine places at which to imbibe, though, mostly tucked away in the *hútòng* behind the roads that line the lakes.

BED BAR Map pp88–9

床吧 **Chuángbā**

Bar

☎ 8400 1554; 17 Zhangwang Hutong, Jiugulou Dajie; 旧鼓楼大街张旺胡同17号; beers from Y25, cocktails from Y40; ☺ 4pm-late Mon & Tue, noon-late Wed-Sun; ◉ Gulou Dajie

One *hútòng* north of Café Sambal is this gem of a bar, situated in a converted courtyard. The bar area leads onto a succession of inner rooms, some with beds, and the overall effect is of a place that's both intimate and spacious. Bed Bar can often be crowded, but there's always a spot where you can hide away. There's a DJ and small dance floor, and it does finger food, too.

LA BAIE DES ANGES Map pp88–9

Bar

天使港法国休闲酒吧 **Tiānshǐ Gǎngwān Fǎguó Xiūxián Jiǔbā**

☎ 6657 1605; 5 Nanguanfang Hutong, Hòuhǎi; 后海南官房胡同5号; wine per glass from Y40; ☺ 6pm-2am summer, 7pm-2am winter, closed Mon; ◉ Gulou Dajie

A few doors down from Hutong Pizza and well away from the Hòuhǎi madness, this laid-back, cool French-run wine bar is great for lovers of the grape. The knowledgeable owners have weekly wine specials, as well as a huge selection of French vintages that start at Y190 a bottle. The space, a former courtyard house, is intimate without being cramped and it offers French-style bar snacks, beer and cocktails as well. There's normally some form of music on Saturday nights.

NO NAME BAR Map pp88–9

Bar

无名酒吧 **Wúmíng Jiǔbā**

☎ 6401 8541; 3 Qianhai Dongyan; 前海东沿3号; beers from Y20, cocktails from Y35; ☺ noon-2am; ◉ Gulou Dajie

Overlooking Qianhai Lake, No Name was the first bar to open in the area and was so successful that it spawned countless imitators. Thankfully, it has resisted going down the overpriced, soulless route taken by most of its competitors. Instead, it's a laid-back joint with pleasant staff where you can sit in a rattan chair and watch the world go by through the large windows,

top picks

DRINKING DESTINATIONS

- **Bed Bar** (left) Lounge on a Qing dynasty–style bed and sip a mojito or three.
- **Face** (p185) Cocktails and pints in a stylish setting.
- **Glen** (p185) Drinking perfection and the best range of whiskies in town.
- **La Baie des Anges** (left) For fans of the grape.
- **Q Bar** (p186) Proper cocktails in an easy-going atmosphere.
- **Saddle Cantina** (p186) Margarita madness on the outside terrace.
- **Salud** (opposite) Raucous fun in the humming *hútòng* (alleyway) of Nanluogu Xiang.

whether over a coffee in the afternoon or a drink in the evening. It's in front of the Nuage restaurant.

OBIWAN Map pp88–9

Bar

☎ 8322 1231; 4 Xihai Xiyan; 西海西沿4号; beers from Y20, cocktails from Y35; ☺ 1pm-2am; ◉ Jishuitan

Perched in splendid isolation by the side of the little-visited Xihai Lake, this three-storey bar is great in summer when its roof terrace comes into its own. But in winter, the 2nd floor is an equally good location for a drink, or to munch on popcorn at Wednesday night screenings of classic '80s movies. Most weekends it runs some sort of event, whether it's Saturday's trance night or the Sunday afternoon reggae jam. It's down the alley to the left of the PLA Theatre.

CHÁOYÁNG 朝阳

The days when Sānlǐtún was the be-all and end-all of Běijīng nightlife are long gone. These days, the main drag of Sanlitun Lu is rather tawdry – at night the touts for massage parlours and hookers emerge – and the bars are strictly for the undiscerning. But Nansanlitun Lu, the road running south from Sanlitun Lu on the other side of Gongrentiyuchang Beilu, has a number of good places, while there's a cluster of lively bars in the streets behind the 3.3 Shopping Centre that attracts younger drinkers. The area around Jianguomenwai Dajie is home to upmarket cocktail bars for the CBD crowd.

DRINKING IN THE CITY

Beer (*píjiǔ*) is Běijing's favourite tipple and the brews you are most likely to encounter are Yanjing Beer, Beijing Beer and Tsingtao. Yanjing is weak and unremarkable, but it's a favourite with Beijingers. A bottle will cost Y2 to Y3 in a local shop. Beijing beer is often served on tap and is very light. Tsingtao, which is brewed from a German recipe in the port of Qingdǎo, tastes more like a European lager, but isn't as strong as most overseas beers. You can pick up a large bottle for around Y3 on the streets.

It is a different story in bars though, where a small bottle of Tsingtao can cost as much as Y25. All bars will have a selection of foreign brews as well, and there are plenty of places around town where you can sup a Stella Artois, chug a Corona or Coopers, or gargle with a Guinness. Expect to pay more, Y30 to Y50, for the privilege of drinking alcohol from overseas. It's well worth checking the local listing mags, which have details of the many happy-hour deals that are available around the city.

The time when a cocktail in Běijing meant a gin and tonic is thankfully long past. Now, there are many bars that can whip up a decent mojito or cosmopolitan. Prices for a drink in a fancy glass start at around Y40. Foreign wine (*pútáojiǔ*) is increasingly available, too. While wine is still an acquired taste for most Chinese, China does now make its own wines, with Great Wall and Dynasty the most popular brands. Most Chinese *vino*, though, is sweet and has a tendency to cling to the teeth.

Far more popular, especially among the young, is whisky. It's often mixed with green tea, which appeals to the Chinese sweet tooth and tastes better than it sounds. The sight of groups of white-collar Chinese 20-somethings downing bottles of Chivas Regal in bars and clubs, while playing finger-guessing games or liars dice, has become something of a cliché in Běijing.

But whisky has a long way to go before it can match the popularity of *báijiǔ*. Despite being loosely translated as wine, it is in fact a clear spirit fermented from sorghum (a type of millet). It's a searing, strong liquor that's very easy to get drunk on – so go easy if you get into a drinking contest with the locals – and has a unique taste that few foreigners can stomach. But if your preferred tipple is nail varnish, or paint stripper, you'll love it. It's supercheap, too; a small bottle of the locally distilled Erguotou will cost around Y5.

ALFA Map pp110-11 — Bar
阿尔法 **Ā'ěrfǎ**
☎ 6413 0086; 6 Xingfu Yicun; 幸福一村6号, 工体北门对面; **beers from Y20, cocktails from Y35**; ⏰ **5pm-late**; ◉ **Dongsishitiao**
With an outside terrace, complete with cushion-strewn booths to lounge in and a water feature to fall into, as well as an in-house Asian-French restaurant to satisfy late-night hunger pangs, Alfa has survived longer than most Běijing bars. It's not the hotspot it was a couple of years ago, but its monthly theme nights – think '80s, Goth and funk – are still popular. It's just down from the Xinjiang Red Rose Restaurant, opposite the north gate of the Workers Stadium.

BAR BLU Map pp110-11 — Bar
蓝吧 **Lánbā**
☎ 6417 4124; 4th fl, Tongli Studio, Sanlitun Beijie; 三里屯北街同里4层; **beers from Y20, cocktails from Y40**; ⏰ **4pm-2am Sun-Thu, 4pm-4am Fri & Sat**; ◉ **Tuanjiehu**
Perennially popular with a younger clientele, Bar Blu's once-huge roof terrace has been cut in half but it's still an acceptable spot in the summer. A pub quiz (Wednes-day), ladies' night on Thursday and karaoke on Sunday help bring in the punters, as does the daily happy hour (4pm to 9pm). Late on weekends, when the DJ is playing party classics, it gets packed.

BEER MANIA Map pp110-11 — Bar
麦霓啤酒吧 **Màiní Píjiǔbā**
☎ 6585 0786; 1st fl, Taiyue Haoting, Nansanlitun Lu; 南三里屯路泰悦豪庭一层; **beers from Y45**; ⏰ **2pm-2am**; ◉ **Tuanjiehu**
With Tintin posters on the walls, this small, simple establishment is a shrine to all things Belgian, but especially their strong beer. Over 70 types are on offer, including Trappist and fruit brews, as well as Stella Artois on tap. The high prices make it worth taking advantage of the daily happy hour (5pm to 7pm). Belgian-style snacks, waffles and chips are available as well.

BLUE FROG Map pp110-11 — Ba
蓝蛙 **Lánwā**
☎ 6417 4030; 3f, S4, Village, 19 Sanlitun Lu; 三里屯路19号院, 4号楼3层; **beers from Y30, cocktails from Y50**; ⏰ **11am-2am Mon-Fri, 10am-2am Sat & Sun**; ◉ **Tuanjiehu**; ✗

A recent Shànghǎi import to the capital, the Frog draws in a mixed, older crowd with drinks promotions, solid burgers and wraps, international sport on the TVs and an outside area in summer. It's still a bit soulless, but if you can drink all 100 shots on its display board, you'll get a free one every day from then. Standard drinks are Y25 on Tuesdays.

CASA HABANA Map pp110-11   Bar
哈瓦那之家 **Hāwǎnà Zhījiā**
☎ 6595 0888; Jinglun Hotel, 3 Jianguomenwai Dajie; 建国门外大街3号京伦饭店; **rum from Y60, cigars from Y80**; ⏰ 9am-midnight; ◉ **Yonganli**

Cuban rum and cigars are the draw at this small bar run by a Beijinger who's spent a lot of time in Havana – check out the photos of him with Fidel Castro that line the walls. The leather armchairs and sofas give the place an exclusive club feel and there's a huge selection of cigars to choose from, as well as humidifiers and cigar cutters for sale. Apart from the rums, there's a reasonable choice of whiskies. It's on the far western corner of the Jinglun Hotel.

CENTRO Map pp110-11   Bar
炫酷 **Xuànkù**
☎ 6561 8833; Kerry Center Hotel, 1 Guanghua Lu; 光华路1号嘉里中心大酒店; **cocktails Y80**; ⏰ 24hr; ◉ **Guomao**

A favourite with foreign business types, as well as locals and expats out to impress, Centro is a swish lounge with a glossy black bar, plenty of sofas and tables, and an eccentric carpet pattern. The service is impressive, there's live jazz during the week and a DJ on the weekends. Centro has an extensive wine list (from Y70 per glass).

CHEERS Map pp110-11   Bar
☎ 135 2044 6062; 2f Tongli Studio, Sanlitun Houjie; 三里屯后街同里商场2层; **beers from Y20, cocktails from Y40**; ⏰ 6.30pm-late; ◉ **Tuanjiehu**

Despite the name, this place has nothing in common with the fictional Boston bar in the eponymous TV series. Instead, it's a loud, wooden-floored drinking den with a pool table and the owner's paintings of nudes adorning the brick walls. It's friendly, though, and has a daily happy hour until 10pm, which makes it a good place to start the night.

CHOCOLATE Map pp110-11   Bar
巧克力 **Qiǎokèlì**
☎ 8561 3988; 19 Ritan Beilu; 日坛北路19号; ⏰ 7pm-7am; ◉ **Chaoyangmen**

There are a number of Russian-style bars around the Ritan Park area, but with its over-the-top, gold-themed decor and cheesy floor shows, as well as a Mongolian midget doorman, this is the closest you will come to a genuine Moscow nightlife experience in Běijīng. Beers start at Y30. This is a place to drink in a group, though, so do as the Russians do and order a bottle of vodka (from Y238). It gets going after midnight.

FACE Map pp110-11   Bar
妃思 **Fēisī**
☎ 6551 6788; 26 Dongcaoyuan, Gongrentiyuchang Nanlu; 工体南路东草园26号; **wine from Y55, cocktails from Y65**; ⏰ 6pm-late; ◉ **Chaoyangmen**

Stylish and expensive, but without the usual accompanying attitude, Face is unique in Běijīng because it's a cocktail bar that also serves pints of Tetley's Bitter and Guinness, as well as a good range of single malt whiskies. The bar is a series of interconnected rooms, all tastefully decorated in a vaguely Southeast Asian theme. There's an outside terrace and two pool tables as well. The bar is down an alley just south of Gongti Nanlu; look for the sign to guide you there.

GLEN Map pp110-11   Bar
☎ 6591 1191; 203 Taiyue Haoting, 16 Nansanlitun Lu; 南三里屯16号泰悦豪庭2层203; **drinks from Y60**; ⏰ 6pm-2am; ◉ **Tuanjiehu**

Precision cocktail-making, a massive malt whisky selection and painstaking attention to detail – shaved ice cubes – make this Japanese-style whisky bar a true connoisseurs' drinking experience. It's not cheap (there's a Y30 cover charge for bar snacks), but the service and setting (whether sitting at the long bar or at the well-spaced tables) are impeccable. It's on the 2nd floor of the office block above Beer Mania; take the stairs on the right-hand side of the building.

LAN Map pp110-11   Bar
兰会所 **Lán Huìsuǒ**
☎ 5109 6012; 4th fl, Twintowers Shopping Mall B-12, Jianguomenwai Dajie; 建国门外大街乙12号LG双子座F层; **cocktails from Y65**; ⏰ 5pm-2am; ◉ **Yonganli**

Despite its incongruous location in an anonymous shopping mall opposite the

Silk Market, this Philippe Starck–designed place is perhaps the most eye-catching bar in Běijīng. Paintings dangle from the ceilings, giant mirrors lean against the walls, red crushed-velvet curtains divide the space, the furniture is a mix of leather armchairs and *fin de siècle* long couches and tables, while the toilets are the most extravagant in the city. There's an attached oyster bar and expensive restaurant. It's popular with movers and shakers, and those who think they fall into that category. There are DJs and sometimes live jazz on the weekends.

MAGGIES Map pp110-11 Bar
美琪 **Màiqí**
☎ 8562 8142/8143; South Gate, Ritan Park; 日坛公园南门; beers from Y30; ✆ 7.30pm-4.30am Sun-Wed, 7.30pm-5am Thu-Sat; ◉ Jianguomen
A Běijīng legend and (in)famous enough for everyone from visiting politicians to Hollywood types, Maggies can be a bit sleazy for some people's tastes. A somewhat mixed, mostly male crowd gathers here, as do many Mongolian ladies. But it is open very late and has a small dance floor, while the spacious bar is a fine spot for people-watching. It serves excellent hotdogs outside as well.

MESH Map pp110-11 Bar
☎ 6417 6688; Bldg 1, Village, 11 Sanlitun Lu; 三里屯路11号院1号楼; cocktails from Y70; ✆ 5pm-1am; ◉ Tuanjiehu
Located inside the achingly trendy Opposite House Hotel (p213), Mesh has been designed to within an inch of its life – white bar, mirrors, fancy light fittings and mesh screens separating its different areas – but the effect isn't overpowering and it can be a fun on the right night. On Thursdays it's gay friendly. The lychee martinis are worth trying.

PADDY O'SHEA'S Map pp110-11 Bar
爱尔兰酒吧 **Ài'érlán Jiǔbā**
☎ 6415 6389; 28 Dongzhimenwai Dajie; 东直门外大街28号; beers from Y20, cocktails from Y40; ✆ 10am-2am; ◉ Dongzhimen
A key spot for watching sport (football and rugby especially) on the big screen and many TVs, Paddy's feels like most overseas Irish pubs – lots of wood panelling and Guinness posters – but it's big, has a proper bar to sit at and the service is warm and ef-

ficient. The alcohol selection is sound, with Kilkenny and Guinness (Y55) on tap and lots of bottled beers. There's a daily happy hour until 8pm, a pool table upstairs and it does pub grub.

PIPES Map pp110-11 Bar
烟斗 **Yāndǒu**
☎ 6553 9513; Gongrentiyuchang Nanmen; 工体南门东100米路北; beers from Y20, cocktails from Y35; ✆ 6pm-2am; ◉ Chaoyangmen
An unremarkable dive with a small dance floor and lots of flashing lights, Pipes switches identity on Saturday nights, when it becomes Běijīng's best-known lesbian hang-out. As such, it attracts a lot of local ladies. To get here, go through the south gate of the Workers Stadium (not the smaller gate by the Blue Zoo) and then hang an immediate right.

Q BAR Map pp110-11 Bar
Q吧
☎ 6595 9239; Top fl, Eastern Inn Hotel, Nansanlitun Lu; 三里屯南路麦霓啤酒吧南100米; cocktails from Y50; ✆ 6pm-late; ◉ Tuanjiehu
Possibly the most amenable cocktail lounge in the city, and one of the most popular, Q Bar benefits from a laid-back atmosphere, a solid music selection (DJs on the weekend) and some of the best-mixed drinks in Běijīng. The bar staff really know their stuff and are always concocting new cocktails. There's a long bar to perch at and sofas to recline in, or you can head to the large roof terrace when the weather is nice. There's a big 'Q' hanging off the side of the Eastern Inn Hotel to guide you there.

SADDLE CANTINA Map pp110-11 Bar
☎ 5208 6005; West Wing, Nali Patio, 81 Sanlitun Beilu; 三里屯酒吧街81号3.3隔壁南边新白楼里边; beers from Y20, cocktails from Y45; ✆ 10am-2am; ◉ Tuanjiehu
The Mexican theme at this spacious, well-managed joint means potent margaritas (Y60) are available, as well as burritos (Y60) and fajitas (Y65 to Y70). That is less important than the attractive 2nd-floor roof terrace, though, which is always heaving in summer with a 20-something crowd. One of Sānlǐtún's hotspots, get here early if you want to sit outside. It's down the alley to the left of the 3.3 Shopping Centre.

TREE Map pp110-11   Bar
树酒吧 Shù Jiǔbā

☎ 6591 6519; 43 Sanlitun Beijie; 三里屯北街
43号; beers from Y15; ⏱ 11am-late Mon-Sat,
1pm-late Sun; Ⓜ Tuanjiehu

Tucked behind a strip of bars that get mad-ousy at weekends, this low-key, long-term favourite attracts a mix of locals, expats and tourists. There's a fine selection of Belgian beers (from Y40) and the thin-crust pizzas (from Y50), cooked in a wood-fired oven in the bar itself, are some of the best in town. It's off the courtyard of the You Yi Youth Hostel.

APERITIVO Map pp110-11   Bar-Cafe
意式餐吧 Yìshì Cānbā

☎ 6417 7793; 43 Sanlitun Beijie; 三里屯北街
南路43楼1号; coffee from Y20, wine & cocktails
from Y38; ⏱ 10am-2am; Ⓜ Tuanjiehu

This Italian-run bar attracts the Euro-crowd, thanks to the continental cafe–like vibe, lengthy wine list and small terrace shielded from the street by some artfully placed shrubs. Inside, it's less appealing but it does offer bar food.

STONE BOAT Map pp110-11   Bar-Cafe
石舫咖啡 Shífǎng Kāfēi

☎ 6501 9986; Southwestern cnr, Ritan Park; 日坛
公园西南角; beers & coffee from Y20, cocktails
from Y35; ⏱ 10am-late; Ⓜ Jianguomen

A lovely bar on a summer evening, this is a place where you can escape the traffic and noise of Sānlǐtún. There's mellow live music, an outside area where you can sit beneath the trees of Ritan Park, and a refreshing ambience that comes with the shock of being so close to nature in Běijīng. By day it functions as a pleasant cafe. To get here after Ritan Park closes, go to the south or west gate of the park and tell the guards you're going to the jiǔbā (bar) and they'll let you in.

WǓDÀOKǑU 五道口

With its concentration of colleges and univer-sities, this district of Hǎidiàn is student land. In summer, there are open-air beer gardens serving cheap draught beer (Y10) close to the subway station.

LUSH Map p125   Bar-Cafe
☎ 8286 3566; 1 Huaqing Jiayuan, Chengfu Lu; 华
清嘉园1号楼2层; beers from Y20, cocktails from
Y35; ⏱ 24hr; Ⓜ Wudaokou

For the hordes of students in Wǔdàokǒu, both foreign and local, all roads lead to Lush. During the day it functions as a cafe with a Western menu, including breakfast (Y30) and sandwiches and salads (from Y35). After dark it becomes the epicentre of nightlife in the area. Every evening offers something different, whether it's movie screenings, live music, a pub quiz, DJs, or an open-mic night for aspiring poets and singers. There's a daily happy hour from 6pm to 10pm and it never closes. It's above the O2 Sun bookstore.

GREATER BEIJING

If you've spent the day exploring the galleries in the 798 Art District, there are some cafes that turn into pleasant spots for a libation in the evening. Or you can head to the nearby Lìdū area, where there are a few bars worth visiting.

FRANK'S PLACE Map pp128-9   Bar
翠欧 Cuì'ōu

☎ 6437 6943; 9-3 Jiangtai Xilu; 将台西路9-3号
珀丽酒店西侧; beers from Y20, cocktails from
Y50; ⏱ 10am-2am; Ⓜ Sanyuanqiao

The oldest bar in Běijīng, Frank's has shifted locations many times in the course of its life. It's now firmly ensconced in the Lìdū area in northeast Cháoyáng, a popular place for expats with families and visiting business types staying in the nearby four-star hotels. Frank's caters to their needs by providing live sport on many TVs, pints of Guinness and Stella (Y50), English-speaking staff and average pub food. The place is chameleon-like; if the NFL is on then it could be an Ameri-can bar, if the football (soccer) is on you could be in England. There's a pool and darts, occasional live music and an outside terrace open in summer. It is west of the Rosedale Hotel.

NIGHTLIFE

China's leaders, President Hu Jintao and Premier Wen Jiabao, may be tucked up in their beds by midnight in the elite residential compound of Zhōngnánhǎi, but plenty of Bei-jingers are out and about in the early hours. Whether it's dancing in a club or listening to pop, punk, metal or jazz at the different venues scattered across town, there are numerous op-tions for night owls.

Běijīng is not Europe or the US, though, and clubbing and watching music live are still the preserve of a minority of locals. Nor are the venues on the same level as those in the West. Clubs, especially, tend to be cut from the same cloth as their competitors, which can lead to a feeling of déjà vu. At the same time, most live-music places are considerably smaller than their equivalents overseas. But if you embrace the differences and head out with a positive attitude, there's plenty of fun to be had in Běijīng.

LIVE MUSIC

There might be an instinctive Chinese fondness for the manufactured, syrupy sound of Canto pop or Taiwanese boy bands, but some of Běijīng's residents have grittier tastes. Having discovered Western rock music in the early '80s via the cassette tapes of foreign students, Beijingers have always been at the forefront of the Chinese rock scene. There are all sorts of acts plugging away on an admittedly limited circuit. The best bands land record contracts with Japanese, Taiwanese or obscure US labels, but most survive by endless gigging. The upside is that most nights there's a band playing somewhere. Běijīng is still a backwater when it comes to international pop and rock acts, though, and few international acts make it here.

You can find live music of varying quality lifting Běijīng's roofs every night of the week and there should be something to suit your sensibilities, whether they be rock, indie, metal, punk, folk or jazz. Check the expat mags (p249) for full listings of who's playing.

2 KOLEGAS Map pp128-9
两个好朋友 Liǎnggè Hǎopéngyǒu
☎ 6436 8998; 21 Liangmaqiao Lu; 亮马桥路 21号 (燕莎桥往东1500米路北汽车电影院 内); admission from Y30; 🕑 8pm-2am Mon-Sat, 10am-9pm Sun; Ⓜ Liangmaqiao, then 🚌 909
Tucked away to the side of Běijīng's drive-in cinema is this great little venue, which hosts local punkers and a fair proportion of out-of-town acts. In summer, you can take a break from the aural assault by sitting outside on the grass with a beer, while munching yángròu chuàn (skewers of lamb).

13 CLUB Map p125
13俱乐部 13 Jùlèbù
☎ 8668 7151; 161 Chengfu Lu; 成府路161号; admission from Y30; 🕑 6pm-late; Ⓜ Wudaokou
Dark and forbidding venue down an alley a few doors east of D-22. A lot of metal acts play here, so if you're a fan of guitar solos

and making the sign of the horns, this is the place for you. Look for the red sign.

CD JAZZ CAFÉ Map pp110-11
北京CD爵士俱乐部 Běijīng CD Juéshì Jùlèbù
☎ 6506 8288; 16 Dongsanhuan Beilu; 农展馆 大门南,东三环北路16号,过街天桥下; 🕑 4pm-2am; Ⓜ Agricultural Exhibition Center
A mainstay on the Běijīng jazz scene, this place has regular live performances on Thursdays, Fridays and Saturdays. On Monday nights it hosts swing dancing. No cover charge, but the drinks start at Y50. The venue is just south of the main gate of the Agricultural Exhibition Center.

D-22 Map p125
☎ 6265 3177; 242 Chengfu Lu; 成府路242号; admission from Y30; 🕑 6pm-2am Tue-Sun; Ⓜ Wudaokou
The focal point of the Běijīng indie scene, this stripped-down but friendly venue out in the student land of Wǔdàokǒu is dedicated to showcasing local bands and the odd visiting foreign act. It's a big muso hang-out and if you're there midweek, you might find yourself propping up the bar with some of the capital's guitar heroes.

EAST SHORE JAZZ CAFÉ Map pp88-9
东岸 Dōng'àn
☎ 8403 2131; 2nd fl, 2 Shichahai Nanyan; 地安 门外大街 什刹海南沿2号楼2层(地安门邮 局西侧); 🕑 1pm-2.30am; Ⓜ Gulou Dajie
Cui Jian's saxophonist, whose quartet play here, opened this chilled venue just off Di'anmenwai Dajie and next to Qianhai Lake. It's a place to hear the best local jazz bands, with live performances from Thursdays to Sundays, in a less precious atmosphere than the CD Jazz Café. There's a small roof terrace open in summer with a nice view of the lake and it's worth booking a table here on weekends, when it gets busy. There's no cover charge and the drinks are reasonably priced.

JIANGJINJIU Map pp58-9
将进酒吧 Jiāngjìnjiǔ Jiǔbā
☎ 8405 0124; 2 Zhongku Hutong; 钟库胡同2号 (鼓楼北门); 🕑 11am-2am; Ⓜ Gulou Dajie
Friendly cafe-bar that puts on lots of Chinese folk and ethnic minority, particularly Uighur, bands. There is no cover charge, and it's situated between the Drum and Bell Towers.

BĚIJĪNG ROCKS

Zhang Shouwang is the lead singer of Carsick Cars. Having supported Sonic Youth on tour in Europe, they are one of the few Chinese bands to have an international profile. The 23-year-old grew up in Hǎidiàn district in northwest Běijīng.

When did you decide you wanted to be a rock star? The first time I heard Velvet Underground I knew I wanted to form a band and make new sounds. I was 17. I met our bass player at my college, the Beijing Institute of Technology. We didn't really know how to play then, so we just made noise. Then we met our drummer and we started getting better.

Is rock music becoming more popular in China? Definitely. I remember the first time we went on tour in 2005, we played a gig in Hángzhōu and there were just two people in the audience. Now, when we play outside Běijīng, we get 300 people coming. A lot of people hear our music online now. Even when we play Hong Kong and Taiwan, there are people who know the lyrics and sing along.

What's the best thing about being in a band in Běijīng? It just feels really exciting. I think Běijīng is the most exciting place in the world for music right now because the scene here isn't very commercial, so we get a lot of freedom. In the UK and the USA, bands can be really famous before they've even put out an album and that can kill the music. We can do what we like and I hope that lasts. The only problem is that there are so many bands in Běijīng now, it can be hard to find a good rehearsal space.

Do you sing about the political situation in China? Not really, I write about my life. Sometimes, if politics affects that, I'll write about it. I think the younger generation doesn't care about politics anymore. The musicians in the '80s and '90s did because society was changing so much and so fast then. But now, people are more interested in getting a good job than politics.

Are you proud to be a role model for younger musicians? I do get kids coming up to me after shows to talk about their bands. I feel pretty honoured to talk to them, because five years ago I was the same as them; I just wanted to be in a band. I'm happy if we can influence people. I think that's better than being popular.

MAO LIVEHOUSE Map pp58-9

光芒 **Guāngmáng**

☎ 6402 5080; 111 Gulou Dongdajie; 鼓楼东大街111号; admission from Y50; ⊗ 8pm-late; ⊖ Andingmen

This midsized venue, opposite the northern entrance to Nanluogu Xiang, has given the capital's music scene a big boost because it's large enough to give the many gigs it hosts a sense of occasion, but small enough to feel intimate. The decor is functional and the sound tight. All sorts of bands play here, but if they're from overseas, the entrance price is sky-high.

STAR LIVE Map pp58-9

星光现场 **Xīngguāng Xiànchǎng**

☎ 6425 5677; 3rd fl, Tango nightclub, 79 Hepingli Xijie; 和平西街79号(糖果3层); admission from Y50; ⊗ 6.30pm-late; ⊖ Yonghegong-Lama Temple

It's a great space and as the only medium-sized venue in Běijīng, it hosts a fair few international bands. The venue hosts occasional dance parties, too.

WHAT? BAR Map pp88-9

什么酒吧 **Shénme? Jiǔbā**

☎ 133 4112 2757; 72 Beichang Jie; 北长街72号(故宫西门往北); admission incl free beer Y30; ⊗ 2pm-late; ⊖ Tiananmen Xi, then 🚌 5

If you like to get up close and personal with the bands you go and see, then visit this easy-to-miss venue. That doesn't mean it is groupie heaven here; rather, it's so small that the audience might as well be on stage with the musicians. Gigs are on Fridays and Saturdays, and it's a good place to hear up-and-coming local talent. Just north of the west gate of the Forbidden City.

YÚGŌNG YÍSHĀN Map pp58-9

愚公移山

☎ 6404 2711; West Courtyard, 3-2 Zhangzizhong Lu; 张自忠路3-2(号段祺瑞执政府旧址西院); admission from Y50; ⊗ 7pm-2am; ⊖ Zhangzizhonglu

Reputedly one of the most haunted places in Běijīng, this historic building has been home to Qing dynasty royalty, warlords and the occupying Japanese army in the 1930s. You could probably hear the ghosts screaming if it wasn't for the array of local and foreign bands, solo artists and DJs who take to the stage here every week. With a very sound booking policy and a decent space to play with, this is perhaps the premier place in town to listen to live music. At other times, it's fine for a drink.

CLUBBING

Běijīng's clubs might not be cutting edge in comparison to Berlin or London, but they're increasingly busy as more and more locals tune into the dance music lifestyle. And thanks to the international DJs who fly in and out of Běijīng on an almost-weekly basis, there's a variety of sounds to hear. The capital's clubs are a good place to observe the cultural divide between East and West. Many Chinese visit nightclubs to knock back expensive whisky with green tea and to play dice games, while refusing to set foot on the dance floor. Consequently, most dancing areas in Běijīng clubs are smaller than the ones you'll find in the West. Bear in mind that if a big-name DJ is playing, admission prices go up and you'll need to get tickets in advance.

BOAT Map pp110-11
☎ 6460 5512; 8 Liangmahe Nanlu; 亮马河南路 8号; ☽ 6pm-3am; ◉ Liangmaqiao
Don't be put off by the alarming list on this ship-based club-cum-bar, which is anchored on the distinctly calm waters of the Liangma River in north Sānlǐtún. You can drink on the top two decks, or descend into the bowels of the ship to dance to the DJs. The drinks are cheap (beers from Y20) and on some nights it's gay friendly.

CARGO Map pp110-11
☎ 6551 6898/78; 6 Gongrentiyuchang Xilu; 工体西路6号; Y50; ☽ 8pm-late; ◉ Chaoyangmen
The best of the cluster of clubs located in the strip just south of the west gate of the Workers Stadium, Cargo consistently flies in some of the bigger names in dance music to play to a locals-dominated crowd. It's busier in the week than the other places nearby.

DESTINATION Map pp110-11
目的地 Mùdìdì
☎ 6551 5138; 7 Gongrentiyuchang Xilu; 工体西路7号; Y60; ☽ 8pm-late; ◉ Chaoyangmen
A club for boys who like boys and girls who want a night off from them, Destination's rough-hewn, concrete-walled interior doesn't stop it being packed on weekends. But then, as Běijīng's only genuine gay club, it doesn't have to worry about any competition.

GT BANANA Map pp110-11
吧那那 Bānànà
☎ 6526 3939; SciTech Hotel, 22 Jianguomenwai Dajie; 建国门外大街22号赛特酒店; Y60; ☽ 8.30pm-4am Sun-Thu, to 5am Fri & Sat; ◉ Jianguomen or Yonganli

It's been around a while but Banana continues to thrive, thanks to its no-nonsense mix of happy and hard house, and other attractions, such as dancers in cages, fire-eaters and bongo players. The upstairs Spicy Lounge offers a more eclectic mix of sounds, depending who's on the decks. It's popular with well-heeled locals.

MIX Map pp110-11
密克斯 Mìkèsī
☎ 6530 2889; Y50; ☽ 8pm-late; ◉ Dongsishitiao
Hip-hop and R&B are the drawcards here and a younger crowd takes to the large (for Běijīng) dance floor in droves. It's opposite Vics, inside the Workers Stadium north gate.

PROPAGANDA Map p125
☎ 8286 3991; ☽ 8.30pm-late; ◉ Wudaokou
Wǔdàokǒu's student crew are drawn like moths to this unprepossessing but long-running club, thanks to cheap drinks, hip-hop sounds and the chance for cultural exchange with the locals. Entry is free and a few doors north of Sculpting in Time; 100m north of the east gate of Huaqing Jiayuan.

VICS Map pp110-11
威克斯 Wēikèsī
☎ 5293 0333; Fri & Sat Y50; ☽ 7pm-late; ◉ Dongsishitiao
Vics is not the most sophisticated nightclub. Nevertheless, it has remained a favourite with the young crowd for many years now, which makes it some sort of institution. The tunes are mostly standard R&B and hip-hop, there's an infamous ladies night on Wednesdays (free drinks for women before midnight), and weekends see it rammed with the footloose and fancy free. If you can't score here, you should give up trying. Entry is free from Monday to Thursday; located inside the Workers Stadium north gate.

WORLD OF SUZIE WONG Map pp110-11
苏西黄 Sūxī Huáng
☎ 6500 3377; West Gate, Chaoyang Park, 1a Nongzhanguan Lu; 农展馆路甲一号朝阳公园西门; Y50; ☽ 7pm-3.30am; ◉ Tuanjiehu
Not as glam or hip as it once was – there's a distinct meat-market feel to it on the weekends – but Suzie Wong's always seem to be jammed, thanks in part to its clever design: opium-den chic with a 21st-century twist. There are traditional wooden beds to recline on while sipping fancy cocktails

KARAOKE

Karaoke is the number one leisure pastime in China. There are well over 100,000 karaoke joints on the mainland, ranging from seedy two-room operations that are often fronts for prostitution, to giant chains where the prices are as high as some of the notes you'll hit. As alien and/or nerve-wracking as it may seem to be sitting in a small room singing along to a TV in front of a group of people, going out to karaoke is one of the best ways of getting to know the locals.

For the Chinese, karaoke is where you go to hang out with friends, or unwind with workmates after a hard week in the office. Westerners can find the experience less relaxing, but if you forget your inhibitions (alcohol comes in handy for that), then you'll be surprised at how quickly crooning along to cheesy pop standards becomes addictive.

If you speak Mandarin, then you can sing along to the latest Mando-pop hits. English speakers will have to content themselves with a smaller and older selection of tunes, but you'll always find something you can sing. At the places listed below, drinks and food are available and sometimes you can persuade the staff to help you out if you need backing vocals to add a semblance of credibility to your singing. Prices depend on the size of the room you want and the time of day. It's always advisable to book ahead at weekends.

Melody (麦乐迪; Màilèdí; Map pp110–11; ☎ 6551 0808; A-77 Chaoyangmenwai Dajie; 朝阳门外大街 A-77号; small room before 8pm per hr Y79, after 8pm per hr Y189; ☯ 8am-2am)

Partyworld (钱柜; Qiángui; Map pp110–11; ☎ 6588 3333; Fanli Bldg, 22 Chaoyangmenwai Dajie; 朝阳门外大街22号泛利大厦; per person Y139; ☯ 7am-2am)

on the 3rd floor, as well as a large square bar on the 2nd floor and an oversubscribed roof terrace. The crowd is a real mix: models and the business types after them, as well as party people and working girls.

THE ARTS
ACROBATICS

Two thousand years old, Chinese acrobatics is one of the best acts to catch in town. Most of today's acrobatic repertoire originates from the works of Zhang Heng (AD 25–120), who is credited with creating such acts as balancing on a high pole, jumping through hoops, swallowing knives and spitting fire. Wuqiao County in Héběi is said to be the original bastion of Chinese acrobatics. In addition to the following listings, you can also find acrobatic performances held at the Dongyue Temple (p109).

The monks of Shaolin from Sōngshān in Hénán province have gained an international reputation for their legendary fighting skills, honed from a recipe of physical deprivation, spiritual illumination, patience and ironclad willpower. They pass through Běijīng to perform on a regular basis and are well worth watching if they are in town. Keep an eye on the local listings mags (p249) for details.

CHAOYANG THEATRE Map pp110-11
朝阳剧场 Cháoyáng Jùchǎng
☎ 6507 2421; 36 Dongsanhuan Beilu; 东三环北路36号; tickets Y180-680; ☯ performances 5.15pm & 7.30pm; ◉ Hujialou

An accessible place for foreign visitors and often bookable through your hotel, this theatre hosts visiting acrobatic troupes from around China who fill the stage with plate spinning and hoop jumping.

TIANQIAO ACROBATICS THEATRE
Map pp118-19
天桥杂技剧场 Tiānqiáo Zájì Jùchǎng
☎ 6303 7449; 95 Tianqiao Shichang Lu Jie; 天桥市场街95号; tickets Y180-380; ☯ performances 5.30pm & 7.15pm; ◉ Qianmen, then ◻ 819
West of the Temple of Heaven Park, this 100-year-old theatre offers one of Běijīng's best acrobatic displays, performed by the Beijing Acrobatic Troupe. Less touristy than the other venues, the high-wire display here is awesome. The entrance is down the eastern side of the building.

UNIVERSAL THEATRE (HEAVEN & EARTH THEATRE) Map pp58-9
天地剧场 Tiāndì Jùchǎng
☎ 6416 0757/9893; 10 Dongzhimen Nandajie; 东直门南大街10号; tickets Y180-680; ☯ performance 7.15pm; ◉ Dongsishitiao
Around 100m north of Poly Plaza, young performers from the China National Acrobatic Troupe perform their mind-bending, joint-popping contortions. A favourite with tour groups, you'll need to book ahead. Tickets are pricier the further from the stage you sit. Keep an eye out for the dismal white tower that looks like it should be in an airport – that's where you buy your tickets (credit cards not accepted).

CLASSICAL MUSIC

The opening of the striking National Centre for the Performing Arts (also known as the National Grand Theatre) has finally given Běijīng's classical and dance scene a real centre. But there are many other venues around town where the city's increasingly cosmopolitan residents can satisfy their highbrow needs. The annual 30-day Beijing Music Festival takes place in October, and is an excellent chance to catch international and domestic classical music. Refer to the listings in expat magazines (p249) for details of what's on and what's coming up.

BEIJING CONCERT HALL Map pp88-9
北京音乐厅 **Běijīng Yīnyuè Tīng**
☎ 6605 7006/5812; 1 Beixinhua Jie; 北新华街
1号; tickets Y80-880; ☯ performance 7.30pm;
☺ Tiananmen Xi or Xidan

The 2000-seat Beijing Concert Hall showcases performances of classical Chinese music as well as international repertoires of Western classical music to hushed, knowledgeable audiences.

FORBIDDEN CITY CONCERT HALL
Map pp58-9
中山公园音乐堂 **Zhōngshān Gōngyuán Yīnyuè Táng**
☎ 6559 8285; Zhongshan Park; 中山公园内;
tickets Y80-880; ☯ performances 7.30pm;
☺ Tiananmen Xi

Located on the eastern side of Zhongshan Park, this is the most central venue for performances of classical and traditional Chinese music. It's also the best acoustically. Tickets can be purchased at the concert hall box office inside the Friendship Store (p150).

NATIONAL CENTRE FOR
THE PERFORMING ARTS Map pp88-9
国家大剧院 **Guójiā Dàjùyuàn**
☎ 6655 0000; 2 Xichang'an Jie; 西长安街
2号; tickets Y80-880; ☯ performances 7.30pm;
☺ Tiananmen Xi

Sometimes called the National Grand Theatre, this spectacular Paul Andreu–designed dome (p91), known to Beijingers as the 'Alien Egg', attracts as many architectural tourists as it does music fans. But it's now *the* place to listen to classical music from home and abroad, despite the slightly dodgy acoustics and the distance of some of the seats from the stage. You can also watch ballet, opera and classical Chinese dance here. Regular minifestivals are staged, too.

POLY PLAZA INTERNATIONAL
THEATRE Map pp58-9
保利大厦国际剧院 **Bǎolì Dàshà Guójì Jùyuàn**
☎ 6500 1188, ext 5126; 14 Dongzhimen Nandajie;
东直门南大街14号; tickets from Y180; ☯ performances 7.30pm; ☺ Dongsishitiao

With a central location in the Poly Plaza right by Dongsishitiao Station, this venue hosts a range of performances, including ballet, classical music, opera and traditional Chinese folk music. It also hosts an increasing number of stage plays by foreign playwrights.

FILM

Movies, both domestic and foreign, are hugely popular in China, as you'd expect from the country with the third-largest film industry in the world. However, a severe shortage of cinemas (diànyǐngyuàn), stringent censorship and a strict quota on the number of foreign films that can be shown each year means the country has never had a big cinema-going culture. In Běijīng, the combination of high ticket prices and rampant DVD piracy ensures that going to the movies is a middle-class pursuit.

Chinese-language films occasionally have English subtitles when shown in cinemas. Before you go to see a Western movie, check if it is screened with subtitles (zìmù) or has been dubbed (pèiyīn) into Chinese. There are a number of alternative venues in Běijīng that show Chinese movies with English subtitles, as well as Western arthouse and classic movies, and they're often the best places to see films. The longest established of them is Cherry Lane opposite. See the expat mags (p249) for Cherry Lane's schedule, as well as for details of the various embassies and cultural institutions around town that have regular screenings of their native cinema.

Apart from that, you can offer up futile prayers for a good movie to be shown on CCTV, or you can tune into your hotel film channels. But if you have a laptop with you or a DVD player in your hotel room, then you won't have to travel far to find someone willing to sell you something to play on it.

For information about Chinese cinema past and present, see p35.

EAST GATE CINEMA Map pp58-9
东环影城 **Dōnghuán Yǐngchéng**
☎ 6418 5931; Bldg B, Basement, East Gate Plaza,
Dongzhong Jie; 东中街东环广场B座地下一
层; admission from Y70, half price before noon;
☺ Dongsishitiao

In a central location, it shows the latest big releases, both domestic and foreign. It's also the only cinema in town that offers double seats (from Y150).

STAR CITY Map pp58-9
新世纪影城 Xīnshìjì Yǐngchéng
☎ 8518 5399; Basement, Oriental Plaza, 1 Dongchang'an Jie; 东长安街1号东方广场地下一层; from Y70; ⊕ Wangfujing
This six-screen cinema is the best place to see Western movies that get released in China because they always have one screening a day with the original, undubbed print (but that doesn't mean it hasn't been cut by the scissor-happy Chinese censors). It's a plush multiplex that feels no different from its equivalents in the West.

Other cinemas around town worth trying include the following:

Cherry Lane (Map pp58–9; www.cherrylanemovies.com.cn; 3-2 Zhangzizhong Lu, Dōngchéng; 张自忠路3-2号段祺瑞执政府旧址西院) Screens contemporary Chinese movies and documentaries with subtitles, many of which never made it to the local cinemas because the censors didn't like them. Films show twice a month (Y50) at Yùgōng Yíshān (p189) and often the directors are present to take questions afterwards.

Dahua Cinema (Dàhuá Diànyǐngyuàn; Map pp58–9; ☎ 6525 0343; 82 Dongdan Beidajie, Dōngchéng; 东单北大街82号)

Drive-in Cinema (Map pp128–9; ☎ 6431 9595; 100 Liangmaqiao Lu; 亮马桥路100号朝阳公园北门对面; ⊕ May-Sep) Opposite the north gate of Chaoyang Park.

UME International Cineplex (Map p125; ☎ 8211 5566; 44 Kexueyuan Nanlu, Wǔdàokǒu; 科学院南路44号)

Xinjiekou Cinema (Map pp88–9; ☎ 6225 2767; 69 Xizhimennei Dajie, Xīchéng; 西直门内大街69号)

BEIJING OPERA

Beijing opera, or Peking opera as it is still sometimes referred to, is one of those aspects of Chinese cultural life that can seem impenetrable to foreigners. Everything about it, from the costumes to the singing style and, of course, the language, conspires to maintain its mystique. But if you've only ever seen it televised, then taking in a live performance will help you understand it better. Bear in mind that the plot lines are simple and not dissimilar to a Shakespearean tragedy, including elements of low comic relief, while the long performances aren't meant to be viewed in stunned silence. The operas have natural highs and lows, which you'll be able to gauge from the reaction of your fellow audience members. Let them be your

guide. Above all, remember Beijing opera is as much a visual experience as a musical one. You can also tune into CCTV 11, which is solely devoted to showing traditional opera.

For more on opera in Běijīng, see p37.

CHANG'AN GRAND THEATRE
Map pp58-9
长安大戏院 Cháng'ān Dàxìyuàn
☎ 5166 4621; Chang'an Bldg, 7 Jianguomennei Dajie; 建国门内大街7号; tickets Y80-800; ⊗ performances 7.30pm; ⊕ Jianguomen
This theatre offers a genuine experience, with the erudite audience chatting away knowledgably among themselves during the weekly performances of Peking opera classics – this is a place for connoisseurs. There are matinees and evening shows, all on the weekend.

HUGUANG GUILD HALL Map pp118-19
湖广会馆 Húguǎng Huìguǎn
☎ 6351 8284; 3 Hufang Lu; 虎坊桥路3号; tickets Y180-680; ⊗ performances 7.30pm; ⊕ Hepingmen, then 🚌 25
With balconies surrounding the canopied stage, the Huguang dates back to 1807. In 1912 the Kuomintang (KMT), led by Dr Sun Yat-sen, was founded here. The interior is magnificent, coloured in red, green and gold, and decked out with tables and a stone floor. Opposite the theatre there's a very small opera museum (admission Y10, free if you have a ticket for a show) displaying operatic scores, old catalogues and other paraphernalia. There are also colour illustrations of the *liǎnpǔ* (types of Beijing opera facial makeup) – examples include the *hóu liǎnpǔ* (monkey face) and the *chǒujué liǎnpǔ* (clown face). Shows here attract a lot of domestic tour groups. There are few English captions.

LAO SHE TEAHOUSE Map pp118-19
老舍茶馆 Lǎo Shě Cháguǎn
☎ 6303 6830; www.laosheteahouse.com; 3rd fl, 3 Qianmen Xidajie; 前门西大街3号3层; evening tickets Y180-380; ⊗ performances 7.50pm; ⊕ Hepingmen or Qianmen
Lao She Teahouse (west of the large KFC on Qianmen Xidajie) has nightly shows, mostly in Chinese. The performances here are a combination of Beijing opera, cross-talk and acrobatics. Prices depend on the type of show and your seat. There are several halls: in the small hall there's folk music (3pm to 5pm Monday to Friday, except Wednesday),

and in the large hall there are folk-music and tea-ceremony performances (3pm to 4.30pm Friday), theatrical performances (2pm to 4.30pm Wednesday and Friday) and matinee Beijing opera performances (3pm to 4.30pm Sunday). It also stages shadow puppet shows (6pm to 7pm daily). Evening performances of Beijing opera, folk and music, acrobatics and magic (7.50pm to 9.20pm) are the most popular. Phone ahead or check the schedule online. The tea house is named after the celebrated Běijīng writer Lao She (p78).

LIYUAN THEATRE Map pp118-19

梨园剧场 Líyuán Jùchǎng

☎ 6301 6688, ext 8860; Qianmen Jianguo Hotel, 175 Yong'an Lu; 永安路175号前门建国饭店; tickets without tea Y200-280, with tea Y380-580; ⏱ performances 7.30pm; ⊜ Hepingmen, then ⛟ 25

This touristy theatre, across the lobby of the Qianmen Jianguo Hotel (p214) and past the mannequins outside, has regular performances for Beijing opera newbies. If you want to, you can enjoy an overpriced tea ceremony while watching. The setting isn't traditional and it resembles a cinema auditorium (the stage facade is the only authentic touch), but it's a gentle introduction to the art form.

THEATRE

Gong Li and Zhang Ziyi, stars of the big screen, might have learned their art at the Central Academy of Drama (Zhōngyāng Xìjù Xuéyuàn), but theatre *(huàjù)* has never commanded much of a following in China. Spoken drama appeared in China only in the 20th century and has never won the hearts of the masses. The great 20th-century playwright Cao Yu penned tragic family tableaux, such as the stifling *Thunderstorm* and *Daybreak*. Lao She is also famed for his ironic social commentary and observations of Běijīng life, with *Teahouse* being his most famous play.

Much of the last century saw drama stubbing its toe on unexpected political corners, such as the Cultural Revolution. As a literary art, creative drama is still unable to express itself fully and remains sidelined. But domestic plays do make it to the stage in small numbers, as do an increasing number of foreign ones, sometimes in English. If you want to know what's waiting in the wings in Běijīng, try some of the venues that follow. The expat magazines (p249) have up-to-date details of what's playing.

CAPITAL THEATRE Map pp58-9

首都剧场 Shǒudū Jùyuàn

☎ 5128 6286; 22 Wangfujing Dajie; 王府井大街22号; tickets Y120-500; ⏱ performances 7.30pm Tue-Sun; ⊜ Wangfujing

Located in the heart of the city on Wangfujing Dajie, the Capital has regular performances of contemporary Chinese productions and is home to a number of theatre companies, including the People's Art Experimental Theatre. Classic plays in the Chinese language often feature.

CHINA PUPPET THEATRE Map pp58-9

中国木偶剧院 Zhōngguó Mù'ǒu Jùyuàn

☎ 6425 4847; 1a Anhua Xili, Beisanhuan Zhonglu; 北三环中路安华西里1a; tickets Y100-380; ⏱ performances 10.30am & 1.30pm Sat & Sun; ⊜ Anzhenmen or Gulou Dajie

This popular theatre puts on shadow play, puppetry, music and dance events on weekends. It's a good place to take kids if they're rebelling against the prospect of more sightseeing.

MEI LANFANG GRAND THEATRE Map pp88-9

梅兰芳大戏院 Méi Lánfāng Dàxìyuàn

☎ 5833 1288; 32 Ping'anli Xidajie; 平安里西大街32号; tickets Y80-1000; ⏱ performances 7.30pm; ⊜ Chegongzhuang

Named after China's most famous practitioner of Peking opera, this theatre opened its doors in 2007 and has since become one of the most popular and versatile venues in town. As well as traditional opera, you can see Shakespeare productions and modern theatre. Contemporary dance companies and international ballet troupes also take to the good-sized stage on a regular basis.

SPORTS & ACTIVITIES

top picks

SPORTS & ACTIVITIES

Long associated with bicycling and taichi, Beijingers have become more adventurous in their quest to maintain the perfect body. Not only are there gyms galore across the city, offering everything from aerobic pole dancing to kickboxing classes, but golf and horse-riding clubs now dot the outer suburbs, while the nearby ski resorts attract a growing number of enthusiasts in winter. In summer, hikers and mountain bikers take to the hills that surround Běijīng.

Would-be Jet Li's will find plenty of places to perfect their Monkey Offers Peach strike (p114); Běijīng is a fine place to study *wǔshù* (martial arts), be it Shaolin kung fu or taichi. Fans of team sports can find just about anything they want, whether it's baseball, cricket, soccer, rugby or Gaelic football. The local listings mags (p249) have details of all the clubs in Běijīng. Less strenuous, but highly popular, is snooker, or you can take to the bowling lanes. Armchair sports fans can follow a number of local teams who play at venues around the city.

But Běijīng also offers more soothing pursuits that are designed to balance the mind. After a day pounding the streets, you can retreat to one of the hundreds of massage centres, or visit a spa, to restore equilibrium. With prices far cheaper than they are in the West, it's a great way to relax and pamper yourself.

HEALTH & FITNESS

MASSAGE

Walking Běijīng's vast distances and dealing with the crowds in the capital can put serious stress on ligaments, muscles and the brain. Thankfully, there are several places in town where you can unwind, while having your feet and body massaged and reinvigorated.

BODHI THERAPEUTIC RETREAT

Map pp110–11

菩提会所 Pútí Huìsuǒ

☎ 6417 9595; 17 Gongrentiyuchang Beilu; 工体北路17号; ☒ 11am-12.30am; ◉ Dongsishitiao

The serene setting, a blend of Thai and Chinese influences just moments away from the madness of Běijīng's traffic, helps you shift gears straightaway, and that's before one of the many masseurs here gets to work in a comfy, private room. Bodhi offers aromatherapy, ayurvedic, Thai- and Chinese-style massage, as well as great foot reflexology massages and a wide range of facial treatments. You get free snacks and drinks, and with TVs in all the rooms you can lie back and watch a DVD while being pummelled into shape. Prices start at Y158 for a massage, but there's a 40% discount before 5pm during the week. It's opposite the north gate of the Workers Stadium, just a few metres from the Xinjiang Red Rose Restaurant.

DRAGONFLY THERAPEUTIC RETREAT

Map pp58–9

悠庭保健会所 Yōutíng Bǎojiàn Huìsuǒ

☎ 6527 9368; 60 Donghuamen Dajie; 东华门大街60号; ☒ 11am-1am; ◉ Tiananmen Dong

Close to the Forbidden City, this popular boutique has a variety of treatments designed to help you de-stress. The two-hour Hangover Relief Massage is self explanatory, but for real pampering go for the Royal Delight (Y360), in which two masseurs get to work at the same time, or the Ultimate Indulgence (Y270), an hour of full-body massage and an hour of foot reflexology. Manicures, pedicures, nails and waxing are also offered. A standard, hour-long body or foot massage costs Y135. There is another branch in Sānlǐtún (Map pp110–11; ☎ 6593 6066; Ground fl, Eastern Inn Hotel, Nansanlitun Lu; ☒ 11am-1am).

YOGA

While older Chinese might choose the more home-grown methods of *qìgōng* (exercise that helps channel *qì*, or energy) and *tàijíquán* (taichi) over the imported variant of yoga, it increasingly popular with younger Chinese

MOUNTAIN YOGA off Map pp128–9

山地瑜珈 Shāndì Yújiā

☎ 6259 6702; www.mountainyoga.cn; 6 Gongzhufen Cun, Fragrant Hills; 香山公主坟村6号

A fine way to escape the crowds and pollution of Běijīng is to head to this homely yoga retreat in the Fragrant Hills. Located in a wooden house, there are lungfuls of fresh air to breathe in and visiting teachers to instruct you. A single day costs Y150, otherwise it costs from Y300 for overnight stays. The price includes accommodation and tasty vegetarian, MSG-free meals. Mountain Yoga can also organise hikes in the hills and occasionally runs yoga retreats to the Great Wall.

YOGA YARD Map pp110-11

瑜珈苑 Yújiā Yuàn
☎ 6413 0774; www.yogayard.com; 6th fl, 17 Gongrentiyuchang Beilu; 工体北路17号6层; ⊕ Dongsishitiao

In the same building as Bodhi Therapeutic Retreat, this friendly English-speaking centre has traditional hatha yoga classes, from beginners to advanced. Ninety-minute lessons are Y100, or it costs Y1000 for an unlimited one-month pass.

GYMS

Many top-end hotels have gyms, as do a few upmarket apartment complexes.

CHINA WORLD FITNESS CENTRE
Map pp110-11

中国大饭店健身中心 Zhōngguó Dàfàndiàn iànshēn Zhōngxīn
☎ 6505 2266, ext 33; 1 Jianguomenwai Dajie; 建国门外大街1号; per day Y200; ⊕ 6am-11pm; ⊕ Guomao

A 20m pool, squash courts, steam bath and Jacuzzi are available here, as well

as yoga, Pilates, ballet and Latin dance. There are posh changing rooms, too. It's in the same complex as the China World Hotel (p213).

OZONE FITNESS CENTRE Map pp110-11

奥力健身中心 Aòlì Jiànshēn Zhōngxīn
☎ 6567 0266; 2nd fl, 2 Dongsanhuan Nanlu; 东三环南路2号瑞赛商务楼2层; per day Y150; ⊕ 6.30am-10.30pm Mon-Fri, 8am-9pm Sat & Sun; ⊕ Guomao

Formerly known as Evolution, there are numerous classes at this fitness centre, including aerobics, tàijíquán, Pilates, Spinning, hip-hop dancing, kickboxing and yoga. Personal training programs, fitness consultation and sports therapy are also available, and there's a 25m five-lane pool. You can also get private wǔshù lessons in English here.

ACTIVITIES
BOWLING
GONGTI 100 Map pp110-11

工体钰泰保玲中心 Gōngtǐ Yùtài Bǎolíng Zhōngxīn
☎ 6552 2688; 6 Gongrentiyuchang Xilu; 工体西路6号; admission Y40; ⊕ 8am-2am; ⊕ Chaoyangmen

Named for the number of lanes here, you can bowl the night away with a mixed crowd of locals, expats and even the occasional celeb. It's above the strip of nightclubs close to the west gate of the Workers Stadium.

TAICHI TIPS

Characterised by its lithe and graceful movements, tàijíquán (literally 'Fist of the Supreme Ultimate'), also known as taichi, is an ancient Chinese physical discipline practised by legions of Chinese throughout the land.

Considerable confusion exists about taichi – is it a martial art, a form of meditation, a qìgōng (exercise that helps channel qì, or energy) style or an exercise? In fact, taichi can be each and all of these, depending on what you seek from the art and how deep you dig into its mysteries.

In terms of health benefits, taichi strengthens the leg muscles, exercises the joints, gives the cardiovascular system a good workout and promotes flexibility. It also relaxes the body, dissolving stress, loosening the joints and helping to circulate qì.

As a system of meditation, taichi makes practitioners feel both centred and focused. Taichi introduces you to Taoist meditation techniques, as the art is closely allied to the philosophy of Taoism. And if you're adept at taichi, it is far easier to learn other martial arts, as you'll have learned a way of moving that is common to all of the fighting arts.

If taking up taichi, a few useful pointers will help you progress in your practice:

- When executing a movement, bodily motion and power is directed by the waist before moving to the hands (observe a skilled practitioner and see how the motion reaches the hands last). The hands never lead the movement.
- When performing a form (as the moving sets are called), keep your head level, neither rising nor dipping.
- Practise taichi as if suspended by an invisible thread from a point at the top of your head.
- Don't lean forward or back and keep your torso vertical.
- Relax your shoulders and let your weight sink downwards.

THIS BIRD HAS FLOWN

With the Olympics a fast-fading memory, the 'Bird's Nest Stadium', the iconic centrepiece of the 2008 games, now stands forlorn and empty. Having staged just one sporting event since the Olympics, as well as a handful of music concerts, the $450 million venue is not so much a shrine to sporting excellence, as a redundant symbol of the most expensive games ever staged.

While a dwindling number of mostly domestic tourists still roll up to have their photos taken on the running track, no one seems sure what to do with the innovative stadium, or how to raise the estimated $15 million a year needed to maintain it. Rumours of theme parks and shopping malls being built next door to the Bird's Nest abound. But until those plans come to fruition, the rust will continue to gather on the intricate steel structure that held the world's attention for one brief month in 2008.

DANCE

DANZ CENTRE Map pp58-9
丹安丝舞蹈中心 Dān'ānsī Wǔdǎo Zhōngxīn
☎ 8041 7745; C/F, Bldg 48, Oriental Kenzo, Dongzhimenwai Dajie; 东直门外大街48号东方银座C层; ☺ afternoon Mon-Fri, from 9am Sat & Sun; ⊙ Dongzhimen
Ballet classes for kids, as well as hip-hop, Latin and jazz for grown-ups. Prices range from Y50 to Y100 per hour, depending on the style.

FOOTBALL

A large number of expat 11-a-side and five-a-side teams play in Běijīng in a variety of leagues. If you are interested in joining a team, get in touch with ClubFootball (☎ 5130 6893; www.clubfootball.com), which organises and coordinates amateur sides for adults and kids.

GOLF

Golf (gāo'ěrfūqiú) enjoys high prestige in China and is becoming such a part of work life that some universities are making golf lessons compulsory for their business students. Běijīng's freezing winters, however, don't lend themselves to a life on the links. Nor is it cheap to get on a course. In fact, you can pick up a basic set of golf clubs in one of Běijīng's many golfing stores for not much more than a day's green fees. Some clubs offer discounts on Mondays. It is advisable to book ahead.

BEIJING GOLF CLUB off Map pp128-9
北京高尔夫球俱乐部 Běijīng Gāo'ěrfūqiú Jùlèbù
☎ 8947 0245/0005; Chaobai River East Bank, Shùnyì; 顺义区潮白河东岸; green fees Mon-Fri Y650, Sat & Sun Y1200; ☺ 7.30am-dusk
One of the cheaper courses, the Beijing Golf Club is northeast of town on the eastern bank of Chaobai River (Cháobái Hé) There's also a four-hole practise course and a driving range. It's 45 minutes by car or taxi from central Běijīng, via the Jingcheng Expressway.

BEIJING INTERNATIONAL GOLF CLUB off Map pp128-9
北京国际高尔夫球俱乐部 Běijīng Guójì Gāo'ěrfūqiú Jùlèbù
☎ 6076 2288; Northwest of Ming Tombs Reservoir Chāngpíng; 昌平区十三陵水库西北; green fees Mon-Fri Y800, Sat, Sun & public holidays Y1400 ☺ 7am-7pm
This Japanese-designed 18-hole course is 35km north of town, close to the Ming Tombs (p229) and north of Shisanling Reservoir. Hitting that little ball around is not cheap, but the greens are in top condition and the scenery is spectacular. You can rent a set of golf clubs and shoes for an additional fee. You will also have to pay the compulsory caddy fee of Y200. A taxi from downtown Běijīng will take 90 minutes via the Badaling Expressway.

HIKING & BIKING

Several groups in Běijīng organise hiking and biking expeditions along the Great Wall and to villages and temples outside town. It's an excellent and convivial way to get out and see the more remote sights. Beijing Hikers (☎ 513 4906, 139 1002 5516; www.beijinghikers.com) organise regular hikes (from Y250 per person) and is open to everyone, including children (Y150 for under 12s). The price includes round-trip transport, snacks and drinks. Hikes are rated from 1 to 5, with 5 being the most strenuous. Mountain Bikers of Beijing (themob@404.com.au) coordinates one-day, 60km to 120km weekend mountain-bike rides around Greater Beijing and in neighbouring Héběi province. The MOB are hard-charging types, though, so you'll need to be fit.

HORSE RIDING

Along with golf, taking to a steed has become popular with the emerging middle class.

EQUULEUS INTERNATIONAL RIDING CLUB off Map pp128-9

北京天星调良国际马术俱乐部 **Běijīng Tiānxīng Tiáoliáng Guójì Mǎshù Jùlèbù**
☎ 6432 4947; www.equriding.com; 91 Shunbai Lu, Sunbaihe Town; 朝阳区孙白河镇顺白路91号; 50min class Y450; ⏰ 7-11am & 3-7pm Tue-Sun summer, 8am-noon & 2-6pm Tue-Sun winter
The closest place to the centre of town to mount up, Equuleus has bilingual trainers and indoor and outdoor riding arenas. It caters to everyone from beginners to advanced equestrians. There are almost 100 horses to choose from.

ICE SKATING

Běijīng's winter chill clamps the city's lakes in sheets of ice – the usual warnings apply about safety and ice thickness for those who want to skate (liū bīng). Popular outdoor venues include Houhai Lake southwest of the Drum Tower, where local entrepreneurs will rent you skates and other paraphernalia, and the lake in Beihai Park.

LE COOL ICE RINK Map pp110-11

国贸溜冰场 **Guómào Liūbīngchǎng**
☎ 6505 5776; Basement 2, China World Shopping Mall, 1 Jianguomenwai Dajie; 建国门外大街1号; per 90min Y30-40; ⏰ 10am-10pm; ⊕ Guomao
Like many of the rinks in Běijīng, Le Cool is not very big. But it's easily accessible and perfect for kids. Visit in the morning or evening if you want to avoid the crowds. Skate hire is included in the price, which varies depending on the time of day. Individual, 40-minute lessons are Y100.

MARTIAL ARTS

Běijīng is an excellent place to stretch a leg. Legions of elderly folk start the day with a bout of tàijíquán, and you'll get used to seeing octogenarians doing the splits without grimacing. Certainly, if you have any interest in China's martial arts heritage, take this opportunity to learn from the experts.

Many visitors will probably settle for a dose of tàijíquán and some qìgōng to limber up, learn some breathing techniques and get the blood circulating. More adventurous souls can dig a bit deeper into China's exciting fighting arts; you never know what you'll unearth.

BEIJING BLACK TIGER ACADEMY
Map pp110-11

黑虎泰拳英雄馆 **Hēihǔ Tàiquán Yīngxióng Guǎn**
☎ 139 1071 2576; www.blacktigerclub.com; Room 906, Bldg 9, Jianwai Soho, 39 Dongsanhuan Zhonglu; 东三环中路39号建外SOHO 9号楼906室; ⏰ afternoons & evenings; ⊕ Guomao
Both a place for fight devotees and fitness fanatics, Black Tiger doesn't restrict itself to Chinese martial arts forms. You can learn Brazilian capoeira, ju-jitsu and Thai boxing here, as well mixed martial arts. The teachers are all certified and conduct classes in English.

JINGHUA WUSHU ASSOCIATION
Map pp110-11

京华武术协会 **Jīnghuá Wǔshù Xiéhuì**
☎ 135 2228 3751; Basement, Pulse Club, Kempinski Hotel, Liangmaqiao Lu; 亮马桥路凯宾斯基地下一层脉搏俱乐部; ⏰ 5.30-7pm Sat & Sun; ⊕ Liangmaqiao
Classes in English from teachers trained in traditional Shaolin forms. Wǔshù, qìgōng and taichi are all taught here. Ten classes cost Y500; there are classes for kids (five years and over), too.

RUNNING

Běijīng's dicey air quality might deter you from sampling extra lungfuls of it, but some groups organise runs in, around and outside town. Hash House Harriers (☎ 139 1131 6130; www.hash .cn) – the eccentric expat organisation ('drinkers with a running problem') that originated with the British in Malaysia – organises 8km to 10km runs most Sundays at 2pm. It costs Y20 just to run; pay Y60 and you'll get all the beer you can drink afterwards, as well as some food.

SKIING

Several ski resorts within reach of Běijīng lure an increasing number of local skiers and snowboarders during the winter months. Bear in mind that the Chinese ski like they drive, so exercise caution. Not many of the slopes will challenge advanced skiers and boarders.

JUNDUSHAN SKI RESORT off Map pp128-9

军都山滑雪场 **Jūndūnshān Huáxuěchǎng**
☎ 6072 5888; www.bjski; 588 Zhènshùn, Cuīcūn, Chāngpíng; 昌平区崔村镇真顺村588号; skiing per day Mon-Fri Y240, Sat & Sun Y380, 1hr Mon-Fri Y60, Sat & Sun Y80, 2hr Mon-Fri Y100, Sat & Sun Y140; ⏰ 8am-10pm
Just 34km from Běijīng, Jundushan has seven trails, as well as a cross-country

path for snowmobiles. Skiing charges vary according to the day of the week and how long you want to ski. You can hire equipment and stay overnight in wooden villas. There is night skiing (Y100) here, too.

LIANHUASHAN SKI RESORT
off Map pp128–9

莲花山滑雪场 Liánhuāshān Huáxuěchǎng

☎ 6148 8333; Zhangzhen Town, Shùnyì; 顺义区张镇; entrance Y20, skiing per day Mon-Fri Y400, Sat & Sun Y340; ⏰ 8.30am-5pm & 6-10pm

Seven ski runs, two of which are optimistically described as advanced, are available at this functional resort. It's 30km from Běijīng's Capital Airport and just over an hour's drive from the city centre.

NANSHAN SKI VILLAGE off Map pp128–9
南山滑雪场 Nánshān Huáxuěchǎng

☎ 8909 1909; www.nanshanski.com; Shengshuitou Village, Henanzhai Town, Miyun County; 密云县河南寨镇圣水头村; entrance Y20, skiing per day Mon-Fri Y220, Sat & Sun Y360; ⏰ 8.30am-5.30pm

The best of the resorts close to Běijīng, Nanshan has 10 well-kept trails for skiers of all abilities. Snowboarders have their own park here, with a half-pipe and six rails, and there's also a 1.3km toboggan run. It's 90 minutes from Běijīng and there are instructors available for coaching. The resort also has accommodation, restaurants and equipment hire.

QIAOBO ICE & SNOW WORLD
off Map pp128–9

乔波冰雪世界 Qiáobō Bīngxuě Shìjiè

☎ 8497 2568; www.qbski.com; Chaobai River National Forest Park, Mǎpō, Shùnyì; 顺义区马坡潮白河国家森林公园内; skiing per hr Mon-Fri Y150, per day Y240, per hr Sat & Sun Y180, per day Y330; ⏰ 8.30am-9pm

The only indoor ski slopes in Běijīng can be found here. The two slopes are not long and experienced skiers will not be excited by them, but it's a good place to head to when the summer heat gets too much.

SNOOKER & POOL

Snooker and pool are both very popular with the Chinese. Many tip China's top player Ding Junhui as a future world champion. You can find pool tables in many bars around town, including Bar Blu (p184), Frank's Place (p187) and Paddy O'Shea's (p186). For snooker, try the

Xuanlong Pool Hall (Map pp58–9; ☎ 8425 5566; 79b Hepingli Xijie; 和平里西街79b; pool/snooker table per hr Y20/Y32; ⏰ 24hr), where there are 28 American-style pool tables and eight full-size snooker tables. It has a bar, too.

SQUASH

The China World Fitness Centre (p197) has squash courts, as do a few five-star hotels. Otherwise, the best option is the Pulse Club (Map pp110–11; ☎ 6465 3388, ext 32; Kempinski Hotel, 50 Liangmaqiao Lu; 亮马桥路50号 凯宾斯基酒店; nonmembers per 45min Y85; ⏰ 6am-10.30pm).

SWIMMING

You can find pools at some four-star and all five-star hotels, but nonguests will have to pay a fee. The China World Hotel (p213) charges Y200, but you get to use the sauna and gym as well. The venerable Friendship Hotel (Map p125; ☎ 6849 8888, ext 32; 1 Zhongguancun Nandajie; 友谊宾馆 中关村南大街1号) has a great Olympic-sized pool, now sadly enclosed, costing Y100 for a day plus a Y100 deposit. Outside hotels try the Ditan Swimming Pool (Map pp58–9; ☎ 6426 4483; 18 Hepingli Zhongjie; 安外和平里中街18号; admission Y30; ⏰ 8.30am-3.30pm & 6.30-10pm Mon-Fri, noon-10pm Sat & Sun).

TENNIS

Tennis (wǎng qiú) is a popular sport in Běijīng that draws enthusiastic crowds, so phone well in advance to make reservations for tennis events or to book a court. Many top-end hotels have tennis courts that can be used by nonguests for a fee. Alternatively, try the International Tennis Center (Map p82; ☎ 6711 3872; 50 Tiantan Donglu; 天坛东路50号; nonmembers per hr Y300; ⏰ 10am-10pm Mon-Fri, 8am-8pm Sat, 9am-9pm Sun), which has indoor courts and is southeast of the Temple of Heaven Park.

SPECTATOR SPORT
FOOTBALL

The Chinese are avid football (zúqiú) fans, but most prefer to watch foreign leagues like the English Premiership, Italy's Serie A and Spain's La Liga, rather than their own China Super League. A succession of match-fixing scandals, dubious refereeing and the generally poor quality of the football means that only a few thousand diehard fans turn out to watch Běijīng Guó'an, the capital's team, play their home matches at the Worker

Stadium. The national team has not impressed in recent years, failing to qualify for the 2010 World Cup.

To watch the beautiful game you can tune into BTV 6 or CCTV 5, which show the big foreign domestic leagues and international matches. If you want some atmosphere while you cheer on your team, a number of bars around town show live matches on ESPN or Star Sports. Try Paddy O'Shea's (p186) or Frank's Place (p187).

BASKETBALL

Basketball is hugely popular and China's gigantic leading player Yao Ming, who plays for the Houston Rockets in the NBA, is a massive star. A number of other young Chinese players have also made the jump from the CBA (the domestic league) to the NBA. The local team is the Beijing Ducks, although they were homeless at the time of writing.

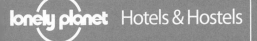

lonely planet Hotels & Hostels

Want more sleeping recommendations than we could ever pack into this little ol' book? Craving more detail — including extended reviews and photographs? Want to read reviews by other travellers and be able to post your own? Just make your way over to **lonelyplanet.com/hotels** and check out our thorough list of independent reviews, then reserve your room simply and securely.

SLEEPING

top picks

Opposite House Hotel (p213)
St Regis (p213)
Aman at Summer Palace (p216)
Park Plaza (p208)
Peking International Youth Hostel (p210)

SLEEPING

Within the space of three decades, Běijīng – and China – has moved from a command-and-control economy to an open market at a blinding pace. The speed of change can leave you spinning, but one way of getting things in perspective is to compare the standard of accommodation then and now in Běijīng.

It wasn't *that* long ago that your average Chinese two-star hotel was caught in an inexorable time warp. *Fúwùyuán* (staff) would burst into the room unannounced (as you changed your trousers) to slam a thermos flask down on the table, sending the dodgy TV reception into a spasm of static. The late-night karaoke would have you chewing your pillow – and so would the 'Western' breakfast. For men, 1am wake-up calls from masseurs were standard.

After three decades of reform and opening up (and the 2008 Olympic Games), things are different now and most of these quirks are thankfully quaint memories. There's still some way to go, but today you can get value for money and you should be able to find what you want whether it's a peaceful courtyard hotel or a five-star luxury tower that pulls out all the stops. For something nonurban, there are several alluring retreats (p215) that can parcel you off into the Běijīng countryside and flush the nitrogen dioxide from your lungs.

Most travellers aim to stay within the Second Ring Rd as that is where most of Běijīng's character survives. The historic districts of Xīchéng and especially Dōngchéng are very well catered for hotel-wise across the budgets. Chóngwén and Xuānwǔ are also areas with a sense of history. Cháoyáng is more modern (and less interesting from a sightseeing point of view), with lively nightlife and a crop of stylish boutique hotels, but has little character. Hǎidiàn is not well supplied with hotels although the Aman at Summer Palace is tempting (if you've won the national lottery).

Good English-language skills remain fitful. Youth hostels typically have excellent English language speakers, as do five-star hotels – it's the ones in between that may not.

Regarding hotel protocol: when checking into a hotel, you will need to complete a registration form, a copy of which will be sent to the local Public Security Bureau (PSB; Gōng'ānjú). If you have a number of China visas in your passport, it's a good idea to find the right one.

Hotels, hostels and guest houses in this chapter are listed by budget within each neighbourhood. In the hotel reviews, we have published the rack rate just to give an idea of which budget the hotel belongs to; rack rates at midrange and top-end hotels, however, very rarely apply (except during the 1 May and 1 October national holiday periods, see p245). Discounting is very much the norm, with discounts of up to 50% or more off the rack rate (although discounts of around 20% to 40% or more are standard). Booking online (see Reservations, p206) is an excellent way to secure the best discounts, but even if you apply at the front desk you will generally be quoted the discounted rate. See the Discounts boxed text, p206, for more information.

Hotel rooms are usually easy to find, although it can sometimes be hard in the peak tourist season from June to September, during Chinese New Year, and especially over the 1 May and October holiday periods, so book ahead if visiting during these times. A 15% service charge is levied at midrange and top-end hotels. Checkout time is usually noon, but exceptions are indicated in hotel reviews. Standard check-in time is also noon (but this can be earlier if the room is empty).

In cheaper midrange and budget hotels, often the only English TV channel is the state-run CCTV 9. It is better than nothing, but some hotels do not have their TVs tuned into the channel, so ask if you want it.

For a list of accommodation-specific Chinese terms, see p257.

ACCOMMODATION STYLES

Unlike Shànghǎi, Hong Kong and Macau, which all have distinguished hotels dating to colonial and foreign concession days, Běijīng has precious few heritage hotels. Instead, if you want history, courtyard hotels (*sìhéyuàn bīnguǎn*) allow you to uncover Běijīng's *hútòng* (alleyway) ambience and inimitable courtyards, and many travellers opt for this. The downside of courtyard hotels the smallish size of the rooms and frugal range of amenities: don't expect a swimming pool, nightclub, views over town or disabled access. Historically, these places didn't function as hotels, but as residences, so they a merely an improvisation. Courtyard hotels do, however, come with an atmosphere that is uniquely Běijīng and a charm that other hotels cannot imitate. The *fēngshuǐ* (geomancy, literally 'wind and water') is also second to none. Courtyard hotels used to be exclusively midrange and top end but are now available for all budgets as entrepreneurs have spotted the gaps in the market.

Youth hostels offer much more than just dorm beds and budget prices. Many are hidden away in heritage buildings down Běijīng's *hútòng*, with comfortable single and double rooms and staff that is tuned into foreign travellers' needs. Travel advice is often honest, impartial and knowledgeable, and the staff frequently speak excellent English. Many hostels have a homely atmosphere, with DVD rooms, Playstations, internet access, wi-fi zones, international breakfasts and other meals, lending libraries, laundry rooms, bicycle hire and useful information boards. Single and double room prices and quality standards frequently nudge hostels into the midrange price bracket.

Some ultracheap guesthouses, known as *zhāodàisuǒ, lǚdiàn* or *lǚguǎn,* still refuse to take foreigners.

If you just want an unfussy room with a guarantee of cleanliness and acceptable comfort, a rapidly mushrooming crowd of lower-midrange business hotel chains offer simple and clean accommodation where the emphasis is on smallish rooms, hygiene and a quick turnaround. They are not luxurious and have little, if any, charm but they are smart enough and good value. Chains include Home Inn (www.homeinns.com), Motel 268 (www.motel268 .com), Piao Home (www.piaohomeinn.com) and Jinjiang Inn (www.jinjianginns.com).

Běijīng's growing crowd of stylish four- and five-star hotels means the top-end bracket is jammed with options in most parts of town. The best five-star hotels offer a standard that equivalent to five-star international hotels abroad, but be warned that some Chinese-managed hotels are only ranked as five stars because they have a swimming pool – other aspects of the hotel may be wanting. Similarly, some four-star hotels can be a star lower when measured against international standards.

If you are in town for a few weeks, it is a good idea to experiment with Běijīng's different accommodation styles, spending a few nights in a courtyard hotel, before checking out a youth hostel or a boutique hotel.

LONGER-TERM ACCOMMODATION

If you are planning to live long-term in Běijīng, you will need to sort out your housing needs. If you are planning to live in a hotel, you should be able to negotiate a good discount for a long-term stay.

Fully furnished serviced apartments are expensive, but offer security, maid service and hotel facilities, including health centres. For information on rents and availability of serviced and other apartments in Běijīng, consult www.moveandstay.com/beijing.

Housing developments and gated communities for the Chinese moneyed class and expats on packages are generally first-rate, with pricey management fees, 24-hour security, sports facilities, swimming pools, kindergartens, and shops selling imported goods and delicacies. While you can find a three-bedroom townhouse in suburban Shùnyì for as little as Y9500 per month, prices can top Y75,000 per month for ultraluxurious apartments or detached villas.

For modern Chinese housing in town (eg apartment blocks; typically called *gōngyù*) rent is substantially lower (from Y4000 per month for a three-bedroom flat), and although standards are lower than typical foreign housing, they're much higher than the average Chinese home (there will be tiles on the floor, decent plumbing, guards at the gate, parking etc). Further down the scale is older housing, where rents can be as low as Y1500 per month for a basic two-bedroom flat.

Many long-term residents dream of living in a Běijīng courtyard house. Located in *hútòng* (alleyways) within the Second Ring Rd, courtyard residences are the *ne plus ultra* of 'old Peking' style, with enviable cachet, an alluring sense of history and none of the sterility of modern high-rises and expat housing developments. Courtyard residents will insist they'll ride out an earthquake, while contemptuously dismissing the high-rises. What you gain in history and character, however, you might sacrifice in amenities: there is frequently nowhere to park the SUV, the toilet might be

PRICE GUIDE

YYY	over Y1000 a night
YY	Y400-1000 a night
Y	under Y400 a night

DISCOUNTS

Rack rates for room prices are listed in hotel reviews in this chapter, but discounting is the norm, so it is imperative to ask what the discount (dázhé) is. Outside high peak times (Chinese New Year and the first weeks of May and October) discounts of 20% to 40% or more are common, but make sure you check whether the discounted price includes the service charge, as this will eat up 10% to 15% of the discount. Also ask about special promotional packages at top-end hotels, especially newly opened ventures. If staying long-term, you should be able to get good deals, especially at top-end hotels; see p205 for more information on long-term accommodation.

If you are arriving in Běijīng without a reservation and are planning to stay in midrange or top-end accommodation, stop by one of the airport's hotel reservations counters, where staff could secure you a discount of up to 50% off the rack rate. Counters are located just outside the arrivals area, after you pass through customs.

Top-end hotels may list their room rates in US dollars, but you will have to pay in local currency. Practically all hotels will change money for guests, and most midrange and top-end hotels accept credit cards. All hotel rooms are subject to a 10% or 15% service charge, but many cheaper hotels don't bother to charge it.

outside, heating and insulation may be poor, and rooms small. But many courtyard homes now have air-con, shower rooms, lavatories and fully equipped kitchens. Rental prices for courtyard houses start at around Y5000 per month, rising to over Y80,000 for the most luxurious. If you want to buy a courtyard house, prices kick off from around Y9000 per sq metre. Using an expat-oriented estate agent is convenient, but far more expensive; if you manage to find a courtyard residence through a Chinese estate agent, it could be much, much cheaper. Look around and compare prices.

Housing laws stipulate that foreigners can live in Chinese housing as long as the owners of the apartment register the foreign resident with the local PSB. Failure to do so could incur a fine for the foreigner of around Y3000 (per person).

If you teach or work for the government, your housing will likely be provided free or at the local Chinese price. If you're coming to study, your school will probably have a dormitory. Homestay is a possibility, either living with a Chinese family and paying rent (from Y1000 per month for a room) or teaching a family's children English in return for free or cut-price accommodation. This can be a good way to learn Chinese and, of course, be exposed to life in a Chinese family context. Take a look at www.chinahomestay.org for details of rent-free homestays. For full-on language immersion and ultracheap rents, weigh up moving in with a Chinese roommate. See the websites, right, for listings.

Foreigners expecting to make Běijīng their permanent home can buy property, and by doing so also gain a residence permit. In most cases, buying actually means leasing the property for 75 years, after which it reverts to state ownership. The Olympic bonanza saw prop-

erty prices in Běijīng heading towards the stratosphere, and they now average around Y8000 per sq metre, although expect to pay much more than that in a desirable part of the city.

Besides word of mouth, the best way to find housing in Běijīng is through a real estate agent or by checking housing ads in the expat mags. The *Beijinger* (www.thebeijinger.com) has regular listings; other useful websites for finding properties or rooms include www.wuwoo.com, www.zhantai.org and beijing.craigslist.org.

RESERVATIONS

It often pays to reserve a hotel room through the hotel's website, where discounts are regularly offered. Also visit travel agencies and browse for the best deals online. Online booking services include Lonely Planet's own website (see boxed text, opposite) and CTrip (☎ 800-8 6666; www.english.ctrip.com).

DŌNGCHÉNG 东城区

Riddled with both *hútòng* and history, Dōngchéng has the best courtyard hotels, most of the best hotels, a bevy of well-located hostels and the cream of the top sights. If there's one district to hang your hat, this has to be it.

RAFFLES BEIJING HOTEL
Map pp58-9   Heritage Hotel Y
北京饭店莱佛士酒店 Běijīng Fàndiàn Láifóshì Jiǔdiàn
☎ 6526 3388; www.beijingraffles.com; 33 Dongchang'an Jie; 东长安街33号; d incl breakfast Y4300; ⓜ Wangfujing;

andwiched between two drab edifices to the east the 1970s lines of the Beijing Hotel, to the west a gawky Soviet-era acade), the seven-storey Raffles oozes cachet and grandeur. The heritage building dates to 1900 when it was the Grand Hotel de Pekin, so pedigree is its middle name. Illuminated in a chandelier glow, the elegant lobby yields to a graceful staircase leading to immaculate standard doubles that are spacious and well proportioned, decked out with period-style furniture and large bathrooms. The ground floor Writer's Bar offers a unique variety of stress-busting tranquillity in deluxe surroundings (with prices to match).

PENINSULA BEIJING

Map pp58–9   Luxury Hotel YYY

王府饭店 **Wángfǔ Fàndiàn**

☎ 8516 2888; www.peninsula.com; 8 Jinyu Hutong; 金鱼胡同8号; d Y3150; ◉ Dengshikou; ✖ ▢ ▣ ⓦ

Owned by the Peninsula Group, this hotel's dated white-tile exterior increasingly seems a bad choice, but the unflinchingly high standards within remain attractive. The restaurants are first-rate, from trendy Jing – announced by a cascade of glass beads in the lobby – to dim sum in the Běijīng courtyard–style Huáng Tíng (p163). The location just off Běijīng's premiere shopping street is supercentral, but if you hanker for tranquillity and zero crowds, behold the customer-free basement shopping arcade.

GRAND HYATT BEIJING

Map pp58–9   Hotel YYY

北京东方君悦大酒店 **Běijīng Dōngfāng Jūnyuè Dàjiǔdiàn**

☎ 8518 1234; www.beijing.grand.hyatt.com; 1 Dongchang'an Jie; 东长安街1号; d Y2600; ◉ Wangfujing; ✖ ✖ ▢ ▣ ♿ ⓦ

A crisp freshness keeps things snappy at this stylish creation lording it over Oriental Plaza – from the grand sweep of its foyer to the brand-name stores downstairs. Standard doubles are not very roomy and views can be limited, but they are attractively (if neutrally) designed. The real advantage is the location off Wangfujing Dajie, 10 minutes' walk east of the Forbidden City and Tiananmen Square; the hotel's range of excellent restaurants, cafes and bars – including the elegant Made in China and

the luxuriant Red Moon Bar (p182) – are further incentives.

HOTEL CÔTÉ COUR SL

Map pp58–9   Hútòng Hotel YYY

☎ 6512 8020; www.hotelcotecoursl.com; 70 Yanyue Hutong; 演乐胡同70号; d Y1489; ◉ Dengshikou; ✖ ▢ ⓦ

With a calm, serene atmosphere and a lovely magnolia courtyard, this 14-room *hútòng* hotel is one of the most charming places to rest your head in town. Like all courtyard hotels, rooms are petite, but this is offset by a spacious rooftop terrace and the central location is both tranquil and 'old Peking'. Perhaps aiming for a members-only exclusive look, there's no sign: it's just beyond Dengcao Hutong (灯草胡同); look out for the colourful, traditional Chinese doorway on your right as you amble east. There's no bell, just knock at the door.

HILTON BEIJING WANGFUJING

Map pp58–9   Hotel YYY

北京王府井希尔顿酒店 **Běijīng Wángfǔjǐng Xī'ěrdùn Jiǔdiàn**

☎ 5812 8888, 800 820 0600; www.wangfujing .hilton.com; 8 Wangfujing Dongdajie; 王府井东大街8号; d Y1550; ◉ Wangfujing; ✖ ✖ ▢ ▣ ⓦ

Still wreathed in a slight chemical aroma when we visited, it was too early to say how the well-located new Hilton would perform before the wrapping was completely off. Muted grey hues come to the fore throughout and much-needed winter warmth is provided by designer gas fires. The snazzy 50-sq-metre standard rooms come with teddy bears and ducks perched on bath tubs and roomy walk-in wardrobes, while the 64-sq-metre superior rooms are effortlessly lovely. The 6th-floor swimming pool has views, and there are Macanese and Chinese restaurants on the 5th floor.

BOOK ACCOMMODATION ONLINE

For more accommodation reviews and recommendations by Lonely Planet authors, check out the online booking service at www.lonelyplanet.com/hotels. You'll find the true, insider lowdown on the best places to stay. Reviews are thorough and independent. Best of all, you can book online.

top picks

HERITAGE HOTELS

- Raffles Beijing Hotel (p206) Civilised blend of pedigree, comfort and elegance.
- Hotel Côté Cour SL (p207) Envelop yourself in the flavours of Qing-dynasty Peking.
- Aman at Summer Palace (p216) Faux-heritage perhaps, but gorgeous nonetheless.
- Red Capital Residence (below) Historic courtyard hotel with a handful of nostalgically styled rooms.
- Changgong Hotel (p215) Old converted guild hall with ultracheap rooms and a quaint yesteryear feel.

RED CAPITAL RESIDENCE
Map pp58-9   Heritage Hotel YYY
新红资客栈 Xīnhóngzī Kèzhàn
☎ 6402 7150; www.redcapitalclub.com.cn; 9 Dongsi Liutiao; 东四六条9号; d Y1488; ⊕ Zhangzizhonglu; ✗ ⚎

Dressed up with Liberation-era artefacts and established in a lovely Qing-dynasty courtyard, this unusual guest house offers a heady dose of nostalgia for a vanished age. Make your choice from five rooms decked out with paraphernalia that wouldn't look out of place in a museum: the Chairman's Residence, the two Concubine Suites (each with their own courtyard); or the two author suites, named after Edgar Snow and Han Suyin. Also in the spirit of pastiche is the Bomb Shelter Bar, where guests are pampered with wine, cigars and propaganda films from a shelter excavated by order of Vice-Chairman Lin Biao. If that's not enough, the hotel can also arrange cruises of Běijīng's streets in Jiang Qing's ageing Red Flag limousine.

REGENT BEIJING Map pp58-9   Hotel YYY
北京丽晶大酒店 Běijīng Lìjīng Dàjiŭdiàn
☎ 8522 1888; www.regenthotels.com; 99 Jinbao Jie; 金宝街99号; d weekday/weekend Y1250/1100; ⊕ Dengshikou; ✗ ⚎ 🖳 🛗 ⚐ 🛆 ⋚

The lavish 500-room Regent has staked out a precious plot of land on the corner of Jinbao Jie and Dongdan Beidajie to the east of Wangfujing Dajie. Guest rooms are good value – luxuriously styled and up to the minute. A full range of health and leisure facilities and five restaurants round off the impressive picture.

EMPEROR Map pp58-9   Hotel YYY
皇家驿栈酒店 Huángjiā Yìzhàn Jiŭdiàn
6526 5566; www.theemperor.com.cn; 33 Qihelou Jie 骑河楼33号; Y1200; ⊕ Dengshikou; ✗ ⚎ 🖳

Attempting to capitalise on a majestic position just east of the Forbidden City, the Emperor's lofty ambitions were undermined by height restrictions so upper-floor rooms merely graze the rooftops of the imperial palace. Nonetheless you can't question the excellent fēngshuǐ this locale brings. The unnumbered rooms are named after emperors: women can join the queue for the Wu Zetian room (named after China's sole female emperor), but is the Chongzhen (who hung himself as rebels swarmed the city walls) room cursed? It's gimmicky perhaps, but the location is regal and views from the rooftop bar, Yin (p182), simply imperial.

GUXIANG20 Map pp58-9   Hotel YY
古巷20号商务会所 Gŭxiàng 20hào Shāngwù Huìsuŏ
☎ 6400 5566; www.guxiang20.com; 20 Nanluogu Xiang; 南锣鼓巷20号; d/ste Y1280/1980; ⊕ Beixinqiao; ✗ ⚎ 🖳

The rooftop tennis court is the first indication that this isn't a bona fide courtyard hotel, despite the deceptive carved stonework, grey-brick styling and traditional furniture. Artful and elegant (some rooms have four-poster beds), with a fantastic perch on the heartland hútòng of Nanluog Xiang, the repro hotel helps fill the gap for midrange comfort in this neighbourhood. Drinking and dining are right on your door step and sightseeing is a breeze.

PARK PLAZA Map pp58-9   Hotel Y
北京丽亭酒店 Běijīng Lìtíng Jiŭdiàn
☎ 8522 1999; www.parkplaza.com/beijingcn; 97 Jinbao Jie; 金宝街97号; d Y850; ⊕ Dengshikou ✗ ⚎ 🖳 ⚐

A good-value riposte to the overblown topflight hotels in the area (see the gaudy Legendale across the road for what not to do), the Park Plaza is a treasured find. If you can or don't want to stretch to a five-star hotel, the Park Plaza has a magnificent location and a comfortable, modern and well-presented four-star finish. The lobby is mildly jazzy and sedate – but not subdued – with chocolate-brown leather seats, while room are stylish and comfortable. Not elegant, b it's modish, the living is easy and you won' be left with a gaping hole in your budget.

't's hidden away behind its hulking sister hotel, the Regent Beijing.

NANJING GREAT HOTEL

Map pp58-9   Hotel YY

北京南京大饭店 Běijīng Nánjīng Dàfàndiàn

☎ 6526 2188; 5 Xi Jie; 西街5号; d Y850; ⊕ Wangfujing; 🖳

This popular midrange hotel right in the centre of town has competitively priced and comfortable rooms. The location, a 10-minute walk east of the Forbidden City and just by Wangfujing Dajie, is a winner, although the staff's English-language skills can be rudimentary.

LUSONGYUAN HOTEL

Map pp58-9   Hútòng Hotel YY

吕松园宾馆 Lǚsōngyuán Bīnguǎn

☎ 6404 0436; 22 Banchang Hutong; 板厂胡同 22号; s/ste Y458/1600, d Y780-880; ⊕ Zhangz-honglu or 🚌 104 to Bei Bingma Si stop; 🍴 🖳

Rooms may be a bit cramped at this hútòng hotel, a courtyard house built by a Mongolian general during the Qing-dynasty era, but the location and setting are big plus points, and guests can sit out quaffing drinks in the courtyard during spring and summer. Pocket-sized singles come with pea-sized baths, the dorms have three beds (with TV, no windows and a common shower), there is just one suite and a handful of double bedrooms – book ahead. Rooms facing the courtyard are slightly more expensive. There's also bike hire (half-/full day Y15/30) and a pricey email centre (open from 7.30am to 10pm; Y5 per 10 minutes).

HOTEL KAPOK Map pp58-9   Boutique Hotel YY

木棉花酒店 Mùmiánhuā Jiǔdiàn

☎ 6525 9988; www.hotelkapok.com; Donghuamen Dajie; 东华门大街16号; d from Y780; ⊕ Tiananmen Dong; 🍴 🖳 🛜

At first glance the exterior knocks your socks off, but the ubiquitous Běijīng dust shows little mercy to the all-glass-grill effect. It's going to need lots of maintenance to keep its edge, but the self-conscious six-floor Kapok offers midrange cool for designer types, the Blackberry generation and those hunting boutique minimalism despite the creeping sensations of a Chinese three-star hotel. A lovely use of space, light and bamboo, but unfortunately things seem to have been knocked out on the

cheap (hence the affordable tariff) – when style is a cornerstone, cost cutting is ill advised. The choice of Chinese titles for the library shelves (including *The Long March* and biographies of Marx and Mao) lacks imagination, but the courtyard 'fashion rooms' on the ground floor are neat.

HAOYUAN HOTEL

Map pp58-9   Hútòng Hotel YY

好园宾馆 Hǎoyuán Bīnguǎn

☎ 6512 5557; www.haoyuanhotel.com; 53 Shijia Hutong; 史家胡同53号; d Y760, deluxe d Y930, ste Y1080-1380, VIP r Y1590; ⊕ Dengshikou; 🖳

Visitors aiming to get into *hútòng* mode could do worse than checking in to this charming courtyard hotel guarded by a pair of stone lions. The eight standard double rooms in the front courtyard are delightfully arranged with traditional Chinese furniture and the red lantern–hung architecture weaves its magical charms. The gorgeous, leafy rear courtyard is even more enchanting. The largest suite's bedroom is set off from a Chinese parlour, complete with calligraphy hangings, vases, rugs and lanterns, while the huge VIP room is there for (wealthy) claustrophobes. The only discernible drawback is the ugly wasteland eyesore opposite the front gate.

DAYS INN Map pp58-9   Hútòng Hotel YY

美国戴斯酒店 Měiguó Dàisī Jiǔdiàn

☎ 6512 7788; www.daysinn.cn; 1 Nanwanzi Hutong; 南湾子胡同1号; d Y548, ste Y998; ⊕ Tiananmen Dong; 🍴 🖳

Communication problems can be a riot at the front desk of this *hútòng*-corner located hotel, where harassed-looking but well-mannered receptionists deal patiently with Western guests. Guests do not recommend the tours arranged through the hotel, but seem happy with the clean and restful, if uninspiring, rooms at this handily located spot that's finished in grey brick. There's only one suite, but it ranges over two floors. A few minutes' walk east of the Forbidden City.

HOTEL PALACE Map pp58-9   Hútòng Hotel YY

北京御城瑞府四合院酒店 Běijīng Yùchéng Ruìfǔ Sìhéyuàn Jiǔdiàn

☎ 6525 6516; www.hotelpalace.cn; 6 Pudusi Xixiang; 普渡寺西巷6号; d Y400-800; ⊕ Tiananmen Dong; 🍴

With some of Běijīng's best-located beds, the small Palace has affordable courtyard-style rooms just a few metres from the Forbidden City. Ensconced within a rebuilt *hútòng*, the location is ultrapeaceful but the Chinese-management isn't particularly adept at dealing with Western guests. Ring the bell for access.

MOTEL 268 Map pp58-9   Motel Y/YY
莫泰连锁旅店 Mòtài Liánsuǒ Lǚdiàn
☎ 5167 1666; www.motel268.com; 19 Jinyu Hutong; 金鱼胡同19号; d Y268-448, f Y538;
🚇 Wangfujing; ✖ 🖳
A fantastic central location right on the edge of Wangfujing Dajie coupled with clean and well-kept rooms make this a good choice from the Motel 268 hotel chain. Rooms are unfussy and low on frills, but this spot is good value for the lower midrange price bracket.

PEKING INTERNATIONAL YOUTH HOSTEL Map pp58-9   Hútòng Hostel Y
北平国际青年旅社 Běipíng Guójì Qīngnián Lǚshè
☎ 6526 8855; pekinghostel@yahoo.com.cn; 5 Beichizi Ertiao; 北池子二条5号; 12-/8-/4-bed dm Y90/100/100, d Y400-500; 🚇 Tiananmen Dong;
✖ 🖳 📶
The discreet, central alleyway location is just the icing on the cake for this hostel, which is tucked away off Nanchizi Dajie and just a guidebook's throw from the Forbidden City. Owned by charming Qīnghǎi lass Fei Fei and her partner Gao Gao, the highly relaxing *hútòng* hostel maintains just the right vibe thanks to the homely lounge area, small and leafy courtyard, good dorms (the doubles are small, though) and an intimate ambience. It's a tad pricier than many other hostels, but prices reduce when it's slack. All the usual hostel suspects are here: internet access (first 30 minutes free), wi-fi, laundry facilities, DVD burning, movies, book lending, blackboard weather forecasts, Playstation2 and bike hire. Book ahead.

CONVENIENT HOTEL Map pp58-9   Hotel Y
北京都市之星快捷酒店 Běijīng Dūshì Zhīxīng Kuàijié Jiǔdiàn
☎ 6402 1188; fax 6402 8557; 216 Dongzhimennei Dajie; 东直门内大街216号; s Y188, d Y228-238;
🚇 Beixinqiao; ✖ 🖳
A short walk from Beixinqiao Station, this aptly named hotel offers a range of no-nonsense, modern, comfortable and clean

rooms amid the bright lights, lanterns and hotpot aromas of Ghost Street (p163). The cheapest twin rooms have no windows, so long stays could spell a double whammy of jaundice and claustrophobia. It may not be stylish, but it's hassle-free, functional and well located for the Airport Express (p233). The sole internet terminal in the lobby sees queues forming.

HÚTÒNGRÉN Map pp58-9   Hútòng Hotel
胡同人
☎ 8402 5238; hutongren@ccthome.com; 71 Xiaoju'er Hutong; 小菊儿胡同71号; r incl breakfast Y260-380; 🚇 Beixinqiao; ✖
With chatty youthful staff, a charming leafy interior, hip alleyway locale and a laid-back no-nonsense vibe, this place could be right up your *hútòng*. Tranquilly positioned off funky Nanluogu Xiang, the courtyard interior has bucket loads of charm but only a handful of rooms, which are decorated with traditional furniture and Buddhist carvings. Three of the nine rooms come with a mezzanine for extra space, and the boss sits out the front, chewing the fat and proffering tea to guests and sundry guitar-strumming wayfarers.

QINGZHUYUAN HOTEL
Map pp58-9   Hútòng Hotel
青竹园宾馆 Qīngzhúyuán Bīnguǎn
☎ 6401 3961; 113 Nanluogu Xiang; 南锣鼓巷 113号; economy r Y150, standard r incl breakfast Y220-260; 🚇 Zhangzizhonglu; ✖ 🖳
With an excellent *hútòng* location and reasonable prices things look good on paper for the Qingzhuyuan, but it hasn't capitalised on a winning hand and is let down by inattentive staff and a vapid approach. However, the Nanluogu Xiang box is well and firmly ticked, which is enough for most. Laundry facilities, bike hire, internet access and rail ticketing are available.

BEIJING CITY CENTRAL INTERNATIONAL YOUTH HOSTEL
Map pp58-9   Hostel
北京城市国际青年旅社 Běijīng Chéngshì Guójì Qīngnián Lǚshè
☎ 6525 8866, 8511 5050; www.centralhostel.com; 1 Beijingzhan Jie; 北京站街1号; 4-8 bed dm Y6_, s with/without shower Y160/120, d Y298;
🚇 Beijingzhan; 🖳
The first youth hostel you hit after exiting Beijing Train Station, the staff at this cent_

...oot understandably looks harassed. The
...lurb optimistically announces: 'Business-
...en's budget hotel, backpacker's deluxe
...otel', which basically means there's zero
...harm in its utilitarian character and a thin
...eneer of style, but rooms still go fast –
...specially to people dragging two-tonne
...ackpacks with little patience to explore al-
...rnatives – so phone ahead. Notice board,
...fo desk, TV and video room, kitchen,
...andy internet cafe on the 2nd floor, the
...iming of the train station clock: they're
...l yours.

...EIJING SAGA INTERNATIONAL
...OUTH HOSTEL

...ap pp58-9   Hútòng Hostel Y

...京实佳国际青年旅社 Běijīng Shíjiā Guójì
...ngnián Lǚshè

... 6527 2773; sagayangguang@yahoo.com; 9
...jia Hutong; 史家胡同9号; 4-bed dm Y65,
...218-238, tr Y258, courtyard r Y268; ⊕ Deng-
...ikou; ⊠ 🖳

...njoying a top location on historic Shijia
...utong, this popular hostel is a grey block
...ut the inside compensates with some
...naracter and staff is friendly. Rooms are
...ell kept, there's a spacious seating area
... the main lobby, a refectory, bar, internet
...ccess (Y8 per hour) and washing (Y10 per
...ad). The mixed dorm rooms are a decent
...e and include private lockers. The build-
...g is modern, but the height has advan-
...ges: head up to the huge open rooftop
...mmon area and directly view the Qing-
...nasty era courtyard below. The three
...all courtyard rooms are at the back.
...scounts to Hostelling International mem-
...rs; breakfast included with some rooms.

...AMA TEMPLE INTERNATIONAL
...OUTH HOSTEL

...p pp58-9   Hútòng Hostel Y

...京雍和宫国际青年旅社 Běijīng
...nghégōng Guójì Qīngnián Lǚshè

... 6402 8663; lama_temple_hostel@yahoo.com
... 56 Beixinqiao Toutiao; 北新桥头条56号;
...6-/4-bed dm Y50/55/60, s/d Y200/220; ⊕ Beix-
...iao; ⊠ 🖳 🛜

...th nearby metro connections pumping
...ht into the heart of town, it's tempting
... make your bed in this historic area, but
... can only recommend this place if all
...hers are full. Summer or late spring stays
... OK, but the hostel often doesn't fire up
... radiators in winter, so rooms can be

top picks

HÚTÒNG HOTELS

- **Côté Cour SL** (p207) Exquisite courtyard hotel tucked away in the centre of Běijīng; pricey, but priceless.
- **City Walls Courtyard** (below) Directly north of the Forbidden City: location, location, location.
- **Haoyuan Hotel** (p209) Qing-dynasty era courtyard charm in Běijīng's historic hútòng heartland.
- **Lusongyuan Hotel** (p209) One of the first courtyard hotels and still going strong, with bundles of character.
- **Hútòngrén** (opposite) Laid-back and leafy abode buried down a small hútòng off Nanluogu Xiang.

arctic even in the Y220 (phone-less) double rooms (and you still have to fork out for soap and towels). The hútòng location is a serious plus, though.

BEIJING DOWNTOWN BACKPACKERS ACCOMMODATION

Map pp58-9   Hútòng Hostel Y

东堂客栈 Dōngtáng Kèzhàn

☎ 8400 2429; www.backpackingchina.com; 85 Nanluogu Xiang; 南锣鼓巷85号; dm Y65, q/tr per bed Y75/85, d Y150-190, ste Y300; ⊕ Beixinqiao; ⊠ 🖳

For backpacking arrivals in town, the central location, helpful staff and lively hútòng aspect are hard to beat. The recently restored doubles are tidy (no TV), with plastic-wood floors and clean shower rooms. Cheaper doubles are without window, pricier rooms come with window or skylight. There's free breakfast plus bike hire (per day Y20, Y300 deposit), internet access (Y6 per hour) and all the nearby bars on Nanluogu Xiang are at your disposal. The hostel also organises trips to the Great Wall.

CITY WALLS COURTYARD

Map pp58-9   Hútòng Hotel Y

☎ 6402 7805; www.beijingcitywalls.com; 57 Nianzi Hutong; 碾子胡同57号; 8-/4-bed dorm Y100/120, d Y380; ⊕ Dongsi; ⊠ 🖳

With lovely rooms and a crumbling hútòng setting, a warm courtyard atmosphere and a bubbly, friendly owner, this excellent hostel – virtually on the line bisecting central Běijīng – is authentically hidden away in one of the city's safest and most historic areas. The maze-like web of *hútòng* can be disorientating: from Jingshan Houjie, look for the *hútòng* opening just east of the playground and the Sinopec petrol station. Walk up the *hútòng* and follow it around to the right and then left – the hostel is on the left-hand side. The north gate of the Forbidden City is merely a few minutes walk away.

BEIJING P-LOFT YOUTH HOSTEL
Map pp58-9   Hútòng Hostel Y

☎ 6402 7218; ploft@yahoo.cn; 29 Paoju Toutiao; 炮局头条29号; 6-/4-bed dm Y40/50, s/tw Y160/180; ⊙ Yonghegong-Lama Temple; ✂ ▯

Embedded in a *hútòng* warren behind the Lama Temple, this place seems to be on the fringe of things, but it's only a short meander to the metro system. The converted-factory feel has a proletarian edge you may or may not warm to, but it's all history outside: next door is where the Qing imperial cannons were once manufactured. Dorms are fine, as are the doubles and singles, both with en suite. A degree on anonymity is guaranteed by the hard-to-find-location; facilities include reading room, bar, internet access, bike hire, laundry, and a roomy sports area for ping pong and pool.

XĪCHÉNG 西城区

Běijīng's other great historic district (after Dōngchéng), Xīchéng is central and close to all the main sights. Several hotels listed here are around the Shichahai Lakes, with their excellent blend of lakeside views, fun bars, *hútòng* restaurants and shopping options.

RITZ-CARLTON BEIJING, FINANCIAL STREET Map pp88-9   Luxury Hotel YYY
北京金融街丽嘉酒店 Běijīng Jīnróng Jiē Lìjiā Jiǔdiàn

☎ 6601 6666; www.ritzcarlton.com; 1 Jinchengfang Dongjie; 金城坊东街1号; d Y4600; ⊙ Fuxingmen; ✂ ▯ ▧ ㋔ ⚟

The magnificent Ritz-Carlton in Běijīng's financial district has further raised the bar in Běijīng's exclusive hotel sector. Spacious rooms are at the apex of luxury, with outrageously comfortable beds, 37in flat screen TVs and more TVs in the bathroom. Occupying an entire floor, the spa and health club has won praise from the pampered guests who can work off the meals they enjoy at the hotel's excellent restaurants.

MARCO POLO BEIJING
Map pp88-9   Hotel Y

北京马哥孛罗酒店 Běijīng Mǎgē Bóluó Jiǔdià

☎ 6603 6688; www.marcopolohotels.com; 6 Xuanwumennei Dajie; 宣武门内大街6号; d/ste Y1080/1580; ⊙ Xidan or Xuanwumen; ▯ ▧

North of the South Cathedral, this unfussy four-star hotel is one of the best in this pa of town. A length in the hotel pool may only take a few strokes, but the basement Clark Hatch Fitness Centre is well equippe and there are handy underground stations nearby.

BAMBOO GARDEN HOTEL
Map pp88-9   Heritage Hotel

竹园宾馆 Zhúyuán Bīnguǎn

☎ 5852 0088; www.bbgh.com.cn; 24 Xiaoshiqiao Hutong; 小石桥胡同24号; s/ste Y380/980, d Y680-880; ⊙ Gulou Dajie; ✂

Within roaming distance of the Drum and Bell Towers and Houhai Lake, the intimate leafy courtyard aspect is impaired by the jarring modern block opposite and occasionally the staff are casual, but this place still gets good reviews. The buildings date to the late Qing dynasty; its gardens once belonged to a eunuch from Empress Cixi' entourage. The small singles are cheap bu ordinary, so upgrading to the more pleasant doubles and suites is recommended. Reception is through the gates on your left.

SLEEPY INN Map pp88-9   Hote
丽舍什刹海国际青年酒店 Lìshè Shíchàhǎi Guójì Qīngnián Jiǔdiàn

☎ 6406 9954; www.sleepyinn.com.cn; 103 Deshengmennei Dajie; 德胜门内大街 103号; dm Y60-80, d Y298; ⊙ Jishuitan

With an adorable lake aspect thanks to its position on the border of Xihai and Houhai Lakes, this popular hotel has well-kept, clean and comfortable rooms in its modern three-storey block. Traditional charm is supplied by one of the halls of the Taoist Zhenwu Temple, incorporated into the main seating area. The terrace, and chirpy, friendly staff are all further perks. Positioned in one of th most *hútòng*-rich areas of Běijīng, there' oodles of charm and the bars of Houhai are nearby. Doubles come without phon or TV; there's internet access and bike h for vanishing into the surrounding labyrinth of alleys.

RED LANTERN HOUSE WEST YARD

Map pp88-9   Hútòng Hotel Y

红灯笼 Hóng Dēnglong

☎ 6656 2181; 111 Xinjiekou Nandajie; 新街口南大街111号; 6-bed dm Y55, s Y140-180, d Y220; ⊙ Ping'anli; ✉ 🖳

ts pretty, open courtyard charms, lazy tempo and helpful staff make this enclave of peace a relaxing proposition, even if t doesn't quite have the character of its relative, Red Lantern House. You can find decent dorm accommodation and good singles and doubles (with or without shower). There's internet, laundry, train, bike hire, plane and ferry ticketing, plus Great Wall trips. It's tucked away off the busy, main drag of Xinjiekou Nandajie; take the small alley to the green door and rummage around for the door bell.

RED LANTERN HOUSE

Map pp88-9   Hútòng Hotel Y

方古园 Fǎnggǔ Yuán

☎ 6611 5771; 5 Zhengjue Hutong; 正觉胡同号; 4-6 bed dm Y55, d Y150; ⊙ Jishuitan; 🖳

With its charming interior, trimmed with red lanterns and opening onto an ample bar area, this is a welcoming hotel. There's also helpful staff and a winning hútòng location, just a short stroll from Houhai Lake. Rooms are on two levels: upstairs doubles are all without shower, but they are comfortable with bright windows. Reserve ahead, and if it's booked out, there's the sibling Red Lantern House West Yard a brief walk west down Xinjiekou Nandajie.

CHÁOYÁNG 朝阳区

Cháoyáng is a vibrant and youthful district for shopping, dining, bars and clubs. It is home to several trendy boutique hotels and a gaggle of top-flight hotels, but it's an area with little discernible history so it can be hard to get under the skin of Běijīng from here. But if you are in the capital for drinking and entertainment, sleeping in this neighbourhood makes perfect sense.

ST REGIS Map pp110-11   Luxury Hotel YYY

北京国际俱乐部饭店 Běijīng Guójì Jùlèbù Fàndiàn

☎ 6460 6688; www.stregis.com/beijing; 1 Jianguomenwai Dajie; 建国门外大街号; d/ste Y3150/3980; ⊙ Jianguomen; 🔊 🖳 🖵 🛓 🛜

Its extravagant foyer, thorough professionalism and tip-top location make the St Regis a marvellous, albeit costly, five-star choice. Sumptuous and soothing rooms ooze comfort, 24-hour butlers are at hand to fine-tune your stay and a gorgeous assortment of restaurants steers you into one of Běijīng's finest dining experiences.

CHINA WORLD HOTEL

Map pp110-11   Luxury Hotel YYY

中国大饭店 Zhōngguó Dàfàndiàn

☎ 6505 2266; www.shangri-la.com; 1 Jianguomenwai Dajie; 建国门外大街1号; d Y2900; ⊙ Guomao; ✉ 🖳 🖵 🛓 🛜

The gorgeous five-star China World Hotel delivers an outstanding level of service to its well-dressed, largely executive travellers. The sumptuous foyer is a masterpiece of Chinese motifs, glittering chandeliers, robust columns and smooth acres of marble, an effect complemented by thoroughly modern and comfortable rooms. The amenities are extensive, dining options are first-rate and shopping needs meet their match at the adjacent China World Shopping Mall (p150).

JIANGUO HOTEL Map pp110-11   Hotel YYY

建国饭店 Jiànguó Fàndiàn

☎ 6500 2233; www.hoteljianguo.com; 5 Jianguomenwai Dajie; 建国门外大街5号; d Y2200; ⊙ Yonganli; 🖳 🛓

A recent refit has modestly galvanised an ageing formula, although old touches persist and the hotel finds itself rather like Běijīng: suspended between two eras. Rooms are pleasant enough, especially the ones in the four-storey building 'A' that have patios and face the strip of garden and water, but rooms opposite Charlie's Bar can be noisy at night. Essentially, it's the location and good discounts that win over guests.

OPPOSITE HOUSE HOTEL

Map pp110-11   Boutique Hotel YYY

瑜舍 Yúshè

☎ 6417 6688; www.theoppositehouse.com; Bldg 1, Village, 11 Sanlitun Lu; 三里屯路11号院1号楼; d Y1950; ✉ ✉ 🖳 🖵 🛜

With see-all open-plan bathrooms, American oak bath tubs, lovely mood lighting, underfloor heating, sliding doors, complimentary beers, TVs on extendable arms and a metal basin swimming pool, this trendy Swire-owned boutique hotel is top-drawer chic. Chinese motifs are muted: this is an international hotel with prices to match. It's not the sort of place to take the kids, but couples can splash out or sip drinks in trendy Mesh (p186). The location is great for shopping, restaurants and drinking, but Sānlǐtún is one of Běijīng's least-charming neighbourhoods, with uniform streets and zero history.

KERRY CENTER HOTEL

Map pp110-11 · Business Hotel YYY

嘉里中心饭店 Jiālǐ Zhōngxīn Fàndiàn

☎ 6561 8833; www.shangri-la.com; 1 Guanghua Lu; 光华路1号; d Y1600; ⊖ Guomao; 🖵 🎌 🕭

Since flinging open the doors 10 years ago, the business-oriented Kerry Center has remained stylish, from the snazzy lobby lines to the svelte female attendants at Centro (p185), the hotel's signature bar. Contemporary and crisp, the 34-sq-metre doubles are comfortable, with sliding doors onto well-designed bathrooms that include a shower and (small) bath. The gym is huge and well equipped, the swimming pool is big enough to get the heart pumping and the adjacent Kerry Mall answers shopping needs.

COMFORT INN Map pp110-11 · Hotel YYY

凯富饭店 Kǎifù Fàndiàn

☎ 8523 5522; fax 8523 5577; 6 Gongrentiyuchang Beilu; 工人体育场北路6号; d/ste Y1380/1580; ⊖ Dongsishitiao, then ⊖ 113; 🗙 🖵 🎌 🕭

Benefiting from proximity to the bars and restaurants of Sānlǐtún, this modern mid-range hotel has rather bland but serviceable rooms, equipped with free internet, and cable and satellite TV. The front lobby looks more like a car salesroom, and the Escher-inspired design behind the lobby counter is derivative, but the hotel is comfortable enough if you are OK with a lack of oomph. There is a top-floor indoor pool.

HOTEL G Map pp110-11 · Boutique Hotel YYY

北京极栈 Běijīng Jízhàn

☎ 6552 3600; www.hotel-G.com; 7a Gongrentiyuchang Xilu; 工体西路甲7号; d with breakfast Y1088; 🎌 🖵 🕭

It is hard to discern the advertised '60s retro-chic style, but this snazzy boutique hotel is certainly distinctive, from its deep purples, charcoal blacks, satins, floral prints and crushed velvet to the fibre-optics by the lobby elevators. Peruse the soothing

pillow menu (six varieties) to complement the gorgeously comfortable beds, snap your iPod into the docking station and Bob's your uncle. At the time of writing the ground-floor bar was due for a makeover: hopefully mufflers will be slapped on it to quiet the earth-moving volume of weekend dance nights. Nintendo Wii and DVD player on request.

SANLITUN YOUTH HOSTEL

Map pp110-11 · Hostel

三里屯青年旅馆 Sānlǐtún Qīngnián Lǚguǎn

☎ 5190 9288; 1 Chunxiu Lu; 春秀路1号; 6-/4-bed dm Y60/70, tw/d Y220/220; ⊖ Dongsishitiao o Dongzhimen; 🗙 🖵 🕭

Situated conveniently inbetween the bar nexus of Sānlǐtún and Line 2 of the underground, this functional four-floor hostel has clean dorms and hygienic common shower rooms, but little character. The hostel is tucked away around 150m north of Gongrentiyuchang Beilu; head through the main gate off Chunxiu Lu to the wall, follow the sign under the arch on your left and it's immediately on the left-hand side. Free internet and wi-fi for guests, bike hire (Y20 per day), Great Wall tours and friendly staff

XUĀNWǓ 宣武区

Riddled with *hútòng* alleyways but possessin grittier, more threadbare charm than eithe Dōngchéng or Xīchéng, Xuānwǔ has a bet ter-value selection of hotels and several yout hostels. Most of the hotels chosen here ar within reach of Tiananmen Square and Tem ple of Heaven Park (in Chóngwén).

QIANMEN JIANGUO HOTEL

Map pp118-19 · Hotel YY

前门建国饭店 Qiánmén Jiànguó Fàndiàn

☎ 6301 6688; www.qianmenhotel.com; 175 Yong'anLu; 永安路175号; d/tr/steY1298/1738/206 ⊖ Hepingmen, then 🚌 25; 🗙 🎌 🖵

Elegant in parts and popular with tour groups, this refurbished and choicely locate hotel has pushed up its prices to reflect its makeover. Business is brisk so the staff are on their toes, but they grab any chance to switch off. The sexually explicit posters in the lobby of massage staff doing their thing send out dodgy messages, but the rooms are spacious, clean, attractively carpeted an bright on the upper floors. You can find the Liyuan Theatre (p194) to the right of the domec atrium at the rear of the hotel.

AUTUMN GARDEN HOTEL

Map pp118-19   Hútòng Hotel YYY

春秋园宾馆 **Chūnqiūyuán Bīnguǎn**

☎ 6315 2881, 6304 4232; 23 Sanjing Hutong; 三井胡同23号; d Y1580; ◉ Hepingmen; ⊠

Handily slung out north of Dashilar in a restful *hútòng* and within strolling distance of Tiananmen Square, this small courtyard hotel in ancient 'Three Wells Hutong' is an attractive choice. Rooms are decked out with traditional furniture but, as with all courtyard hotels, they're on the titchy side. Good discounts often bring rooms down to around Y780.

QIANMEN HOSTEL

Map pp118-19   Heritage Hostel Y

前门客栈 **Qiánmén Kèzhàn**

☎ 6313 2370, 6313 2369; www.qianmenhostel.com; 33 Meishi Jie; 煤市街33号; 6-8 bed dm Y60, 4-bed dm Y70, tw Y200-240, d Y240, tr Y240-300; ◉ Qianmen; ⊟ ⊠

A five-minute trot southwest of Tiananmen Square, this heritage hostel offers a relaxing environment with able staff. Close the door on the busy street outside and appreciate the high ceilings, original woodwork and charming antique buildings. An affable old-hand, hostel owner Genghis Kane may enthusiastically show you his environmentally sound heating apparatus (fired with dried pellets of plant matter), or you can surf the net (Y1 per 10 minutes) in the skylight-lit foyer. The heritage rooms are simple with spongiform mattresses; the purpose-built rooms are more modern. Western breakfasts available.

HANGGONG HOTEL

Map pp118-19   Heritage Hotel Y

汉宫饭店 **Hánggōng Fàndiàn**

☎ 5194 8204; changgong_hotel@yahoo.com.cn; 1 Yingtao Xiejie; 樱桃斜街11号; 4-/6-bed dm Y40, tw without shower Y60, d/tr with shower Y180/210; ⊠ ⊟

The marvellous former Guizhou Guild Hall, opposite the disintegrating Guanyin Temple on Yingtao Xiejie, is a cavernous old Qing-dynasty era building stuffed with fantastic tiling and period details. Arranged over two floors linked by a vertigo-inducing flight of stairs, the hotel's excellent-value doubles are spacious, if rather threadbare. The friendly staff speaks good English, but there's often someone perched waxwork-like at the sole internet terminal, the hotel's echo-chamber acoustics amplify every murmur and winters can be frosty. That said, it's a bargain.

FAR EAST INTERNATIONAL YOUTH HOSTEL

Map pp118-19   Hútòng Hostel Y

远东国际青年旅社 **Yuǎndōng Guójì Qīngnián Lǚshè**

☎ 5195 8811; 113 Tieshu Xiejie; 铁树斜街113号; 4-6 bed dm Y45-60; ◉ Hepingmen; ⊠ ⊟

This hostel is in a pretty, old courtyard opposite the hotel of the same name. It is an extremely pleasant and clean place with loads of character, internet, kitchen, washing facilities and a fine bar-cafe. There is also a handy tourist office and guests can lounge around in the courtyard when the weather is warm. Rooms come without TV, phone or shower. The Far East Hotel (Map pp118–19; s/d/tr Y238/398/378, q per person Y75) opposite is an unremarkable two-star hotel, but the quads downstairs are clean with wooden floors and well-kept bunk beds.

HǍIDIÀN 海淀区

A huge and sprawling district of northwest Běijīng with a mere handful of sights, Hǎidiàn is a peripheral area of town that is mainly of interest to business travellers.

SHANGRI-LA HOTEL

Map p122   Hotel YYY

香格里拉饭店 **Xiānggé Lǐlā Fàndiàn**

☎ 6841 2211; www.shangri-la.com; 29 Zizhuyuan Lu; 紫竹园路29号; d incl breakfast Y1370; ⊠ ⊟ ⅋

The Shangri-La's air-freshened lobby and muted Chinese motifs may not match the majesty of its sibling China World Hotel, but the rates here are far lower. The Olympics and high-occupancy rates prompted the construction of a new tower brimming with spacious 'Horizon' rooms. Modest-sized swimming pool.

GREATER BEIJING

COMMUNE BY THE GREAT WALL

off Map pp128-9   Luxury Hotel YYY

长城脚下的公社 **Chángchéng Jiǎoxià de Gōngshè**

☎ 8118 1888; www.communebythegreatwall.com; d Y2500; ⊠ ⊟ ⅋ ⌐

The Commune by the Great Wall is seriously expensive but the cantilevered geometric architecture, location and superb panoramas are simply standout. Positioned at the Shuiguan Great Wall off the Badaling Hwy, the Kempinski-managed Commune may have a proletarian name but the design and presentation are purely for the affluent. Take out another mortgage and treat yourself – this is the ultimate view, with a room. There is a kid's club to boot.

AMAN AT SUMMER PALACE

Map pp128-9   Heritage Hotel YYY

颐和安缦 **Yíhé Ānmàn**

☎ 5987 9999; 15 Gongmenqian Jie; 宫门前街 15号; r US$480, courtyard r US$580, ste US$780; 🅇 🖭 🖳 🕭 🛜

Just round the corner from the Summer Palace, the sedate Aman resort is a rare and privileged escape from central Běijīng's fuggy and noisy streets. Stepping through the ceremonial-looking gate and past the stone lions takes you to a completely different world – the discreet reception area in the lobby suggests a highly intimate service (and an exclusive tariff). The courtyard rooms are simply gorgeous and just the ticket if you want gilt-edged memories of Běijīng. Choice restaurants, a spa, a library, a cinema, pool and squash courts round off the refined picture.

RED CAPITAL RANCH

off Map pp128-9   Ranch YYY

☎ 8401 8886; www.redcapitalclub.com; 28 Xiaguandi Village, Yanxi, Huairou County; 怀柔县雁 栖镇下关地村28号; d 1425; 🅇 🖭 🖳

Doing its own thing miles from civilisation, Red Capital Ranch is *the* Běijīng escapist option. Sooner or later, the capital's particular fusion of ear-splitting noises, toxic air and honking cars will have you sprinting for the exit. If so, why not check into one of the 10 individually styled villas at this Manchurian hunting lodge on a 20-acre estate north of town – settle down for a long, stress-free siesta. If the mountain setting – complete with Great Wall remains running through the estate – doesn't dissolve your stress, the Tibetan Tantric Space Spa will. Try to get you Běijīng sightseeing out of the way before staying here – it's quite a hike into town.

HOLIDAY INN LIDO BEIJING

Map pp128-9   Hotel Y

北京丽都假日饭店 **Běijīng Lìdū Jiàrì Fàndiàn**
☎ 6437 6688; www.beijing-lido.holiday-inn.com; cnr Jichang Lu & Jiangtai Lu; 机场路和将台路 交叉口; d Y820; 🅇 🖭 🖳 🕭 🛜

On the way to the airport, this hotel – the first Holiday Inn built in China – has virtually everything you may need, with excellent amenities and a well-resourced shopping mall.

EXCURSIONS

EXCURSIONS

The flatland of central Běijīng inevitably reinforces a lopsided and two-dimensional urban view of China. The Middle kingdom has its sparkling skyscrapers, heaving flyovers and high-intensity inner-city pressures, while the rest of the nation is largely agricultural and hilly. Excursions into the surrounding landscape don't just help blow the nitrogen dioxide and construction dust from your hair and lungs, they round out the picture.

China is only occasionally the shimmering vision of modernity dished up by glossy international magazines to wide-eyed jetsetters. Parts of Běijīng, Shànghǎi, Guǎngzhōu and Shēnzhèn are indeed ultramodern, but China's GDP per capita is on a par with Namibia's. So don't fall for the endless glamour portrayed in high-end advertisements, get out of town and see something of rural China. You've made it this far, so why not go that extra mile and dig a bit deeper into the China experience: otherwise it's a bit like going to get a book you've always wanted to read and returning with the dust jacket.

For charming glimpses of traditional Chinese village life visit Chuāndǐxià, a few hours west of the city. Remoteness has protected its alleys and buildings from development and the hillside community provides a fascinating snapshot of a traditional way of life that is disappearing in China.

Several famous temples lie within reach of town, including Tanzhe Temple and Jietai Temple. But consider travelling further to Chéngdé, 255km northeast of Běijīng, with its magnificent scenery, imperial estate and a distinctive crop of hillside temple architecture. Zhèngdìng is a historic, walled temple town that can be visited in a day trip from Běijīng, while the Ming-dynasty garrison town of Shānhǎiguān allows travellers to skirt the edge of China's mighty northeast while exploring sections of the Great Wall north of town and over the border in Manchuria. If you are after some fresh air, consider a trip to Shídù, where you can go hiking.

The Ming Tombs are routinely pedalled as a mandatory sight and while the stately burial place of 13 of the Ming emperors can be tied in with trips to some sections of the Great Wall, they are rarely the highlight of anyone's trip to Běijīng, although some visitors find the scenic valley setting a great antidote to Běijīng's flatness.

You can't see it from the moon, but you can get up close to the Great Wall by travelling a couple of hours from Běijīng. The brick bastion is certainly China's number-one, must-see sight. It's important to cherry-pick the right section to visit because some of the most famous areas are overdeveloped, over-run and inauthentic; consult the Journey to the Great Wall chapter (p97) for the low-down on where to go for a unique experience. For suggestions on accommodation options near or alongside the wall, see the Greater Beijing section in the Sleeping chapter (p215).

CHÉNGDÉ 承德

Once known as Jehol, Chéngdé is an 18th-century imperial resort area where the remnants of the largest regal gardens in China sit among the Héběi hills.

The site was rescued from obscurity in 1703 when Emperor Kangxi – lured by hunting opportunities and the area's proximity and semblance to the Manchu homelands – began building a summer palace with all the court trappings, including a throne room. More than a home away from home, Chéngdé became a seat of government, since wherever the emperor went his seat went, too. Kangxi called the Imperial Summer Villa 'Bìshǔ Shānzhuāng', which means Fleeing-the-Heat Mountain Villa.

By 1790, during the reign of Kangxi' grandson Qianlong, the villa grounds had mushroomed to the size of Běijīng's Summer Palace and the Forbidden City combined. Qianlong built replicas of minority architecture (an initiative begun by Kangxi) so that envoys could feel right at home.

Qianlong was particularly eager to promote Tibetan and Mongolian Lamaism, hence the pronounced Tibetan and Mongolian features of some of the monasteries; there is even a mini-replica of the Potala Palace in Lhasa.

The year 1861 was a dreadful one for Chéngdé's royal patronage. The Emperor Xianfeng died here, permanently warping its fēngshuǐ (geomancy, literally 'wind and water') and tipping the Imperial Summer Villa toward long-term decline. It was never again used by

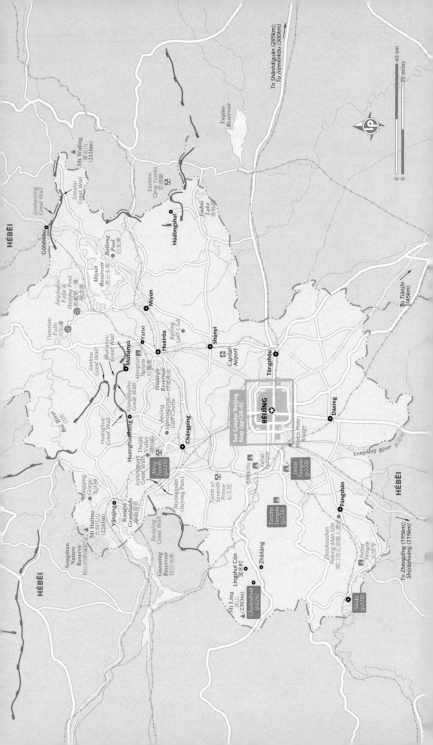

CHÉNGDÉ

0   2 km
0   1 mile

A   **B**   **C**   **D**

Arhat Hall Ruins
(Luohan Tang)
罗汉堂

Guangan Temple
广安寺

16   18   Guangyuan
Temple
广缘寺

19

Shizigou Lu 舞子沟路

17

20

Xibei Gate
西北门

Shizi Gouche

Wulie

Beizhen
▲Twin Peaks
北枕双峰

Wulie River

10

To Club Rock (1.5km);
Toad Rock (1.5km)

30

Imperial Summer Villa
(Bishǔ Shānzhuāng)
避暑山庄

Huodiji Gate
惠迪吉门

22

15

21

Bifeng Gate
碧峰门

Xi Dajie 西大街

Birengmen Donglu

14

Fragrant
Garden House
(Fangyuanju)
芳园居

Puren
Temple
溥仁寺

Shanzhuang Donglu 山庄东路

11

Delhui Gate
德汇门

24

12   13
3   7
26   23

27

Lizhengmen Dajie 丽正门大街

9

6
28

Nanxinglong
Xiaochi Jie

Dutongfu Dajie
都统府大街

Qinglong Jie

Shaanxiying Jie 陕西营街

Nanyingzi Dajie 南营子大街

29

Chaichang
Hutong
柴厂胡同

Wu Lu

4
8

Luoshan
Mountain
罗汉山

Shidongzi Gou 石洞子沟

Cuiqiao Lu

25

Xinhua Lu

Chengde
Train Station
承德火车站

2

5   Chezhan Lu 车站路

To East Bus
Station (8km)

...the emperors, who shunned its associations with misfortune. Even Henry Puyi – the wishy-washy 'last emperor' – gave it a wide berth when his world was collapsing around him.

Today Chéngdé has slipped back into being the provincial town it once was, its grandeur long decayed and its emperors long gone. The town is no oil painting and could easily pass itself off as any other medium-sized Chinese city, but the Imperial Summer Villa is on the Unesco World Heritage list, along with Chéngdé's magnificent brood of temples.

Autumn visits are recommended as tourists swarm like termites during summer. Winter is face-numbingly cold, but visitors are few and far between.

The train from Běijīng to Chéngdé passes level fields, dark mountains, factories, terraced slopes, occasional pagoda-capped hills and crumbling lengths of the Great Wall, including Jīnshānlǐng (p105).

IMPERIAL SUMMER VILLA 避暑山庄

Sprawling over 590 hectares, the Imperial Summer Villa (Bìshǔ Shānzhuāng; summer/winter Y90/60, guide Y50; park 5.30am-6.30pm, palace 7am-5pm) is a colossal park bounded by a splendid 10km wall. Only a small portion of the grounds contain architecture: around 90% is taken up by lakes, hills, mini-forests, plains and hunting grounds. Passing through the Main Gate (Lìzhèng Mén) you reach the Front Palace (Zhèng Gōng), containing the main throne hall. Inside, the refreshingly cool Hall of Simplicity & Sincerity is fashioned from an aromatic hardwood called *nánmù*; there is a carved throne on display. There are also the emperor's fully furnished bedrooms, as well as displays of ceramics, drum stones and calligraphy.

The double-storey Misty Rain Tower (Yǔ Lóu), on the northern side of the main lake, was an imperial study. Further north is the Wenjin Chamber (Wénjīn Gé) built in 1773 to house a copy of the *Sìkùquánshū*, a major anthology of classics, history, philosophy and literature commissioned by Qianlong.

In the east, the tall green-and-yellow Yongyousi Pagoda (Yǒngyòusì Tǎ) soars above the fragments of its vanished temple and dominates the area.

Just beyond the main palace are electric carts that buzz around the grounds (Y40); further on is a boat-rental area (Y10 to Y50 per hour). Most of the forested section is out of bounds during the fire-prone dry season (November to May), but the rest of the park is easily big enough to bring you to your knees.

GUANDI TEMPLE 关帝庙

Also called the Wumiao, the Guandi Temple (Guāndì Miào; Lizhengmen Dajie; admission Y20; 8am-5pm) is a Taoist temple first built in 1732 and home to a band of Taoist monks, garbed in distinctive jackets and trousers, their long hair twisted into topknots. In the courtyard at the rear are two steles, supported on the backs of a pair of disintegrating and distressed-looking *bìxì* (mythical tortoise-like dragon creatures). The Hall of the Three Clear Ones stands at the rear to the left.

EIGHT OUTER TEMPLES & OTHER SIGHTS 外八庙

The scenic foothills outside the northern and northeastern walls of the Imperial Summer Villa are strewn with one of China's most captivating clusters of temples. Not all temples have been restored or are open, but there are more than enough to keep you busy. Built between 1750 and 1780, the temples are 3km to 5km from the Imperial Summer Villa's front gate; take bus 6 to the northeast corner or bus 118 along Huancheng Beilu. Travelling by bike is a breezier and more panoramic option.

The most jaw-dropping spectacle is at Puning Temple (Pǔníng Sì; Puningsi Lu; summer/winter Y50/40; summer 7.30am-6pm, winter 8am-5pm) – the Temple of Universal Tranquillity – a Chinese-style temple with more Tibetan-style features at the rear. Enter the temple grounds to a stele pavilion with inscriptions by Emperor Qianlong in Chinese, Manchu, Mongol and Tibetan. Behind are halls arranged in the typical Buddhist-temple layout, featuring the Hall of Heavenly Kings (Tiānwáng Diàn) and the Mahavira Hall (Dàxióng Bǎodiàn) beyond. Steep steps then rise (the temple is arranged on a mountainside) to a gate tower, a terrace and the breathtaking Mahayana Hall. The highlight of the temple is the heart-arresting gilded statue

of the Buddhist Goddess of Mercy (Guanyin) in the Mahayana Hall. The effigy is astounding: it's over 22m high (the highest of its kind in the world) and it radiates a powerful sense of divinity. Hewn from five kinds of wood (pine, cypress, fir, elm and linden), Guanyin has 42 arms, with each palm bearing an eye, and each hand holds instruments, skulls, lotuses and other Buddhist devices. On Guanyin's head sits the Teacher Longevity Buddha (Shīzūn Wúliàng Shòufó). To her right stands Shancai, a male guardian and disciple, opposite his female equivalent, Longnü (Dragon Girl).

If you're lucky, you can clamber up to the first gallery (Y10) for a closer inspection of Guanyin; torches (flashlights) are provided to cut through the gloom and help you pick out the uneven stairs (take care). Sadly, the higher galleries are often out of bounds, so an eye-to-eye with the goddess may be impossible. If you want to climb up, aim to come in the morning as it is often impossible to get a ticket in the afternoon (especially outside of summer).

Puning Temple has a number of friendly lamas who manage their domain, so be quiet and respectful at all times. You can catch bus 6 from the front of the Mountain Villa Hotel to Puning Temple.

If it looks familiar, it's because the largest of Chéngdé's temples, Putuozongcheng Temple (Pǔtuózōngchéng Zhī Miào; Shizigou Lu; summer/winter Y40/30; 8am-6pm), is based upon Lhasa's Potala Palace. Also called the Little Potala Palace (小布达拉宫; Xiǎo Bùdálā Gōng), the temple

---

TRANSPORT: CHÉNGDÉ

Distance from Běijīng 255km

Direction Northeast

Train Regular trains run between Běijīng and Chéngdé; the fastest take just over four hours (hard/soft seat Y41/61), slower trains take much longer. The first train from Běijīng departs at 6.30am, arriving in Chéngdé at 10.48pm. In the other direction, the first train to Běijīng leaves at 5.45am, arriving at 11am, or the 1.30pm from Chéngdé is a useful train, arriving at 5.48pm.

Long-distance bus Buses (Y56 to Y74, four hours) to Chéngdé depart hourly from the Liuliqiao and Sihui Long-Distance Bus Stations in Běijīng. Minibuses for Běijīng (Y65, four hours, last bus 6.30pm) leave every 20 minutes from Chengde Train Station and just down the road from the Yunshan Hotel. For Shānhǎiguān (p224), first take bus 118 or a taxi (Y10) to the East Bus Station (东站; Dōngzhàn), 8km south of Chengde Train Station, and then take a bus to Qínhuángdǎo (Y90, four hours, five per day); then take local bus 33 to Shānhǎiguān.

Local transport Taxis are Y5 at flag fall, which should get you to most destinations in town, but be warned: most drivers don't use meters. There are several bus lines (Y1), including buses 5 and 11 from the train station to the Imperial Summer Villa and bus 6 to the Eight Outer Temples. Biking around town is a fine idea; at the time of writing the only place renting bikes was Battle (Wulie Lu; per hr/day Y20/60, Y300 deposit). Also ask at your hotel.

Tours Minibus tours from hotels start out at 8am. The cheapest bus tours (check at the Mountain Villa Hotel) are Chinese-speaking only; a personal tour should cost around Y100, excluding admission prices. Consider hiring a taxi for the day, which should cost around Y150.

is a striking sight on a clear day, its vast red walls standing out against the mountain backdrop. Preceded by squeaking prayer wheels and flapping flags, the Red Palace (also called the Great Red Terrace) encloses the majority of main shrines and halls. Press on past an exhibition of *thangkas* (Tibetan sacred art) in a restored courtyard and look out for the marvellous sandalwood pagodas further up. Both are 19m tall and contain 2160 effigies of the Amitabha Buddha. Among the many exhibits are displays of Tibetan Buddhist objects and instruments, including a *kapala* bowl, made from the skull of a young girl; all captions are in Chinese. The main hall is housed at the very top, surrounded by several small pavilions; the climb to the top is rewarded by fabulous views.

The monumental Temple of Sumeru, Happiness & Longevity (Xūmífúshòu Zhī Miào; Shizigou Lu; summer/winter Y30/20; 8am-5.30pm) is around 1km to the southeast of the Putuozongcheng Temple. In honour of the sixth Panchen Lama (who stayed here in 1781) the temple was built in imitation of a temple in Shigatse, Tibet, and incorporates Tibetan and Han architectural elements. Note the eight, huge glinting dragons (each said to weigh over 1000kg) that adorn the roof of the main hall.

Pule Temple (Pǔlè Sì; summer/winter Y30/20; 8am-5pm) was built in 1776 for the visits of minority envoys (Kazakhs among them). At the rear of the temple is the unusual round pavilion, reminiscent of the Hall of Prayer for Good Harvests at the Temple of Heaven Park (p80) in Běijīng. Bus 10 can get you to the temple.

East of Puning Temple is Puyou Temple (Pǔyòu Sì; admission Y20; 8am-6pm). While dilapidated and devoid of its main hall, a contingent of merry gilded *luóhàn* (Buddhists, especially monks, who achieved enlightenment and passed to nirvana at death) wait in the side wings, although a fire in 1964 incinerated many of them. Note that the temple to the east (Guangyuan Temple) is unrestored and inaccessible.

It's a 30-minute hike to Club Rock (Bàngchuí Fēng) from the Pule Temple – the rock is said to resemble a club used for beating laundry dry. Nearby is Toad Rock (Háma Shí). Enjoy the pleasant hiking, good scenery and commanding views of the area. You can save yourself a steep climb by taking the chairlift to the base of Club Rock/Toad Rock (Y20/40 return), but it's more fun to walk if you're reasonably fit.

Anyuan Temple (Ānyuǎn Miào; admission Y10; 8am-6.30pm) is a copy of the Gurza Temple in Xīnjiāng. Only the main hall remains and

it contains deteriorating Buddhist frescoes. Note that the temple further south (Puren Temple) is not open to the public.

Located northwest of the Imperial Summer Villa and surrounded by a low red wall, Shuxiang Temple (Shūxiàng Sì) is sometimes closed, although it may open in the summer months (unless it is being restored). A gate in the eastern wall swings open so you can take a peek inside, but there are signs about dangerous dogs – explore at your own risk! Just to the west of Shuxiang Temple there is a sensitive military zone where foreigners are not allowed access, so don't wander around.

INFORMATION

It is possible to store luggage at the East Bus Station ticket hall and at the train station ticket hall.

Bank of China (Zhōngguó Yínháng; 4 Dutongfu Dajie) ATM access.

Chaosu Internet Cafe (Cháosù Wǎngbā; Chezhan Lu; per hr Y2; 24hr) Northwest of the train station.

CITS (Zhōngguó Guójì Lǚxíngshè; 0314-202 4816; 2nd fl, 3 Wulie Lu) This service for international travellers is in the building on your right in a dishevelled courtyard on the western side of Wulie Lu; not much use. There's also a small branch on Bifengmen Donglu.

Kodak Express (Kēdá; 5-7 Lizhengmen Dajie) CD burning (Y15 per disc) available. Opposite the Guandi Temple.

No 5 Hospital (Dìwǔ Yīyuàn; Chezhan Lu)

Post office (Yóujú; cnr Lizhengmen Dajie & Dutongfu Dajie; 8am-6pm) A smaller branch exists on Lizhengmen Dajie just east of the Main Gate of the Imperial Summer Villa.

Public Security Bureau (PSB; Gōngānjú; 0314-202 2352; 9 Wulie Lu; 8.30am-5pm Mon-Fri)

Tiancheng Internet Café (Tiānchéng Wǎngbā; Chaichang Hutong; per hr Y1.50; 24hr)

Xiandai Internet Cafe (Xiàndài Wǎngbā; Chezhan Lu; per hr Y2; 24hr) Northwest of the train station.

EATING

Chéngdé's local speciality is wild game and you can find deer (*lùròu*) and pheasant (*shānjī*) dishes all over town.

Xiláishùn Fànzhuāng (0314-202 5554; 6 Zhonggulou Dajie; dishes Y10-40) An excellent choice for those fleeing Chinese staples, this Muslim restaurant cooks up a fine beef fried with coriander (*kǎo niúròu*; Y24) and sesame duck kebabs (*zhīma yāchuàn*; Y25).

Dongpo Restaurant (Dōngpō Fànzhuāng; ☎ 0314-210 6315; Shanzhuang Donglu; meals Y30) Hung welcomingly with red lanterns and located a short walk east of the Imperial Summer Villa, this popular eatery has a good range of spicy Sichuān dishes and a menu lightly peppered with English. Another branch can be found across from the train station.

Dadi Beijing Roast Duck Restaurant (Dàdì Jiǔjiā; ☎ 0314-202 2979; 5-12 Lizhengmen Dajie; duck Y68; 9am-9pm) The round tables dwarf small groups, but the duck comes roasted over fruit-tree wood. You may have to wait a thumb-twiddling 45 minutes for your duck – if so, you can choose to order, pay up front and come back later. Pancakes for the roast duck are Y3, sauce Y1.

SLEEPING

Touts around the train station can often find you a room in a family hotel near the station for around Y80 to Y100.

Yiyuan Hotel (Yíyuán Bīnguǎn; ☎ 0314-202 8430; 7 Lizhengmen Dajie; 丽正门大街7号; d Y330-380, ste Y480) The exterior is shabby and service is run of the mill, but the location is marvellous and double rooms generally discounted to a very budget-friendly Y120.

Mountain Villa Hotel (Shānzhuāng Bīnguǎn; ☎ 0314-209 1188; www.hemvhotel.com; 11 Lizhengmen Lu; 丽正门路11号; d Y280-480, tr Y210;) The Mountain Villa is a strong budget-to-midrange choice, but preview the rooms first to weigh up the variety and standards. The location is winning – near the Imperial Summer Villa and within striking distance of the temples. Take bus 7 from the train station and from there it's a short walk.

Qiwanglou Hotel (Qíwànglóu Bīnguǎn; ☎ 0314-202 2196; 1 Bifengmen Donglu; 碧峰门东路1号; tw Y500-800;) With peacocks strolling around the green grounds, the attractive and secluded setting of this hotel next to the Imperial Summer Villa is alluring, but the cheaper rooms are iffy and you will have to strain for views of the villa grounds over the treetops. Aim for the newer rear building.

Yunshan Hotel (Yúnshān Dàjiǔdiàn; ☎ 0314-205 5888, fax 0314-205 5885; 2 Banbishan Lu; 半壁山路2号; d/ste Y780/1600;) The numbing exterior (white tiles, office-block style) is an unfortunate composition and the location is unimpressive, but rooms at this four-star hotel are clean, elegant and spacious. The hotel has a business centre, Western restaurant, sauna and lobby bar.

SHĀNHĂIGUĀN
山海关

The Great Wall meets the sea at Shānhǎiguān in Héběi province, where a strategic pass leads to northeast China. Shānhǎiguān came into its own in 1381, when it was developed into a fortified garrison town with four gates at the compass points and two major avenues running between them. The Manchus

SHĀNHĂIGUĀN

stormed the pass in 1644 before enslaving China for over 250 years.

Recent destruction and rebuilding within the old walled enclosure has sapped the town of some charm, but Shānhǎiguān still packs enough history into its old, dusty courtyards that sit on the east–west running *hútòng* (narrow alleyways) to warrant exploration, and the nearby Great Wall is a major drawcard. The Drum Tower at the heart of Shānhǎiguān's old town has been rebuilt, along with several *páilou* (decorated archways) running east and west from it, a handful of temples and much of the main streets. These structures are not original, but possess flavours – although fabricated – of old China.

First Pass Under Heaven (Tiānxià Dìyī Guān; cnr Dong Dajie & Diyiguan Lu; admission Y40; ☺ 7.30am-6.30pm, to 5.30pm Oct-Apr) is also known as East Gate (东门; Dōng Mén; also called 东关; Dōng Guān). The Great Wall here is 12m high and the principal watchtower – a two-storey structure with double eaves and 68 arrow-slit windows – is a towering 13.7m high, while decayed sections of battlements trail off into the hills. Several other watchtowers can also be seen and a *wèngchéng* (enceinte) extends east from the Wall. Admission includes entry to the newly expanded Great Wall Museum (Chángchéng Bówùguǎn; Diyiguan Lu; admission without First Pass Under Heaven ticket Y10; ☺ 8am-6pm), which displays memorabilia relating to the Wall. The nearby Wang Family Courtyard House (Wángjiā Dàyuàn; 29-31 Dongsantiao Hutong; admission Y25, joint ticket with First Pass Under Heaven Y40; ☺ 6.30am-6.30pm) is a large, historic *hútòng*-style residence faced by a spirit wall.

Old Dragon Head (老龙头; Lǎolóngtóu; admission Y50; ☺ 7.30am-5.30pm), 4km south of Shānhǎiguān, was the serpentine conclusion of the Great Wall. The name derives from the legendary and now-vanished carved dragon head that once faced the waves. What you see now was reconstructed in the late 1980s. Avoid buying the pricey ticket and instead take the left-hand road to the sea (under the arched gate) where you can walk along the sandy beach to Old Dragon Head or ride a horse (Y20). Watch out for touts who will do anything to pull you into a peripheral attraction of no interest. To get here take bus 25 (Y1) from Shānhǎiguān's South Gate.

Recently rebuilt temples and historic monuments include the four halls of the Dabei Pavilion (Dàbēi Gé) in the northwest of town, and the Taoist Sanqing Temple (三清观; Sānqīng Guàn; Beihou Jie), outside the walls.

Shānhǎiguān's Drum Tower (Gǔlóu) has been similarly resurrected with lines of recently constructed páilou running off east and west along Xi Dajie and Dong Dajie.

The unrestored North Gate (Běi Mén) stands in a state of dreary neglect, but you can climb up onto the overgrown sections of the city wall attached to it if you head up the brick steps to the east of the gate (go through the compound). The city gates once had circular enceintes attached to them – the excavated outlines of the enceinte outside the West Gate (Xī Mén) are discernible, as are slabs of the original Ming dynasty road, lying around 1m below the current level of the ground.

A half-hour walk (taxi Y10; motor tricycle Y5) beyond the North Gate and 3km north of Shānhǎiguān is Jiǎo Shān (角山; admission Y30;

TRANSPORT: SHĀNHĂIGUĀN

Distance from Běijīng 285km

Direction East

Train The fastest and most convenient train from Beijing Train Station is the sleek D5 (two hours) soft-seat express to Shěnyáng, which leaves Beijing Train Station at 9.20am and pulls into Shānhǎiguān at 11.27am. An earlier alternative is the D21 (Y75, two hours) to Hā'ěrbīn from Beijing Train Station, which leaves at 7.20am and reaches Qínhuángdǎo at 9.19am, from where you can take bus 33 to Shānhǎiguān (Y2, 30 minutes). In the other direction, the D10 leaves Shānhǎiguān at 11.12am, reaching Běijīng at 1.19pm.

Long-distance bus These buses are slower than trains and leave from Běijīng's Bawangfen Station for Qínhuángdǎo (Y85, 3½ hours, depart regularly from 7.30am to 6pm) and Sihui Long-Distance Bus Station (Y78, 3½ hours, five per day); in Qínhuángdǎo take bus 33 (Y2, 30 minutes) to Shānhǎiguān. There are also direct buses from Qínhuángdǎo to Chéngdé (Y90, four hours, five per day). Buses also run regularly from Capital Airport to nearby Qínhuángdǎo.

Air There's a small airport between Shānhǎiguān and Qínhuángdǎo, with flights to several cities.

Local transport Taxis are Y5 at flag fall and Y1.40 per kilometre after that. Shānhǎiguān seethes with motor tricycles, which cost Y2 for trips within town.

DETOUR: JIǓMÉNKǑU

Over the border in Liáoníng province (erstwhile Manchuria) is Jiumenkou Great Wall (九门口长城; Jiǔménkǒu Chángchéng), where the brick fortification traverses the Jiujiang River. Named after its nine arches ('Jiǔménkǒu' literally means 'Nine Gates') and China's only section of the bastion to ford a river, the Wall is pinched between two sections that rise steeply up the hillsides. The setting is both magnificent and little visited (especially on weekdays), offering peaceful views of the rampart in a unique setting. Jiǔménkǒu is 15km northeast of Shānhǎiguān; a round trip in a taxi from Shānhǎiguān will cost Y70.

☺ 7am-sunset), where the Great Wall mounts its first high peak. It's a trying 20-minute clamber from the base, but a cable car can yank you up for Y20 return. The views are spectacular on a clear day. Continue along the Wall or hike over to Qixian Monastery (栖贤寺; Qixián Si; admission Y5).

Mengjiangnü Temple (孟姜女庙; Mèngjiāngnǚ Miào; admission Y40; ☺ 7am-5.30pm) is a famous and historic temple 6km east of Shānhǎiguān. A taxi there should cost around Y12.

INFORMATION

Bank of China (Zhōngguó Yínháng; Nanhai Xilu; ☺ 8.30am-5.30pm) Foreign-exchange facilities; US dollars only.

Kodak Express (Kēdá; Nanhai Xilu) CD burning (Y15 per disc) available; located next to Bank of China.

Lüdao Kongjian Internet Café (Lǜdǎo Kōngjiān Wǎngbā; per hr Y2; ☺ 24hr) In between Friendly Cooperate Hotel and the post office.

Post office (Yóujú; Nanhai Xilu; ☺ 8am-6pm) Just west of the Friendly Cooperate Hotel.

Public Security Bureau (PSB; Gōngānjú; ☎ 0335-505 1163) Opposite the entrance to First Pass Under Heaven, on the corner of a small alleyway.

EATING

Mike Hamn Fast Food (Màikè Hànmǔ; Guancheng Nanlu; meals Y20) Anywhere else and this fast-food spot would sink without trace, but here in Shānhǎiguān it's where you can get fried chicken, chips, coffee and cheesy '80s numbers on the stereo.

Shuānghé Shāokǎo (☎ 0335-507 6969; Xishun Chengjie; meals Y30) This is a popular kebab restaurant a short stroll south of the South Gate. Occupy one of the grill-equipped booth seats and flag down the waitress for bottles of beer, oodles of lamb kebabs (Y15 per plate), chicken kebabs (Y12 per plate) and eggplant kebabs (Y8 per plate).

SLEEPING

Jiguan Guesthouse (Jíguān Zhāodàisuǒ; ☎ 0335-505 1938; 17 Dongsitiao; 东四条17号; tw Y100-180; ☒) This pleasant hotel has a hútòng location and courtyard aspect. Cheaper rooms are showerless, but have clean, tiled floors and TV. The guesthouse is about 50m down Dongsitiao hútòng on the north side and there's no English sign.

Longhua Hotel (Lónghuá Dàjiǔdiàn; ☎ 0335-507 7698; 1 Nanhai Dajie; 南海大街1号; s/d/large d Y188/188/288; ☒) Recently refurbished (in some parts) with decent and affordable rooms; 20% discounts are the norm.

Friendly Cooperate Hotel (Yíhé Jiǔdiàn; ☎ 0335-593 9777; 4-1 Nanhai Xilu; 南海西路4-1号; tw/tr/d Y380/420/560; ☒) This large two-star hotel has large, cleanish double rooms with water cooler, TV, phone and bathroom. The staff is pleasant, there's a restaurant next door and regular 40% discounts.

CHUĀNDĬXIÀ 川底下

Nestled in a windswept valley 90km west of Běijīng and overlooked by towering peaks is Chuāndǐxià (admission Y20), a gorgeous cluster of historic courtyard homes with old-world charm. The backdrop is lovely: terraced orchards and fields with ancient houses and alleyways rising up the hillside. Two hours is more than enough to wander around the village because it's not big.

Chuāndǐxià is also a museum of Maoist graffiti and slogans, especially up the incline among the better-preserved houses. Despite their impressive revolutionary credentials, Chuāndǐxià's friendly residents sensed the unmistakable whiff of the tourist dollar on the north-China breeze long ago and flung open their doors to overnighting visitors. There are several places to stay overnight, such as Bǎishùn Kèzhàn (百顺客栈

DETOUR: LÍNGSHUǏ CŪN

If taking a taxi to Chuāndǐxià, consider paying an extra Y20 or so for your driver to take you back via the nearby village of Língshuǐ Cūn (灵水村), another historic village dating back to the Tang dynasty.

TRANSPORT: CHUĀNDĬXIÀ

Distance from Běijīng 90km
Direction West
Local bus A daily bus (Y10, two hours) departs for Chuāndĭxià from Pingguoyuan Station in Běijīng at 7.30am and 12.30pm, returning at 10.30am and 3.30pm. Taking the late bus may mean spending the night in Chuāndĭxià unless you find a taxi or taxi van to bring you back. Alternatively, take bus 929 – make sure it's the branch line (支线; zhīxiàn) rather than the regular bus – from the bus stop 200m west of Pingguoyuan Station to Zhāitáng (斋堂; Y8, two hours), then hire a taxi van (Y20). The last bus returns from Zhāitáng to Pingguoyuan at 4.20pm. If you miss the last bus, a taxi will cost around Y80 to Pingguoyuan. Taxi drivers waiting at Pingguoyuan Station will charge around Y140 to Y50 for a round trip.
Tours Some hostels, such as the Peking International Youth Hostel (p210), arrange tours to Chuāndĭxià.

43 Chuandixiacun), an attractive courtyard hotel with loads of charm located behind the spirit wall at Chuandixiacun at the foot of the village.

In the hills east of the village stands a small Qing dynasty Guandi Temple. For panoramic bird's-eye-view photos of the village climb the hill south of Chuāndĭxià in the direction of the Niangniang Temple.

ZHĒNGDÌNG 正定

Do-able as a day trip from Běijīng, Zhèngdìng is a quaint portrait of old China, its streets littered with needy Taoist soothsayers and temple remains. Climb Zhèngdìng's South Gate and admire the silhouettes of the four pagodas that jut prominently above the sleepy town. Nicknamed the town of 'nine buildings, four pagodas, eight great temples and 24 golden archways', Zhèngdìng may have lost a number of its standout buildings and archways, but enough remain to recall its former grandeur.

Four to five hours in town is adequate for an on-foot tour of the main sights. Commencing at the Dafo Temple, you can see almost everything by walking west until reaching Yanzhao Nandajie and then heading south to the city gate. There's a small map (in Chinese) on the back of the through ticket. The through ticket (通票; tōngpiào; Y60) gets you access to all sights except Linji Temple, making a saving of Y25 if you see everything. Opening hours are from 8am to 6pm.

Zhèngdìng's most famous monastery is Longxing Temple (隆兴寺; Lóngxìng Sì), more popularly known as Dafo Temple (大佛寺; Dàfó Sì; 109 Zhongshan Donglu; admission Y40, student 30) or Big Buddha Temple, which is located in the east of town. The standout hall is the vast Pavilion of Great Mercy (大悲阁; Dàbēi Gé), where

a bronze 21.3m colossus of Guanyin rises, cast in AD 971 and sporting a third eye.

About five minutes, west of Dafo Temple is Tianning Temple (天宁寺; Tiānníng Sì; admission Y5) and the climbable 41m-high Tang-dynasty Lofty Pagoda (凌霄塔; Língxiāo Tǎ) – also called Mùtǎ or Wooden Pagoda – originally dating from AD 779. The octagonal, nine-eaved and spire-topped pagoda is in fine condition and typical of Tang brickwork pagodas.

Further west on Zhongshan Xilu, past the intersection with Yanzhao Nandajie, stands the unassuming Confucius Temple (文庙; Wén Miào; admission Y5); however, there is little to see.

South along Yanzhao Nandajie stands the Kaiyuan Temple (开元寺; Kāiyuán Sì; admission Y15), which originally dates from AD 540. Destroyed in 1966, little remains of the temple itself beyond the bell tower and the drawcard, dirt-brown Xumi Pagoda (须弥塔; Xūmí Tǎ), a well-preserved and unfussy early-Tang-dynasty brickwork, nine-eaved structure topped with a spire. Its round, arched doors and carved stone doorway are particularly attractive, as are the carved figures on the base.

The active monastery of Linji Temple (临济寺; Línjì Sì; Linji Lu; admission Y8), around 700m south-

MONKEY BUSINESS

A Unesco World Heritage site, the Zhoukoudian Peking Man Site (Zhōukǒudiàn Yuánrén Yizhǐ; ☎ 010-6930 1272; admission Y30), 50km from the capital at Zhōukǒudiàn (周口店), was the location of several excavations in the 1920s that unearthed the fossilised remains of homo erectus, who inhabited this region half a million years ago. The fossils themselves vanished during WWII and remain missing to this day, but the museum at Zhōukǒudiàn explains the anthropological importance of the find. Bus 917 runs to Zhōukǒudiàn from Tianqiao.

TRANSPORT: ZHÈNGDÌNG

Distance from Běijīng 250km

Direction Southwest

Train The fastest way to reach Zhèngdìng is to take an express train (Y86 to Y103, two hours) from Beijing West Train Station to the Héběi capital of Shíjiāzhuāng and then catch a bus (see below). The earliest train is the D573 (Y86 to Y103, two hours), which leaves Beijing West Train Station at 6.45am, arriving in Shíjiāzhuāng at 8.48am. The next express is the D565, leaving Běijīng at 9.29am and reaching Shíjiāzhuāng at 11.31am. There are two further express trains, one leaving Běijīng in the midafternoon and the other in the early evening. Returning from Shíjiāzhuāng, the D572 departs for Beijing West Train Station at 5.35pm.

Bus From Shíjiāzhuāng, minibus 201 (Y3, 45 minutes, departing between 6.30am and 7pm) runs regularly to Zhèngdìng from Daocha Jie, slightly south of the main bus stop in the Shíjiāzhuāng train station square. The minibus goes to Zhèngdìng Bus Station, from where you can take minibus 1 to Zhèngdìng's Dafo Temple (Y1). Minibuses also run from outside Zhèngdìng's Kaiyuan Temple for Shíjiāzhuāng (Y3, last bus 5pm).

Air Shíjiāzhuāng's international airport is 40km northeast of town.

Local transport Taxis in Shíjiāzhuāng are Y5 at flag fall, then Y1.60 per kilometre thereafter.

east of Kaiyuan Temple, is notable for its tall, elegant, carved brick Chengling Pagoda (澄灵塔; also called the Green Pagoda) that is topped with an elaborate lotus plinth, plus a ball and spire. The temple is also notable for the main hall behind, with a large gilt effigy of Sakyamuni and 18 golden *luóhàn*.

Nothing remains of Guanghui Temple (广惠寺; Guǎnghuì Sì; admission Y10) further south, except its unusual Indian-style pagoda decorated with lions, elephants, sea creatures, púsà (bodhisattvas) and other figures. You can climb to the top.

At the southern end of the Yanzhao Dajie is Changle Gate (长乐门; Chánglè Mén; admission Y10; 8am-6pm), also known as Nanchengmen or South Gate. You can climb the gate, where there is a small exhibition. Extending away from the gate to the east and west are the dilapidated remains of the city wall, stripped of its trees and sprouting grass.

If you want to stay overnight in Shíjiāzhuāng, the city is packed with hotels and restaurants, many of which are near the train station.

TANZHE TEMPLE & JIETAI TEMPLE
潭柘寺、戒台寺

The largest of all Běijīng's temples, Tanzhe Temple (Tánzhé Sì; adult Y35; 8.30am-6pm) dates as far back as the 3rd century but has been modified considerably since those days.

The Buddhist temple is attractively placed amid trees in the mountains and its ascending temple grounds are overlooked by towering cypress and pine trees – many of which are so old that their gangly limbs are supported by metal props. Don't miss the small Talin Temple (塔林寺; Tǎlín Sì) by the forecourt where you disembark the bus, with its assembly of stupas. Visits to Tanzhe Temple around mid-April are recommended, as the magnolias are in bloom.

About 10km southeast of Tanzhe Temple the smaller Jietai Temple (Jiètái Sì; adult Y35; 8am-6pm) was originally built in the 7th century. The main complex is dotted with ancient pine trees. One of these, Nine Dragon Pine, is claimed to be over 1300 years old, while the Embracing Pagoda Pine does just what it says.

TRANSPORT: TANZHE TEMPLE & JIETAI TEMPLE

Distance from Běijīng 10km to 20km

Direction West and southwest

Train & bus Take Line 1 of the subway west to the Pingguoyuan stop and hop on bus 931 (Y3) to the last stop for Tanzhe Temple – ensure you don't take the bus 931 branch line (支线; zhīxiàn). This bus also stops near Jietai Temple; the temple is a 10-minute walk uphill from the bus stop.

SHÍDÙ 十渡

Known as the 'Guìlín of the North' and best visited during the summer rainy season, Shídù's pinnacle-shaped rock formations, pleasant rivers and general beauty make it a great place to hike. Shídù means '10 ferries or '10 crossings': before the new road and bridges were built, visitors had to cross the Juma River 10 times while travelling along the gorge from Zhāngfāng (张坊) and Shídù village.

In addition to its trekking options, there's a bundle of activities at hand, from excellent rock climbing to bungee jumping; numerous restaurants exist where you can grab some calories.

MING TOMBS 十三陵

The Ming Tombs (Shísān Líng; 8am-5.30pm) are the final resting place of 13 of the 16 Ming emperors (the first Ming emperor, Hongwu, is buried in Nánjīng, which means 'Southern Capital' and was the first capital of the Ming dynasty). Billed with the Great Wall as Běijīng's winning double act, the imperial graveyard can be a dormant and lifeless spectacle, unless you pack a penchant for ceremonial tomb architecture or Ming imperial genealogy.

The Ming Tombs follow a standard imperial layout. In each tomb the plan consists of a main gate (*líng mén*), leading to the first of a series of courtyards and the main hall. Beyond this lie gates or archways leading to the Soul Tower (Míng Lóu), behind which rises the burial mound (tumulus).

Three tombs have been opened to the public – Cháng Líng, Dìng Líng and Zhāo Líng. The road leading up to the tombs is a 7km stretch called the Spirit Way. Commencing with a triumphal arch, the path enters the Great Palace Gate, where officials once had to dismount, and passes a giant *bìxì*, which bears the largest stele in China. A guard of 12 sets of stone animals and officials ensues.

The most imposing of the Ming Tombs, Cháng Líng (☎ 010-6076 1334; summer/winter Y45/30) is the burial place of Emperor Yongle. Its magnificent halls lie in a series beyond its yellow-tiled gate. Seated upon a three-tiered marble terrace, the standout structure is the Hall of Eminent Favours (灵恩殿; Líng'ēn Diàn), containing a recent statue of Yongle and a breathtaking interior with vast *nánmù* (cedar wood) columns. The pine-covered burial mound at the rear of the complex is yet to be excavated and is not open to the public.

Dìng Líng (☎ 010-6076 1424; summer/winter Y65/40) is the burial place of Emperor Wanli, who died at age 56 in 1620. The tomb contains a series of subterranean interlocking vaults, and the remains of the various gates and halls of the complex. Excavated in the late 1950s, some visitors find this tomb of more interest, as you are allowed to descend into the underground vault.

Accessing the vault down the steps, you are confronted by the vast marble self-locking doors that sealed the chamber after it was

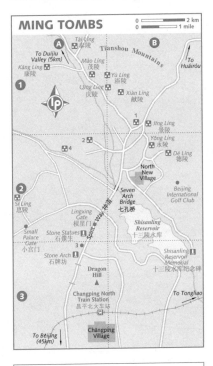

TRANSPORT: MING TOMBS

Distance from Běijīng 50km
Direction Northwest
Local bus Take bus 345 (Y6, one hour) from Deshengmen (德胜门) to the terminus Chāngpíng Běizhàn (昌平北站) stop and transfer to bus 314 for the tombs. A taxi from Chāngpíng to the Mong Tombs will cost you somewhere around Y20.
Tour bus The most convenient transport option is tour bus. Many hostels and hotels run handy tours to the Great Wall at Bādálǐng and the Ming Tombs. The Line A bus (Y160, departures 6am to 10.30am) runs to Bādálǐng and Dìng Líng at the Ming Tombs from the Beijing Sightseeing Bus Centre (Běijīng Lǚyóu Jísàn Zhōngxīn; Map pp58–9; ☎ 010-8353 1111), which is west of Front Gate (p69) in Běijīng; the tour price includes entrance tickets and lunch.

vacated. Note the depression in the floor where the stone prop clicked into place once the door was finally closed.

The resting place of the 13th Ming emperor Longqing, Zhāo Líng (☎ 010-6076 3104; summer/winter Y30/20), follows quite an orthodox layout and is a tranquil alternative if you discover that the other tombs are too busy to enter.

The rest of the tombs in the area are in various stages of dilapidation and are sealed off by locked gates.

TRANSPORT

Because Běijīng is the national capital, getting there and leaving are straightforward. Air connections link the capital to cities across China and overseas, trains speed to towns throughout the land (including Tibet) and abroad, while fleets of buses honk their way en masse to provincial destinations.

Central Běijīng's roads may be of orderly design, but the huge distances and traffic make surface travel gruelling. Down below it's a different story: the subway has benefited from ambitious expansion plans that have installed a first-rate metro system, which continues to grow. The size and affordability of Běijīng's bus system looks appealing, but you don't see many foreigners riding the network because it's crowded and hard to fathom, and traffic jams can be pernicious. If you have to take to the road, hop in a taxi. They are cheap and efficient, but avoid the rush hour and prepare for sudden gridlock. Combining the underground with taxi rides is a fast and efficient way of covering large distances.

Tackling Běijīng by bicycle is a fascinating and effective way of getting about, especially in the centre of town. Walking about on foot is only realistic over short distances – some of Běijīng's foot-numbing roads seem to go on to the very ends of the earth. Rickshaws look tempting but are best avoided as they are slow and overcharging comes as standard.

You can book flights, tours and rail tickets online at www.lonelyplanet.com/travel_services.

AIR

Tickets for Chinese carriers flying from Běijīng can be booked through most midrange and top-end hotels, at any one of the ubiquitous air ticket offices (*hángkōng shòupiào chù*) around town (one can be found to the east of the entrance to Beijing Train Station) or from the Aviation Building (Mínháng Yíngyè Dàshà; Map pp88–9; ☎ 6656 9118, domestic within China 6601 3336, international 6456 3604; 15 Xichang'an Jie, Xīchéng; ☺ 7am–midnight).

Make enquiries for all airlines at Běijīng's Capital Airport (首都机场; off Map pp128–9; ☎ 6512 8931, in Běijīng 962580). Call ☎ 6459 9567 for information on international arrivals and departures, and ☎ 1689 6969 for information

on domestic flights. Online, click on www.bcia.com.cn/en/index.jsp or the websites of individual airlines, listed below.

Airlines

Chinese carriers in Běijīng:

Air China (Map pp88–9; ☎ 6601 7755; www.airchina.cn; Aviation Bldg, 15 Xichang'an Jie, Xīchéng)

China Eastern Airlines (☎ 6464 1166; www.ce-air.com)

China Southern Airlines (☎ 95539; www.csair.com/en; 2 Dongsanhuan Nanlu, Cháoyáng)

Shanghai Airlines (Map pp88–9; ☎ 6606 1260; www.shanghai-air.com; Aviation Bldg, 15 Xichang'an Jie, Xīchéng)

International airlines in Běijīng:

Air Canada (Map pp110–11; ☎ 6468 2001; www.aircanada.cn; Room C201, Lufthansa Center, 50 Liangmaqiao Lu, Cháoyáng)

Air France (Map pp110–11; ☎ 4008 808 808; www.airfrance.com.cn; Room 1606-1611, Bldg 1, Kuntai International Mansion, 12A Chaoyangmenwai Dajie, Cháoyáng)

British Airways (Map pp110–11; ☎ 8511 5599; www.britishairways.com; Room 210, 2nd fl, SciTech Tower, 22 Jianguomenwai Dajie, Cháoyáng)

Cathay Pacific (Map pp110–11; ☎ 10800 852 1888; www.cathaypacific.com; 28th fl, East Tower, Twintowers Shopping Mall, 12b Jianguomenwai Dajie, Cháoyáng)

Dragon Air (Map pp110–11; ☎ 4008 886 628; www.dragonair.com; 28th fl, East Tower, Twintowers Shopping Mall, 12b Jianguomenwai Dajie, Cháoyáng)

Japan Airlines (Map pp110–11; ☎ 6513 0888; www.jal.com; 1st fl, Changfugong Office Bldg, Hotel New Otani, 26a Jianguomenwai Dajie, Cháoyáng)

KLM Royal Dutch Airlines (Map pp110–11; ☎ 4008 808 222; www.klm.com; Rm 1606-1611, 16th fl, Kuntai International Mansion, 12a Chaoyanmenwai Dajie, Cháoyáng)

Lufthansa Airlines (Map pp110–11; ☎ 6468 8838; www .lufthansa.com; Room 101, Lufthansa Center, 50 Liangma- qiao Lu, Cháoyáng)

Qantas Airways (Map pp110–11; ☎ 6567 9006; www .qantas.com.au; 10th fl, West tower, Twintowers Shopping Mall, 12b Jianguomenwai Dajie, Cháoyáng)

Singapore Airlines (Map pp110–11; ☎ 6505 2233; www .singaporeair.com; Room 801, China World Trade Center, 1 Jianguomenwai Dajie, Cháoyáng)

Thai Airways International (Map pp58–9; ☎ 8515 0088; www.thaiairways.com; Units 303, Level 3, Office Tower 3, Oriental Plaza, 1 Dongchang'an Jie, Dōngchéng)

United Airlines (Map pp110–11; ☎ 800 810 8282, 6463 1111; www.united.com; C/D1 Unit, 15th fl, Tower A, Gateway, 18 Xiaguangli, Cháoyáng)

Airports

Běijīng's Capital Airport, comprising three terminal buildings, is 27km northeast of the city centre. If you need to exchange currency, several banks (open 24 hours) can be found in the arrivals hall. The banks offer a similar exchange rate to those in the city and probably a better rate than at your hotel. There are also several ATMs with international access, where you can draw local currency. Post of-fices and public telephones are available at the airport, as are left-luggage facilities (from Y25; maximum seven days) and mobile-phone charging stations. Trolleys are available free of charge. A small clinic is also located here. A free shuttle bus (every 10 minutes from 6am to 11pm; every 30 minutes from 11pm to 6am) whizzes between the three terminals.

There is a branch of the Beijing Tourist In-formation Center (see p252) in the arrivals hall, where you can pick up a map and literature on Běijīng, or book a hotel room. Other desks in the arrivals hall also provide hotel bookings, and you can often obtain substantial discounts on accommodation.

Airport restaurants and shops are gener-ally expensive. If you're doing last-minute souvenir shopping, do it in town.

International/domestic departure tax is Y90/50 and is included in the price of your air ticket.

Capital Airport's stunningly massive third terminal building, which was designed by Norman Foster, opened in 2008. The world's largest-ever airport expansion project, the new terminal is essential to Capital Airport's ambitions to deal with 60 million arrivals by 2015.

Travel Within China

Daily flights connect Běijīng to every major city in China. There might not be daily flights to smaller cities throughout the country, but

---

CLIMATE CHANGE & TRAVEL

Climate change is a serious threat to the ecosystems that humans rely upon, and air travel is the fastest-growing con-tributor to the problem. Lonely Planet regards travel, overall, as a global benefit, but believes we all have a responsibility to limit our personal impact on global warming.

Flying & Climate Change

Pretty much every form of motor transport generates CO_2 (the main cause of human-induced climate change) but planes are far and away the worst offenders, not just because of the sheer distances they allow us to travel, but because they release greenhouse gases high into the atmosphere. The statistics are frightening: two people taking a return flight between Europe and the US will contribute as much to climate change as an average household's gas and electricity consumption over a whole year.

Carbon Offset Schemes

Climatecare.org and other websites use 'carbon calculators' that allow jetsetters to offset the greenhouse gases they are responsible for with contributions to energy-saving projects and other climate-friendly initiatives in the developing world – including projects in India, Honduras, Kazakhstan and Uganda.

Lonely Planet, together with Rough Guides and other concerned partners in the travel industry, supports the carbon offset scheme run by climatecare.org. Lonely Planet offsets all of its staff and author travel.

For more information check out our website: www.lonelyplanet.com.

GETTING INTO TOWN

Běijīng's Capital Airport is 27km from the centre of town; about 45 minutes to one hour by car, depending on traffic.

Faster than the bus and much cheaper than a taxi, the Airport Express (Y25; 16 minutes; from Dongzhimen first/last train 6am/10.30pm; from Terminal 2 first/last train 6.35am/11.10pm; from Terminal 3 first/last train 6.21am/10.51pm) rail link to town is highly convenient, running regularly and swiftly from Terminal 2 and Terminal 3 to Dongzhimen Station (a station on Line 2 of the underground), via Sanyuanqiao Station (on Line 10).

Several express bus routes (☎ 6459 4375, 6459 4376) run regularly to Běijīng every 10 to 15 minutes during operating hours. Tickets on all lines are Y16. Line 3 (first bus 7am, last bus meets arrival of last flight) is the most popular with travellers, running to the Beijing International Hotel and Beijing Train Station via Chaoyangmen. Line 2 (first bus 7am, last bus meets arrival of last flight) runs to the Aviation Building (Mínháng Yíngyè Dàshà; Map pp88–9; ☎ 6656 9118, domestic 6601 3336, international 6456 3604; 15 Xichang'an Jie, Xichéng; ⏰ 7am-midnight) in Xidan, via Dongzhimen. Line 1 (first/last bus 7am/11pm) runs to Fāngzhuāng, via Dàběiyáo, where you can get onto subway Line 1 at Guomao.

Public bus 359 (Y3) runs to Dongzhimen from the airport, from where you can get on the subway.

Travelling from the city to the airport, the most useful place to catch the bus is at the west door of the Beijing International Hotel (Map pp58–9; 9 Jianguomennei Dajie, Dōngchéng), where buses leave every half-hour between 6am and 7.30pm (Y16). You can also take a bus (☎ 6459 4375/4376) from the eastern end of the Aviation Building (the CAAC ticket office) on Xichang'an Jie in Xidan district (Y16, one hour, departures are every 30 minutes between 5.45am and 7.30pm).

Many top-end hotels run shuttle buses from the airport. Ask at the hotel desks at the airport upon arrival or check with the hotel beforehand. You do not necessarily have to be a guest of the hotel to use these, but you do have to pay for the service. The price for the minibuses is higher than that for the regular airport buses.

A taxi (using its meter) should cost between Y80 and Y100 from the airport to the centre of town, including the Y15 airport-expressway toll; make sure the driver uses the meter. Queue for your taxi outside and never take a taxi from touts inside the arrivals halls, where a well-established illegal taxi operation attempts to lure weary travellers into a Y300-plus ride to the city (one man acts as a taxi pimp for a squad of drivers).

Don't expect to be able to rent a car at the airport, unless you have a residence permit and a Chinese driving licence.

---

there should be at least one flight a week. You can buy tickets from the Aviation Building (p231), one of the numerous airline offices in Běijīng or through your hotel. Discounts for domestic flights are generally available; however, full fare may be effective at weekends and public holidays. The domestic airfares listed here are approximate only and represent the nondiscounted air fare from Běijīng.

Destination	One-way fare (Y)
Dàlián	570
Guǎngzhōu	1700
Guìlín	1940
Hángzhōu	1050
Hong Kong	2860
Kūnmíng	1940
Lhasa	2430
Nánjīng	1010
Qīngdǎo	820
Shànghǎi	1130
Ürümqi	2410
Wǔhàn	1080
Xī'ān	840

There are also handy buses from Capital Airport's Terminal 3 to Qínhuángdǎo (Y126, every two hours, 9am to 8pm) for Shānhǎiguān, p224, and Tiānjīn (Y70, every 30 minutes, 7am to 11pm).

BICYCLE

Flat as a mah jong table, widely supplied with bicycle lanes and riddled with alleys, central Běijīng is ideally suited to cyclists. Běijīng's streets can be hazardous, however, so keep your wits about you at all times. Whenever possible, opt for a route through the city's quieter and more car-free *hútòng* (alleyways) – they typically run in straight lines and at right angles to each other, so just follow the grid. The air on the main roads can also have you holding your breath till you're blue in the face; it's less muggy in the *hútòng*. If you get caught up in one of spring's monumental dust storms, you'll get a free exfoliation.

If you take to the main roads, prepare for unpredictable vehicle movements and pedestrians impulsively crossing the road. Someone walking at the roadside will suddenly peel off, without looking, to cross the street directly in the path of a truck. This is all quite natural in Běijīng. Chinese drivers are used to wild and irrational behaviour on the streets – but you may not be. Furthermore, pedestrians are regularly ejected onto the road by clutter on the pavement. As if that wasn't enough, night-time brings a whole new set of risks: few Chinese bikes have lights, and both pedestrians and cyclists tend to wear dark clothes (reflective strips are rarer than hen's teeth). Car drivers will sometimes wait for their pupils to fully dilate before turning on their lights.

Remember you will be on the lowliest transportation device in town and buses, trucks, taxis, cars and scooters will all honk at you, in that pecking order (just ignore them). Cars often don't look or give way when driving from minor to more major roads or when leaving private driveways.

With all of these warnings in mind, however, cycling in Běijīng is exhilarating, fun and cheap. Parking your bike in one of the more secure pavement bike parking lots found all over town costs around Y0.50. Very cheap roadside repairs can be found down Běijīng's numerous alleyways. Look out for the characters 修车 (xiūchē; bicycle repairs).

Bike hire is easy, and purchase is straightforward: you can buy a mountain bike for as little as Y250 at hypermarkets, such as Carrefour. Bikes need to be taxed, with a disc displayed; the bike shop will usually arrange this, and hypermarkets have a dedicated counter.

Hire

A handy network of bike-hire stations (Beijing Bicycle Rental Co Ltd) can be found outside numerous underground stations, principally on Lines 2 and 5. Bikes (Y5 per hour, Y10 for four hours, Y20 per day, Y70 per week; Y400 deposit, Y100 service charge, both refunded on return of bike; 24 hours) can be hired and returned to different underground station outlets. The bicycle rental shop (Map pp118–19; 77 Tieshu Xiejie, Xuānwǔ; Y10, deposit Y200; ☿ 7am-11pm) is one of several along this road and in the vicinity. Budget hotels can also hire you a bike for around Y20 per day; hire at upmarket hotels is far more expensive. Pricier tourist-oriented hire stations tend to be found in the vicinity of the top tourist sites. When hiring a bike it's safest to use your own lock(s) in order to prevent bicycle theft, a common problem in Běijīng.

BOAT

The nearest port for international ferries is at Tánggū, 50km from Tiānjīn, itself 30 minutes away by train (Y58 to Y69; at least every half-hour) from Beijing South Train Station. Long-distance buses also run direct to Tánggū from Běijīng. From Tánggū there are weekly ferries to Kōbe (from Y1875, 48 hours) in Japan and two weekly boats to Incheon (Y888 to Y1590, 28 hours) in South Korea.

BUS

'Be not afraid of going slowly but only afraid of standing still.'

Chinese proverb

Relying on buses (gōnggòng qìchē) to get swiftly from A to B can be frustrating unless it's a short hop. Getting a seat may be impossible, especially during rush hour. Fares are typically Y1 depending on the distance, although air-conditioned buses are slightly more expensive (Y2). You generally pay the conductor, rather than the driver, once aboard the bus. Běijīng's fleet of aged leviathans is busily being replaced with modern low-pollution green buses running on compressed natural gas (CNG).

Buses run from 5.30am to 11pm daily or thereabouts, and stops are few and far between. Routes on bus signs are all in Chinese, with no English. It's important to work out how many stops you need to go before boarding. If you can read Chinese, a useful publication (Y5) is available from kiosks listing all of the Běijīng bus lines; alternatively, tourist maps of Běijīng illustrate some of the bus routes.

One- and two-digit bus numbers are city core; 100-series are trolleys; 200-series are night buses (yèbān gōnggòng qìchē); 300-series are suburban lines; and 900-series are long-distance buses. Minibuses (xiǎobā) follow some routes and cost from around Y2. If you work out how to combine bus and subway connections you'll find the subway will speed up much of the trip.

Special double-decker buses run in a circle around the city centre. They are slightly more expensive but spare you the traumas of normal public buses, and you should be able to get a seat.

The following double-decker routes are useful:

2 Qianmen, north on Dongdan Beidajie, Dongsi Nandajie, Dongsi Beidajie, Lama Temple, Zhonghua Minzu Yuan (Ethnic Minorities Park), Asian Games Village

3 Jijia Miao (the southwest extremity of the Third Ring Rd), Grand View Garden, Leyou Hotel, Jingguang New World Hotel, Tuanjiehu Park, Agricultural Exhibition Center, Lufthansa Center

4 Beijing Zoo, Exhibition Center, Second Ring Rd, Holiday Inn Downtown, Yuetan Park, Fuxingmen Dajie flyover, Qianmen Xidajie, Qianmen

Useful standard bus routes:

1 Runs along Chang'an Jie, Jianguomenwai Dajie and Jianguomennei Dajie: Sihuizhan, Bawangfen, Yong'anli, Dongdan, Xidan, Muxidi, Junshi Bowuguan, Gongzhufen, Maguanying

4 Runs along Chang'an Jie, Jianguomenwai Dajie and Jian-guomennei Dajie: Gongzhufen, Junshi Bowuguan, Muxidi, Xidan, Tiananmen Xi, Dongdan, Yong'anli, Bawangfen, Sihuizhan

5 Deshengmen, Di'anmen, Beihai Park, Xihuamen, Zhong-shan Park, Qianmen

15 Beijing Zoo, Fuxingmen, Xidan, Hepingmen, Liulichang, Tianqiao

20 Beijing South Train Station, Tianqiao, Dashilar, Tiananmen Square, Wangfujing, Dongdan, Beijing Train Station

44 outer ring Xinjiekou, Xizhimen, Fuchengmen, Fuxing-men, Changchunjie, Xuanwumen, Qianmen, Taijichang, Chongwenmen, Dongbianmen, Chaoyangmen, Dongzhi-men, Andingmen, Deshengmen, Xinjiekou

52 Beijing West Train Station, Muxidi, Fuxingmen, Xidan, Gate of Heavenly Peace, Dongdan, Beijing Train Station, Jianguomen

103 Beijing Train Station, Dengshikou, China Art Gallery, Forbidden City (north entrance), Beihai Park, Fuchengmen, Beijing Zoo

332 Beijing Zoo, Weigongcun, Renmin Daxue, Zhongguan-cun, Haidian, Beijing University, Summer Palace

For more information, you can check the Beijing Public Transport website: www.bjbus com/english/default.htm.

Travel Within China

No international buses serve Běijīng, but there are plenty of long-distance domestic routes. Although most domestic travel is by train, roads are improving, buses are cheaper and it's easier to book a seat. Sleeper buses are widely available and recommended for over-night journeys.

Běijīng has numerous long-distance bus stations (*chángtú qìchēzhàn*), positioned on the city perimeter. Choose the one that's roughly in the direction you want to head. The most useful bus stations for travellers are: Bawangfen Long-Distance Bus Station (Bāwángfén Chángtú Kèyùnzhàn; Map pp110–11; ☎ 8771 8844) in the east of town; Sihui Long-Distance Bus Station (Sihuì Chángtú Qìchēzhàn; Map pp110–11; ☎ 6557 4804); Liuliqiao Long-Distance Bus Station (Liùlíqiáo Chángtúzhàn; Map pp128–9; ☎ 8383 1716), southwest of Beijing West Train Station; and Lianhuachi Long-Distance Bus Station (Liánhuāchí Chángtú Qìchēzhàn; Map pp128–9; ☎ 6332 2354). Other useful stations are at Zhaogongkou (Map pp128–9; ☎ 6711 9491) in the south and the Dongzhimen Transport Hub Station (Map pp58–9).

Buses range in both type and quality, from simple minibuses to luxury air-conditioned buses equipped with TV sets, toilets, reclining seats and hostesses handing out free mineral water. For long journeys it is advisable to spend a bit more so that you can travel in comfort.

CAR

The authorities remain twitchy about foreigners taking off around China, so you can only hire a car if you have a residency permit and a Chinese driving licence.

Taxis (see p236) are cheap, however, and you can hire a basic taxi with a driver for Y400 per day from taxi firms such as Beijing Beiqi Taxi (☎ 8661 1062).

SUBWAY & LIGHT RAILWAY

Massively expanded over recent years from its once-modest two-line extents, the Běijīng subway system (地铁; ditiě; www.bjsubway.com) is usually the fastest and most stress-free way to get around town. If you include the Air-port Express, the subway now runs to eight lines, with a further line under construction. The subway is also excellent value, costing a mere Y2 anywhere (apart from the Air-port Express, which costs Y25). Paper tickets have now been replaced by electronically read tickets that are fed into turnstiles; the stored-value transport card (*jiāotōng kǎ*) is worthwhile if you aim to do a lot of travel-ling (it saves queuing up). The subway runs from 5am to 11pm daily; platform signs are in Chinese characters and Pinyin. Some sta-tion platforms have pay toilets. Trains, which can get very crowded, run at a frequency of one every few minutes during peak times. Stops are announced in English and Chi-nese. You'll find a detailed subway map of Běijīng in the colour map section at the back of this book.

To recognise a subway station (dì tiě zhàn) look for the subway symbol, which is a blue English capital 'D' with a circle around it. Another identifying sign is the enormous cluster of bicycles.

Line 4, linking northwest Běijīng with the south of the city, was due to open in 2009 and should be operating by the time you read this. A further east–west line, Line 6, was under construction at the time of writing.

Line 1 一号地铁线

With 23 stations, Line 1 runs from Sihuidong to Pingguoyuan, a western suburb of Běijīng. The transfer stations with Line 2 are at Fuxingmen and Jianguomen. The transfer station for Line 5 is at Dongdan. Passengers for the Batong line transfer at Sihuixi or at Sihuidong. Line 1 intersects with Line 10 for transfers at Guomao.

Line 2 二号地铁线

With 18 stations, including Beijing Train Station (Běijīngzhàn), this 16km line intersects with Line 1 at Fuxingmen and Jianguomen. Passengers for Line 13 transfer at Dongzhimen or Xizhimen, while Line 5 intersects Line 2 at Chongwenmen and Yonghegong Lama Temple. The Airport Express leaves from Dongzhimen on Line 2.

Line 5 五号地铁线

With 23 stations, this line runs from Songjiazhuang in the south of town to Tiantongyuan North in the north of Běijīng. Passengers for Line 2 can transfer at Chongwenmen and Yonghegong Lama Temple. The line intersects with Line 1 at Dongdan; for Line 10, the transfer station is Huixinxijie Nankou; for Line 13 you can transfer at Lishuiqiao.

Line 8 八号地铁线

With only four stations, Line 8 connects Beitucheng with South Gate of Forest Park, stopping at Olympic Sports Center and Olympic Green. The line connects with Line 10 at Beitucheng.

Line 10 十号地铁线

With 22 stations, this line connects Jinsong in the southeast with Bagou in the northwest. Transfer stations include: Guomao for Line 1, Sanyuanqiao for the Airport Express,

Shaoyaoju and Zhichunlu for Line 13, Huixinxijie Nankou for Line 5 and Beitucheng for Line 8 (for the Olympic Green).

Line 13 十三号地铁线

Classified as part of the subway system but actually a light-rail link, Line 13 runs in a northern loop from Xizhimen to Dongzhimen in the north of Běijīng, with a total of 16 stations (approximately three minutes per station) in between (first/last train 6am/9pm). Passengers can transfer at Shaoyaoju and Zhichunlu for Line 10 and at Lishuiqiao for Line 5.

Airport Express 机场快轨

The Airport Express runs from Dongzhimen on Line 2 to Terminal 2 and Terminal 3 of Capital Airport, via Sanyuanqiao. The Airport Express line intersects with line 10 at Sanyuanqiao. Tickets are Y25.

Batong Line 八通地铁线

Batong Line stations are Sihuixi, Sihuidong, Gaobeidian, Communication University of China, Shuangqiao, Guanzhuang, Baliqiao, Tongzhoubeiyuan, Guoyuan, Jiukeshu, Liyuan, Linheli and Tuqiao.

TAXI

Taxis (chūzūchē) are everywhere, and finding one is only a problem during rush hour and (infrequent) rainstorms or spring sandstorms.

Běijīng taxis have red stickers on the side rear window declaring the rate per kilometre. Y2 taxis are Y10 for the first 3km and Y2 per kilometre thereafter (a night rate also applies from 11pm to 6am: Y11 flag fall for the first 3km and Y3 per km afterwards). Taxis are required to switch on the meter for all journeys (unless you negotiate a fee for a long journey out of town). Taxis are air-conditioned; but rear seatbelts may not work. A new fleet of silver London cabs, offering extra comfort and leg room, is now roaming the Běijīng streets.

Běijīng taxi drivers speak little, if any, English, despite encouragement from the authorities to learn 100 basic phrases in the run up to the 2008 Olympic Games. If you don't speak Chinese, bring a map or have your destination written down in characters (grab your hotel business card). Also take a mobile phone so that you can hand your taxi driver over to a speaker of Chinese (eg your hotel concierge)

Taxis can be hired by distance, by the hour, or by the day (a minimum of around Y400 per day). Taxis can be hailed in the street, summoned by phone, or you can wait at one of the designated taxi zones or outside hotels. Call ☎ 6835 1150 to register a complaint. Ask the driver to give you a receipt (*fāpiào*), which will include the driver's number; if you accidentally leave anything in the taxi, you'll be able to located them. There is no need to tip.

The taxi driver may try to dissuade you from wearing a seatbelt – ignore them and prepare yourself for Běijīng's atrocious driving (p250). Watch out for tired drivers; they work long and punishing shifts.

If you're staying for a long time and you meet a taxi driver you like or trust, ask for a name card. Most drivers have home phones or mobile phones and can be hired for the day. Alternatively, Beijing Beiqi Taxi (☎ 8661 1062) can hire you a taxi plus driver from around Y400 per day, useful for trips to the Great Wall or further afield.

TRAIN

The Chinese have travelled by train for decades like total naturals, but the contemporary passion for trains was hardly love at first sight. Railways were strongly resisted in the 19th century for fear they would disturb ancestors' graves and obstruct *fēngshuǐ* (geomancy, literally 'wind and water'); Běijīng was also anxious that railroads would accelerate the military domination of China by foreign powers. Today, however, China's extensive passenger rail network covers every province except the island of Hǎinán; it has also famously made inroads into Tibet. At any given time it is estimated that over 10 million Chinese are travelling on a train in China, except at the Chinese New Year, when the entire nation is on the move and the system pushed to breaking point.

Chinese train travel – especially by sleeper (p238) – is a magnificent subculture; if you have time to travel around China, you should try to incorporate at least one train journey into your itinerary. Train travel offers an entertaining ride and brings you together with Chinese travelling the land. An increasing number of comfortable high-speed routes has opened up the land to rapid exploration. The safety record of the train system is also good, but keep an eye on your belongings.

The new fleet of trains that run intercity routes is a vast improvement on the old models. The new Z-class express trains (eg from Běijīng to Shànghǎi and Xī'ān) are very plush, with mobile-phone charging points, well-designed bunks, and meals thrown in on some routes. D-class bullet trains are very swift, good-looking and comfortable. Trains nationwide are punctual and depart on the dot.

Buying Tickets

It's cheapest to buy tickets at the train station, but for a small surcharge you can get them at most hotel counters and ticket counters around the city or through travel agents. For telephone bookings, call the Ticket Center Hotline (☎ 9510 5105) to book your ticket up to 10 days in advance.

Avoid buying from the touts who gather outside the train station, unless you are desperate for a ticket. If you do buy from a tout, examine the ticket carefully to check the date of travel and the destination before handing over your money.

Tickets for most trains can be purchased up to 10 days in advance, which includes the day you buy the ticket and the day you depart. Reservations for Z-class express trains can be made up to 20 days in advance. Note that your chances of getting a sleeper (hard or soft) are good if you book quite a few days ahead. Never just turn up and expect to be able to buy a ticket to a distant destination for same-day travel. Train tickets to and from Běijīng can be booked solid for almost a week around National Day (1 October); the rail network is also totally congested during Chinese New Year. Return tickets to Běijīng are also available.

The queues at the Beijing Train Station ticket office (*shòupiàotīng*) can be overwhelming. There is usually at least one ticket window offering some kind of English-language service, and at the time of writing this was at window 1. Go to windows 82 to 84 in the east of the concourse to buy tickets from Beijing West Train Station. Purchase tickets for high-speed trains to Tiānjīn from windows 70 and 71; windows 63 to 65 are for sleeper tickets to Shànghǎi on the evening express. If you want to see someone off, platform tickets (*zhàntái piào*) can be bought from window 81. Refunds and ticket returns can be made at windows 25 and 26.

A foreigner's ticketing office can be found on the 2nd floor of Beijing West Train Station (☽ 24hr).

Complicated paperback train timetables for the entire country are published every April and October, available in Chinese only. You can consult www.travelchina guide.com/china-trains, which allows you to enter your departure point and destination, and gives you the departure times, arrival times and train numbers of trains running that route.

Classes

Trains on longer routes are divided into classes. Hard seat (*yìng zuò*) is actually generally padded, but it can be hard on your sanity, painful on long hauls and packed to the gills. Your ticket should have an assigned seat number, but if seats have sold out ask for a standing ticket (*wúzuò* or *zhànpiào*), which at least gets you on the train – you can then find a seat or find the conductor and upgrade (*bǔpiào*) yourself to a hard sleeper, soft seat or soft sleeper if there are any available.

On short express journeys (such as Běijīng to Tiānjīn) trains generally have soft-seat (*ruǎn zuò*) carriages. Seats are two abreast, carriages are often double-decker and overcrowding is not permitted.

Hard-sleeper (*yìng wò*) carriages consist of doorless compartments with half a dozen bunks in three tiers. The lowest bunk (*xiàpù*) is the most expensive and the top bunk (*shàngpù*) is the cheapest, although there is not a huge difference in price. The middle bunk (*zhōngpù*) is preferable, as all and sundry use the lower berth as a seat during the day, and the top bunk has little headroom. Lights and speakers go out at around 10pm. Each compartment is equipped with its own hot-water flask (*rèshuǐpíng*), which is filled by an attendant.

Soft sleepers (*ruǎn wò*) are expensive (about twice the hard-sleeper price), with four comfortable bunks in a closed, carpeted compartment. Express Z-class trains (eg Běijīng–Shànghǎi) are the most modern, with mobile-phone charging points, free meals (on some routes) and well-made bunks (four to a compartment). Z-class deluxe soft sleepers are two to a compartment, with their own toilet and wardrobe.

Services

Travellers arrive and depart by train at Beijing Train Station (Běijīng Huǒchē Zhàn; Map p82; ☎ 5101 9999) or Beijing West Train Station (Běijīng Xī Zhàn; Map pp118–19; ☎ 5182 6253). Beijing Train Station is served by its own underground station, making access simple. International trains to

Moscow, Pyongyang and Ulaanbaatar arrive at and leave from Beijing Train Station; trains for Hong Kong and Hanoi leave from Beijing West Train Station. Buses 122 and 721 connect Beijing Train Station with Beijing West Train Station.

Two other stations of significance are the new Beijing South Train Station (Běijīng Nánzhàn; Map pp118–19) – for high-speed trains to Tiānjīn (Y58 to Y69, at least every half hour) and Beijing North Train Station (Běijīng Běizhàn; Map pp88–9; ☎ 5186 6223) for trains to Inner Mongolia.

Left-luggage counters (*jìcúnchù*) and lockers can be found at most train stations; prices are around Y10 per hour.

A host of the new, fast Z-class overnight express trains depart from Beijing Train Station to destinations as diverse as Sūzhōu (hard sleeper Y309, 10 hours 50 minutes), Hángzhōu (soft sleeper Y554, 12 hours 50 minutes), Héféi (hard sleeper Y263, nine hours 20 minutes), Chángchūn (hard seat Y116, hard sleeper Y215, seven hours 50 minutes), Ha'ěrbīn (nine hours 15 minutes) and Nánjīng (soft sleeper Y417, nine hours 10 minutes).

From Beijing Train Station, overnight Z-class soft-sleeper express trains (lower/upper bunk Y499/478) do the trip to Shànghǎi in 12 hours, with several trains departing nightly from 7pm to around 8pm.

Fast Z-class express trains from Beijing West Train Station include Fúzhōu (hard seat Y253, hard sleeper Y458, 19 hours 4 minutes), Nánchāng (hard sleeper Y319, 11 hours 30 minutes), Wǔchāng (hard sleeper Y281, 10 hours), Hànkǒu (hard sleeper Y281, 10 hours) and Xī'ān (soft sleeper Y417, 11 hours).

TO RUSSIA

On the *Trans-Mongolian Railway*, Train K3 leaves Beijing Train Station on its five-day journey at 7.45am every Wednesday (arriving in Moscow on the following Monday at 2.28pm), passes through Dàtóng and travelling via Ulaanbaatar and Novosibirsk. From Moscow, train K4 leaves at 9.35pm on Tuesday, arriving in Běijīng on the following Monday at 2.04pm. Departure and arrival times may fluctuate slightly. Travellers on the *Trans-Mongolian Railway* will need a Russia and Mongolia visa as well as a China visa.

On the *Trans-Manchurian Railway*, train K19 departs Běijīng at 10.56pm Saturday (arriving in Moscow the following

Friday at 5.57pm), travels through Tiānjīn, Shānhǎiguān, Shěnyáng, Chángchūn and Hā'ěrbīn before arriving at the border post Mǎnzhōulǐ, 2347km from Běijīng. Zabaykal'sk is the Russian border post and the train continues from here to Tarskaya, where it connects with the Trans-Siberian line. Train K20 leaves Moscow at 11.55pm every Friday, arriving in Běijīng on the following Friday at 5.31am. Note that departure and arrival times may fluctuate slightly. Travellers on the *Trans-Manchurian Railway* will need a Russia visa as well as a China visa.

In Běijīng, tickets can be conveniently purchased from CITS (Zhōngguó Guójì Lǚxíngshè; Map pp58–9; ☎ 6512 0507; Beijing International Hotel, 9 Jianguomennei Dajie, Dōngchéng). Abroad, tickets can be bought from Intourist Travel (www.intourist .com), which has branches in the UK, the USA, Canada, Finland and Poland.

BUSINESS HOURS

China officially has a five-day working week. Banks, offices and government departments are normally open Monday to Friday, roughly from 9am until 5pm or 6pm (some closing for two hours in the middle of the day). Some banks have branches that are open at weekends as well. Saturday and Sunday are both public holidays, but most Běijīng museums stay open on weekends and close on one weekday (usually Monday). Museums tend to stop selling tickets half an hour before they close. Bank of China branches are generally open weekdays from 9am to noon and 2pm to 4.30pm, and 24-hour ATMs (see p248) are plentiful. Travel agencies, foreign-exchange counters in tourist hotels and some of the local branches of the Bank of China have similar opening hours, but are generally open on weekends as well, at least in the morning. Shops are generally open from 10am to 10pm, while restaurants tend to run from 10.30am to 11pm, although some shut in the afternoon between the hour of 2pm and 5.30pm. Internet cafes are either open 8am to midnight or are open 24 hours. Note that many businesses in Běijīng have interruptions in their service or close at three points in the year: the three days following 1 May, the week after National Day on 1 October and the week following the Spring Festival in January or February.

Parks are generally open from 6am to around 9pm or later, although they can open later and shut earlier in winter. Opening hours for sights are listed under each entry in the Neighbourhoods chapter.

Běijīng's entertainment sector is working increasingly long hours, and it's possible to find something to eat and somewhere to drink at any hour of the day.

CHILDREN

The Chinese have a deep and uncomplicated love of children and openly display their affection for them.

Baby food and milk powder are widely available in supermarkets, as are basics such as nappies, baby wipes, bottles, creams, medicine, clothing, dummies (pacifiers) and other paraphernalia. Few cheap restaurants, however, have baby chairs, and finding nappy-changing rooms can be hard. Check the Health section (p243) for information on recommended vaccinations for children.

Admission prices to many sights and museums have children's rates, usually for children under 1.1m to 1.3m in height. Infants under the age of two fly for 10% of the full airfare. Children between the ages of two and 11 need to pay half the full price for domestic flights, and 75% of the full price for international flights.

Always ensure that your child carries a form of ID and your hotel's card, in case they get lost.

See the Top Picks for Children boxed text, p94, for recommended diversions and activities for kiddies.

For more information on travelling with children, turn to the following books:

Travel with Children (Brigitte Barta)

The Rough Guide to Travel with Babies & Young Children (Fawzia Rasheed de Francisco)

Take the Kids Travelling (Helen Truszkowski)

Travelling Abroad with Children (Samantha Gore-Lyons)

Babysitting

If you need a babysitter (āyí) or nanny (bǎomǔ), contact Century Domestic Services (☎ 6498 8220; per hr from Y10-15, live-in nanny per month from Y500), who can supply an English-speaking āyí. Chinese-speaking nannies (many of whom come from Hénán or Ānhuī) are cheaper and an excellent idea if you want your child (and yourself) to learn Chinese, but ensure they speak Mandarin (preferably without a Fujianese accent).

CLIMATE

Běijīng is largely very dry with four distinct seasons. Summer (May to August) is long and scorching, with heavy rainfall in July and August

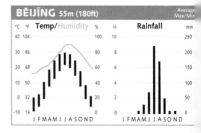

Gorgeous autumn (September and October) is over swiftly before the punishing winter (November to February/March) sets in, with the mercury falling as low as -20°C in January. Spring (March to April/May) is pleasant, apart from the billowing sandstorms that sweep in from the Gobi Desert. For more information on the best time to visit the capital, see p12.

COURSES

Whether it's learning Chinese, making Chinese kites or delving into the mysteries of taichi, the China Culture Center (CCC; Map pp128–9; ☎ weekdays 6432 9341, weekends 6432 0141; www.chinaculture enter.org; Kent Center, 29 Anjialou, Liangmaqiao Lu, Cháoyáng) offers a range of cultural programs, taught in English and aimed squarely at foreign visitors and expats. The centre also conducts popular tours around Běijīng and expeditions to other – including off-the-beaten-track – parts of China, and presents lectures on a variety of subjects, including Chinese art, philosophy and film. The Neighborhood Chinese Club (☎ 8450 789; www.chineseneighbor.com) offers a range of cultural activities from Chinese-language classes to Chinese cookery and Chinese music.

Chinese

Chinese – Mandarin specifically – has become one of the world's must-learn languages and learning to speak it isn't as hard as you may think. And where better to study the lingo than in Běijīng, home of the Mandarin dialect (see p45 for more information). If you don't have the time to sign up for a semester at a university, such as Peking University (☎ 6275 1230; www.pku.edu.cn) or Beijing Normal University (☎ 5880 960; www.bnu.edu.cn), there are hordes of private schools (which can be more up-to-date in their teaching methods) to choose from. It pays to hunt around, however, as the rapidly expanding market regularly produces schools of suspect quality. Check out how long the school has been in business and if possible, talk to students attending classes there. One-on-one classes should start from around Y110 per hour; group classes start at about Y60 per hour. For language exchange partners, consult the classified pages of English magazines such as the *Beijinger* (www.thebeijinger.com). The following language schools are reputable and either offer tuition in the Chinese language or Chinese culture, and occasionally both:

Academy of Chinese Language Study (ACLS; ☎ 5869 425; www.acls.com.cn) Variety of Chinese-language courses for all ages with intensive four-week language courses and holiday camps.

Berlitz (Map pp110–11; ☎ 6593 0478; www.berlitz.com; Room 801, Sunjoy Bldg, 6 Ritan Lu, Cháoyáng) Group and one-on-one classes in Chinese, including effective immersion lessons for complete novices.

China Cultural Center (see left) Cultural programs aimed at foreigners and expats.

Executive Mandarin (Map pp110–11; ☎ 6561 2486; www.ecbeijing.com; Hanwei Bldg, 7 Guanghua Lu, Cháoyáng) Immersion programs, Mandarin and Cantonese, and business Chinese.

Global Village (☎ 6253 7737) Popular school offering value-for-money classes in Mandarin. A taster lesson is available. Located on the west side of Wudaokou Station.

Martial Arts

The Běijīng air won't do wonders for your *qì* (energy), but the capital is an excellent place to learn taichi and other Chinese martial arts and techniques. A host of English-speaking teachers advertise in the classified pages of the free expat mag the *Beijinger*; some of whom teach on a daily basis in Ritan Park (see boxed text Monkey Offers Peach in Ritan Park, p114) and other locations around town. If you are not sure what it is you want to study, you can go along and look at what is being taught and then make your choice. For further information on martial arts courses in Běijīng, see p199.

Traditional Chinese Medicine

Traditional Chinese medicine is a popular interest for would-be acupuncturists and students of moxibustion. The China Academy of Traditional Chinese Medicine (Map pp58–9; ☎ 6401 4411; 16 Dongzhimennei Nanxiaojie, Dōngchéng) has courses in Chinese for greenhorn and intermediate level students. The Beijing University of Chinese Medicine (Map pp128–9; ☎ 6428 6322; www.bjucmp .edu.cn; 11 Beisanhuan Donglu, Cháoyáng) has full programs in Chinese or shorter programs taught in English.

CUSTOMS REGULATIONS

Chinese customs generally pay tourists little attention. There are clearly marked 'green channels' and 'red channels' at the airport. Duty free, you're allowed to import 400 cigarettes or the equivalent in tobacco products, 1.5L of alcohol and 50g of gold or silver. Importation of fresh fruit and meat is prohibited. There are no restrictions on foreign currency;

however, you should declare any cash that exceeds US$5000 (or its equivalent in another currency).

Pirated DVDs and CDs are illegal exports from China as well as illegal imports into most other countries. If they are found, they will be confiscated.

Objects considered antiques require a certificate and red seal to clear customs. To get the proper certificate and seal, your antiques must be inspected by the Relics Bureau (Wénwù Jiàndìng; ☎ 6401 4608), where no English is spoken. Anything made before 1949 is considered an antique and needs a certificate, and if it was made before 1795 it cannot legally be taken out of the country.

DISCOUNT CARDS

An International Student Identity Card (ISIC; www.isiccard.com) may be useful as you could get half-price entry to some sights. Chinese signs at many sights clearly indicate that students pay half price – so push the point. If you are studying in China, your school will issue you with a student card, which is more useful for discounts on admission charges.

Tickets must be purchased for virtually every sight in Běijīng and beyond, and there is little that one can do for free (for a list of free sightseeing ideas, see the boxed text, p141). The annual Y80 Beijing Museum Pass (p73) is a good investment.

ELECTRICITY

Electricity is 220 volts, 50 cycles AC. There are four types of plug – three-pronged angled pins (as in Australia), three-pronged round pins (as in Hong Kong), two flat pins (US style but without the ground wire) or two narrow round pins (European style). Conversion plugs are easily purchased in Běijīng. For more information on electricity and adaptors in China, see www.kropla.com.

EMBASSIES

Embassies in Běijīng are open from 9am to noon and from 1.30pm to 4pm Monday to Friday, but visa departments are often only open in the morning. There are two main embassy areas: Jiànguóménwài and Sānlǐtún.

The following embassies are in the Jiàn-guóménwài area:

India (Map pp110–11; ☎ 6532 1908; www.indian embassy.org.cn; 1 Ritan Donglu, Cháoyáng)

Ireland (Map pp110–11; ☎ 6532 2691; www.embassy ofireland.cn; 3 Ritan Donglu, Cháoyáng)

Japan (Map pp110–11; ☎ 6532 2361; www.cn.emb -japan.go.jp; 7 Ritan Lu, Cháoyáng)

Mongolia (Map pp110–11; ☎ 6532 1203; www.mongol embassychina.org; 2 Xiushui Beijie, Cháoyáng)

New Zealand (Map pp110–11; ☎ 6532 2731; www .nzembassy.com/china; 1 Ritan Dong'erjie, Cháoyáng)

North Korea (Map pp110–11; ☎ 6532 1186; fax 6532 6056; Ritan Beilu, Cháoyáng)

Philippines (Map pp110–11; ☎ 6532 1872; 23 Xiushui Beijie, Cháoyáng)

Singapore (Map pp110–11; ☎ 6532 1115; www.mfa.gov .sg/beijing; 1 Xiushui Beijie, Cháoyáng)

South Korea (☎ 8351 0700; www.koreaemb.org.cn; 20 Dongfang Donglu, Cháoyáng)

Thailand Embassy (Map pp110–11; ☎ 6532 2151; www .thaiembassy.org/beijing; 40 Guanghua Lu, Cháoyáng); Vis Section (Map pp110–11; ☎ 8528 8771; Huabin International Bldg, 8 Yong'an Dongli)

UK Embassy (Map pp110–11; ☎ 5192 4000; www.uk.cn 11 Guanghua Lu, Cháoyáng); Visa & Consular Section (Map pp110–11; ☎ 8529 6600; 21st fl, Kerry Center, 1 Guanghua Lu, Cháoyáng)

US (Map pp110–11; ☎ 6532 3831; http://beijing.us embassy-china.org.cn; 3 Xiushui Beijie, Cháoyáng)

Vietnam (Map pp110–11; ☎ 6532 1155; fax 6532 5720; 32 Guanghua Lu, Cháoyáng)

The Sānlǐtún area is home to the following embassies:

Australia (Map pp110–11; ☎ 5140 4111; www.austemb .org.cn; 21 Dongzhimenwai Dajie, Cháoyáng)

Cambodia (Map pp110–11; ☎ 6532 2790; fax 6532 3507; 9 Dongzhimenwai Dajie, Cháoyáng)

Canada (Map pp110–11; ☎ 6532 3536; www.beijing .gc.ca; 19 Dongzhimenwai Dajie, Cháoyáng)

France (Map pp110–11; ☎ 8532 8080; www.ambafranc -cn.org; 3 Dongsanjie, Cháoyáng)

Germany (Map pp110–11; ☎ 8532 9000; www.deutsch ebotschaft-china.org; 17 Dongzhimenwai Dajie, Cháoyáng)

Italy (Map pp110–11; ☎ 8532 7600; www.italian embassy.org.cn; 2 Sanlitun Dong'erjie, Cháoyáng)

Kazakhstan (Map pp110–11; ☎ 6532 6182; www .kazembchina.org; 9 Sanlitun Dongliujie, Cháoyáng)

Laos (Map pp110–11; ☎ 6532 1224; 11 Dongsijie, Cháoyáng)

Myanmar (Map pp110–11; ☎ 6532 0351; www.myan marembassy.com; 6 Dongzhimenwai Dajie, Cháoyáng)

Nepal (Map pp110–11; ☎ 6532 1795; www.nepal embassy.org.cn; 1 Sanlitun Xiliujie, Cháoyáng)

Netherlands (Map pp110–11; ☎ 8532 0200; www hollandinchina.org; 4 Liangmahe Nanlu, Cháoyáng)

Pakistan (Map pp110–11; ☎ 6532 2504/2558; www embassyofpakistan-beijing.org.cn; 1 Dongzhimenwai Dajie, Cháoyáng)

Russia (Map pp58–9; ☎ 6532 1381; www.russia.org.cn; Dongzhimen Beizhongjie, Dōngchéng)

Sweden (Map pp110–11; ☎ 6532 9790; www.sweden broad.com; 3 Dongzhimenwai Dajie, Cháoyáng)

EMERGENCY

Important telephone numbers in Běijīng include the following:

Ambulance (☎ 120)

Directory inquiries (☎ 114)

Fire (☎ 119)

International directory inquiries (☎ 115)

Police (☎ 110)

Public Security Bureau (PBS; ☎ foreigners' section 8402 0101)

Tourist Hotline (☎ 6513 0828)

Weather (☎ 121) In English and Chinese.

GAY & LESBIAN TRAVELLERS

Even though the Chinese authorities take a dim view of homosexuality, which was officially classified as a mental disorder until 2001, a low-profile gay and lesbian scene exists in Běijīng. For an informative and up-to-date lowdown on the latest gay and lesbian hotspots in Běijīng (and the rest of China) have a look at the Utopia (www.utopia-asia.com pschin.htm) site or invest in a copy of the *Utopia Guide to China*.

HEALTH

Except for the thick layer of air pollution that sometimes blankets the city, Běijīng is a reasonably healthy city and you needn't fear tropical bugs such as malaria. Bear in mind more immediate dangers – the greatest saftey issue you will probably face is crossing the road (p250).

It's worth taking your own medicine kit so you have remedies at hand. It is advisable to take your own prescription drugs with you

---

HEALTH ADVISORIES

It's a good idea to consult your government's travel-health website before departure, if one is available.

Australia (www.dfat.gov.au/travel)

Canada (www.travelhealth.gc.ca)

New Zealand (www.mfat.govt.nz/travel)

UK (www.dh.gov.uk) Search for travel in the site index.

US (www.cdc.gov/travel)

---

because they could be more expensive or hard to find in the capital. Until recently, antibiotics *(kàngjūnsù)*, sleeping pills *(ānmiányào)*, antidepressants and other medications could be picked up prescription-free from many chemists in Běijīng, but this is no longer the case. If you require a specific type of drug, ensure you take an adequate supply. When looking for medications in Běijīng, make sure you take along the brand and the generic name so that pharmacy staff can locate it for you.

Vaccinations

Proof of vaccination for Yellow Fever is required if entering China within six days of visiting an infected country. If you are travelling to China from Africa or South America, check with a travel medicine clinic about whether you need the vaccine.

The following vaccinations are recommended for those travelling to China:

Adult diphtheria/tetanus (ADT) A booster is recommended if it is more than 10 years since your last shot. Side effects include a sore arm and fever.

Hepatitis A One shot provides almost 100% protection for up to a year; a booster after 12 months provides another 20 years' protection. Mild side effects include a sore arm, fever and headaches.

Hepatitis B Now considered a routine vaccination for most travellers. Given as three shots over six months, this vaccine can be combined with Hepatitis A (Twinrix). In most people the course gives lifetime protection. Mild side effects include a sore arm and headaches.

Measles/mumps/rubella (MMR) Two lifetime doses of MMR are recommended unless you have had the diseases. Many adults under the age of 35 require a booster. Occasionally a rash and flu-like illness occur about a week after vaccination.

Typhoid Needed if spending more than two weeks in China. A single injection provides around 70% protection for two to three years.

Varicella (chickenpox) If you haven't had chickenpox, discuss this vaccine with your doctor. Chickenpox can be a serious disease in adults and has such complications as pneumonia and encephalitis.

Under certain circumstances, or for those at special risk, the following vaccinations are recommended. Discuss these with a doctor who specialises in travel medicine.

Influenza If you are over 50 years of age or have a chronic medical condition such as diabetes, lung disease or heart disease, you should have an influenza shot annually.

Japanese encephalitis There is risk only in rural areas of China. Recommended if travelling to rural areas for more than a month during summer.

Pneumonia (Pneumococcal) This vaccine is recommended for travellers over 65 or those with chronic lung or heart disease. A single shot is given, with a booster in five years.

Rabies Recommended if spending more than three months in China. Three injections given over a one-month period are required.

If you are pregnant or breast feeding, consult a doctor who specialises in travel medicine before having any vaccines.

Diseases

AIDS & SEXUALLY TRANSMITTED DISEASES

The Chinese government is starting to take AIDS seriously as the country is said to be on the brink of a major epidemic. Although most cases so far have occurred in intravenous drug users or from contaminated blood products, the virus is increasingly being spread via heterosexual sex.

Always use condoms if you have sex with a new partner, and never share needles. If you have had unsafe sex while travelling, get a check-up and immediately seek medical advice if you develop pain, a rash or a discharge.

BIRD FLU

'Bird flu' or Influenza A (H5N1) is a subtype of the type A influenza virus. This virus typically infects birds and not humans; however, in 1997 the first documented case of bird-to-human transmission was recorded in Hong Kong. As of 2008 there have been 27 confirmed human cases in China, of whom 18 have died. Currently very close contact with dead or sick birds is the principal source of infection and bird-to-human transmission does not easily occur.

Symptoms include high fever and typical influenza-like symptoms with rapid deterioration, leading to respiratory failure and often death. At this time it is not recommended for travellers to carry antiviral drugs such as Tamiflu; rather, immediate medical care should be sought if bird flu is suspected.

There is currently no vaccine available to prevent bird flu. For up-to-date information check the websites www.who.int/en and www.avianinfluenza.com.au.

HEPATITIS A

This virus is transmitted through contaminated food and water, and infects the liver causing jaundice (yellow skin and eyes), nausea and extreme tiredness. There is no specific treatment available; you just need to allow time for the liver to heal, which might take many weeks.

HEPATITIS B

This disease is common in China and is transmitted via infected body fluids, including through sexual contact. The long-term consequences can include liver cancer and cirrhosis.

INFLUENZA

Flu is common in Běijīng in winter. This virus gives you high fevers, body aches and general symptoms, such as a cough, runny nose and sore throat. Antibiotics won't help unless you develop a complication, such as pneumonia. Anyone travelling in winter should think about vaccination, but it is particularly recommended for the elderly or those with underlying medical conditions.

TRAVELLER'S DIARRHOEA

This is the most common problem faced by travellers in Asia. Most traveller's diarrhoea is caused by bacteria and thus responds rapidly to a short course of appropriate antibiotics. How soon you treat your diarrhoea will depend on individual circumstances, but it is a good idea to carry treatment in your medical kit.

TUBERCULOSIS (TB)

This is a rare disease in travellers that's contracted after prolonged close exposure to a person with an active TB infection. Symptoms include a cough, weight loss, night sweats and fevers. Children under the age of five spending more than six months in China should receive

BCG (Bacillus Calmette-Guérin) vaccination. Adults are rarely immunised.

TYPHOID
This serious bacterial infection is contracted from contaminated food and water. Symptoms include high fever, headache, a cough and lethargy. The diagnosis is made via blood tests, and treatment is with specific antibiotics.

Environmental Hazards

AIR POLLUTION
Běijīng is one of the 10 most polluted cities in the world (p120). Although the government improved the situation prior to the 2008 Olympics and kept certain measures in place after the games (eg restricting car use), those with chronic respiratory conditions should ensure they have adequate personal medication with them in case symptoms worsen.

WATER
Don't drink the tap water or eat ice. Bottled water (but check the seal is not broken on the cap), soft drinks and alcohol are fine.

HOLIDAYS
Holiday periods in China, like five-year plans and other government campaigns, are highly structured. The main holiday periods for the Chinese are the days following the 1 May holiday, National Day on 1 October and the Spring Festival, each of which is known as 'Gold Week', when the Chinese take a break from graft and blow some of their savings. Travelling in China during these periods can be nightmarish as tourist sights are swamped particularly the major ones, such as the Summer Palace) and bus, train and air tickets are scarce (especially during the Spring Festival). The 1 May holiday used to run to an entire week, but has now been sliced back to three days, with the extra days lent to the Tomb Sweeping Festival (p13) in April.

Also refer to Festivals (p12) in the Getting Started chapter for a list of Běijīng's big festival periods.

Public Holidays
New Year's Day 1 January

Spring Festival (Chinese New Year) Generally held in January or February; 14 February 2010, 3 February 2011

International Women's Day 8 March

Tomb Sweeping Day 5 April (4 April in leap years)

International Labour Day 1 May

Youth Day 4 May

International Children's Day 1 June

Birthday of the Chinese Communist Party 1 July

Anniversary of the founding of the People's Liberation Army 1 August

Double Ninth 9 September

National Day 1 October

INTERNET ACCESS
Many midrange and top-end hotels provide free broadband internet access as standard; many also have wi-fi areas. Most youth hostels levy internet charges of around Y10 per hour, but some offer free access.

Internet cafes are generally easy to find (except in the very centre of town) tucked away down side streets and above shops. They rarely have English signs, so memorise the characters 网吧 (wǎngbā) for 'internet cafe'.

Rates should be around Y2 to Y4 per hour for a standard no-frills outlet, but there are different priced zones – the common area (pǔtōng qū) is the cheapest. Rates can also vary depending on what time you go online, with daytime cheapest and night-time more expensive. In most internet cafes you will be given a card with a number (zhèngjiànhào)

THE GREAT FIREWALL
Chinese internet censorship – known as the 'Great Firewall of China' – is Draconian, with a group of 30,000 censors working nonstop to stem the tide of undesirable electronic data from corrupting Chinese minds. Anything that the Běijīng leadership disapproves of (pornography, Taiwan independence information, criticism of the Chinese Communist Party, BBC news in Chinese) is susceptible to censorship. A temporary relaxation of censorship during the 2008 Olympics (as Běijīng was bound to provide complete internet access to journalists covering the event) took place but the firewall was later reinstalled. Internet monitors (known as the 'five máo gang' as they reputedly earn five máo per posting) are employed to discreetly usher online chat room discussions on topical and sensitive issues in authorised directions; Chinese monitors fluent in English are also suspected of attempting to manipulate foreign opinion in the international online media.

WI-FI ACCESS

Wi-fi (wireless internet) zones are increasingly common in hotels, cafes and restaurants around town. All of the cafes in the Entertainment chapter (p180) come equipped with wi-fi.

and password (mìmǎ or kǒulìng) to enter into the on screen box before you can start. Internet cafes are generally open 24 hours. Smoking is often tolerated in internet cafes (as you will discover when your neighbour lights up his fifth cigarette in an hour).

It is increasingly common for bars and cafes, such as those along Nanluogu Xiang, to offer free internet access and wi-fi. Be prepared for occasionally slow connections and the sudden disappearance of sites for periods. Many internet cafes do not allow the use of a USB stick.

Internet cafes in Běijīng are required to see your passport before allowing you to go online, and a record of your visit may be made. You will be filmed or digitally photographed at reception by a rectangular metal box that sits on the counter of each licensed internet cafe in town.

The following internet cafes are centrally located:

Biyuan Xianjing Internet Cafe (Bìyuán Xiānjīng Wǎngbā; Map pp88–9; 73 Xinjiekou Nandajie, Xīchéng; per hr Y3; 24hr)

Dayusu Internet Cafe (Dáyǔsù Wǎngbā; Map pp118–19; 2 Hufang Lu, Xuānwǔ; per hr Y3; 8am-midnight) No English sign, but it's around three shops north of Bank of China on Hufang Lu.

Internet Cafe (Wǎngbā; Map pp58–9; 432-1 Dongsi Beidajie, Dōngchéng; per hr Y2; 24hr)

Internet Cafe (Wǎngbā; Map pp58–9; 2nd fl, 1 Beijing-zhan Jie, Dōngchéng; per hr Y5; 24hr) Above the Beijing City Central International Youth Hostel.

Internet Cafe (Wǎngbā; Map pp58–9; 30 Wusi Dajie, Dōngchéng; per hr Y2; 24hr)

Internet Cafe (Wǎngbā; Map pp110–11; Shop 2601, 2nd fl, Soho New Town, Cháoyáng; per hr Y3; 24hr) Next to Dawanglu Station exit B.

Internet Cafe (Wǎngbā; Map pp110–11; 2nd fl, 1 Chunxiu Lu, Cháoyáng; per hr Y2; 24hr) Above the Sanlitun Youth Hostel.

Internet Cafe (Wǎngbā; Map pp110–11; Cháoyáng; per hr Y4; 24hr) On the 2nd floor, up the fire escape, just east of Bookworm.

LEGAL MATTERS

Anyone under the age of 18 is considered a minor in China; the minimum driving age is also 18. The age of consent for marriage is 22 years for men and 20 years for women. No minimum age restricts the consumption of cigarettes or alcohol.

China's laws against the use of illegal drugs are harsh, and foreign nationals have been executed for drug offences (trafficking in more than 50g of heroin can result in the death penalty).

The Chinese criminal justice system does not ensure a fair trial, and defendants are not presumed innocent until proven guilty (China conducts more judicial executions than the rest of the world combined). If arrested, most foreign citizens have the right to contact their embassy.

LIBRARIES

Bookworm (Shūchóng; Map pp110–11; ☎ 6586 9507; www.beijingbookworm.com; Bldg 4, Nansanlitun Lu, Cháoyáng; 9am-2am) The Bookworm has wriggled its way into a commanding lead in the lending-library stakes and its copious lending library is a source of bliss for Běijīng bibliophiles. The bookshop-library-restaurant is also the venue of the fantastic annual International Literary Festival (p13).

Le Petit Gourmand (Xiǎo Měishíjiā; Map pp110–11; ☎ 6417 6095; www.lepetitgourmand.com.cn; 3rd fl, Tongli Studios, Sanlitun Beijie, Cháoyáng; 9am-midnight) There's an excellent and lovingly looked-after horde of books at this restaurant-cum-library. Maximum two books per loan; membership costs Y150 for six months.

National Library (Guójiā Túshūguǎn; Map p122; ☎ 8854 5593; 33 Zhongguancun Nandajie, Hǎidiàn; 9am-9pm) Large collection of English titles and books in other languages, for reference only. Reading charges Y5 per month.

MAPS

English-language maps of Běijīng can be bought from newspaper kiosks and the Foreign Languages Bookstore (p145). They can also be picked up for free at most big hotels and branches of the Beijing Tourist Information Center (p252). The concierge at your hotel may be able to supply you with a quality English language map of town.

Street vendors hawk cheap maps near subway stations around Tiananmen Square and Wangfujing Dajie – make sure you check they have English labelling before purchasing from pushy vendors. The so-so English-language *Beijing Tourist Map* (Y8) is labelled in English and Chinese, but shows little detail on lesser streets and alleys. Ensure you buy the current edition as old, out-of-date copies are also hawked. Open the map on the reverse side (which depicts the 'Tourist Sketch Map of Beijing Suburbs') and inspect the bottom left-hand corner where the publication date can be found (for example, '2009 年 2 月' means the map was last printed in February 2009).

The Wangfujing Bookstore (north of Oriental Plaza) has a wide range of (largely Chinese-language) detailed maps and guides to Běijīng. For readers of Chinese, detailed street maps in book form that show bus routes, such as the *Mapple Beijing City Map*, are available from Chinese-language bookshops.

For a fascinating copy of a Chinese map showing how Běijīng looked in 1950 (before the huge reshaping of the town), look out for the *1950 Beijing City Street Map* available from bookshops and published by the China Map Publishing House.

MEDICAL SERVICES

As the national capital, Běijīng naturally sports some of China's best medical facilities and services.

Clinics

A consultation with a doctor in a private clinic will cost between Y200 and Y800, depending on where you go. It will cost Y10 to Y50 in a state hospital.

Bayley & Jackson Medical Center (Map pp110–11; ☎ 8562 9998; www.bjhealthcare.com; 7 Ritan Donglu, Cháoyáng) Full range of medical and dental services; attractively located in a courtyard next to Ritan Park.

Beijing Union Hospital (Xiéhé Yīyuàn; Map pp58–9; ☎ 6529 6114, emergency 6529 5284; 53 Dongdan Beidajie, Dōngchéng; ☼ 24hr) A recommended Chinese hospital operating from a wonderful building off Wangfujing Dajie, with a wing reserved for foreigners in the back building. Open 24 hours with a full range of facilities for inpatient and outpatient care, plus a pharmacy.

Beijing United Family Hospital (Map pp128–9; ☎ 6433 3960, 24hr emergency hotline 6433 2345; www.unitedfamilyhospitals.com; 2 Jiangtai Lu, Cháoyáng; ☼ 24hr) Can provide alternative medical treatments along with a comprehensive range of inpatient and outpatient care. There is a critical care unit. Emergency room staffed by expat physicians.

Hong Kong International Medical Clinic (Map pp58–9; ☎ 6553 2288; www.hkclinic.com; 9th fl, Office Tower, Hong Kong Macau Center, Swissôtel, 2 Chaoyangmen Beidajie, Cháoyáng; ☼ 9am-9pm) There's a 24-hour dental and medical clinic, including obstetric and gynaecological services and facilities for ultrasonic scanning, and immunisations can also be performed. Prices are more reasonable than at International SOS.

International SOS (Map pp110–11; ☎ clinic appointments 6462 9199, dental appointments 6462 0333, 24hr alarm centre 6462 9100; www.internationalsos.com; Suite 105, Wing 1, Kunsha Bldg, 16 Xinyuanli, Cháoyáng; ☼ 9am-6pm Mon-Fri) Offering 24-hour emergency medical care, with a high-quality clinic with English-speaking staff.

Pharmacies

Pharmacies (药店; *yàodiàn*) are identified by a green cross. Several sizeable pharmacies on Wangfujing Dajie stock both Chinese (*zhōngyào*) and Western medicine (*xīyào*). As with many large shops in Běijīng, once you have chosen your item you are issued with a receipt that you take to the till counter (*shōuyíntái*) where you pay, then you return to the counter where you chose your medicine to collect your purchase. Note that many chemists are effectively open 24 hours and have a small window or slit through which you can pay for and collect medicines through the night. Watson's (Map pp58–9; CC17, 19, CC21, 23 Oriental Plaza, 1 Dongchan'an Jie, Dōngchéng) has many branches and is geared towards selling cosmetics, sunscreens, deodorants and the like. Try Wangfujing Medicine Shop (Wángfǔjǐng Yīyào Shāngdiàn; Map pp58–9; ☎ 6524 0122; 267 Wangfujing Dajie, Dōngchéng; ☼ 8.30am-9pm) for a large range of Western and Chinese drugs.

MONEY

For information regarding exchange rates, see the Quick Reference section on the inside front cover. The Costs & Money section in the Getting Started chapter (p14) gives you an idea of the costs you are likely to incur during your stay in Běijīng.

The basic unit of Chinese currency is the *yuán*, designated in this book by a capital 'Y'. In spoken Chinese, the word *kuài* or *kuàiqián* is often substituted for *yuán*. Ten *jiǎo* – in spoken Chinese, it's known as *máo* – make up one *yuán*. Ten *fēn* make up one *jiǎo*, but these days *fēn* are very rare because they are worth next to nothing.

Renminbi (RMB), or 'people's money', is issued by the Bank of China. Paper notes are issued in denominations of one, two, five, 10, 20, 50 and 100 *yuán;* one, two and five *jiǎo;* and one, two and five *fēn.* Coins are in denominations of one *yuán;* one, two and five *jiǎo;* and one, two and five *fēn.*

ATMs

Most ATMs in Běijīng now accept foreign credit cards and bank cards connected to Plus, Cirrus, Visa, MasterCard and Amex; there could be a small withdrawal charge levied by your bank (or the local bank). ATMs are often open 24 hours; Bank of China (中国银行; Zhōngguó Yínháng), the Industrial and Commercial Bank of China (工商银行; Gōngshāng Yínháng), the China Construction Bank (中国建设银行; Zhōngguó Jiàn-shè Yínháng) and the Agricultural Bank of China (中国农业银行; Zhōngguó Nóngyè Yínháng) all have extensive ATM networks. ATM screens frequently offer the choice of English or Chinese operation. There are ATMs in the arrivals hall at Capital Airport, and in many large department stores and hotels, or you can check www.moveandstay.com/beijing/guide_banks.asp for a list of ATMs in Běijīng.

Banks

Citibank (Huāqí Yínháng; Map pp58–9; ☎ 6510 2933, nationwide 800 830 1880; www.citibank.com; 1st fl, Tower 2, Bright China Chang'an Bldg, 7 Jianguomennei Dajie, Dōngchéng) One of three branches.

HSBC (Huìfēng Yínháng; Map pp58–9; ☎ 6526 0668, nationwide 800 820 8878; www.hsbc.com.cn; 1st fl, Block a, COFCO Plaza, 8 Jianguomennei Dajie, Dōngchéng) One of four branches in the capital.

Changing Money

Foreign currency and travellers cheques can be changed at large branches of banks, such as the Bank of China, CITIC Industrial Bank, the Industrial and Commercial Bank of China and the China Construction Bank, at the airport, hotel money-changing counters and at several department stores, as long as you have your passport. You should be able to change foreign currency into renminbi at foreign-exchange outlets and banks at large international airports outside China, but rates may be poor. Hotels usually give the official rate, but some will add a small commission. Some

upmarket hotels will change money for their own guests only. Avoid changing money on the black market.

You can find foreign-exchange counters in the Bank of China branches at Oriental Plaza on Wangfujing Dajie (Map pp58–9), the Lufthansa Center (Map pp110–11) and the China World Trade Center (Map pp110–11).

As renminbi is not fully convertible on international markets, you need to have a few exchange receipts if you want to change any remaining renminbi back into another currency at the end of your trip.

Counterfeit Bills

Counterfeit notes are a problem across China, Běijīng included. Very few shopkeepers will accept a Y50 or Y100 note without first running it under an ultraviolet light.

Credit Cards

Although living on credit is not popular with the Chinese, most tourist hotels, restaurants and travel agencies, department stores and tourist shops (even small ones) accept credit cards. If there aren't credit card signs posted at the shop entrance, check at the till before purchasing items.

It's possible to get cash advances on Visa cards at branches of the Bank of China and HSBC and at Plus-equipped ATMs. You can get cash advances at CITIC Bank (Map pp110–11; CITIC Bldg, 19 Jianguomenwai Dajie, Cháoyáng), or the Bank of China's Sundongan Plaza (Map pp58–9) and Sānlǐtún branches, but there is a steep (4%) commission. You can also cash personal cheques if you have an Amex card at CITIC Industrial Bank (Map pp110–11; CITIC Bldg, 19 Jianguomenwai Dajie, Cháoyáng) and large branches of the Bank of China.

Money Transfers

If you need cash in a dash, Western Union (☎ 800 820 8668; www.westernunion.com) arrange money transfers that arrive in just 15 minutes. Counters can be found all over town at branches of China Post and the Agricultural Bank of China.

Travellers Cheques

Besides increased security, travellers cheques are useful to carry in China because the exchange rate is more favourable than the rate for cash. Cheques from most of the world's eading banks and issuing agencies are acceptable in Běijīng – stick with the major players such as Citibank, Amex and Visa and you should be fine. Note that although cashing travellers cheques is easy at branches of the Bank of China and tourist hotels in Běijīng, don't expect to find anywhere to cash your cheques in small towns elsewhere in China.

Amex (Map pp110–11; ☎ 6505 2838; Room 2313, Tower , China World Trade Center, 1 Jianguomenwai Dajie, Cháoyáng)

Citibank (Huāqí Yínháng; Map pp58–9; ☎ 6510 2933, nationwide 800 830 1880; www.citibank.com; 1st fl, Tower , Bright China Chang'an Bldg, 7 Jianguomennei Dajie, Dōngchéng)

NEWSPAPERS & MAGAZINES

Copies of popular imported English-language international magazines, such as *Time*, *Newsweek*, *Far Eastern Economic Review* and the *Economist*, can be bought from the bookshops of four- and five-star hotels. These hotels also stock European magazines in French or German and newspapers, such as the *Times*, the *International Herald Tribune*, the *Asian Wall Street Journal*, the *Financial Times* and the *South China Morning Post*. Most English-language newspapers and magazines are accessible online from Běijīng. For a wide-ranging and across-the-board selection of glossy magazines, including women's magazines, pop into the Bookworm (see p148).

Běijīng has a lively galaxy of English-language rags available free at most five-star hotels and expat bars and restaurants. The *Beijinger* (www.thebeijinger.com) has its finger on Běijīng's ever-quickening pulse and can point you in exactly the right direction. After problems with its licence, *Time Out Beijing* (www.timeout.com/beijing) is back on the ball. *City Weekend* (www.cityweekend .com.cn) is a useful and up-to-the-minute bi-weekly.

The *China Daily* (www.chinadaily.com .cn), the government's favourite English-language mouthpiece, is generally an unappetising blend of censorship and pro-government opinion, but it's slowly improving and the weekend culture section, 'Beijing Weekend', is useful for arts listings, events and ideas for trips out of Běijīng. Among the countless Chinese-language newspapers is the state's flagship paper, the *Renmin Ribao* (People's Daily), and papers of more specialist leanings, such as the *Nongmin Ribao* (Farmer's Daily).

If you are a reader of Chinese, be on your guard against fake Chinese newspapers (see boxed text, p117).

For a country expected to shape the course of the 21st century, the media outlook in China is grim; for more information, see p44.

ORGANISED TOURS

The recommended China Cultural Center (CCC; Map pp128–9; ☎ weekdays 6432 9341, weekends 6432 0141; www.chinaculturecenter.org; Kent Center, 29 Anjialou, Liangmaqiao Lu, Cháoyáng) offers a range of fascinating tours geared towards expats and foreign tourists. Destinations range from Běijīng to off-the-beaten-track locations around China; it also offers a variety of stimulating courses on Chinese language and culture.

Other recommended tour agencies, which all offer trips to the Great Wall, include the following:

90 Percent Travel (☎ 5962 6850; www.90percenttravel .com) A company focused on experiential travel.

Beijing Sideways (☎ 139 1103 4847; www.beijingside ways.com) Trips outside town in a motorcycle sidecar.

Intrepid Travel (Map pp58–9; ☎ 6406 8022; www .intrepidtravel.com; Room 608, 94 Dongsishitiao, Beijing Wanxin Business Bldg, Dōngchéng)

Pixie Adventures (☎ 8402 6713; www.pixieadventures .com) Tours around Běijīng and China for small groups.

PASSPORTS

You must have a passport with you at all times; all hotels will insist upon seeing it. The Chinese government requires that your passport be valid for at least six months after the expiry date of your visa (for information on visas, see p253). You'll need at least one entire blank page in your passport for the visa.

Have an ID card with your photo in case you lose your passport and make photocopies of your passport so that if you lose it, your embassy can issue a new one (a process that can take weeks). Also report the loss to the local Public Security Bureau (PSB; Gōng'ānjú). Long-term visitors should register their passport with their embassy.

POST

Large post offices are generally open daily between 8.30am and 6pm. Convenient post offices can be found in the basement of the China World Trade Center (Map pp110–11), east of Wangfujing Dajie on Dongdan Ertiao

(Map pp58–9), on the south side of Xichang'an Jie west of the Beijing Concert Hall (Map pp88–9) and just east of the Qianmen Jianguo Hotel on Yong'an Lu (Map pp118–19). You can also post letters via your hotel reception desk, or at green post boxes around town.

Letters and parcels marked 'Poste Restante, Beijing Main Post Office' will arrive at the International Post Office (Map pp110–11; ☎ 6512 8114; Jianguomen Beidajie, Cháoyáng; ⏲ 8am-7pm Mon-Sat), 200m north of Jianguomen Station. Outsized parcels going overseas should be sent from here (parcels can be bought at the post office); smaller parcels (up to around 20kg) can go from smaller post offices. Both outgoing and incoming packages will be opened and inspected. If you're sending a parcel, don't seal the package until you've had it inspected.

Letters take around a week to reach most overseas destinations. China charges extra for registered mail, but offers cheaper postal rates for printed matter, small packets, parcels, bulk mailings and so on.

Express Mail Service (EMS) is available for registered deliveries to domestic and international destinations from most post offices around town.

Courier Companies

Several private couriers in Běijīng offer international express posting of documents and parcels, and have reliable pick-up services as well as drop-off centres:

DHL (☎ 800 810 8000; www.cn.dhl.com) Branches in the China World Trade Center, Cháoyáng and COFCO Plaza.

FedEx (Federal Express; Map pp128–9; ☎ toll free landline 800 988 1888, toll free mobile phones 400 886 1888; www.fedex.com/cn_english; Room 101, Tower C, Lonsdale Center, 5 Wanhong Lu) FedEx also has self-service counters in Kodak Express shops around town.

United Parcel Service (UPS; Map pp110–11; ☎ 800 820 8388; www.ups.com; Room 1818, China World Tower 1, 1 Jianguomenwai Dajie, Cháoyáng)

RADIO

The BBC World Service can be picked up on 17760kHz, 15278kHz, 21660kHz, 12010kHz and 9740kHz. Reception can often be poor, however, and Voice of America (VOA) is often a bit clearer at 17820kHz, 15425kHz, 21840kHz, 15250kHz, 9760kHz, 5880kHz and 6125kHz. There is tuning information for the BBC on the web at www.bbc.co.uk/world service/tuning, for Radio Australia at www .abc.net.au/ra and for VOA at www.voa.gov Crystal-clear programs from the BBC World Service can be heard online: follow the links on www.bbc.co.uk/worldservice.

China Radio International (CRI) broadcasts in about 40 foreign languages, as well as in pǔtōnghuà (the standard form of the Chinese language) and several local dialects.

RELOCATING

If you're moving things like furniture or household goods, you'll need an international mover or freight forwarder. In Běijīng, contact one of the following international companies but note that their rates are typically around US$500 to US$1000 per cubic metre:

Allied Pickfords (Map pp110–11; ☎ 5870 1133; www .alliedpickfords.com.cn; Room 812, Bldg a, Space International Centre, 8 Dongdaqiao Lu, Cháoyáng)

Asian Express (Map pp110–11; ☎ 8580 1471/2/3; www .aemovers.com.hk; Room 1612, Tower d, SOHO New Town, 88 Jianguo Lu, Cháoyáng)

Crown Worldwide (☎ 6585 0640; www.crownworld wide.com; Room 201, West Tower, 1a Golden Bridge Bldg, Jianguomenwai Dajie, Cháoyáng)

SAFETY

Generally speaking, Běijīng is a very safe city compared to other similarly sized cities around the world. Serious crime against foreigners is rare, although on the rise.

Guard against pickpockets, especially on public transport and crowded places such as train stations. A money belt is the safest way to carry valuables, particularly when travelling on buses and trains. Hotels are usually safe places to leave your stuff and older establishments may have an attendant watching who goes in and out on each floor. Staying in a dormitory carries its own set of risks, and while there have been a few reports of thefts by staff, the culprits are more likely to be other guests. Use lockers as much as possible.

The greatest hazard may well be crossing the road, a manoeuvre that requires alertness and dexterity. Like Běijīng's chaotic surge onto its metro carriages, it's a mad scramble on the streets. Cars defy the laws of physics by pouring themselves into each and every tiny crevice of space. It's an unremitting war of attrition and drivers have to be sharp: if they drop their guard for an instant, the impossibly minute space in front of them is seized by the brake lights of a green Santana taxi

Traffic comes from all directions, and a reluctance to give way holds sway. If right of way is uncertain, drivers tend to dig in their heels. Safe crossing points are indicated by zebra crossing markings and/or pedestrian lights, although cars are not obliged to stop at zebra crossings and never do. The green 'cross now' light doesn't necessarily mean that traffic won't try to run you down, as cars can still turn on red lights.

Scams

Be wary of anyone luring you to cafes, tea houses or art galleries on Wangfujing Dajie, Tiananmen Square and other popular tourist areas. Foreigners have been scammed by English-speaking people who invite them to vastly overpriced tea ceremonies or art shows (see boxed text, p78, for more information).

At Capital Airport never take a taxi from touts inside the arrivals halls, where a well-established illegal taxi operation attempts to lure weary travellers into a Y300-plus ride to the city (one man acts as a taxi pimp for a squad of drivers). Also beware of fraudsters trying to sell you departure tax (now included in the price of your ticket) at Capital Airport.

Whenever taking a ride in a rickshaw, ask the driver to write the amount down on a piece of paper first (have a pen and paper ready), so there is no ambiguity about how much the trip will cost, otherwise you could be ripped off.

TAXES

Four- and five-star hotels add a service charge of 15%, and smarter restaurants levy a service charge of 10%.

TELEPHONE

International and domestic calls can be made easily from your hotel room or from public telephones, which are plentiful. Local calls from hotel-room phones are usually free, while international calls are expensive. If making a domestic phone call, public phones at newspaper stands (报刊亭; *bàokāntíng*) and hole-in-the-wall shops (小卖部; *xiǎomàibù*) are useful; make your call and pay the owner (a local call is around five *jiǎo*). Most public phones take IC cards (see Phonecards, p252).

When making domestic long-distance or international calls in China, it's cheapest to use an IP card (see Phonecards, p252). Domestic long-distance and international phone calls

can also be made from main telecommunications offices or 'phone bars' (*huàbā*).

The country code to use to access China is 86; the code for Hong Kong is 852 and Macau is 853. To call a number in Běijīng from abroad, dial the international access code (00 in the UK, 011 in the USA and so on), dial the country code (86) and then the area code for Běijīng (010), dropping the first zero, and then dial the local number. For telephone calls within the same city, drop the area code (*qūhào*).

Important city area codes within China include the following:

City	Area code
Běijīng	010
Chéngdū	028
Chóngqìng	023
Guǎngzhōu	020
Hángzhōu	0571
Hāěrbī	0451
Hong Kong	852
Jǐnán	0531
Kūnmíng	0871
Nánjīng	025
Qīngdǎo	0532
Shànghǎi	021
Shíjiāzhuāng	0311
Tiānjīn	022
Xiàmén	0592

The English-language Běijīng *Yellow Pages* is available at most business centres, and you might find it provided in your hotel room; alternatively, you can go online at www.yellowpage.com.cn or pick up your own copy at 65 Jianguomennei Dajie (☎ 6512 0400).

Mobile Phones

Mobile phone shops (手机店; *shǒujīdiàn*) such as China Mobile and China Unicom sell SIM cards, which cost from Y60 to Y100 and include Y50 of credit. Note that numbers containing 4s are avoided by the Chinese, making them cheaper. You can top up credit with Y50 or Y100 credit-charging cards (充值卡; *chōngzhí kǎ*). Cards are available from the ubiquitous newspaper kiosks and corner shops displaying the China Mobile sign.

The mobile phone you use in your home country should work (as long as it has not been locked by your network – check with your phone company) or you can buy a phone locally. China Mobile's local, nonroaming city call charge is seven *jiǎo* per minute if calling a landline and 1.50 *jiǎo* per minute if calling another mobile phone. Receiving calls on your mobile is free from mobile phones and seven *jiǎo* from landline phones. Roaming charges cost an additional two *jiǎo* per minute and the call receiving charge is the same. Overseas calls can be made for Y4.80 per minute plus the local charge per minute by dialling ☎ 17951 – then follow the instructions and add 00 before the country code. Otherwise you will be charged the International Dialling Code call charge plus seven *jiǎo* per minute.

If you have an English-speaking Chinese contact, mobile phones can be particularly useful for communicating a message to non-English speakers. Just phone your friend, tell him/her what you want to say and hand the phone over to whoever you are trying to communicate with.

Phonecards

For domestic calls, IC (Integrated Circuit; *IC kǎ*) cards, available from kiosks, hole-in-the-wall shops, internet cafes and China Telecom offices, are prepaid cards in a variety of denominations that can be used in most public telephones. Note that some IC cards can only be used locally while other cards can be used in phones throughout China, so check this when you purchase one.

For international calls on a mobile phone or hotel phone and for long-distance domestic calls buy an IP (Internet Phone; *IP kǎ*) card. International calls on IP cards are Y1.80 per minute to the USA or Canada, Y1.50 per minute to Hong Kong, Macau and Taiwan, and Y3.20 to all other countries; domestic long-distance calls are Y0.30 per minute. Follow the instructions on the reverse; English-language service is usually available. IP cards come in various denominations, typically with a big discount (a Y100 card should cost around Y40). IP cards can be found at the same places as IC cards. Again, some IP cards can only be used locally, while others can be used nationwide, so it is important to buy the right card (and check the expiry date).

TELEVISION

The national TV outfit, Chinese Central TV (CCTV), has an English-language channel (CCTV 9) that is useful for news and programs on cultural topics, but is markedly bland. The news is heavily censored and often the lead story is reserved for news about the latest government meeting, however minor. Most TVs in hotel rooms have CCTV 9, but some do not, so if you want it enquire before you book your room. CCTV 4 also has some English programs. Tourist hotels may have ESPN, Star Sports, CNN or BBC News 24. Sports programs and some live sports matches can be picked up on CCTV 5 (in Chinese) or on BJTV, otherwise you will have to find a bar with sports TV.

TIME

All of China runs on the same time as Běijīng, which is set eight hours ahead of GMT/UTC (there's no daylight saving time during summer). When it's noon in Běijīng it's 4am in London, 5am in Frankfurt, Paris and Rome, noon in Hong Kong, 2pm in Melbourne, 4pm in Wellington, and, on the previous day, 8pm in Los Angeles and 11pm in Montreal and New York.

TOILETS

Over the last decade the capital has made its toilets less of an assault course of foul smells and primitive appliances, but many remain pungent. Make a beeline for fast-food outlets, top-end hotels and department stores for more hygienic alternatives. Toilet paper is rarely provided in streetside public toilets so keep a stash with you. Toilets are often squat versions. As a general rule, if you see a wastebasket next to the toilet, that's where you should throw the toilet paper; otherwise the loo could choke up and flood.

Remember that the symbol for men is 男 and women is 女.

TOURIST INFORMATION

Staff at the chain of Beijing Tourist Information Centers (Běijīng Lǚyóu Zīxún Fúwù Zhōngxin; ☽ 9am-5pm) – with uniform turquoise facades – generally have limited English-language skills and are not always helpful, but you can grab a free tourist map of town, nab handfuls of free literature and, at some branches (eg Cháoyáng), rustle up train tickets. Useful branches include the following:

Beijing Train Station (Map pp58–9; ☎ 6528 4848; 16 Laoqianju Hutong)

Capital Airport (首都机场; ☎ 6459 8148)

Cháoyáng (Map pp110–11; ☎ 6417 6627, 6417 6656; chaoyang@bjta.gov.cn; Gongrentiyuchang Beilu)

Háidiàn (Map p125; ☎ 8262 2895; haidian@bjta.gov.cn; 40 Zhongguancun Dajie)

Xuānwǔ (Map pp118–19; ☎ 6351 0018; xuanwu@bjta .gov.cn; 3 Hufang Lu)

The Beijing Tourism Hotline (☎ 6513 0828, press 1 for English; ☻ 24hr) has English-speaking operators available to answer questions and hear complaints. CITS (China International Travel Service; Map pp58–9; ☎ 8511 8522; www.cits.com.cn; Room 1212, CITS Bldg, 1 Dongdan Beidajie, Dōngchéng) is more useful for booking tours.

Hotels can offer you advice or connect you with a suitable tour, and some have useful tourist information desks that can point you in the right direction.

Some bars also informally address themselves to the needs of travellers: Passby Bar (p181) has travel-oriented staff who are keen to help, as long as you order a drink or two.

TRAVELLERS WITH DISABILITIES

If you are wheelchair bound or have a mobility disability, Běijīng can be a major obstacle course. Pavements are often crowded and in a dangerous condition, with high curbs often preventing wheelchair access. Many streets can be crossed only via underground or overhead walkways with steps. You will also have to stick to the main roads, as parked cars and bicycles often occupy the pavements of smaller alleys and lanes, forcing others on to the road. Escalators in subways normally only go up, but wheelchair lifts have been installed in numerous stations (although you may have to send someone down to find a member of staff to operate them). Getting around temples and big sights such as the Forbidden City and the Summer Palace can be trying for those in wheelchairs. It is recommended that you take a lightweight chair so you can collapse it easily when necessary, such as to load it into the back of a taxi. Most, but not all, hotels will have lifts, and while many top-end hotels do have rooms for those with disabilities as well as good wheelchair access, hotel restaurants may not.

Those with sight, hearing or mobility disabilities must be extremely cautious of the traffic, which almost never yields to pedestrians.

VISAS

Unless you are a citizen of Japan, Singapore and Brunei, you need a visa to visit the People's Republic of China, but at the time of writing visas were not required for most Western nationals to visit Hong Kong or Macau. For the majority of travellers, the type of visa required is an L, from the Chinese Pinyin word for travel (*lǚxíng*). This letter is stamped on the visa.

Visas are available from Chinese embassies and consulates in most Western and many other countries. A standard 30-day, single-entry visa from most Chinese embassies abroad can be issued in three to five working days. A visa mailed to you will take up to three weeks to arrive. Express visas cost twice the usual fee. You normally pay up front for the visa, rather than on collection. You can get an application form in person at the embassy or consulate, or obtain one online through a consular website. Rather than going through an embassy or consulate, you can also make arrangements at certain travel agencies. Visa applications require at least one photo. Your passport will need at least one blank page to accommodate the stick-on visa and will need to be valid for at least six months after the expiry date of your visa.

On the application form you will be asked where you are going and your occupation. If you write that you plan to visit places such as Tibet or western Xīnjiāng, or that you work in the media, are a journalist or writer, it might raise eyebrows and slow down the application process.

Thirty-day, 60-day and 90-day visas are activated on the date you enter China, and must be used within three months of the date of issue. Until recently, 60-day and 90-day visas were becoming easier to obtain, but restrictions on visa applications are occasionally enforced, and longer-stay visas are susceptible to the vagaries of politics. For example, in the run up to, during and after the 2008 Olympic Games, restrictions were imposed on certain types of visas and some travellers were flatly denied visas.

A Chinese visa covers virtually the whole of China, although some restricted areas exist that will require an additional permit from the PSB, at a cost. If you are planning on travelling to Tibet, you will need to check that the Tibet Autonomous Region is open to foreigners (it is periodically shut); if Tibet is open, you will still need to obtain a Tibetan Travel Permit and further permits are required for more extensive exploration of the region away from the main tourist areas.

When you check into a hotel, there is a question on the registration form asking what type of visa you hold. The letter specifying what type of visa you have is usually stamped on the visa itself. There are eight categories of visas, as follows:

Type	Description	Chinese name
L	travel	旅行; lǚxíng
F	business or student	访问; fǎngwèn
D	resident	定居; dìngjū
G	transit	过境; guòjìng
X	long-term student	学生; xuéshēng
Z	working	工作; gōngzuò
J	journalist	记者; jìzhě
C	flight attendant	乘务; chéngwù

Getting a Visa in Hong Kong

Hong Kong is usually a good place to pick up a visa for China or to reapply when your China visa and extensions expire. Almost any travel agent can obtain a visa for you or you can apply directly to the Visa Office of the People's Republic of China (☎ 852 3413 2300; 7th fl, Lower Block, China Resources Centre, 26 Harbour Rd, Wan Chai, Hong Kong; ☼ 9am-noon & 2-5pm Mon-Fri, closed public holidays). Visas processed here in one/two/three days cost HK$400/300/150. Double/six-month multiple/one-year multiple visas cost HK$220/400/600 (plus HK$150/250 if you require express/urgent service). Be aware that US and UK passport holders must pay considerably more for their visas. You must supply two photos, which can be taken at photo booths in the MTR (Mass Transit Railway) and at the visa office for HK$35.

Visas for China can be arranged by China Travel Service (CTS; ☎ 852 2522 0450; www.ctshk.com; Ground fl, China Travel Bldg, 77 Queen's Rd Central, Hong Kong; ☼ 9am-6pm Mon-Fri, to 7.30pm Sat, 9.30am-5pm Sun) or more cheaply at other Hong Kong travel agencies, such as Phoenix Services Agency (☎ 852 2722 7378; info@phoenixtrvl.com; Room 1404-5, 14th fl, Austin Tower, 22-26a Austin Av, Tsim Sha Tsui, Hong Kong; ☼ 9am-6pm Mon-Fri, to 4pm Sat) and Traveller Services (☎ 852 2375 2222; www.taketraveller.com; Room 1813, Mirimar Tower, 132 Nathan Rd, Tsim Sha Tsui, Hong Kong; ☼ 9am-6pm Mon-Fri, to 1pm Sat).

If you enter Hong Kong or Macau on a China visa, you will either need a multiple-entry visa or a new visa to be allowed back into China.

Residence Permit

The 'green card' is a residence permit, issued to English teachers, foreign expats and long-term students who live in China. Green cards are issued for a period of six months to one year and must be renewed annually. Besides needing all the right paperwork, you must also pass a health examination (for which there is a charge). If you lose your card, you'll pay a hefty fee to have it replaced.

Visa Extensions

The Foreign Affairs Branch of the local PSB – the police force – handles visa extensions. The visa office at the PSB main office (Běijīngshì Gōng'ānjú Chūrùjìng Guǎnlǐchù; Map pp58–9; ☎ 8402 0101, 8401 5292, 2 Andingmen Dongdajie, Dōngchéng; ☼ 8.30am-4.30pm Mon-Sat) is on the 2nd floor on the east side of the building – take the escalator up. You can also apply for a residence permit here.

First-time extensions of 30 days are easy to obtain and are issued on any tourist visa, but further extensions are harder to get and might give you only a further week. Offices of the PSB outside Běijīng might be more lenient and more willing to offer further extensions, but don't bank on it.

Visa extensions vary in price, depending on your nationality. US travellers pay Y185, Canadians pay Y165, UK citizens pay Y160 and Australians pay Y100; and prices can go up or down. Expect to wait several days for your visa extension to be processed and be prepared to stay in the same hotel for the duration (as you will need your passport to register at a new hotel). You can obtain passport photographs at the PSB main office (Y30 for five).

The penalty for overstaying your visa in China is up to Y500 per day. Some travellers have reported having trouble with officials who read the 'valid until' date on their visa incorrectly. For tourist (L) visas, the 'valid until' date is the date by which you must enter the country, not the date upon which your visa expires. Your visa is activated once you enter the country and expires 30 days, 60 days or what have you, after that time. Note that you must enter China within three months of the date the visa is issued.

Visa extensions can also be obtained for a fee through private visa services in Běijīng. Look in the classified section of the expat mags for listings, or try to get a personal recommendation from someone.

WOMEN TRAVELLERS

Women travellers generally feel safe in Běijīng. Chinese men are not macho and respect for women is deeply ingrained in Chinese culture.

As with anywhere else, you will be taking a risk if you travel alone. If you are concerned, a self-defence course can equip you with extra physical skills and boost your confidence before your trip. A whistle or small alarm can be a useful defence against an unpleasant encounter. If travelling to towns outside Běijīng, stick to hotels near the city centre. For further tips, consult www.oculartravel.com, which has a very useful section for women travellers. Another handy website is www.journeywoman.com.

Tampons *(wèishēng miántiáo)* can be found almost everywhere. It may be advisable to take supplies of the pill *(bìyùnyào)*, although you will find brands like Marvelon at local pharmacies.

WORK

Over the past decade it has become easier for foreigners to find work in Běijīng, although having Chinese-language skills is becoming increasingly important.

Teaching jobs that pay by the hour are usually quite lucrative. If you have recognised ELT qualifications, such as TEFL and/or experience, teaching can be a rewarding and profitable way to earn a living in Běijīng. International schools offer salaries in the region of Y6000 to Y10,000 per month to qualified teachers, with accommodation often provided. More basic (and plentiful) teaching positions will offer upwards of around Y100 per hour. Schools regularly advertise in the English culture magazines, such as the *Beijinger*; you can visit its classified pages online at www.thebeijinger.com. Also hunt for teaching jobs on www.teachabroad.com.

There are also opportunities in translation, freelance writing, editing, proofreading, the hotel industry, acting, modelling, photography, bar work, sales and marketing, and beyond. Most people find jobs in Běijīng through word of mouth, so networking is the key.

Doing Business

Difficulties for foreigners attempting to do business have eased up, but the China work environment can still be frustrating. Renting properties, getting licences, hiring employees and paying taxes can generate mind-boggling quantities of red tape. Many foreign businesspeople who have worked in China say that success is usually the result of dogged persistence and finding cooperative officials.

See p43 for recommended books on Chinese economics and politics, including *Mr China: A Memoir* by Tom Clissold and other cautionary tales.

If you are considering doing business in China, plenty of preliminary research is recommended. In particular, talk to other foreigners who are already working there. Alternatively, approach a firm of business consultants for advice or approach the Běijīng business associations that follow:

American Chamber of Commerce (Map pp58–9; ☎ 8519 1920; www.amcham-china.org.cn; Room 1903, China Resources Bldg, 8 Jianguomen Beidajie, Dōngchéng)

British Chamber of Commerce (Map pp110–11; ☎ 8525 1111; www.pek.britcham.org; Room 1001, China Life Tower, 16 Chaoyangmenwai Dajie, Cháoyáng)

Canada-China Business Council (Map pp110–11; ☎ 8526 1820; www.ccbc.com; Suite 18-2, 18th fl, CITIC Bldg, 19 Jianguomenwai Dajie, Cháoyáng)

China-Australia Chamber of Commerce (Map pp58–9; ☎ 6595 9252; www.austcham.org; E fl, Office Tower, Beijing Hong Kong Macau Centre, 2 Chaoyangmenbei Dajie, Dōngchéng)

China Britain Business Council (CBBC; Map pp110–11; ☎ 8525 1111; www.cbbc.org; Room 1001, China Life Tower, 16 Chaoyangmenwai Dajie, Cháoyáng)

European Union Chamber of Commerce in China (Map pp110–11; ☎ 6462 2066; www.europeanchamber.com .cn; Room S-123, Lufthansa Center, 50 Liangmaqiao Lu, Cháoyáng)

French Chamber of Commerce & Industry (Map pp58–9; ☎ 6512 1740; www.ccifc.org; 6th fl, Novotel Xinqiao, 2 Dongjiaomin Xiang, Dōngchéng)

US-China Business Council (☎ 8526 3920; www.uschina.org)

Business Cards

Business cards in China are essential, even if you don't do business. Cards are exchanged much in the same way as handshakes are in the West. To be caught without a card in a business setting is like attending an official function in jeans and sneakers. Try to get your name translated into (simplified) Chinese and have it printed on the reverse of the card. You can get name cards made cheaply at local printers, but it's better to have some made before you arrive (try your local Chinatown). When proffering and receiving business cards, emulate the Chinese method of respectfully using the thumb and forefinger of both hands.

LANGUAGE

The official language of the PRC is based on the dialect spoken in Běijīng. In the West, this language is usually referred to as Mandarin, but the Chinese call it *pǔtōnghuà* (common speech). The total number of Mandarin speakers worldwide is estimated at 800 million, making it the most widely spoken language in the world.

If you're not one of the millions, you'll be pleased to know that a growing number of Beijingers also speak some English; at tourist hotels, restaurants and major sights you'll get along OK without Mandarin. But if you venture into shops, neighbourhoods or conversations that are off the tourist track, you may find yourself lost for words. Learning some of the local lingo will greatly enrich your travel experience. And you'll find that locals genuinely appreciate travellers trying their language, no matter how muddled you may think you sound.

If you want to learn more Mandarin than we've included here, pick up a copy of Lonely Planet's comprehensive and user-friendly *Mandarin Phrasebook*.

PRONUNCIATION
Pinyin

In 1958 the Chinese adopted a system of writing their language using the Roman alphabet, known as *Pīnyīn*. Pinyin is often used on shop fronts, street signs and advertising billboards, but very few Chinese are able to read or write it.

The pronunciation of a few consonants in Pinyin may cause confusion when compared to their counterparts in English:

c	as the 'ts' in 'bits'
ch	as in 'chop', but with the tongue curled back
q	as the 'ch' in 'cheese'
r	as the 's' in 'pleasure'
sh	as in 'ship', but with the tongue curled back
x	as the 'sh' in 'ship'
z	as the 'dz' sound in 'suds'
zh	as the 'j' in 'judge', but with the tongue curled back

Tones

The Chinese language has a large number of words with the same pronunciation but a different meaning; what distinguishes them are 'tones' – rises and falls in the pitch of the voice on certain syllables. The word *ma*, for example, has four different meanings depending on tone:

high tone	mā	(mother)
rising tone	má	(hemp, numb)
falling-rising tone	mǎ	(horse)
falling tone	mà	(to scold, to swear)

Mastering tones is tricky for newcomers to Mandarin, but with a little practice it gets a lot easier.

SOCIAL
Meeting People

Hello.
你好。 Nǐ hǎo.

Goodbye.
再见。 Zàijiàn.

Please.
请。 Qǐng.

Thank you.
谢谢。 Xièxie.

Thank you very much.
太谢谢了。 Tài xièxie le.

Yes.
是的。 Shìde.

No. (lit: don't have)
没有。 Méi yǒu.

No. (lit: not so)
不是。 Búshì.

Do you speak English?
你会说英语吗? Nǐ huì shuō yīngyǔ ma?

Do you understand?
懂吗? Dǒng ma?

I understand.
我听得懂。 Wǒ tīngdedǒng.

I don't understand.
我听不懂。 Wǒ tīngbudǒng.

Could you please …?
你能不能 …?
Nǐ néng bunéng …?
  repeat that
  重复   chóngfù
  speak more slowly
  慢点儿说   màn diǎnr shuō
  write it down
  写下来   xiě xiàlái

Going Out

What's on …?
… 有什么娱乐活动?
… yǒu shénme yúlè huódòng?
  locally
  本地   běndì
  this weekend
  这个周末   zhège zhōumò
  today
  今天   jīntiān
  tonight
  今天晚上   jīntiān wǎnshang

Where are the …?
… 在哪儿?
… zài nǎr?
  clubs
  俱乐部   jùlèbù
  gay venues
  同性恋场所   tóngxìngliàn chángsuǒ
  places to eat
  吃饭的地方   chīfàn de dìfang
  pubs
  酒吧   jiǔbā

Is there a local entertainment guide?
有当地娱乐指南吗?
Yǒu dāngdì yúlè zhǐnán ma?

PRACTICAL

Question Words

Who?
谁?   Shuí?
What?
什么?   Shénme?
When?
什么时候?   Shénme shíhou?
Where?
哪儿?   Nǎr?
How?
怎么?   Zěnme?

Numbers & Amounts

1	一/幺	yī/yāo
2	二/两	èr/liǎng
3	三	sān
4	四	sì
5	五	wǔ
6	六	liù
7	七	qī
8	八	bā
9	九	jiǔ
10	十	shí
11	十一	shíyī
12	十二	shí'èr
13	十三	shísān
14	十四	shísì
15	十五	shíwǔ
16	十六	shíliù
17	十七	shíqī
18	十八	shíbā
19	十九	shíjiǔ
20	二十	èrshí
21	二十一	èrshíyī
22	二十二	èrshíèr
30	三十	sānshí
31	三十一	sānshíyì
40	四十	sìshí
50	五十	wǔshí
60	六十	liùshí
70	七十	qīshí
80	八十	bāshí
90	九十	jiǔshí
100	一百	yìbǎi
200	两百	liángbǎi
1000	一千	yìqiān
2000	两千	liǎngqiān
10,000	一万	yíwàn
20,000	两万	liǎngwàn
100,000	十万	shíwàn
200,000	二十万	èrshíwàn
1,000,000	一百万	yībǎiwàn

Days

Monday	星期一	xīngqīyī
Tuesday	星期二	xīngqièr
Wednesday	星期三	xīngqīsān
Thursday	星期四	xīngqīsì
Friday	星期五	xīngqīwǔ
Saturday	星期六	xīngqīliù
Sunday	星期天	xīngqītiān

Accommodation

hotel
饭店/酒店   fàndiàn/jiǔdiàn
youth hostel
青年旅馆   qīngnián lǚguǎn
single room
单人间   dānrénjiān

double room		
双人间	shuāngrénjiān	
triple room		
三人间	sānrénjiān	
quad room		
四人间	sìrénjiān	
suite		
套房	tàofáng	
nonsmoking room		
无烟房间	wúyān fángjiān	

air-con	空调	kōngtiáo
bathroom	卫生间	wèishēngjiān
bed	床	chuáng
blanket	被子	bèizi
breakfast	早饭	zǎofàn
check-out	退房	tuìfáng
discount	折扣	zhékòu
lift	电梯	diàntī
luggage storage	寄存	jìcún
passport	护照	hùzhào
pillow	枕头	zhěntou
reception	总台	zǒngtái
remote control	遥控器	yáokòngqì
satellite TV	卫视	wèishì
shower room	卫生间	wèishēngjiān
taxi	出租车	chūzūchē
telephone	电话	diànhuà
toilet paper	卫生纸	wèishēngzhǐ
TV	电视	diànshì
wake-up call	叫醒	jiàoxǐng
	电话	diànhuà
window	窗户	chuānghù

Banking

I'd like to …
我想 …
Wǒ xiǎng …
    cash a cheque
    支票   zhīpiào
    change money
    换钱   huàn qián
    change travellers cheques
    换旅行支票   huàn lǚxíng zhīpiào

Excuse me, where's the nearest …?
请问, 最近的 … 在哪儿?
Qǐng wèn, zuìjìnde … zài nǎr?
    ATM
    自动柜员机
    zìdòng guìyuánjī
    foreign exchange office
    外汇兑换处
    wàihuì duìhuànchù

Post

Where's the post office?
邮局在哪里?
Yóujú zài nǎlǐ?

I'd like to send a …
我想寄 …
Wǒ xiǎng jì …
    fax
    传真   chuánzhēn
    letter
    信   xìn
    package
    包裹   bāoguǒ
    postcard
    明信片   míngxìnpiàn

I'd like to buy (a/an) …
我想买 …
Wǒ xiǎng mǎi …
    aerogram
    航空邮简   hángkōngyóujiǎn
    envelope
    信封   xìnfēng
    stamps
    邮票   yóupiào

Internet

Is there a local internet cafe?
本地有网吧吗?
Běndì yǒu wǎngbā ma?
Where can I get online?
我在哪儿可以上网?
Wǒ zài nǎr kěyǐ shàng wǎng?
Can I check my email account?
我查一下自己的email户, 好吗?
Wǒ chá yīxià zìjǐ de email hù, hǎo ma?

computer	
电脑	diànnǎo
email	
电子邮件/email	diànzǐyóujiàn/email
internet	
因特网	yīntè wǎng

Phones & Mobiles

I want to make …
我想打 …
Wǒ xiǎng dǎ …
    a call (to …)
    打电话 (到 …)
    diànhuà (dào …)
    a reverse-charge/collect call
    对方付费电话
    duìfāng fùfèi diànhuà

Where can I find a/an …?
哪儿有 …?
Nǎr yǒu …
I'd like a/an …
我想要 …
Wǒ xiǎng yào …

adaptor plug
转接器插头
zhuǎnjiēqī chātóu

charger for my phone
电话充电器
diànhuà chōngdiànqì

mobile/cell phone for hire
租用移动电话
zūyòng yídòng diànhuà

prepaid mobile/cell phone
预付移动电话
yùfù yídòng diànhuà

SIM card for your network
你们网络的SIM卡
nǐmen wǎngluò de SIM kǎ

I want to buy a phone card.
我想买电话卡。
Wǒ xiǎng mǎi diànhuà kǎ.

Transport

What time does the … leave/arrive?
… 几点开/到?
… jǐdiǎn kāi/dào?

boat
船   chuán
bus
汽车   qìchē
train
火车   huǒchē
plane
飞机   fēijī

When is the … bus?
… 汽车几点开?
… qìchē jǐdiǎn kāi?

first
头班   tóubān
last
末班   mòbān
next
下一班   xià yìbān

Is this taxi available?
这车拉人吗?
Zhèi chē lā rén ma?

Please use the meter.
打表。
Dǎ biǎo.

How much (is it) to …?
去 … 多少钱?
Qù … duōshǎo qián?

I want to go to …
我要去 …
Wǒ yào qù …

this address
这个地址
zhège dìzhǐ

EMERGENCIES

It's an emergency!
这是紧急情况!
Zhèshì jǐnjí qíngkuàng!

Could you help me please?
你能不能帮我个忙?
Nǐ néng bunéng bāng wǒ ge máng?

Call the police/a doctor/an ambulance!
请叫警察/医生/救护车!
Qǐng jiào jǐngchá/yīshēng/jiùhùchē!

Where's the police station?
警察局在哪儿?
Jǐngchájú zài nǎr?

HEALTH

Excuse me, where's the nearest …?
请问, 最近的 … 在哪儿?
Qǐng wèn, zuìjìnde … zài nǎr?

chemist
药店   yàodiàn
chemist (night)
药店 (夜间)   yàodiàn (yèjiān)
dentist
牙医   yáyī
doctor
医生   yīshēng
hospital
医院   yīyuàn

Is there a doctor here who speaks English?
这儿有会讲英语的大夫吗?
Zhèr yǒu huì jiǎng yīngyǔ de dàifu ma?

Symptoms

I have (a/an) …
我 …
Wǒ …

diarrhoea
拉肚子   lādùzi
fever
发烧   fāshāo
headache
头疼   tóuténg

FOOD & DRINK

breakfast	早饭	zǎofàn
lunch	午饭	wǔfàn
dinner	晚饭	wǎnfàn
snack	小吃	xiǎochī
eat	吃	chī
drink	喝	hē

Can you recommend a …?
Nǐ néng bunéng tuījiàn yíge …?
你能不能推荐一个 …?

bar/pub
jiǔbā/jiǔguǎn 酒吧/酒馆
cafe
kāfēiguǎn 咖啡馆
restaurant
fànguǎn 餐馆

Is service/cover charge included in the bill?
帐单中包括 Zhàngdān zhōng
服务费吗？ bāokuò fúwùfèi ma?

I don't want MSG.
我不要味精。 Wǒ bù yào wèijīng.

I'm vegetarian.
我吃素。 Wǒ chī sù.

Not too spicy.
不要太辣。 Bù yào tài là.

menu
菜单 càidān
bill (cheque)
买单/结帐 mǎi dàn/jiézhàng
set meal
套餐 tàocān

Let's eat!
吃饭！ Chī fàn!

Cheers!
干杯！ Gānbēi!

Food Glossary
BASICS

báifàn	白饭	rice
bīngde	冰的	ice cold
chāzi	叉子	fork
dāozi	刀子	knife
hújiāo	胡椒	pepper
húluóbo	胡萝卜	carrots
jiàngyóu	酱油	soy sauce
jīdàn	鸡蛋	egg
jīròu	鸡肉	chicken
kuàizi	筷子	chopsticks
làjiāo	辣椒	chilli
miàntiáo	面条	noodles
niúròu	牛肉	beef
qīngjiāo	青椒	green peppers

rède	热的	hot
sháozi	勺子	spoon
shūcài	蔬菜	vegetables
tāng	汤	soup
táng	糖	sugar
tǔdòu	土豆	potato
xīlánhuā	西兰花	broccoli
yán	盐	salt
yángròu	羊肉	lamb
yùmǐ	玉米	sweet corn
zhūròu	猪肉	pork

RICE DISHES

jīròu chǎofàn 鸡肉炒饭
fried rice with chicken
jīdàn chǎofàn 鸡蛋炒饭
fried rice with egg
jīdàn mǐfàn 鸡蛋米饭
steamed white rice
shūcài chǎofàn 蔬菜炒饭
fried rice with vegetables
xīfàn/zhōu 稀饭/粥
watery rice porridge (congee)

NOODLE DISHES

húntun miàn 馄饨面
wontons and noodles
jīsī chǎomiàn 鸡丝炒面
fried noodles with chicken
jīsī tāngmiàn 鸡丝汤面
soupy noodles with chicken
májiàng miàn 麻酱面
sesame paste noodles
niúròu chǎomiàn 牛肉炒面
fried noodles with beef
niúròu miàn 牛肉面
soupy beef noodles
ròusī chǎomiàn 肉丝炒面
fried noodles with pork
shūcài chǎomiàn 蔬菜炒面
fried noodles with vegetables
tāngmiàn 汤面
noodles in soup
xiārén chǎomiàn 虾仁炒面
fried noodles with shrimp
zhájiàng miàn 炸酱面
bean and meat noodles

BREAD, BUNS & DUMPLINGS

cōngyóu bǐng 葱油饼
spring onion pancakes
guōtiē 锅贴
pot stickers/pan-grilled dumplings
mántou 馒头
steamed buns
ròu bāozi 肉包子
steamed meat buns

shāobǐng 烧饼
clay-oven rolls
shuǐjiān bāo 水煎包
pan-grilled buns
shuǐjiǎo 水饺
boiled dumplings
sùcài bāozi 素菜包子
steamed vegetable buns

SOUP

húntun tāng 馄饨汤
wonton soup
sān xiān tāng 三鲜汤
three kinds of seafood soup
suānlà tāng 酸辣汤
hot and sour soup

BEEF DISHES

háoyóu niúròu 蚝油牛肉
beef with oyster sauce
hóngshāo niúròu 红烧牛肉
beef braised in soy sauce
gānbiǎn niúròu sī 干煸牛肉丝
stir-fried beef and chilli
niúròu fàn 牛肉饭
beef with rice
tiěbǎn niúròu 铁板牛肉
sizzling beef platter

CHICKEN & DUCK DISHES

háoyóu jīkuài 蚝油鸡块
diced chicken in oyster sauce
hóngshāo jīkuài 红烧鸡块
chicken braised in soy sauce
jītuǐ fàn 鸡腿饭
chicken leg with rice
níngméng jī 柠檬鸡
lemon chicken
tángcù jīdīng 糖醋鸡丁
sweet and sour chicken
yāròu fàn 鸭肉饭
duck with rice
yāoguǒ jīdīng 腰果鸡丁
chicken and cashews

PORK DISHES

biǎndòu ròusī 扁豆肉丝
shredded pork and green beans
gūlū ròu 咕噜肉
sweet and sour pork
guōbā ròupiàn 锅巴肉片
pork and sizzling rice crust
háoyóu ròusī 蚝油肉丝
pork with oyster sauce
jiàngbào ròudīng 酱爆肉丁
diced pork with soy sauce

jīngjiàng ròusī 京酱肉丝
pork cooked with soy sauce
mù'ěr ròu 木耳肉
wood-ear mushrooms and pork
páigǔ fàn 排骨饭
pork chop with rice
qīngjiāo ròu piàn 青椒肉片
pork and green peppers
yángcōng chǎo ròupiàn 洋葱炒肉片
pork and fried onions

SEAFOOD DISHES

géli 蛤蜊
clams
gōngbào xiārén 宫爆虾仁
diced shrimp with peanuts
háo 蚝
oysters
hóngshāo yú 红烧鱼
fish braised in soy sauce
lóngxiā 龙虾
lobster
pángxiè 螃蟹
crab
yóuyú 鱿鱼
squid
zhāngyú 章鱼
octopus

VEGETABLE & BEAN CURD DISHES

báicài xiān shuānggū 白菜鲜双菇
bok choy and mushrooms
cuìpí dòufu 脆皮豆腐
crispy skin bean curd
hēimù'ěr mèn dòufu 黑木耳焖豆腐
bean curd with wood-ear mushrooms
jiāngzhī qīngdòu 姜汁青豆
string beans with ginger
lǔshuǐ dòufu 卤水豆腐
smoked bean curd
shāguō dòufu 砂锅豆腐
clay pot bean curd
tángcù ǒubǐng 糖醋藕饼
sweet and sour lotus root cakes
hóngshāo qiézi 红烧茄子
red cooked aubergine
sùchǎo biǎndòu 素炒扁豆
garlic beans
sùchǎo shūcài 素炒蔬菜
fried vegetables
yúxiāng qiézi 鱼香茄子
'fish-resembling' aubergine
jiācháng dòufu 家常豆腐
'home style' bean curd

ALCOHOLIC DRINKS

bái pútáo jiǔ 　白葡萄酒
white wine

báijiǔ 　白酒
white spirits

hóng pútáo jiǔ 　红葡萄酒
red wine

mǐjiǔ 　米酒
rice wine

píjiǔ 　啤酒
beer

NONALCOHOLIC DRINKS

chá 　茶
tea

dòujiāng 　豆浆
soya bean milk

kāfēi 　咖啡
coffee

kāi shuǐ 　开水
water (boiled)

kěkǒu kělè 　可口可乐
Coca-Cola

kuàngquán shuǐ 　矿泉水
mineral water

nǎijing 　奶精
coffee creamer

niúnǎi 　牛奶
milk

qìshuǐ 　汽水
soft drink (soda)

suānnǎi 　酸奶
yoghurt

yézi zhī 　椰子汁
coconut juice

GLOSSARY

arhat – Buddhist, especially a monk who has achieved enlightenment and passes to nirvana at death

běi – north; the other points of the compass are nán (south), dōng (east) and xī (west)

bīnguǎn – tourist hotel

bìxì – mythical tortoise-like dragons often depicted in Confucian temples

bodhisattva – one worthy of nirvana but who remains on earth to help others attain enlightenment

bówùguǎn – museum

bǔpiào – upgrade

CAAC – Civil Aviation Administration of China

cānting – restaurant

catty – unit of weight, one catty (jīn) equals 0.6kg

CCP – Chinese Communist Party, founded in Shànghǎi in 1921

Chángchéng – the Great Wall

cheongsam (Cantonese) – originating in Shànghǎi, a fashionable tight-fitting Chinese dress with a slit up the side

chop – see name chop

CITS – China International Travel Service; the organisation deals with China's foreign tourists

CTS – China Travel Service; CTS was originally set up to handle tourists from Hong Kong, Macau, Taiwan and overseas Chinese

dàfàndiàn – large hotel

dàjiē – avenue

dàshà – hotel, building

dàxué – university

dìtiě – subway

dōng – east; the other points of the compass are běi (north), nán (south) and xī (west)

dòngwùyuán – zoo

fàndiàn – hotel or restaurant

fēng – peak

fēngshuǐ – geomancy, literally 'wind and water', the art of using ancient principles to maximise the flow of qì, or vital energy

Fifth Generation – a generation of film directors who trained after the Cultural Revolution and whose political works revolutionised the film industry in the 1980s and '90s

gé – pavilion, temple (Taoist)

gōng – palace

gōnggòng qìchē – bus

gōngyì – crafts

gōngyuán – park

gùjū – house, home, residence

gǔwán – antiques

hé – river

hú – lake

huàjù – theatre

Huí – ethnic Chinese Muslims

hútòng – a narrow alleyway

jiāng – river

jiǎo – see máo

jìcúnchù – left-luggage counters

jiē – street

jié – festival

jīn – see catty

jīngjù – Beijing opera

jiǔdiàn – hotel

kàngjūnsù – antibiotics

kǎoyādiàn – roast duck restaurant

kuài – colloquial term for the currency, *yuán*

Kuomintang – Chiang Kaishek's Nationalist Party, the dominant political force after the fall of the Qing dynasty

lama – a Buddhist priest of the Tantric or Lamaist school; it is a title bestowed on monks of particularly high spiritual attainment

líng – tomb

lóu – tower

lù – road

lǚguǎn – cheap hotel

luóhàn – see *arhat*

máo – colloquial term for *jiǎo*, 10 of which equal one *kuài*

mén – gate

miào – temple

name chop – a carved name seal that acts as a signature

nán – south; the other points of the compass are *běi* (north), *dōng* (east) and *xī* (west)

páilou – decorated archway

pedicab – pedal-powered tricycle with a seat to carry passengers

Pinyin – the official system for transliterating Chinese script into the Roman alphabet

PLA – People's Liberation Army

Politburo – the 25-member supreme policy-making authority of the CCP

PRC – People's Republic of China

PSB – Public Security Bureau; the arm of the police force set up to deal with foreigners

pǔtōnghuà – the standard form of the Chinese language used since the beginning of the 20th century and based on the dialect of Běijīng

qì – flow of vital or universal energy

qiáo – bridge

qìgōng – exercise that channels *qì*

qílín – a hybrid animal that only appeared on earth in times of harmony

rénmín – people, people's

renminbi – literally 'people's money', the formal name for the currency of China; shortened to RMB

ruǎn wò – soft sleeper

ruǎn zuò – soft seat

shān – hill, mountain

shāngdiàn – shop, store

shěng – province, provincial

shìchǎng – market

Sixth Generation – a generation of film directors whose dour subject matter and harsh film style contrasts starkly against the lavish films of the Fifth Generation

sì – temple, monastery

sīchóu – silk

sìhéyuàn – courtyard house

tǎ – pagoda

tàijíquán – the graceful, flowing exercise that has its roots in China's martial arts; also known as taichi

tíng – pavilion

wǎngbā – internet cafe

wǔshù – martial arts

xī – west; the other points of the compass are *běi* (north), *nán* (south) and *dōng* (east)

yángróngshān – cashmere

yáng – positive, bright and masculine; the complementary principle to *yīn*

yīn – negative, dark and feminine; the complementary principle to *yáng*

yìng wò – hard sleeper

yìng zuò – hard seat

yuán – the Chinese unit of currency; also referred to as RMB (see also *renminbi*)

zhāodàisuǒ – basic lodgings, a hotel or guest house

zhēng – 13- or 14-stringed harp

zhíwùyuán – botanic gardens

zhōng – middle, centre

BEHIND THE SCENES

THIS BOOK

This 8th edition of *Beijing* was written by David Eimer and Damian Harper, who also coauthored the previous edition. The History section of the Background chapter was based on the previous edition's content, written by Jasper Becker. This guidebook was commissioned in Lonely Planet's Oakland, California, office and produced by the following:

Commissioning Editor Emily K Wolman

Coordinating Editor Anna Metcalfe

Coordinating Cartographers Hunor Csutoros, Jolyon Philcox

Coordinating Layout Designer Aomi Hongo

Managing Editor Bruce Evans

Managing Cartographers David Connolly, Herman So

Managing Layout Designer Sally Darmody

Assisting Editors Kim Hutchins, Kristin Odijk

Assisting Cartographers Diana Duggan, Corey Hutchison, Peter Shields

Cover Image Research provided by lonelyplanetimages .com

Language Content Coordinators Laura Crawford, Annelies Mertens

Project Manager Chris Love

Thanks to Lucy Birchley, Sabrina Dalbesio, Craig Kilburn, Lauren Meiklejohn, Wayne Murphy, Raphael Richards, Navin Sushil, Ji Yuanfang

Cover photographs Chinese Theatre, Beijing, Jon Arnold Images/Photolibrary (top), Chinese New Year Spring Festival: lantern decorations on a restaurant front, Beijing, John Warburton Lee Photography/Photolibrary (bottom).

Internal photographs p97, p104 (top right) Damian Harper; p8 (#1) Peter Bruce /Hemis/Photolibrary; p8 (#2) Maison Boulud. All other photographs by Lonely Planet Images: p102 Sean Caffrey; p5 (#3), p8 (#3) Jinghui Cai; p6 (#1) p103 (bottom left) Bob Charlton; p2, p4 (#3), p5 (#1), p6 (#2), p7 (#2, #3), p104 (top left), p106 Greg Elms; p100 Anthony Giblin; p3, p4 (#1) Richard l'anson; p98 Diana Mayfield; p6 (#3) Martin Moos; p101 Nicholas Pavloff; p4 (#2), p7 (#1), p99, p108 Keren Su; p103 (bottom right) Sune Wendelboe; p5 (#2), Rodney Zandbergs.

All images are copyright of the photographer unless otherwise indicated. Many of the images in this guide are available for licensing from Lonely Planet Images: www .lonelyplanetimages.com.

THANKS
DAMIAN HARPER

Thanks as always to my wife Dai Min for her patience and good humour. My two children also deserve special praise for being so cherubic and cheerful. A glass is raised to David Eimer for his invaluable suggestions and companionship. Thanks also to Dai Lu and Alvin for helping out. Cheers also to the residents of Běijīng for being such great people and thanks to the staff at Lonely Planet for all their help and support.

DAVID EIMER

Special gratitude goes to Li Ying for her invaluable assistance. Thanks to all those people who, knowingly or unwittingly, passed on tips. Thanks also to Damian Harper for his patience and to Emily Wolman and David Connolly at Lonely Planet.

OUR READERS

Many thanks to the travellers who used the last edition and wrote to us with helpful hints, useful advice and interesting anecdotes:

Scott Byrne, Julie Campbell, Jun Keung Cheung, Creighton Connolly, John Crosland, Maurizio D'Angelo, Jamison Folland, Clare Graydon, Cathrin Hoefs, Hans Jayatissa, Martina Johansson, Denise Jost, Caitlin Kelly-Sneed, Josie Knapp, Dan Kretzer, Andrew Laub, Bonnie Liu, Nickolas Liu, Iain McConnell, Talita PM, Jane Robertson, Anthony Rocchi, Filip Rollé, Gonzalo Scanferla, John Schaub, Max Smith, Maggie Tan, Jolanda Van Dongen, Greg Van Fulpen, Ilse Van Kesteren, Helen Voss, Mengzhu Wang, Rosamund Whiting, Al Sing Yuen.

SEND US YOUR FEEDBACK

We love to hear from travellers — your comments keep us on our toes and help make our books better. Our well-travelled team reads every word on what you loved or loathed about this book. Although we cannot reply individually to postal submissions, we always guarantee that your feedback goes straight to the appropriate authors, in time for the next edition. Each person who sends us information is thanked in the next edition and the most useful submissions are rewarded with a free book.

To send us your updates — and find out about Lonely Planet events, newsletters and travel news — visit our award-winning website: lonelyplanet.com/contact.

Note: we may edit, reproduce and incorporate your comments in Lonely Planet products such as guidebooks, websites and digital products, so let us know if you don't want your comments reproduced or your name acknowledged. For a copy of our privacy policy visit lonelyplanet.com/privacy.

Notes

Notes

INDEX

798 Art District 133-4, **5**

A

accommodation 204-16,
see also Sleeping *subindex*
Cháoyáng 213-14
costs 205
discounts 206
Dōngchéng 206-12
Greater Beijing 215-16
Hǎidiàn 215
internet resources 207
language 257-8
long-term 205-6
reservations 206, 207
Xīchéng 212-13
Xuānwǔ 214-15
acrobatics 191
activities 196-202, *see
also individual
activities*, Sports &
Activities *subindex*
air travel 231-3
airlines 231-2
airports 232
to/from airport 233
within China 232-3
alleyways 46-50, **7**
ambulance 243
aquariums 95
architecture 37-40, *see
also* building & develop-
ment
Olympic buildings
114-15
notable buildings 41
sìhéyuàn 47-8
area codes 251

000 map pages
000 photographs

art 31-4
contemporary scene 33
shopping 153
arts 28-37, *see also*
Entertainment *subindex*
ATMs 248

B

babysitting 240
Bādàchù 134
Bādálǐng 101-2, **99**, **101**
banks 248
bargaining 144
bars & cafes 180-7, **2**,
see also Entertainment
subindex
business hours 180
Cháoyáng 183-7
Dōngchéng 181-2
Greater Beijing 187
Wǔdàokǒu 187
Xīchéng 182-3
basketball 201-2
Beihai Park 87-90, **91**
Běijīng municipality **219**
Beijing Museum Pass 73
Beijing Music Festival 14
Beijing opera 37, 193-4
bicycling, *see* cycling
bike hire 234
bike riding, *see* cycling
Bird's Nest 114, 198
blogs 15, 45
boat travel 234
books, *see also* literature
economics 43
fiction 29
history 16
politics 43
bowling 197
building & development
26-7, 40
bus travel 234-5
within China 235
business hours 240, *see also
inside front cover*
bars & cafes 180
food 161
shopping 144-5
business in China 255

C

cabs, *see* taxis
Cǎochǎngdì 134

Capital Airport 232
car travel 235
cathedrals, *see* Sights
subindex
CCP, *see* Chinese Communist
Party
CCTV Building 113-14, **7**
censorship 44-5, 245
Chairman Mao Memorial
Hall 68-9
changing money 248
Cháoyáng 109-15, **110-11**
accommodation 213-14
bars & cafes 183-7
food 172-7
shopping 148-51
transport 109
Chen Kaige 35
Chéngdé 218-24, **220**
children, travel with 94, 240
Chinese Communist Party
42-4
Chóngwén 80-6, **82**
food 169-71
shopping 147
transport 80
Christianity 27
Christmas Day 14-15
Chuāndǐxià 226-7
churches, *see* Sights *subindex*
cinemas 192-3, *see also* film,
Entertainment *subindex*
Cixi, Empress Dowager 21-2
classical music 192, *see
also* live music, music,
Entertainment *subindex*
climate 12, 240-1
climate change 232
clubs 190-1, *see also*
Entertainment *subindex*
communism in China 23-7
Communist Revolution 23-5
Confucius Temple 71-2, **6**
consulates 242-3
costs 14-15, 242
accommodation 205
food 161
counterfeit bills 248
courses 241
courtyard hotels 204-5
courtyard houses 47-8
credit cards 248
Cultural Revolution 24
slogan tour 75

customs regulations 241-2
cycling 198, 233-4
tours 140-2, **140**

D

dance 198
Dashilar 151
desertification 42
Diary of a Madman 29-30
disabilities, travellers
with 253
discounts 242
accommodation 206
museums 73
Dōngchéng 56-79, **58-9**
accommodation 206-12
bars & cafes 181-2
food 162-9
shopping 145-7
transport 57
Dongyue Temple 109-13
drinks 181, 184
drinking, *see* bars & cafes,
Entertainment *subindex*
Drum Tower 74
duck, *see* Peking duck

E

eating, *see* food, Eating
subindex
economy 14
books 43
electricity 242
embassies 242-3
emergencies 243, *see also
inside front cover*
environmental issues 41-2
etiquette
food 156-7, 159
events 12-14
exchange rates, *see inside
front cover*
exchanging money 248

F

ferry travel 234
festivals 12-14, *see also
individual festivals*
Fifth Generation directors 35
film 35-7, 192-3, *see
also* Entertainment
subindex
food 156-78, 162, 170, *see
also* Eating *subindex*
business hours 161

INDEX

MAP LEGEND
ROUTES

	Freeway		Mall/Steps
	Primary		Tunnel
	Secondary		Pedestrian Overpass
	Tertiary		Walking Tour
	Lane		Walking Tour Detour
	Under Construction		Walking Trail
	Unsealed Road		Walking Path
	One-Way Street		

TRANSPORT

	Metro		Cable Car, Funicular
	Rail		

HYDROGRAPHY

	River, Creek		Water

BOUNDARIES

	International		Regional, Suburb
	State, Provincial		Ancient Wall

AREA FEATURES

	Airport		Land
	Area of Interest		Mall
	Building		Market
	Cemetery, Christian		Park
	Cemetery, Other		Sports
	Forest		Urban

POPULATION

✪ CAPITAL (NATIONAL)		◉	CAPITAL (STATE)
●	Large City	●	Medium City
●	Small City	○	Town, Village

SYMBOLS

Information

⊖	Bank, ATM	
⊘	Embassy/Consulate	
⊕	Hospital, Medical	
⊕	Information	
@	Internet Facilities	
⊛	Police Station	
⊜	Post Office, GPO	
☏	Telephone	
⊕	Toilets	

Sights

🕌	Buddhist
🏰	Castle, Fortress
✝	Christian
🏛	Confucian

☪	Islamic
▯	Monument
🏛	Museum, Gallery
●	Point of Interest
⊡	Ruin
☯	Taoist
▣	Zoo, Bird Sanctuary

Shopping

🛍	Shopping

Eating

🍴	Eating

Entertainment

🎭	Entertainment

Sports & Activities

▣	Pool

Sleeping

🛏	Sleeping

Transport

✈	Airport, Airfield
▣	Bus Station
P	Parking Area

Geographic

▣	Lookout
▲	Mountain, Volcano
▣	National Park
⊗	Waterfall

Published by Lonely Planet Publications Pty Ltd
ABN 36 005 607 983

Australia (Head Office)
Locked Bag 1, Footscray, Victoria 3011,
☎03 8379 8000, fax 03 8379 8111,
talk2us@lonelyplanet.com.au

USA 150 Linden St, Oakland, CA 94607,
☎510 250 6400, toll free 800 275 8555,
fax 510 893 8572, info@lonelyplanet.com

UK 2nd fl, 186 City Rd, London, EC1V 2NT,
☎020 7106 2100, fax 020 7106 2101,
go@lonelyplanet.co.uk

© Lonely Planet 2009
Photographs © as listed (p264) 2009

Printed through Colorcraft Ltd, Hong Kong.
Printed in China.

Mixed Sources
Product group from well-managed
forests and other controlled sources
www.fsc.org Cert no. SGS-COC-005002
© 1996 Forest Stewardship Council

FSC